The Complete Encyclopedia of

golf

SECOND EDITION

First published in 2005

This edition published in 2010

10 9 8 7 6 5 4 3 2

Copyright © Carlton Books Limited 2010

A CIP catalogue record of this book is available from the British Library

ISBN 978-1-84732-506-8

Editor: Chris Hawkes
Project Art Direction: Darren Jordan
Design: Kathie Wilson
Picture Research: Tom Wright
Production: Kate Pimm

Printed in Dubai

All statistics correct as of April 2010

The Complete Encyclopedia of golf

TED BARRETT WITH CHRIS HAWKES

SECOND EDITION

CARLTON
BOOKS

CONTENTS

Augusta: Phil Mickelson leaps in the air after his birdie to take the Masters in 2004.

INTRODUCTION

Golf as it is known today – with its lucrative tours spread around the globe and its multi-millionaire players – is as far removed from the game played over 150 years ago as it is possible to be. How the early pioneers of the game – who, in the main, were club-makers from Scottish links villages – must look down in awe at the incredible transformation that has taken place within the game whose gospel they spread in the latter part of the 19th century.

The Complete Encyclopedia of Golf is the amazing story of the events that have taken place over the centuries. It is the story of those early pioneers, through to the individuals who took up their cause and who, in turn, became celebrated characters of their day: the history of golf is dotted with such characters.

From Allan Roberston and Old Tom Morris, to the first group of players who became household names, the Great Triumvirate of Harry Vardon, James Braid and J.H. Taylor, to the inimitable Walter Hagen and the game's first true superstar, Bobby Jones. And then on to the arrival of Arnold Palmer, whose charisma appealed so much to golf's brand-new audience – those sitting in their living rooms watching tournaments unfold on television.

Palmer's exploits spawned another great new rivalry. The Big Three – Palmer, Jack Nicklaus and Gary Player – enthralled a new generation of fans, picking up tournament victories around the world and helping to inspire the leading players of today, led by the game's biggest star, Tiger Woods – the man who has become one of the best-known faces on the planet and the sport's first billionaire.

This book traces the tournaments in which these men made their names – most notably the competitions that have become known as golf's four major tournaments. It also looks at the team events: although golf is an individual sport, special feelings arise for both players and fans when they group together for a single cause – as a result, the Ryder Cup, in particular, has become one of the most eagerly anticipated events on the sporting calendar.

The book also celebrates the courses which were the settings for great feats: every actor, no matter how good, needs a stage upon which to perform. As a result, golf architects have played a leading role in the spread of the game around the world and their legacies – the courses that they created – still stand today for all to admire. For the most part, these architects moulded the land upon which they stood, and created stunning results.

So please sit back and enjoy the story of this simple game …

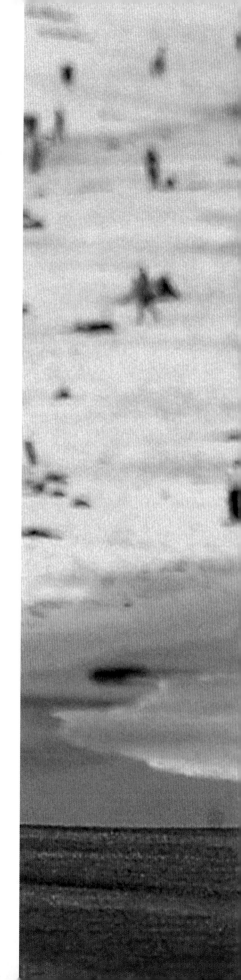

Pebble Beach: Jack Nicklaus hits out from the ninth fairway during the 2000 US Open. Overleaf: Nick Faldo plays out of the sand at Valderrama in the Ryder Cup, 1997.

PART ONE:

THE STORY OF GOLF

As with most ancient sports, the true origins of golf have been lost in the mists of time. What is certain, however, is that the game as we know it today can trace its roots to the linkslands of Scotland and, although the technology that is now used - from clubs to balls - may have altered dramatically in the intervening centuries, the fundamentals of the game of golf have altered little over the years.

The great Bobby Jones in action at Hoylake, 1930.

1502
James IV, the first recorded golfer, buys clubs and balls

1513
James IV killed at Flodden

1553
Archbishop of St Andrews confirms right to play over links

1567
Mary Queen of Scots accused of playing golf a few days after the murder of her husband, Lord Darnley

1592
Golf at Leith forbidden for interfering with worship on Sunday

1603
James I (and VI of Scotland) ascends English throne: he appoints a royal club-maker and encourages both of his sons to play

THE EARLY HISTORY OF GOLF

The Dutch game of *kolven* could well be the predecessor of the game of golf.

Golf belongs to the group of sports best described as target ball games. This also includes snooker, pool, ten-pin bowling, bowls, pétanque, croquet, curling and several varieties of billiards. Yet it stands proudly apart from them all, for only golf can claim to be both Royal and Ancient.

Eleven years before his death in 1513 during the disastrous Scottish defeat at Flodden, James IV of Scotland had golf clubs made by a Perth artisan whose usual stock in trade was bows and arrows. More clubs and balls were bought the following year for a match with the Earl of Bothwell.

These purchases by James, the record of whose golf transactions is the earliest historical evidence of a golfer's name, were utterly at variance with previous royal attitudes to golf. In the previous century several bans on "futeball, golfe and uther sik unproffitable sportis" were imposed by the Scottish parliament, the last as late as 1491.

The reasoning behind the bans was that time wasted on "the green" – the old Scots term for a course, and not just the putting surface, hence greenkeeper and Green Committee – should have been spent in mastering the martial arts, the better to discomfort the English.

Yet this game despised by the Scottish leadership has conquered vast areas of land in every continent, and, like football, the allegiance of millions. The English have never quelled the Scots half as effectively as this Scottish game has colonized the five continents.

The relatively sudden change of heart in the Stuart camp followed close upon James's marriage to the daughter of Henry VII of England. The royal alliance did not, as Flodden and the Jacobite uprisings of the 18th century attest, mean the immediate end of war between the two nations, but longer spells of peace and prosperity supervened.

Moreover, for more than 180 years – until William of Orange replaced James II of England – there was an unbroken line of royal Stuart golfers, including Mary Queen of Scots, who may or may not have been insensitive enough to have played golf shortly after the murder of her husband, Lord Darnley, but whose reputation has suffered ever since from the suspicion that she did. Mention of William, who, like the Hanoverians who followed him on the English throne, was no golfer, reopens the great debate as to whether the game is utterly Scottish, or an adaptation of pastimes like *kolven*, popular in Holland, or *chole*, from Belgium and northern France, or *jeu de maille*, a pursuit of Louis XIV. *Jeu de maille*, however, contains even fewer of the essential elements of golf than *kolven* which, as clearly shown in a Rembrandt drawing, was played with a ball the size of a cricket ball, usually in a courtyard or on a frozen river, or even in churches in the days before pews. The object was to drive the ball against a mark or post.

Chole, which dates from at least as early as the middle of the 14th century, was a cross-country event, with the target a distant door or pillar. Golf historian Robert Browning believes *chole* may have been brought back and adapted to Scottish usages by Scots fighting on the side of the French in the Hundred Years' War after Henry V's victory at Agincourt.

Chole had hockey-like features absent from golf, since a player was at liberty to hit his opponent's ball into trouble if he had failed to hit the target within the number of strokes he had declared, something that is directly opposed to the principles of golf.

There are pictures, dating from the early 17th century, showing the playing of *kolven* and *chole* that

c.1600
Feathery ball is introduced

1618
James I approves of Sunday play ... after worship

1637
Boy is hanged in Banff, Scotland, for stealing golf clubs

1646
Charles I (prisoner of the Scots) plays at Newcastle-upon-Tyne

1650
Charles II plays after being crowned King of Scotland

1689
Royal link with golf is broken as William III succeeds James II

are convincing arguments that these games are the forerunners of golf.On the other hand, golfers must have been active, to the annoyance of the Scottish parliament, well before that body first banned the sport in the middle of the 15th century; since Scotland was not rich in graphic art in that era, all we know for certain is that golf was being played two centuries before *kolven* pictures were being painted.

Moreover, there is no known form of the Scottish word golf that begins with a "k" sound.

Mary Queen of Scots is one of many royals to have played the game.

The novelist Sir Walter Scott doubted that the word golf came from the verb "to gowff", meaning to hit. Others theorize that the verb derived from the game. The correlation between verb and game seems too close and too clear, however, to be mere coincidence.

Another possible origin is shinty, but no recorded variant of this ancient Celtic hockey-like game has ever included mention of putting a ball into a hole, though in an early 16th-century German book of religious and sporting illustrations on vellum there is a depiction of a child apparently putting a ball into a depression. These fragmentary clues, like the club-swinging figure in a stained-glass window in Gloucester Cathedral in England (dating from the middle of the 14th century), provide no definite answers.

Putting the ball into the hole is the crucial, and some would say, diabolical, contribution of golf to the cross-country target ball game. The other contribution, which can be seen in courses throughout the world, is the nature of the Scottish landscape over which golf was developed. Great sums of money have been spent around the world on earth-moving, carried out frequently on a vast scale in order to replicate in turf and sand what are the characteristic features of natural Scottish courses.

The worldwide spread of golf received a racing start when Elizabeth I died without issue, and the Stuarts assumed the English throne in 1603 in the person of James I of England and VI of Scotland. He was the son of Mary Queen of Scots and the unfortunate Lord Darnley, and the great-grandson of Margaret Tudor. Margaret was the English wife of James IV, none other than our first (known) golfer.

No doubt exists that James I was a powerful influence in favour of golf. Though a century had passed since the Scottish ban on golf had been lifted, James I was moved to make his view known that the common people's right to enjoy sport on Sunday was to be respected, as long as religious observances had been completed first. Charles I repeated this sentiment a few years later. James I, Charles I and II and James II all golfed, and so did Bonny Prince Charlie, who succeeded James II as pretender to the throne of England.

Many a 40-shilling fine was imposed on those who persisted in playing "in tyme of sermonis" - notably in Scotland, where the kirk looked down upon such flibbertigibbet behaviour. Despite these hindrances, golf flourished, like cricket, in all classes of the community. Early in James I's reign, bishops, noblemen, and folk of every rank were busy on Scottish links, while James's two sons were making golf fashionable south of the border by taking it up at their father's behest. The eldest son, Henry, died at 18, the second son Charles surviving to succeed to the crown, only to lose his head after the Civil War. Charles was golfing on Leith Links, near Edinburgh, on the day he received the news of a rebellion in Ireland.

The Restoration of the Monarchy in 1660 brought royal golfers into play again, the most notable being James, Duke of York, later James II. James is credited with setting up and playing in the first international match, partnered by a Scottish shoemaker called Patersone, who was no novice at the tee. This Scottish team of Stuart and shoemaker beat two English noblemen, and Patersone was rewarded with enough cash to build a house in Cannongate, Edinburgh (which stood until 1961).

Not until the middle years of the following century did golf take the next great step forward. The engine of golf's further development was the social device of the club, until then strictly a political entity. No matter how powerful the ruling bodies of the game, no matter how rich the professional tours become, it is the club that remains the beating heart of the game.

A golf course was just that, a place where people could play golf. They did not pay for the privilege: there was no one to pay, no committee and no greenkeeping costs, since the land over which the game took place was common land, untended apart from grazing animals and rabbits and the more damaging attentions of wind and tide. The links at St Andrews in Fife had, since 1552, been given under licence by Archbishop Hamilton for free and unfettered use of citizens at football, golf and other games. That was the only formal convention.

The rules under which people played were a matter of local custom, on-the-spot agreements and wagers. Scorecards were yet to be thought of. All golf was of the matchplay variety, and handicaps a rudimentary give and take between individuals, be they dukes or cobblers. Leading players were, however, already sufficiently celebrated to be the subject of poetry. The next step was to see who was the best player of all.

1744

John Rattray, Edinburgh surgeon, wins first club competition for Honourable Company of Edinburgh Golfers' Silver Cup. First recorded code of rules

1754

St Andrews men set up similar Silver Cup contest

1759

St Andrews men change Silver Cup knock-out to strokeplay

1766

Foundation of Blackheath club, first in England

1786

First mention of golf in the US: Charleston club is founded

1848

Gutta-percha ball is introduced

1856

Continent of Europe's first club is founded at Pau, France

THE 18TH AND 19TH CENTURIES

The defining moment came in 1744, when a group of players, "gentlemen of honour" it goes without saying, well known on Leith Links, presented a petition to the City of Edinburgh to provide a prize for the winning player in an open competition. This was granted in the shape of a Silver Club by the magistrates, who were quick to indemnify themselves, after the fashion to be expected from careful guardians of public funds in those days, from any further expenditure which might be incurred in running the competition.

The new trophy was carried on the appointed day through the streets of Edinburgh, to the tuck of drums. The entry (of ten) in the event was strictly a local one. An Edinburgh surgeon called John Rattray came out on top, and repeated the dose the following year. A year earlier, the poet Mathison had sung of "Rattray for skill ... renowned".

This man of medicine was certainly a cool hand. He went at Bonny Prince Charlie's behest to the aid of the wounded in the Young Pretender's army during the second Jacobite rebellion of 1745. Owing perhaps to the leading Edinburgh golfers having

a heavy presence in the law – they still do – he was not arraigned for treason as he might well have been. His escape has been attributed mainly to the efforts of Duncan Forbes of Culloden, which only goes to show what useful contacts can be made at golf clubs, since Forbes was himself a "Gentleman Golfer".

After Rattray's second victory, the aftermath of the Jacobite troubles prevented further competition for the Silver Club for two years.

Ten years after the Edinburgh initiative, 22 "Noblemen and Gentlemen" of St Andrews subscribed for a Silver Club of their own. As at Edinburgh, competition for the silver trophy was the only cement binding together the group of local players. The winner each year was named captain of the group, and was entrusted with the resolution of any disputes between players. Not for another 80 years did the St Andrews men have a regular meeting place, and even then they shared it with the local Archers' Club.

A second key date in the slow, piecemeal development of the idea of a club came in 1764 when, with no

sign as yet of the hoped-for challenge for the Silver Club from other parts of Britain, the Edinburgh men moved to restrict entry to competition to "admit such Noblemen and Gentlemen as they approve to be members of the Company of Golfers". The cornerstone of the Honourable Company of Edinburgh Golfers had been laid 20 years earlier, and thus, in 1994, the Company celebrated their 250th anniversary – ten years before their rivals in St Andrews were at liberty to do so.

Edinburgh also scored a first in the matter of setting up a code of rules. This they did in 1744, to govern play for their Silver Club, though it is possible that the players at Leith had already put together a rudimentary list of dos and don'ts. The St Andrews men,

One of the oldest, and certainly the most well-known, stretches of linksland was at St Andrews in Fife, Scotland.

1857
Inter-Club foursomes, first Championship Meeting, is suggested by Prestwick; won by Blackheath

1858
Robert Chambers wins first individual championship

1859
Death of leading professional Allan Robertson

1860
Willie Park wins Championship Belt offered by Prestwick for annual championship, beating seven other professionals

1861
Tom Morris Sr wins first "Open" as championship is widened to admit amateurs

1864
Westward Ho! (Royal) North Devon Club, founded

following suit in 1754, were to abide by a similar codification, employing the principles of simplicity and brevity.

Today's mighty tomes detailing definitions and settling abstruse queries are a world away from the 13 rules issued in 1754: "back to basics" is an inadequate description. The first of the 13 makes strange reading to the modern golfer, since it directs that the player must tee off within a club's length of the hole, which gives an immediate and daunting idea of what the putting surfaces must have been like in the mid- 18th century. The main burden of the other 12 rules is "Play it as it lies", except when the player's ball comes to rest against that of his opponent, or is unplayable in "water or watery filth", in which latter case the player may lift his ball, but must allow his opponent a stroke. Removing "stones, bones, or any break-club for the sake of playing your ball" was forbidden, except "upon the fair green, and that only within a club length of your ball". Putting green standards obviously improved over the next hundred years, and needed to be protected, because halfway through the 19th century Rule 1 was relaxed to the extent that the ball was allowed to be teed as much as six club lengths away from the hole.

All these early rules were, as has been indicated, for matchplay. Once strokeplay became widespread – and strokeplay has always been the most popular form of the game in America – the need arose for exact definitions as to what constituted, to give an obvious example, an unplayable ball. A competitor at strokeplay needed to know precisely whether the circumstances involved a penalty or not. Otherwise it would be impossible for him to continue his round and complete his card.

A century after the first simple codification of the rules, an attempt by the St Andrews club to define "unplayable" required almost as many words as the whole of the original 13 rules. The process of devoting further words to this intractable problem has used up a quantity of ink since then.

With the Leith Links deteriorating as the city pressed in upon them, the Honourable Company had to move, initially to Musselburgh, while the duties of regulators and adjudicators were assumed little by little by the men from St Andrews. Finally they were shared by the United States Golf Association, and, in 1951, a conference made the first real attempt to provide a code for golf worldwide. In doing so, it also got rid of the hated stymie.

Within a few years, the irresistible attractions of golf were spreading south of the border. Just as with the two pioneer Scottish clubs, the presentation of a trophy in 1766 set Blackheath golfing activities in motion in Kent, to the south of London. Not surprisingly, Blackheath's foundation owed much to the presence of expatriate Scots. Such men were often prime movers in helping the game spread further afield.

It did so with great rapidity and, in 1810, came the first mention of a women's competition, at Musselburgh. There had already been reports of Scottish officers playing in New York, and of the formation (in 1786) of a club in South Carolina, though the game was slow to take root in the United States, a process

The term "caddie" derives from the French *cadet*, which dates to the time of Mary Queen of Scots.

which took more than another 100 years, and was pre-dated by the founding of Royal Montreal in 1873.

Golf had already followed the Union flag to Calcutta in 1829, and Bombay in 1842. Conversely, although the British began business in Hong Kong in the 1840s, golf did not flower there until 1889. Nor did it make the short journey to the Continent until 1856, when Pau, in the shadow of the Pyrenees, was founded for holiday visitors. Scottish soldiers of the Duke of Wellington's Peninsular Army are said to have played at Pau in 1814, some of them returning 20 years later on holiday – which places them among the very first of the great army of golf tourists, though many English players belonged to the leading Scottish clubs and journeyed north for their regular silver club and gold medal meetings.

Australia joined the throng in 1870, with the Royal Adelaide Club, and South Africa in 1885, with the Royal Cape Club.

The rate of golf course construction in the Britain was prodigious in Victorian times, mostly with horse, cart and shovel. The railways helped, from St Andrews to Blackheath, and from Sheringham, where the line ran within a few feet of the 17th green, to Aberdovey in west Wales, and from Ganton in Yorkshire to Lytham in Lancashire, where there were also gas trams on a line that was later electrified.

Course building reached a feverish pitch in the 1890s, as proved by the number of clubs celebrating their centenaries in the last decade of the 20th century. Curiously, there had been little golf in Ireland before the boom of the '90s, though Belfast set up their club in 1881. Unsurprisingly,

1869
(Royal) Liverpool Club formed at Hoylake, former race-track

1870
Young Tom Morris lands hat-trick of Opens at 19 and retains Championship Belt

1872
Silver claret jug offered by Prestwick, St Andrews and Honourable Company of Edinburgh Golfers as perpetual trophy for Open. Young Tom wins again

1875
Young Tom dies, aged 24, soon after wife's death in childbirth

1885
Royal Liverpool organize first British Amateur Championship, won by Hoylake member A F Macfie from Scotland

1888
Formation of St Andrew's Club, Yonkers, New York, named after the "Apple Tree Gang"

it was a Scot, Sir David Kinloch, who brought the game to Dublin.

The popularity of the game had greatly increased because it was given a focus by two competitions. 1860 saw the staging of what has gone down history as the first "Open" Championship, though as we shall see in the next section it was not "Open" at all, and the crucial value of the events of that year took many years to make themselves apparent. Second, 25 years later, came what was eventually styled as the Amateur Championship, which meant that for players both paid and unpaid there was a summit to strive towards.

Among the catalysts leading to the foundation of golf's first major championship was Blackheath's victory, gained by George Glennie and Lieut. J C Stewart, in the Inter-Club Foursomes of 1857, a competition suggested by the Prestwick club. This constituted the first Championship Meeting to be played at St Andrews, and the host club were beaten finalists. The St Andrews club had assumed authority as the game's law-givers, and their decision to cut the number of holes on their course from 22 to 18 made 18 the magic number worldwide.

Significantly the winning pair in 1857 were both Scots; Glennie's natural talent was such that when he was studying at St Andrews University his fellows insisted he should play with only one club. He still won.

The following year a singles event was held, attracting a field of 28 from which the publisher, Robert Chambers, emerged victorious. In 1859, another publisher, Robert Clark, who wrote about golf, was much fancied to win,

but a big hitter called George Condie strolled to the title 6&5.

These three competitions were amateur, but the leading players were celebrated in newspaper reports and verse, and attained the status of national sporting heroes.

The links were the haunt of a great variety of folk quite apart from the gentlemen amateurs, some of whom played in tall hats – a powerful inducement to keep the head still – and their caddies, whose name, it seems clear, derives from the French word cadet. This was the term used to describe the young French noblemen who came to Edinburgh with Mary Queen of Scots when she returned after her years at the French court.

Scottish humour, ever sardonic, extended the usage to mean something less complimentary, and in a classic sequence of semantic change, the meaning of cadet journeyed by way of "hanger-on" and "odd jobber" to "porter". Latterly, over the last two centuries, the word has slowly gone up-market again, certainly in the world of the major tours, to mean well-paid golf-bag carriers who keep their player dry when it is wet, watered when it is dry, fed when hungry and well supplied with advice at all times on how far it is to the hole, which way the wind is blowing and exactly how far the next putt will swing on its way to the hole.

Many wanderers across the courses were simply out to take the air; others kicked a ball about, or flew kites. Soldiers drilled, horses were raced, cricket matches were played: but on the days of big challenge matches, sometimes with hundreds of pounds at stake, crowds surrounded the growing

band of professionals. They got much closer to the action than would be countenanced today. The classlessness of the game, at least in Scotland, is indicated by the story of the caddie who, when he judged that spectators were getting a little too close, grabbed one, who happened to be a magistrate, by the ear, and invited him to stick his nose into the hole, so that he could feel whether the ball was there.

After the success of the events they had set in motion in 1857–59, the innovative members of Prestwick turned their attention to the professionals, many of whom started their golfing life as caddies.

It hardly needs saying that the professionals around the middle of the 19th century could not make a living from tournament winnings alone: there was no programme of events, and what money they won with their clubs, which they usually fashioned themselves, came from challenge matches for cash.

Club-making, which in the early days seemed to become the natural fiefdom of bow-makers, was, along with the manufacture of feathery golf balls and teaching, the staple source of income for the early Victorian professional. This state of affairs continued long after the establishment of the first regular Open events.

Allan Robertson, the first golfer to beat 80 at St Andrews, was accepted as the leading player of the day. With his assistant Tom Morris, Robertson ran a thriving feathery-ball business out of the window of their workshop, which was the kitchen of Robertson's house. Stuffing a top hat full of feathers into a leather casing was a job for an expert,

Allan Robertson, a club-maker from St Andrews, was widely accepted as the leading golfer of his day.

though even the best could manage no more than three balls a day.

The era of the feathery, which was almost certainly preceded by lathe-turned wooden balls as used in such games as chole, ended, to Robertson's dismay, with the development of the solid gutta-percha ball during the last years of his life: he died in 1859, aged only 44. The popularity of the cheaper "gutty" must have been an especially severe shock to Robertson, because the family feathery trade had been in existence for so long, run by his grandfather Peter and father Davie before him. The gutty was a solid ball made from the juice of the Malayan

1890	1891	1893	1894	1895	1896	1898
John Ball is the first amateur and Englishman to win the Open, at Prestwick	R&A rule hole width at 4½ in, minimum 4in deep	Ladies' Golf Union founded in Britain. Lady Margaret Scott wins first championship	United States Golf Association formed	USGA stages first Amateur Championship, won by Charles Macdonald from Chicago; US Open won by Horace Rawlins, an English pro; and Women's Amateur won by Mrs Charles Brown	Harry Vardon, Channel Islander, wins British Open	Coburn Haskell patents ball with gutta-percha cover over rubber bands wound under tension around a core

percha tree and, unlike the feathery, could be remoulded when damaged – the feathery simply burst open when mistreated, especially in wet weather.

Moreover, the Robertson and Co. output is reckoned to have been well in excess of 2,000 featheries a year. At half a crown each (12.5 pence in sterling metric terms, or about 20 US cents) that came to an annual revenue of about £300, a fair sum in the mid-19th century. The high cost of a feathery in the last days of its dominance no doubt kept many would-be golfers off the course. Robertson proved himself the complete professional, for after first declaring of the new projectile, "It's nae gowff", he reacted positively to the playing problems set by the new ball, which was much less responsive and more difficult to get into the air than the feathery. He made much greater use of the mid- and short irons to fly the ball to the target. Pitching had previously been performed with wooden clubs. Never a long hitter, Robertson obeyed the first rule of golf: he kept the ball in play, and used his new iron technique to get close to the hole with his approach shots.

His death posed the question: who is champion now? Prestwick provided a way of finding out in October 1860, with the game's first formal competitive tournament at strokeplay, what we know as the British Open. The golfing calendar has for nearly a century been dominated by this and three other majors: two of them, both amateur events, were replaced as social changes re-shaped golf. How appropriate that the youngest of the majors, the Masters, is the first great international event of the year.

DEVELOPMENT OF BALLS AND CLUBS

As the game evolved, so did the equipment that the players were using. It seems certain that the early golf balls were of the lathe-turned wooden variety. These were replaced by the feathery which, as the name suggests, were made from feathers stuffed into a leather case. But these were problematic: they were expensive to produce and, when wet, difficult to play with. Along came the gutta percha, a solid rubber-like ball made from the juice of the Malayan percha tree. The fact that they could be produced on a mass scale, and that they could be remoulded when damaged, saw the demise of the feathery: they still weren't perfect, though.

It was down to chance that the "golf ball revolution" occurred and the conspirator of this uprising was none other than Coburn Haskell. Standing in the factory of a friend Coburn was idly winding some rubber bands around a ball: the ball slipped out of his hand. Its liveliness when it hit the ground gave him an idea that would change the game of golf forever and which would lead to the need to lengthen courses and cause bunkers to be repositioned.

It wasn't plain sailing, though ... literally. The Haskell ball, as it came to be known, was not the most obedient of balls: ball flight was difficult to control, to say the least. Until, that is, James Foulis, the 1896 US Open champion, placed some new Agrippa "blackberry bump" patented covers on a batch of gutties ... or so he thought.

Intriguingly, one of the balls flew through the air better than any of the others. When he cut it open he discovered that it was none other than a Haskell ball: he had found a cure for its flight problems.

The technology may have changed somewhat over the years, but the principles behind golf ball manufacture remain the same to this day: rubber wound around a core with a plastic, dimpled, covering.

From Nibliks to Hippos – Club-making was traditionally the preserve of bow-makers, and then became an art passed down through families. And so it remained, with wooden- and iron-headed clubs being the norm until the 1920s, when metallurgical progress ushered in the steel shaft and the production of matched sets of clubs began. At that point, endearing names such as niblick, mashie and brassie were confined to the history books, as clubs started to be known solely by their number.

Early examples of golf balls and clubs.

THE EARLY CLUBS AND THEIR MODERN EQUIVALENTS

brassie	=	two-wood	midmashie	=	three-iron
mashie	=	five-iron	pitching niblick	=	eight-iron
spoon	=	three- or four-wood	mashie iron	=	four-iron
spade mashie	=	six-iron	niblick	=	nine-iron
mashie-niblick	=	seven-iron			

CHRONOLOGY OF THE 20TH AND 21ST CENTURIES

1900
Vardon tours US and wins US Open by two shots from J.H. Taylor

1901
James Braid wins the first of his five British Open titles, at Muirfield

1902
Sandy Herd pioneers Haskell "Bounding Billy" ball to win British Open

1903
Vardon wins the British Open title at Prestwick by six strokes

1904
Walter J Travis lands first US victory in British Amateur at Royal St George's

1905
British women's team beats US 6-1 at Cromer, Norfolk

Willie Anderson completes a hat-trick of US Open wins

1906
The British Open returns to Muirfield and James Braid repeats 1901 success

Scot Alex Smith triumphs in the US Open

1907
Frenchman Arnaud Massy is the first foreigner to win the British Open

1913
Bostonian Francis Ouimet, aged 20, is first amateur to win US Open, beating Harry Vardon and Ted Ray in a play-off at Brookline

1914
Walter Hagen wins his first US Open

1916
PGA of America founded: Jim Barnes wins first US PGA title

1919
R&A take over management of major British championships

1923
Bobby Jones wins the US Open for the first time

1924
Joyce Wethered wins fifth English Ladies' Amateur in a row

1925
British Open played at Prestwick for the last time and is won by Jim Barnes

1926
Britain defeats US 13½-1½ in unofficial professional international at Wentworth

Bobby Jones wins British Open at Lytham

Jess Sweetser first American to win British Amateur title

1927
Hagen wins fourth US PGA title in a row, his fifth in all

US beats Britain in the first Ryder Cup match at Worcester, Ma

1928
Last appearance of members of the Great Triumvirate at the British Open at Sandwich

1929
Hagen wins his fourth British Open

R&A legalize steel-shafted clubs, following USGA lead of 1926

1930
Bobby Jones wins grand slam: wins US and British Opens, British and US Amateurs in same year

1938
Britain and Ireland score first Walker Cup win at St Andrews

1939
Dick Burton wins the last British Open to be staged before the onset of the Second World War

1940
Johnny Laidlay, the true inventor of the "Vardon" grip, dies aged 80

1943
Pam Barton, first woman to win the British and American Amateurs in the same year (1936), dies in RAF air crash

1945
Byron Nelson wins 19 events in 31 starts, 11 of them in a row

1946
First Women's US Open is played

1947
Lew Worsham beats Sam Snead in play-off for US Open at St Louis in first championship to be televised (locally)

Babe Zaharias first American to win British Women's Amateur

1948
Ben Hogan wins first US Open, at Los Angeles

1908
Old Tom Morris dies at St Andrews, aged 87

1909
Dorothy Campbell from North Berwick is the first to gain British and US titles in one season

1910
James Braid breaks the 300-mark for the first time in a British Open held at St Andrews

1911
Johnny McDermott is the first American-born winner of the US Open

1912
Jamie Anderson, British Open winner from 1877-79, dies in Perth Poorhouse

1920
British Open played for first time since halted for First World War: tournament won by George Duncan

Bobby Jones plays in the US Open for the first time

1921
Jock Hutchison is the first to take the British Open trophy to the US

R&A and USGA rule ball must not be more than 1.62oz in weight and 1.62in in diameter

US beat Britain 9-3 in unofficial amateur international at Hoylake

Britain pros beat US 10½-4½ in unofficial international at Gleneagles

1922
Walter Hagen, first American-born player to win British Open

US win inaugural Walker Cup match

Gene Sarazen: the first player to complete the grand slam.

1931
British Open played at Carnoustie for the first time. Tommy Armour wins by one stroke from José Jurado

1932
Inaugural Curtis Cup match: US beat Britain 5½ -3½

1933
Gene Sarazen wins US PGA to complete wins in all three of the major tournaments

1934
Henry Cotton is first Briton to win the British Open since 1923

1935
Gene Sarazen becomes the first player to complete the career grand slam with his victory in the Masters

1936
Horton Smith wins the Masters for the second time in three years

1937
First US Ryder Cup away win, by 8-4, at Southport and Ainsdale

Harry Vardon, record six-time winner of British Open, dies

1949
Ben Hogan is almost killed in road crash in Texas

1950
Ben Hogan recovers to win second US Open

James Braid, five-time winner of the British Open, dies aged 80

1951
R&A/USGA Rules conference to rationalize golf throughout world: major decision abolishes stymie

1952
Britain and Ireland gain first Curtis Cup win over US

1953
Ben Hogan becomes the first (and only) golfer to win Masters, US Open and British Open in the same year

World Cup is played for the first time

1954
Peter Thomson wins the first of his five British Open titles

1955
Last day of British Open at St Andrews is televised: Peter Thomson wins

1956
Babe Zaharias, "Athlete of the Century", dies aged 42

1957
Dai Rees leads Britain
and Ireland to first
Ryder Cup win over US
in 34 years at Lindrick,
Nottinghamshire

1958
Arnold Palmer wins his first major, the Masters
at Augusta

PGA Tour prize money reaches record $1 million

US PGA reverts to a strokeplay format:
Dow Finsterwald wins

1959
Sam Snead's team
regains the Ryder Cup by
five points in California

1960
Palmer wins Masters and
US Open, then fails by a
shot to catch Kel Nagle
in the Centenary
British Open

1969
Tony Jacklin becomes first
Briton to win his national
Open since 1951

Walter Hagen dies, aged 76

1970
Tony Jacklin wins the
US Open by seven strokes

1971
Lee Trevino wins US, Canadian and British Opens in three weeks

Bobby Jones dies, aged 69

John Hudson holes successive tee shots at 11th (195 yards) and
12th (311 yards) in Martini Tournament at Royal Norwich, Norfolk

Jack Nicklaus came to the fore when he won the US Open in 1962.

1979
Severiano Ballesteros
wins the British Open,
via the BBC parking lot

US Ryder Cup foes now
Europe, who lose, 17-11,
in West Virginia

1980
Ballesteros
becomes the
first European
to win the
Masters

1981
The US fields
their strongest-
ever Ryder
Cup team and
trounce Europe
18½-9½ at
Walton Heath

1982
Tom Watson
wins both the
British Open
and the
US Open

1983
Ballesteros wins
the Masters for the
second time

US retain the Ryder
Cup with a single point
margin of victory

1984
Ballesteros wins the
British Open for a
second time

1985
Europe beat Trevino's
US team in the Ryder
Cup at The Belfry

1986
Nicklaus becomes the
oldest Masters winner,
aged 46. Sixth win is also
a record

1999
Jean Van de Velde loses three-stroke lead going into the final hole
of the British Open at Carnoustie. Paul Lawrie emerges from play-
off as surprise champion

Payne Stewart wins US Open and is killed in plane crash later in year

US regain Ryder Cup amid controversial scenes at Brookline

2000
A year of records for
Tiger Woods as he wins
three of the year's four
majors – and completes
career grand slam with
victory at the British
Open at St Andrews

2001
Victory at the Masters
means that Woods is
the only player in the
history of the game
to hold all four
major trophies at
the same time

2002
Tiger Woods wins first two majors of the year,
but dreams of a grand slam are blown away
during a blustery third-round at the
British Open at Muirfield. Ernie Els emerges
from the carnage to win

Europe regain Ryder Cup with win at The Belfry

2003
All four majors are
won by first-time
winners

2004
Phil Mickelson wins the Masters

Vijay Singh wins the US PGA and
ends year as world number one

Europe retain Ryder Cup by
crushing the US

1961
Bernard Darwin, greatest of golf writers, dies aged 85

1962
Jack Nicklaus, aged 22, beats Palmer in US Open play-off

1963
Bob Charles is the first lefthander to win a major - British Open

J H Taylor, last survivor of the Great Triumvirate, dies, aged 91

1964
World Matchplay is held for the first time: Arnold Palmer beats Neil Coles 2&1 in the final

1965
Peter Thomson wins his fifth British Open title, at Royal Birkdale

Gary Player wins the US Open to complete the career grand slam

1966
Tony Lema, 1964 British Open champion, dies in air crash

Jack Nicklaus completes career grand slam with victory in the British Open at Muirfield

1967
Francis Ouimet dies, aged 74

1968
Tour pros win fight for new US PGA division to run own affairs

Croquet-style putting banned

1972
Britain and Ireland's second Walker Cup win in 50 years

European Tour gets under way

1973
Jack Nicklaus wins the US PGA: it was his 12th major victory to take him past Walter Hagen as the winner of the most major tournaments

1974
Gary Player wins British Open, with now-obligatory 1.68in ball, at Lytham

Jack Nicklaus becomes the first player to win the Masters five times

1975
British tour pros gain large measure of autonomy in separate PGA division

1976
Johnny Miller shoots final-round 66 to win British Open by six shots. Unknown 19-year-old Spaniard Severiano Ballesteros finishes in second place

British Women's Open is held for the first time

1977
Tom Watson beats Jack Nicklaus in what is widely regarded as the greatest British Open of all time, at Turnberry

1978
Jack Nicklaus wins his third British Open title: his second triumph at St Andrews

Gary Player wins the Masters for the third time

1987
Nick Faldo wins his first British Open with final round of 18 pars

Ryder Cup further revitalized with European victory in Ohio

1989
Europe retain Ryder Cup with second-ever tie in the series

1990
Faldo wins second successive Masters, then wins British Open at St Andrews

1991
Europe lose Ryder Cup "War on the Shore" at Kiawah Island

US regain Walker Cup at Portmarnock

1992
Nick Faldo wins British Open for the third time

1994
Nick Price (British Open, US PGA), Ernie Els (US Open) and José-Maria Olazabal (Masters) leave US without "major" winner

1995
Europe regain the Ryder Cup

1996
Nick Faldo overcomes a six-shot final-day deficit to win his third Masters

1997
Tiger Woods, aged 21, becomes the youngest winner of the Masters

Europe retain the Ryder Cup, played on the Continent for the first time

1998
Mark O'Meara completes the best year of his golfing career when he wins both the Masters and the British Open

2005
Tiger Woods wins two of the season's four majors (the Masters and the British Open), his ninth and tenth, to move ahead of Gary Player and Ben Hogan on the all-time list

2006
Phil Mickelson wins his second Masters

Tiger Woods win the British Open and the US PGA to move ahead of Walter Hagen on the all-time list (with 12 majors)

Europe retain the Ryder Cup

2007
The season starts with three first-time major winners - Zach Johnson (Masters), Angel Cabrera (US Open) and Padraig Harrington (British Open) - before Tiger Woods win the US PGA to collect his 13th major

2008
Tiger Woods injured en route to winning the US Open

Padraig Harrington becomes the first European to win back-to-back majors - the British Open and the US PGA

The United States regain the Ryder Cup in emphatic fashion

2009
Angel Cabrera wins the Masters

Stewart Cink ended Tom Watson's fairytale in a four-hole play-off to win the British Open

YE Yang becomes the first Asian-born player to win a major when he wins the US PGA Championship

THE HISTORY OF THE SWING

Some players, such as Bobby Jones and Sam Snead, are born great; some achieve greatness by sheer persistence, such as Ben Hogan and Henry Cotton; lesser mortals, short on both counts, labour somewhere in between.

The ball shapes the swing

Every bat and ball game is at the mercy of the men who make the ammunition, the ball. The golf ball has gone through radical changes, notably with its composition: boxwood, feathers stuffed into a leather sphere, gutta percha, wound rubber bands, liquid cores, solid cores, two-piece, three-piece, constant improvement of dimple patterns on the cover ... and at every stage different demands, complicated by wind and weather, have been made on the mechanics of making the ball fly.

One thought about the golf ball and how to propel it has remained a favourite through the years. As expressed by Horace Hutchinson in his classic and comprehensive 1891 study of the game in *Badminton Golf*: "it's a swing, not a hit" ... very short and simple words containing a truth universally admired but, all too often, forgotten.

Hutchinson held that "hit" means a jerk with tensed muscles, whereas the golf swing involves gradual acceleration with flexible muscles. This does not preclude the application of great strength, but does preclude its misapplication.

Hutchinson played in the era that started with the solid gutty ball, which arrived in the middle of the 19th century, and finished with the lively

Haskell, patented in 1898, with its wound rubber interior. Before these innovations, the light and responsive feathery ball made its own swing rules. It fairly sprang off the clubface, performing best in the dry. In the wet, especially when clumsily hit, the feathery would burst its stitches, and a careless iron shot would cut it.

Therefore it was necessary to sweep the ball away, so what is thought of as the old St Andrews swing was flat, and sent the ball flying away over the wide open spaces of what is now the Old Course. The favoured stance was closed, that is, with left foot in advance of the right, which had the additional advantage on windswept links courses (there were few of any other type) of keeping the ball low and running.

This method contrasts sharply with the model swing of today, which has become more and more upright, though Lee Trevino's swing, while scarcely a throwback to Victorian times, has resisted the trend, and won him a fortune. Jack Nicklaus, himself an exemplar of the upright swing, defines Trevino's as "effective, in that it is wonderfully well grooved". In other words, it is an action Trevino can repeat exactly and almost endlessly, an action that has stood the test of time deep into his Senior status.

The coming of the solid gutty ball called for immediate adjustments. The player now had to master the art of clipping the gutty into flight, which called for accurate timing of the shot and firm wrists, and increased the value of iron-club shots that came down hard on the ball, enabling the player to pitch the ball positively and stop it on the greens.

Every golfer has a friend who, once in a while, will excitedly make the claim that he has discovered the "secret" of golf. For Hutchinson, whose steadiness under pressure made him such a fine match player, the secret was accuracy in bringing the club back to the position it was in when addressing the ball. This, he wrote, "can best be accomplished by keeping under firm control all parts of the body whose free movement is not essential to speed of swing."

Thus there should be no swaying to the right (the movements of a right-handed player are specified throughout this section) involved in turning the body on its own axis. This simple idea of building up power by means of the body swivelling around the axis of the spine was scarcely challenged in essentials for half a century until refined by American researchers into the full impact, and potential, of the Haskell and its derivatives as propelled by steel-shafted clubs.

Hutchinson was not the first to publish an instruction manual. H. B. Farnie's *A Keen Hand*, which

The great English player Harry Vardon was one of the first golfers to use the overlapping grip: the Vardon grip carries his name today, even though he was not the inventor.

appeared in 1857, described the clubs involved and their purpose, but fell far short of an attempt to analyse the mechanics of the swing.

Hutchinson's work, in contrast, was a bold and specific analysis. His starting point was a closed stance, with the right foot two to three inches behind the left, as was the method of the feathery players, with their long-shafted, long-headed clubs that swept the ball away. This, he wrote, was the practice of most fine players, who lifted their left foot onto the toe at the top of the backswing, with the sole of the left shoe facing towards the green.

Though he did not speak of posture as often as modern teachers, he was making a related point when he insisted that the upward swing was important because it must forecast the nature of the downswing to the ball. He held that the left hand provided power, the right guidance, so that the grip should be tight with the left hand and lighter with the right.

John Ball, the Hoylake champion, changed all this with a more upright, open stance that proved a winner, because it allowed a plane of swing that got the gutty up in the air. Ball was a ball-manoeuvrer supreme, and he would have been scornful of the modern professional practice of carrying wedges for all occasions.

He was able to open or close the clubface to achieve his ends, which included keeping the ball low into the wind, or getting it up, with backspin, to pull it up quickly on the green. Bernard Darwin considered Ball's swing even more pleasing to watch than Bobby Jones's.

J H Taylor added significantly to the golfer's armoury with the spin he imparted to his iron shots, and his control over the ball in bad weather. The story is told of him that while giving a playing lesson on course to Tommy Armour, he was asked how he contrived to get so much "stop" on the ball. Taylor replied that he would instruct Armour on that art as soon

Byron Nelson who, in 1945, produced the best year that golf has ever seen, used his legs to help drive the club through the ball.

as he showed some signs of being able to hit his ball up to the hole.

Vardon officiates at a marriage

Harry Vardon was the next great innovator. He made a successful adaptation of the overlapping grip, with the little finger of the right hand crooked over the index finger of the left, first employed by Johnny Laidlay, the Scottish amateur. By this means it was possible, in Vardon's phrase, "to wed the hands". The highest and lowest points at which the club is grasped are well separated, the thumb and first finger of the right hand at the lowest point of the hands, and the third, fourth and fifth fingers of the left at the highest.

Adding this to matchless timing,

for he was said never to force a shot, Vardon created a classic model admired on both sides of the Atlantic. A contemporary account has it that the outstanding impression of watching Vardon play was of "utter ease and lack of physical effort".

He began his swing in a fashion not taught today, dragging the club back and the hands inward: at the top of the backswing his arm was not merely bent but at a right angle. He held that the force of the swing would cause the arm to straighten at impact, which refutes accusations that he "hit from the top". Further proof is in pictures of Vardon taken at an advanced stage in his downswing. They show he was as late a hitter as the golfing world has seen, bringing his wrists into the equation at the last fraction of a second.

The only other player to attract as much veneration and fulsome praise as Vardon was Bobby Jones. Jones's instructional films and the flick books of his swing display an upright swing with an effect of unbroken, rounded symmetry. This is as different as can be from pictures of golfers in the late gutty days.

A search for means to control the lively Haskell-type ball quickly became a top priority as the 20th century dawned. Americans supplied the best answers, especially in approach shots, though Jock Hutchison's deeply grooved clubs that brought him the British Open in 1921 also brought action from the authorities.

Henry Cotton's doctrine of the crucial importance of hand action, and training the fingers by practice to take up the correct tension on the

Ben Hogan honed the erratic swing of his early days to such an extent that he remains the most controlled hitter of a golf ball ever to have played the game.

swing, ever since the days when Hutchinson was insisting that there should be no lateral swaying.

Vardon had implied that the use of the legs was part of the required swing sequence, in his practice of bringing the left heel back to the ground as he began his downswing. Now Nelson went further, and harnessed the power of his legs, yet achieved a straightness few could rival, and runs of tournament success no one has ever equalled.

Ben Hogan progressed from youthful hooker, by way of prodigies of practice, to perhaps the most complete master of ball control from tee to green that the game has seen. Hogan's slight fade and low flight were an insurance policy that paid off handsomely.

Comparing photographic studies of Hogan's action in the early years of his domination with its full flowering in the early 1950s, the impression is inescapable that everything became tighter: less flamboyant leg action and all other physical movements became a paradigm of economy. The impression was that the whole production was so compact, there was so little left to chance, that very little could go wrong.

"Grooved" was indeed the name of his game; and of American teacher-technology since the Second World War. Jack Nicklaus and Tom Watson, in particular, have carried on in that grooved tradition, Watson with one of the most upright swings of all – sharp, speedy, yet compact.

Shedding light on putting

Frank Thomas and his USGA team of researchers are brave, or foolhardy, enough to be going into the mystic business of putting. At the 1994 US Open at Oakmont, and at certain 1995 PGA events, laser beams were used to take exhaustive measurements of putts as to length, slope, speed and borrow. Pro tour statistics over the last 20 years also came into the equation.

Early tees were, by rule, so close to holes that putting surfaces could scarcely be velvety in texture, and putting was sometimes better tackled as a chipping manoeuvre, a useful skill in any case in the days of the stymie. There is, therefore, a fine irony in the fact that it was largely through his putting supremacy that Willie Park Sr became the first winner of the Championship Belt back in 1860. He also won the British Open on three other occasions, despite a tendency to foolhardy gambles through the green. Once on it, though, he usually proved the master.

Nowadays it is a useful putter who gets round, consistently, in less than 30 strokes on the greens. Pros on majors tours must aspire to around 28. The arrival of better greens made it clear that putting is a game within a game. It still is, and one at which success has suddenly eluded even the greatest players, from Harry Vardon to Nick Faldo and Tom Watson. When it happened to Watson, he had already written one of the most useful of all instructional books, *Getting Up and Down*, subtitled "How to Save Strokes from 40 Yards and In". It is a genuine stroke-saver. It is rather sad to read, in Jack Nicklaus's foreword to the book: "He [Watson] knows he isn't going to miss many short putts, so he can be aggressive and take a run at a long putt or chip. Someday maybe he'll start missing some short putts and come back into the real world ..." This last conjecture is exactly what has happened to Watson, who would otherwise have added several majors to his tally.

This suggests that, however good the putting method, it will fail unless nerve and inspiration support it. Park believed in a pendulum-stroke principle, using hands and arms. Watson's major points are keeping the eye over the ball, hands locked with forearms so that the putter is moved with the arms, which are locked to the shoulders, and (a crucial point) a consistent angle of bend in the

club, helped him become the envy of all for his straightness off the tee. He believed teachers inflicted damage on their pupils by their injurious emphasis on body action. He did not need a full swing to send the ball enormous distances, and his swing attracted the epithet "grooved" before the American development of the notion.

Byron Nelson's great contribution to the swing, as he collected one prize after another before and after the Second World War, was his ability to make best use of the firmer and more obedient steel shafts by virtue of using his legs, both of them, to drive through the ball. Hitting against the braced left side had long been the accepted gospel of the left elbow. Extending the arm, he believes, must break the bond with the shoulders.

Watson uses the term pendulum, but only as a tip to maintain a good rhythm: after hitting the putt, he advises, count one before looking up. As with all other strokes, deceleration of the clubhead as it reaches the ball is a cardinal sin, often caused by taking the putter too far back.

In between Park and what might be called the classic American "straight-line" putting technique espoused by Watson, there were all sorts of contrivances, notably croquet putting, banned in 1968, and the Sam Snead side-winder style: a development of croquet putting, but with the left hand high on the shaft and the right hand much lower. This involved pushing the putter head through the ball while both feet remain the same side of the line of putt, i.e. in a legal position.

Desperate measures have been taken to combat putting failures. Henry Longhurst's cure, most radical of all, ensured that he never missed another short putt: he retired from the game. Faldo has tried left hand below right, gone back to orthodoxy, then returned to left hand below right, and so on. Others have garages packed with putters, and many have gained comfort from the broomhandle putter, long enough to cuddle under the chin, with one hand acting as a fulcrum, while the other pushes the putter head through.

Bernhard Langer's valour in the face of putting terrors is unrivalled. He has twice been in the depths, but rebuilt his game on the greens with his much-copied ploy of gripping well down the shaft with his left hand, while holding his left forearm against the upper part of the shaft with his right hand. The shaft is thus made to act as a splint for his left wrist. He has since reverted, with considerable success, to the broomhandle putter.

The far from encouraging fact for each and every struggler on the green

Putting is a crucial but often overlooked aspect of golf: Bobby Locke, the South African, is considered by many to have been its finest exponent.

is that the list of consistently great putters is much shorter than that of golf's "Legends". The six giants of the putting game are Walter Travis (once described as "a killer" on the green), Walter Hagen, Bobby Jones (who had no weaknesses, least of all perhaps when it came to a "must" putt), Billy Casper, Bobby Locke and Bob Charles.

Hagen's strength as a putter was two-fold. His hands, firstly, were those of a musician, with long slender fingers. Wrapping these around the grip, and with his weight on his left foot, he stroked through the ball in the approved US style of the straight-line putter, continuing the clubhead's path towards the hole for as long as possible.

Secondly, his mental toughness was renowned. Who else would have asked for his closest rival at the climax of a US Open to come out and watch him putt for a win? Hagen rimmed the hole, went out on the town for most of the night, then beat his man in a play-off the next day.

Casper's method was almost frightening to watch: his stroke was the antithesis of Hutchinson's swing-not-hit gospel, for he gave his putts a thorough-going rap with an action that was almost all wrist. His putting average in winning the 1959 US Open was 28, and at Winged Foot too, notorious for its slopes.

Locke is held by many to be the greatest putter of them all. John

Reece tells the story of how Norman Sutton gave an off-form and worried Locke a putting lesson just before the 1949 Open. Sutton had spotted that Locke was moving his body at impact. By the end of the lesson, Locke had holed 50 putts in a row from 4ft without moving any part of his body apart from his hands, with which, Sutton diagnosed, Locke had been gripping too tightly. Locke won that Open, after single-putting eight of the nine holes at which he had to escape from sand.

It is worth noting that even the greatest of putters took a lesson. As Watson asked the weekend golfer: "How many do you know who've ever taken a putting lesson?"

THE RULES OF GOLF

Golf is a target ball game of stark simplicity, but it is governed by a wide-ranging and detailed set of rules and circumscribed by a code of conduct and an etiquette that are throwbacks to a more gentlemanly age.

In the beginning, and for several centuries after the game emerged as a cross-country sport, matchplay was the only form of golf. The object was to strike a ball with a club from point A (called a tee) into a hole at point B in fewer strokes than one's opponent. The contest was played over a stipulated number of holes in a set order. It could be single combat or between pairs of players.

Games were organized person to person, on a private and individual basis, on the common land of such courses as Leith Links and St Andrews. The idea of the club, as a sporting institution, is far younger than the game of golf: before the founding of the Gentlemen Golfers of Edinburgh (now the Honourable Company of Edinburgh Golfers) just over two and a half centuries ago, clubs were political in function.

There came a time when golfing man's competitive instincts reached a stage when a search for the best player became imperative. Hence the gift of the Silver Club by the City of Edinburgh to the Gentlemen Golfers of that city. The winner of the Silver Club was to become Captain of the Golf: in modern parlance, champion. As such he was to settle all points of dispute concerning the rules.

John Rattray, winner of the first two Silver Club contests (1744-45), was undoubtedly concerned with the first code of rules, copied in 1754 by the St Andrews men away to the north in Fife.

To lift, or not to lift

These rules are simple and unequivocal. Though the player is never adjured in so many words to play the ball as it lies, the underlying thrust of the rules is unmistakably to that effect. Only if the ball landed in water or "watery filth", or shots came to rest so close together that strokes were impeded, could the ball be lifted. A player must, for the privilege of lifting his ball out of water, dropping it behind the hazard and playing on towards the hole, give up a stroke to his opponent. Obstructions, termed "break clubs", such as stones, were not to be removed, except upon "the fair green" - the putting surface. A lost ball cost a stroke too, the substitute to be played from the location of the errant shot.

St Andrews golfers played for their Silver Club from 1754 until 1759 not by a knock-out process, but on the basis that he who won more holes in his match than anyone else in theirs was the victor. This would clearly not do: a weak opponent, rather than a brilliant winner, might settle the issue.

So it was decreed that the trophy would go to "whoever puts in the ball at the fewest strokes over the field, being 22 holes" ... for not until 1764 did St Andrews amend their course to the now universally accepted 18 holes for a round. This invention of strokeplay brought its problems.

The old play-it-as-it-lies rule of thumb could not survive in all circumstances. It was slow to die, however. Charles Macdonald, the first US amateur champion, a pupil of Old Tom Morris in the 1870s, wrote: "Touching a ball in play without penalty was anathema to me, a kind of sacrilegious profanity."

Provision had to be made in strokeplay for golfers to complete their rounds and submit a score no matter what difficulties they ran into. So punishments for hitting into trouble, penalties for escaping from it, and definitions for every facet of play had to be minted and, over the years, reminted and refined. So varied is the nature of courses throughout the world that conundrums for the Rules of Golf Committees of the USGA and the R&A will never cease to present themselves. So their work is never done: for it is their joint responsibility to exercise authority worldwide, keeping the rules up to date amid changes in conditions and equipment and responding to the curious scrapes that golfers get into.

Modern terminology

There is plenty of variety in the forms golf can take. On top of the linchpins of single combat at matchplay and strokeplay, there are threesomes, in which one plays against two, and each side plays one ball; foursomes (two against two, each side playing one ball); threeball (three playing one another, with a ball apiece); bestball (one plays against the better ball of two or the best ball of three); fourball (two play their better ball against the better ball of two other players). In the foursome format, the partners play tee-shots at alternate holes, thereafter playing alternate shots; playing out of turn costs the hole in matchplay, two strokes in strokeplay.

Disqualification follows in strokeplay if the error is not corrected before teeing off at the next hole, or, where the last hole is concerned, leaving the putting green without declaring the intention to correct the error.

American terminology is now accepted worldwide where scoring is concerned: par means the score expected on each hole of a first-class, i.e. scratch, player. Birdie (one-under par), eagle (two under), the rare double-eagle or albatross (three under) developed from the day in 1899 at Atlantic City after George Crump's second shot at a par four fell close to the hole after hitting a bird in flight. There is an alternative version, that the origin is a comment about "a bird of a shot". Bogey is one-over par (double- and triple-bogey, etc. being self-explanatory).

Bogey used to mean the score achieved by the mythical Colonel Bogey, who made no mistakes, and therefore turned in the perfect score. The American system is clearly far more explicit, though the Colonel lingers on in older dictionaries.

The variations of the golf game are infinite, especially where the myriad betting formulas are concerned. Rules Committees have

an opinion on betting, too; it is a frosty one. Since private wagers are beyond the reach of the game's rulers, they make no attempt to police such gambling, and bookmakers take bets worldwide on professional tournaments. Where amateur play is concerned, the authorities frown on large-scale Calcutta sweepstakes and, on days of major club competitions, the purchase of shares in competitors with a view to receiving a dividend if investment has been made in the winning player.

"Vive la politesse"

Almost alone among sports, golf demands, but does not always elicit, total respect for opponents. Generally speaking, the better the golfer, the closer he or she comes to the USGA/R&A ideal. Etiquette comes first in the book of rules, the concept wedded to safety and consideration for others.

Players must be alert lest their practice swing injures a bystander, while absolute silence and immobility is demanded when a player prepares to hit the ball. Players must not dawdle, strike the ball before players in front are out of range, or fail to call following players through when a ball is being sought; three- or fourball matches must let twoball matches through, and golfers must not delay in leaving the green (by inference, this means also not standing about filling in scorecards before moving off). A group losing more than one clear hole on the players in front should invite the following group to go through.

It would be folly to suggest that all these counsels are followed with saintly forbearance, or even that the vast majority of players are aware of every one of the foregoing,

At the 1999 British Open, Frenchman Jean Van de Velde felt the full force of the "play the ball as it lies" rule – an errant shot into the water cost him the championship.

not to mention further points of etiquette, such as that "Any match playing a whole round is entitled to pass a match playing a shorter round" and "A single player has no standing and should give way to a match of any kind".

There is also the matter of consideration for the course, in that players should smooth over marks they make in bunkers, repair pitch-marks (dents made in greens by approach shots), replace "divots" (portions of fairway turf dislodged in play ... though turf damaged on tees should not be replaced, lest a tee peg shift in a loose divot) and avoid damage to the holes themselves. Damage caused on greens by shoe spikes should be repaired only after putting is completed. However, repairs to old hole plugs and turf damaged by ball impact can be repaired before putting out.

In the writer's experience, one point of etiquette that is seldom ignored is that the great majority of players do take care not to walk on the line of other players' putts.

Professionals in general and top-class amateurs in particular will go further than the rule book on etiquette. On the tee, they will not drive off while a player is putting on a nearby green. This may lead to a minor delay, but it seldom causes ill feeling. The major cause of high blood pressure on golf courses is the failure to yield to other groups on the basis of the rules of precedence outlined above.

A basic cause of slow play, especially where groups of three or four are concerned, is the dis-inclination of players to get ready to play as soon as it is their turn. No. 2 of a quartet will delay his pacing out and surveying of his putt until No. 1 has performed the same sequence.

The rules are not the same for strokeplay and matchplay. Suppose a player thinks his ball is damaged and unfit for play when he reaches his drive. Before lifting his ball

to check, he must "announce his intention to his opponent in matchplay or his marker or a fellow competitor in strokeplay". Then he must mark the position of the ball. He must not clean it (mud on the ball does not make it unfit for play). He must allow his opponent, marker or fellow-competitor the chance to examine the ball.

The ball can be changed if it is found to be unfit for play. (When a ball breaks into pieces the stroke is cancelled, and another ball played from the same spot.) Any deviation from this procedure is punished in matchplay by the loss of the hole; in strokeplay by a two-stroke penalty.

Since the usual penalty in strokeplay for breaking a rule is two strokes, and in matchplay the loss of the hole, it is not permitted to indulge in both forms of the game at the same time: so a player keeping count of his opponent's strokes for submission for handicap purposes, of which more later, while also competing with him at matchplay has, according to the letter, and spirit, of the law, lost at matchplay and compiled an inadmissible card at strokeplay.

It's no handicap

Golf has unique charms for spectator and player. It is possible to get a close-up view of players even in major championships. Furthermore, while an overweight, none-too-fit businessman of 45 would never survive on a lawn tennis court even with the world's 100th-ranked player, or do more than just get in the way as a linebacker with the Dallas Cowboys, he could enjoy a game of golf against a top-class amateur, or a leading professional, and even hope to win if he played to his handicap. By which is meant the number of strokes that his ruling body consider to represent the difference between our plump businessman's golfing skills and those of the expert.

In principle, a player's handicap is, or should be, an accurate assessment of his ability to play to the standard scratch score (SSS) of a course. Great minds have been applied to the intricate and thankless task of making these judgements which affect a golfer's prospects every time he enters a competition, or even plays a friendly match. Until 1983, a great many British players could not, consistently, play to their handicaps because they were awarded on the basis of their best scores.

Since 1983, performances are reckoned against the SSS of courses, after a model developed by the Australian Golf Union. The SSS computation starts with the length of a course. At 7,001 yards the provisional SSS is 74; at 4,100 it is 60.

The final SSS might be increased or lowered on consideration of general layout, sizes of greens and whether watered or unwatered, difficulties imposed by hazards, width of fairway, trees, rough, and prevailing weather conditions, together with the degree to which the ball runs on landing. Therefore the total par of a course will not necessarily equal the SSS, which must not be allocated hole by hole, but given only as a total for the course.

In the first place a player can obtain a handicap by submitting scorecards. The national union or a delegated area authority is responsible for ratifying the handicaps of players with low or plus handicaps.

A player's handicap is effective wherever he plays, and can only be obtained by a member of a club affiliated to the national union. The USGA operates a patented system that depends on evaluation of 20 scores against two assessments of a course's playing difficulty, one for scratch players and one for players inferior to that standard.

The player in receipt of strokes from his betters on a golf course

cannot choose where he will take them. The card of the course includes a stroke index, which will decree that if two strokes are to be given, they will be, for instance at Royal St David's, Harlech, taken at the tenth hole (stroke index 1) and the third (SI 2). If 14 strokes were to be given, the receiver would get them at every Royal St David's hole except the second, ninth, 11th and 18th. The SI figure is not an indication of a hole's degree of difficulty.

Point scoring

One of golf's principal benefactors was Dr Frank Stableford, who has been called the patron saint of club golfers. His eponymous points system not only allows single matches to involve players of varying ability in a meaningful contest, but any number of players on a course - or courses. His system was first used at Wallasey on Merseyside in the early 1930s. A scratch player receives four points for an eagle, three for a birdie, two for par, one for bogey, none for double-bogey. A player who has a stroke on any particular hole receives an extra point at each stage of this progression, so a par brings him three points, a birdie four.

Recent converts to golf cannot fully appreciate it, but those who were playing before 1952 may consider that the 1951 R&A/USGA rules conference included a majority of saintly figures. The conference was the first of its kind between the two ruling bodies, and issued uniform rules effective worldwide from 1952. One conference decision ended a hoary, old and bitter controversy: the "stymie" was abolished.

A player was "stymied" on the green if he was unable to putt to the hole because his opponent's ball lay in the way. Unless the balls lay within six inches of each other, the only solution was either to loft the ball, or use the contours of the green to circumvent the obstacle:

Old Tom Morris had remarked how skilful Allan Robertson had been at finding the crumbling edge of a hole in such circumstances.

Traditionalists wanted to keep the stymie, to some degree because it had been part of the game for so long, but also because ending the stymie rule offered another opportunity to lift the ball, anathema to the old school of play-it-as-it-lies. Abolitionists considered that the essence of golf was that players should never be baulked in this way.

The USGA, among others, agonized about the matter, and polled the larger associations about it: 22 said keep the stymie, which had been in force since 1812, apart from one year. That was when the R&A abandoned the rule in 1833, but re-imposed it the following year. Twenty-four associations said the stymie should be abolished.

Controversy was periodically renewed when famous matches were decided by stymies, as in Bobby Jones's 19th-hole win over Cyril Tolley on his way to the first leg of his grand slam in 1930, and the defeat, six years later, of the Scot, Jack McLean, in the US Amateur final by Johnny Fischer from Kentucky. English hackles were raised when the final of the English Close Amateur Championship in the crucial year of 1951 ended at the 39th hole when G.P. Roberts of Southport and Ainsdale beat H. Bennett of Buxton with the cruellest of stymies.

Seventeen years later the conference outlawed croquet-style putting: players may not putt with one foot on either side of the line of putt, as if with a croquet mallet. Like many other players, especially older ones who had developed a twitch using the traditional stance, Sam Snead had to resort to a posture known as the "side-winder", holding the top of the shaft with the left hand, then stroking the ball forward with the right hand lower down the shaft. Few believed that putting in the croquet style was consistent with the traditions of the game.

Such are the complexities of golf's rules nowadays that even the top professionals seek advice on the course from tournament officials.

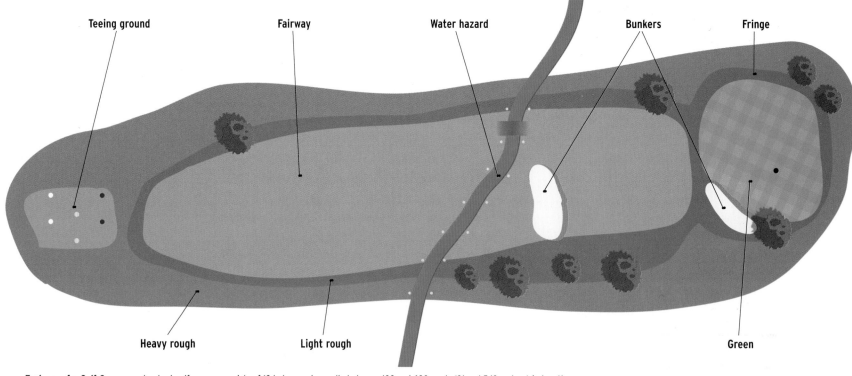

Teeing ground   **Fairway**   **Water hazard**   **Bunkers**   **Fringe**

Heavy rough   **Light rough**   **Green**

Features of a Golf Course: a standard golf course consists of 18 holes, each usually between 100 and 600 yards (91 and 549 metres) in length.

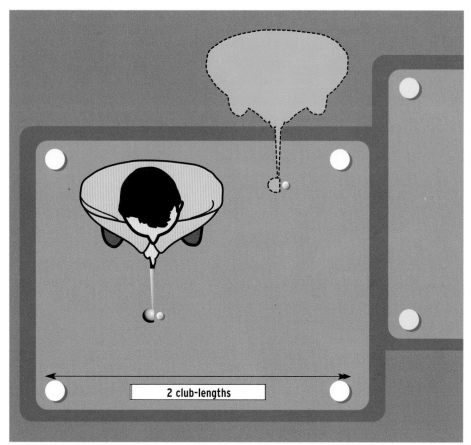

2 club-lengths

Teeing Ground: tee-shots must be struck from within a rectangle two club lengths in depth – but players can stand outside to hit their shots.

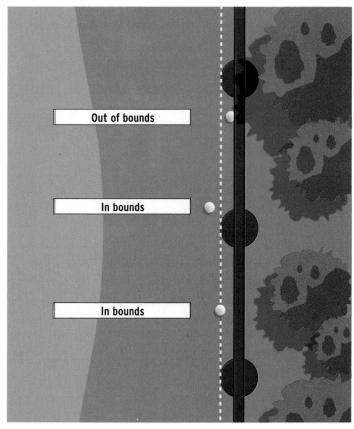

Out of bounds

In bounds

In bounds

Out of Bounds: the out-of-bounds line is that which joins inside points of fence posts at ground level. Therefore, the ball at the top is out of bounds; the other two are in bounds.

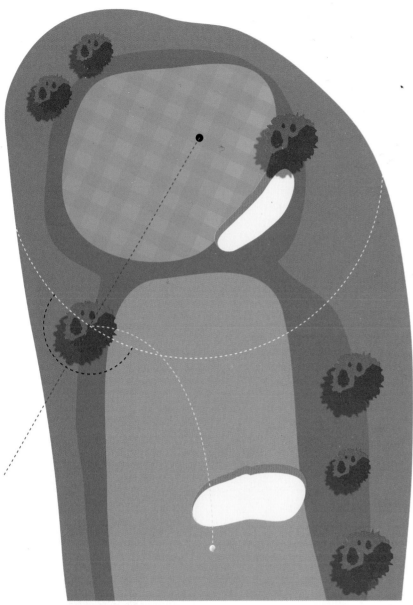

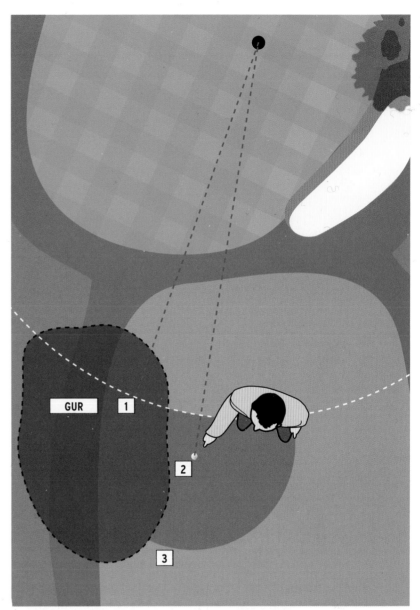

Unplayable Ball: if a ball is declared unplayable in a bush, the player can (under penalty of one stroke): (i) go back to play from where the previous stroke was played, (ii) drop a ball within two club lengths of where the ball was declared unplayable, not nearer the hole, as shown in the diagram, (iii) drop a ball behind the point where the ball lay, keeping that point directly between the hole and the spot on which the ball is played, with no limits to how far behind that point the ball may be dropped.

Where and How to Drop: a ball lying in ground under repair (GUR) at 1 must be lifted and dropped (without penalty) within one club-length of the nearest point of relief (2), and not nearer the hole (i.e. not between the dotted line and the hole). The ball is still in play as long as it rolls to no further back than 3, two club-lengths from 2. If the stance to the dropped ball is inside the GUR, the ball must be redropped. To drop the ball, stand erect with the arm outstretched to the front or side and release the ball. The ball must not be dropped over the shoulder.

One waive and you're out

Anyone who has served in the military will recognize the third section of Rule 1 (The Game) for what it is ... golf's version of that service charge prohibiting conduct prejudicial to good order and discipline which, as every soldier, sailor or airman knows, means any conduct of which the Service

remotely disapproves.

Golf's version is entitled "Agreement to Waive Rules", and says: "Players shall not agree to exclude the operation of any Rule or to waive any penalty incurred."

Rule 1 has already, in section two, brought the player to the realization that he is on his own. It makes

clear that neither he, nor any other player, nor his caddie shall take any action to influence the position or the movement of a ball except in accordance with the rules. Nor is he to give advice on play, or choice of club, to anyone except a partner, or their caddies ... nor seek it, with the same exceptions. The penalty:

the loss of the hole in matchplay, two strokes in strokeplay. Penalties henceforward will be given in that order: first for matchplay, then strokeplay.

Man is a litigious animal, and legislators are frequently outflanked by the expertise of the general public, aided by sharp-eyed lawyers, in finding loopholes in statutes. After more than 260 years of refinement, the rules of golf present a brick wall to the cheat. Admittedly, this is a strange claim to make of a game where cheating is easy, because the player is often out of sight of his fellows and, in theory at least, could do anything to improve his lot.

Here is the inner appeal of the game for, in effect, as the totality of the rules make clear, the golfer's only opponent is himself. If he cheats, he has lost and the game has won: it usually does whether he cheats or not, but the difference is between honourable and dishonourable defeat. The stigma attached to the latter is a destroyer of character, and a quick way to lose club membership. Henry Beard has written, tongue in cheek one assumes *The Official Exceptions to the Rules* with a subtitle of "At last a rule book that makes cheating legal" – but the official rule book accepts no exceptions to observing the rules.

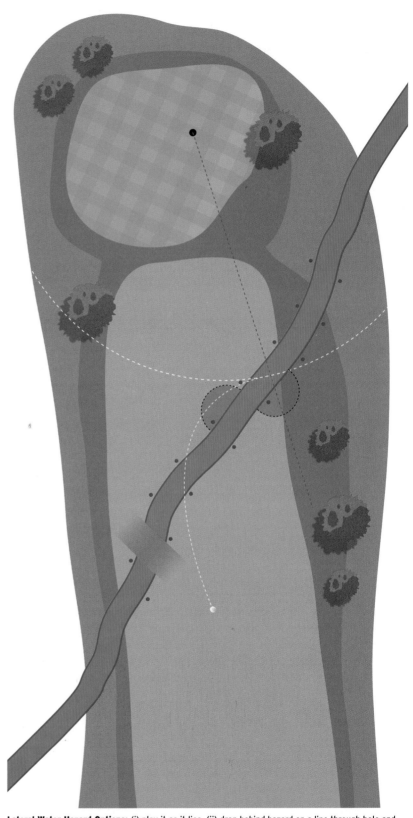

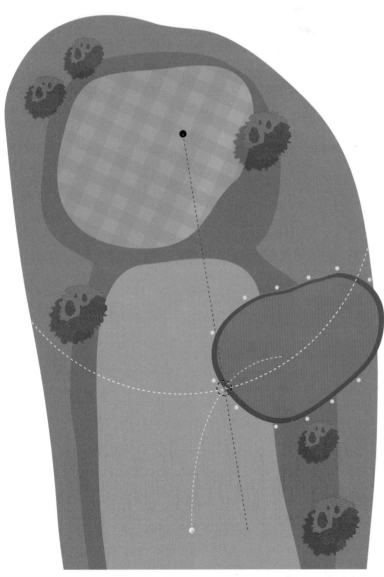

Water Hazard Options: (i) play the ball as it lies without penalty, (ii) drop, not nearer the hole, on an extension of line from hole through the line of entry: penalty, one stroke, (iii) return to the point where the previous stroke was made: penalty, one stroke.

Lateral Water Hazard Options: (i) play it as it lies, (ii) drop behind hazard on a line through hole and point of entry, (iii) play from point of previous stroke, (iv) play from shaded area, i.e. within two club-lengths of point of entry, no nearer hole or (v) shaded area on opposite side of hazard. Options ii, iii, iv and v cost one stroke.

Playing the Ball as it Lies: do not improve the lie of the ball (e.g. by pressing the foot into long grass behind the ball). Principle: play the ball as it lies. Penalty for violation: matchplay, loss of hole; strokeplay, two strokes.

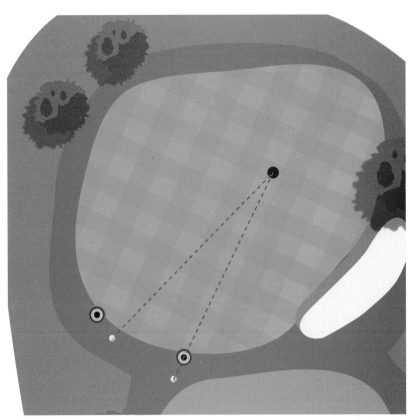

Sprinkler Blockage: the ball shown on the right must be played as it lies, as the sprinkler head is not interfering with stance. The ball on the left can be lifted as the sprinkler head is interfering with stance (though not in the case of a left-hander). No penalty.

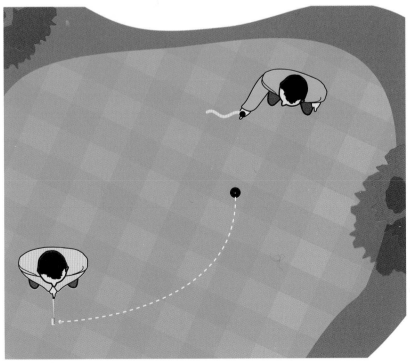

Indicating the Line of a Putt: a caddie or partner may indicate line of putt, but must not touch the green or mark it. Penalty: loss of hole or two strokes.

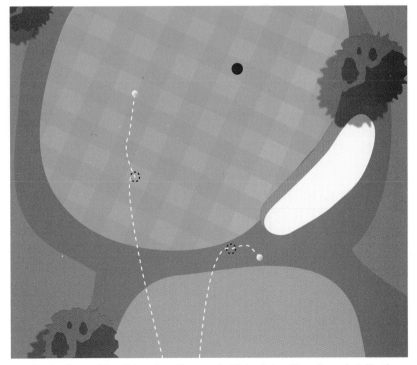

Running Repairs: repairing pitch marks on the green (top) is legal – repairing spike marks is illegal. Repairing ball marks off the green is a violation, but is permitted after putting out (below).

Playing by the rules

Let us now start at the beginning, on the tee. The player must arrive there with no more than 14 clubs in his bag. Six or seven was the usual complement for Harry Vardon and his rivals in the days of wooden, usually hickory, shafts. With the coming of steel clubs (legalized by the USGA in 1924, but not until 1929 by the R&A) and particularly with the refinement of matched sets, the temptation to carry a club for every length and variety of shot was powerful.

Lawson Little, winner of both the British and US Amateur Championships in 1934-35, carried as many as 25. Opponents always of excess, and eager to encourage shot-making skills (veteran golfers were scornful of players who couldn't play a half shot with a six-iron to make up for lack of a seven-iron), the authorities called a halt at 14 clubs in 1938. Penalties are heavy for the unwary: one hole for each hole at which the infraction occurred to a maximum of two holes, or two strokes per hole, maximum four strokes per round. The clubs, too, must conform to strict regulations as to configuration.

The ball must conform to USGA/R&A specifications, and much money and effort is expended to make sure that they do. Briefly, its weight must be no more than 1.62oz (45.93g), and its diameter no less than 1.68in (42.67mm). Crucially, the initial velocity of the ball must be no greater than 250ft (76.2m) per second, within a tolerance of two per cent.

Suitably equipped, which means without "artificial device or unusual equipment" and certainly without means of measuring distance or gauging the conditions, the golfer makes a start, mindful always that "the ball shall be fairly struck at with the head of the club and must not be pushed, scraped or spooned". Hitting the ball twice

in the execution of a stroke costs a penalty stroke, i.e. the one blow counts as two. The golfer must be careful to take his rightful turn on the tee according to the rules of precedence. In a competition, that means following the draw order issued by the committee, in the absence of which the order "should be decided by lot".

Low-handicap golfers do not gain the honour, as the right to strike the first blow is called, because of respect for their greater expertise, though they often do by custom in friendly matches. Thereafter, the honour falls to whoever last won a hole.

Our man should be equally careful not to place his ball nearer the hole than a line joining the twin tee-markers. Nor can he play from more than two clubs' lengths behind that line. At last, he steps up to make a start, only to find his ball has toppled off his tee-peg (not an essential item for teeing off) before he could make a swing at it. He is at liberty to replace the ball, and carry on: if this happens no penalty is involved, since no attempt to hit the ball was made.

If the ball falls off during the downswing, and the golfer cannot check his swing, too bad – it counts as a stroke, even if the club makes no contact with it.

A tee shot struck from outside the proper teeing ground can be recalled by your opponent. You must play again: apart from this there is no penalty, but in strokeplay the penalty is two strokes, and play again.

That would make three off the tee, which is also the answer when a ball is lost, or flies out of bounds. The scorecard outlines what the boundaries of the course are, and what marks them: a line, itself out of bounds (OOB), a ditch, a fence, wall or stakes, where the OOB line is the nearest inside points of the stakes or fence posts at ground

level, excluding angled supports. The principle follows the soccer model: the ball is out of bounds when all of it lies out of bounds.

The player who fears his ball is lost can, to save time and an irritating walk back after a fruitless search, play a provisional ball. This constitutes the stroke and distance rule, in this case being provisionally followed in case the ball cannot be found in the statutory five minutes allowed. Opponent(s) or marker must be informed of the intention to play a provisional, which must be done before searching for the first ball starts: normally, that is before leaving the tee. The provisional can be played again, up to the point where the player believes his original ball might be.

If that stays lost, the provisional ball becomes the ball in play. A second ball can also be played when a disagreement occurs between players in a group about the right way to proceed, for example, what penalty should be imposed if any, or relief received. The player whose position is in doubt may play the first ball as it lies, the second with a drop, make a note of the score from both, and seek an official ruling at the end of the round, remembering not to sign the card until the issue has been settled.

The rules allow a golfer to declare his ball unplayable at any time, except in a water hazard.

The "unplayable" decision is entirely up to the golfer's sense of fair play. First, at the cost of a stroke, he can follow the stroke and distance procedure, taking the ball back to where it was last struck. Second, he can drop his ball, again with a stroke penalty, within two club-lengths, but not nearer to the hole. Finally, the ball may be dropped any desired distance behind the unplayable spot, keeping that spot between the new position of the ball and the hole. This, too, costs a shot. "Drop" means

releasing the ball while standing erect with ball at arm's length.

The most frustrating misfortune in golf is undoubtedly playing the wrong ball: which is why a distinguishing mark on a ball is a good and potentially match- or card-saving precaution. For the penalty for playing the wrong ball, except in a hazard, is the loss of the hole, or two strokes. Disqualification follows in strokeplay if the error is not put right before the miscreant tees off at the next hole. If the wrong ball played in strokeplay belongs to an opponent, it must be replaced as nearly as possible to the position of the first stroke played in error.

The golfer is at liberty to lift his ball to identify it, if it is not in a hazard, and to replace it, but he may not clean it. If the ball was found in deep grass or mud, thence it must be returned.

Since lifting a ball to identify it in a hazard is not permitted, the golfer may play a ball in a hazard (defined below) when he cannot definitely identify it. This carries no penalty.

Next the golfer must be aware of penalties and rights attached to hazards, defined as any bunker (usually termed a "trap" in America) or water hazard. Grassy ground near a bunker is not part of a bunker, which is basically a hollow filled with sand. Grassed areas within a bunker are not part of it. Little dells lined with grass are neither bunkers nor hazards.

A water hazard is "any sea, lake, pond, river, ditch, surface drainage ditch or other open water course (whether or not it contains water) and anything of a similar nature".

There are options in both types of hazards. Play it as it lies is always an option, though the club must not touch the hazard except when the ball is being struck: so the club must not be grounded before the stroke is made. It is a good pre-caution never to ground a club in the rough either, for the grass, being disturbed, may move the ball, for which there is a one-stroke penalty.

A ball in a bunker which is also lying in casual water, ground under repair (usually delineated with a white line and labelled GUR by the greenkeeper) or in casts made by a burrowing animal can be dropped in the bunker without penalty, or outside it with a penalty stroke. It is sometimes impossible to find a spot clear of water in a bunker. Casual water is defined as a temporary accumulation of water visible before or after the player takes his stance.

Water hazards marked with yellow stakes or lines differ from lateral water hazards, which have red markings. Islands within a water hazard are deemed to be part of it. The first option with a ball in either is to play it as it lies ... easier when the area is dry, but not impossible when wet. But the player has to remember that the club must not be grounded.

If there is "reasonable evidence" that the ball is lost in the hazard, the player may, at the cost of a stroke, play a ball as nearly as possible at the spot from which the original ball was last played; or "drop a ball behind the water hazard, keeping the point at which the original ball last crossed the margin of the water hazard directly between the hole and the spot on which the ball is dropped, with no limit to how far behind the water hazard the ball may be dropped". In the case of a lateral water hazard, the procedure is different; it lies along the general direction of play, so it is not possible to drop behind it, so a ball may be dropped within two club-lengths of either the point where the original ball last crossed the margin of the water hazard or at a point on the opposite margin of the hazard equidistant from the hole.

Loose impediments (natural objects such as leaves and stones) and obstructions (artificial, man-made) present different options. The former may be moved, as long as they and the ball are not in a hazard: boundary fences and the like are not obstructions. Movable obstructions are what their name suggests ... the rules are highly literal in their wording ... but where immovable obstructions are concerned, relief without penalty is the general rule, unless the ball is in a water hazard.

The over-riding instruction is still to play the course as you find it, avoiding any temptation to improve lies or "moving or bending or breaking anything fixed or growing except in fairly taking your stance of making your swing".

Having finally reached the green, the golfer must never make a mark upon it to indicate a line for his putt, nor hit the flagstick with his putt, which costs the hole or a two-stroke penalty. Sand and loose soil are loose impediments only on greens, and can be brushed aside (but not pressed down), and balls may be cleaned before putting.

When a putt overhangs the hole, the golfer, having reached the hole "without unreasonable delay", is allowed ten additional seconds to make sure the ball is at rest. If it falls in after that, the player is deemed to have holed out with his last stroke, but a penalty stroke is added.

Golfers must be men of their word to the last. If a putt is conceded, the offer may not be refused. The offer, once made, may not be withdrawn.

A golfer who seeks to absorb golf's 34 rules by competing at a board game called Masterstroke can be secure in the knowledge that this is by no means a Trivial Pursuit. Masterstroke has been put together by an acknowledged rules expert, Bruce Adams.

Here are a few of the posers on offer:

Ace decision
Fearing his tee shot at a par three was lost, a golfer played a provisional, and could not find his original ball in a five-minute search. It was later found in the hole. Ruling: an ace, his play on the hole was complete once the ball was holed.

Water torture
Just out of bounds there is casual water in which a player must stand to hit his ball which is just in bounds. Can he claim relief? No, such a condition must be "on the course".

Lucky bounce
A player's ball hit a rock and flew backwards into woods. He declared it unplayable, and dropped at the original lie. His opponent's objection, on grounds that he was getting nearer the hole without playing a stroke, was rejected.

Taking the rap
When can a player not send for a replacement for a broken club? When it was not broken "in the normal course of play" - as when Ben Crenshaw in the 1987 Ryder Cup rapped his putter on the ground and snapped it.

In the cart
Players A and B were sharing a caddie car, in which B was sitting when A's shot hit it during strokeplay. Ruling: his ball was stopped by their (mutual) equipment: two-stroke penalty on A.

Living things
Andy Bean won at Doral after escaping penalty when his practice swing near a tree detached leaves. It was ruled that this had not assisted him. Sam Torrance was penalized two strokes in Austria for bringing down a small branch with a practice swing.

Caning for slow coaches
Golf's legislators anxiously sought an effective procedure for eradicating slow play for about as long as they agonized about abolishing the stymie. The nettle was grasped by radically expanding Rule 6-7, which required players to play without undue delay.

From 1996 this had to be done, "in accordance with any pace of play guidelines which may be laid down by the committee." The penalty for breaking the rule in this instance: loss of hole or two strokes, and "for subsequent offence - disqualification". This, think some, is a sure-fire source of bad blood at club level, especially if "pace of play" is not clearly set out and impartially enforced - an error avoided to great effect at the celebrated Sunningdale Foursomes in 1997, when the draw sheet was accompanied by set time limits for shots, holes and courses: the rounds had to be completed in 3hr 32min for both the Old and New courses.

The professionals' rulers are also now very specific. For instance, the European Tour has been empowered to impose a one-stroke penalty and a fine of £500 on players who are guilty of three "bad times". A "bad time" is acquired by a group spoken to by a Tour official once they got out of position, which means more than ten minutes behind the group in front. Further monitoring follows, with specific timings allowed for playing a shot or putting. There is a penalty schedule in place for those who offend: one bad time = no action, two = a warning, three = a stroke plus a £500 fine, and so on till five costs two strokes plus £1,000 fine. Seven brings a £1,000 fine and disqualification.

There is absolutely no pity or waiting on the PGA Tour, where officials stroll over to the offending party and say, "That'll be a $1,000."

CHAPTER TWO:
THE MAJOR CHAMPIONSHIPS

With the increasing popularity of golf throughout the 20th century, four championships have so captured the imagination of players and public alike that they have become known as the majors. The four majors march through the calendar nowadays like this: the Masters (held in April), the United States Open (in June), the British Open (in July) and the US PGA (in August) ... careful attempts over the years to fashion a fifth major have failed.

There are other tournaments that capture the public's imagination - largely the Ryder Cup, the biennial clash between the United States and, since 1979, Europe. An International team has got in on the act as well, playing the Americans in non-Ryder Cup years in an event called the President's Cup.

Tiger Woods on the fairway at St Andrews.

THE MASTERS

It may be the youngest major of them all, but the Masters, played over the Augusta course, has become one of the best known.

It took a long time for the full effects of the years 1930-34 to register upon the world of golf. Indeed, things were never the same again from the moment Bobby Jones, at the age of 28, retired from competitive golf. He had no more peaks to climb after 1930, when he exceeded even the massive expectations of his adoring public on both sides of the Atlantic by winning all four of what were then accepted as the four major championships in one season – the British and United States Opens, and the Amateur championships of the same two countries.

Arnold Palmer and Jack Nicklaus have won ten green jackets between them and have had some famous Augusta showdowns over the years, none more so than in 1964 and 1965.

Masters Results at Augusta National, Georgia

Year	Winner	Runner-up	Score
1934	H Smith	C Wood	284
1935	G Sarazen	C Wood	282
	won 36-hole play-off 144 to 149		
1936	H Smith	H Cooper	285
1937	B Nelson	R Guldahl	283
1938	H Picard	R Guldahl	285
1939	R Guldahl	S Snead, W Burke, W Lawson Little	279
1940	J Demaret	L Mangrum	280
1941	C Wood	B Nelson	280
1942	B Nelson	B Hogan	280
	won 18-hole play-off 69 to 70		
1943-45	No tournament		
1946	H Keiser	B Hogan	282
1947	J Demaret	B Nelson, F Stranahan	281
1948	C Harmon	C Middlecoff	279
1949	S Snead	J Bulla, L Mangrum	282
1950	J Demaret	J Ferrier	283
1951	B Hogan	S Riegel	280
1952	S Snead	J Burke Jr	286
1953	B Hogan	P Oliver Jr	274
1954	S Snead	B Hogan	289
	won 18-hole play-off 70 to 71		
1955	C Middlecoff	B Hogan	279
1956	J Burke Jr	K Venturi	289
1957	D Ford	S Snead	283
1958	A Palmer	D Ford, F Hawkins	284
1959	A Wall Jr	C Middlecoff	284
1960	A Palmer	K Venturi	282
1961	G Player	A Palmer, C Coe	280
1962	A Palmer	G Player, D Finsterwald	280
	won 18-hole play-off 68 to 71 to 77		
1963	J Nicklaus	A Lema	286
1964	A Palmer	D Marr, J Nicklaus	276
1965	J Nicklaus	A Palmer, G Player	271
1966	J Nicklaus	T Jacobs, G Brewer	288
	won 18-hole play-off 70 to 72 to 78		
1967	G Brewer	R Nichols	280
1968	R Goalby	R de Vicenzo	277
1969	G Archer	T Weiskopf, W Casper, G Knudson	281
1970	W Casper	G Littler	279
	won 18-hole play-off 69 to 74		
1971	C Coody	J Miller, J Nicklaus	279
1972	J Nicklaus	T Weiskopf, B Crampton, R Mitchell	286
1973	T Aaron	JC Snead	283
1974	G Player	D Stockton, T Weiskopf	278
1975	J Nicklaus	J Miller, T Weiskopf	276
1976	R Floyd	B Crenshaw	271
1977	T Watson	J Nicklaus	276
1978	G Player	R Funseth, H Green, T Watson	277
1979	F Zoeller	T Watson, E Sneed	280
	won play-off at second extra hole		

Year	Winner	Runner-up	Score
1980	S Ballesteros	G Gilbert, J Newton	275
1981	T Watson	J Nicklaus, J Miller	280
1982	C Stadler	D Pohl	284
	won play-off at first extra hole		
1983	S Ballesteros	B Crenshaw, T Kite	280
1984	B Crenshaw	T Watson	277
1985	B Langer	C Strange, R Floyd, S Ballesteros	282
1986	J Nicklaus	T Kite, G Norman	279
1987	L Mize	S Ballesteros, G Norman	285
	won play-off at second extra hole		
1988	S Lyle	M Calcavecchia	281
1989	N Faldo	S Hoch	283
	won play-off at second extra hole		
1990	N Faldo	R Floyd	278
	won play-off at second extra hole		
1991	I Woosnam	J-M Olazabal	277
1992	F Couples	R Floyd	275
1993	B Langer	C Beck	277
1994	J-M Olazabal	T Lehman	279
1995	B Crenshaw	D Love III	274
1996	N Faldo	G Norman	276
1997	T Woods	T Kite	270
1998	M O'Meara	F Couples, D Duval	279
1999	J-M Olazabal	D Love III	280
2000	V Singh	E Els	278
2001	T Woods	D Duval	272
2002	T Woods	R Goosen	276
2003	M Weir	L Mattiace	281
	won play-off at first extra hole		
2004	P Mickelson	E Els	279
2005	T Woods	C DiMarco	276
	won play-off at first extra hole		
2006	P Mickelson	T Clark	281
2007	Z Johnson	R Sabbatini, R Goosen, T Woods	289
2008	T Immelman	T Woods	280
2009	A Cabrera	K Perry, C Campbell	276
	won play-off at second extra hole		
2010	P Mickelson	L Westwood	272

After finishing runner-up in 1939, Sam Snead finally came good ten years later and went on to triumph in the Masters on two more occasions (in 1952 and in 1954).

It is difficult for a golf fan under 80 who has not skimmed the contemporary media to take on board the scale of the adulation, respect, affection and general awe commanded by Jones, even before the grand slam. Jones's fame eclipsed that of such outstanding professionals as Walter Hagen and Gene Sarazen. Besides, they could not play for the two amateur titles, and though the Professional Golfers' Championship, founded in 1916, was gaining in importance, its quality was never franked by the presence of the undisputed top golfer, Jones.

Three years after Jones retired, Johnny Goodman won the US Open. No amateur has won it since, or won any other major. So the amateur titles rapidly lost their honoured position at the topmost level of the game. Playing in high-class amateur golf cost money, and there was little about in the depths of the Depression.

Another major, open to paid and unpaid, was needed, and there was more than a touch of poetic justice in the fact that the greatest amateur of all, Jones, provided it, unknowingly, in 1934. His offering was a uniquely lovely course and an event which admitted pros and amateurs, and would, in time, slot into the calendar alongside the two main Opens and the US PGA Championship, which was to move into the top bracket of competition now that the amateur challenge had faded.

Jones had decided to return to his law practice on retirement and to make some money with instructional films and books. He also intended to fulfil a long-held ambition: to found a golf club with a superior course, somewhere near his home in Georgia, which his golfing friends could join. A year before his retirement, Jones had spoken on the subject with course architect Dr Alister Mackenzie at Pebble Beach during the US Amateur Championship, in which Jones was beaten by Goodman from Nebraska. Mackenzie and Jones sought a different marque of course, one which Mackenzie characterized as "adventurous". With the assistance of a New York businessman, Clifford Roberts, who had started out as a suit salesman and enjoyed golf trips to Georgia and friendship with Jones, Thomas Barrett, of the Augusta Chamber of Commerce, the journalist Grantland Rice and several financiers, the project took a big step forward when Barrett suggested the purchase of what had been one of the first nurseries in Georgia, Fruitlands.

Jones fell in love with the site at once. "It seemed that this land had been lying here for years waiting for someone to lay a golf course upon it." The money for the purchase was obtained piecemeal.

Once the purchase had been underwritten, however, more cash flowed in from all over the world to meet the building costs. Augusta National, as it was to be called, was built to Mackenzie's design in about a year, incorporating the latest in irrigation systems. Jones struck a great many balls to verify shot values around the hilly layout, which was designed with massive fairways and greens, little rough and few bunkers. Instead of these, mounds were used to produce a rolling topography much after the style

Between 1958 and 1964, Arnold Palmer won the Masters on four occasions – his final visit, in 2004, triggered a wave of emotion around the Augusta fairways.

NICKLAUS v. MILLER v. WEISKOPF, 1975 Masters

The outcome of the 1975 Masters tournament at Augusta depended on what might be called a two-way head-to-head. It involved Jack Nicklaus, looking for a fifth green jacket, Johnny Miller and Tom Weiskopf.

Neither Miller nor Weiskopf had won at Augusta, but both were particularly dangerous opponents. Weiskopf had been second three times, twice in the previous three years; Miller had been shooting awesomely low scores on the PGA winter Tour, including 24-under par (Phoenix) and 25 under (Tucson).

There was no luck for the tournament's first black golfer, Lee Elder, but plenty for the galleries, who saw what Masters regulars still recall as the most exciting finish of them all, perhaps because it concerned three golfers with a penchant for the spectacular.

Miller, seven behind Nicklaus on the opening day with 75, improved to 71 and then 65 on the third, with six birdies in a row from the second hole. That still left him three behind Nicklaus, whose grip had been loosened by his third-round 73, and four behind Weiskopf, he of the huge and stately swing arc, who had moved ahead on 207 thanks to a majestic third round of 66. Miller was in much the same course-burning vein on the final day, and close on the heels of his rivals, who were level at the turn.

The odd putt was clearly going to decide it. That seemed to have been achieved by Weiskopf, for he birdied the 14th. Now Nicklaus hears the commotion behind him, and gets down to the problem of fashioning a birdie, quick. He is standing on the fairway of the par-five 15th, 242 yards from the hole. It is reachable with a wood, but Nicklaus decides to use the club he trusts best, his one-iron. His ball tears straight at the pin, rolls close by the hole, but 20ft past. He is to rate this one of the "three finest maximum pressure one-irons" of his career. His two-putt birdie is timely, because Weiskopf birdies the 15th, too, and moves ahead. Miller almost eagles the 15th.

Both stand on the 16th tee watching Nicklaus putt for a two. Nicklaus is playing with Tom Watson, who has put two balls in the lake that makes this 170-yard hole almost all carry. Watson, three months away from his first major, the British Open at Carnoustie, putts first, on the same line as the 45-footer Nicklaus faces.

Nicklaus takes in the huge swing on Watson's putt, is convinced he can see the right line with crystal clarity, and strikes firmly up the slope ... and holes out for his two, celebrating with an atypical (for Nicklaus) golfer's gavotte. This is not only a positive move for Nicklaus, but has a negative effect upon Weiskopf, who three-putts the 16th.

A roar from the 17th checks Nicklaus as he shapes up to his birdie putt on the 18th. He is anxious to know who has saved the shot there, and is relieved to know it is Miller. So he lags his putt for a safe par four. His cool analysis of the situation gives a clue as to why he kept winning over so many years. Now he can only wait by the 18th green.

Both Weiskopf and Miller drive superbly. Their second shots leave Miller a 15-footer, Weiskopf an eight-footer. The putts are roughly on the same line, but Miller misses left, Weiskopf right. He is second for the fourth time, and this pressure cooker of a Masters provides Nicklaus with his fifth triumph.

1975 Masters at Augusta, Ga

Pos	Name	Score				
1	Jack Nicklaus	68	67	73	68	276
2	Johnny Miller	75	71	65	66	277
3	Tom Weiskopf	69	72	66	70	277

of Jones's beloved St Andrews. One of the underlying aims had been to produce a course which would look far more difficult than it really was. Jones wanted all of his friends, expert or not, to enjoy the course.

By the time the first Augusta National Invitation was issued in 1934, the final touch had been added – that every hole should be named after a blossom, and decorated with that blossom, among others.

The idea that this was no more than a jolly spring meeting for Jones's friends at the close of the professional winter tour lasted no time at all. No one knows if Roberts had a long-term vision of Augusta as a world-class event, but his promotional skills and the box office appeal of Jones did the trick with

bewildering speed. Roberts made a fuss of the Press, always a good public relations move, and paid old-time pros to sit around in front of the clubhouse. He later hit a promotional jackpot by enrolling Eisenhower as a member: schmaltz, class and flowers make a potent mixture. Roberts persuaded Jones to play in the first and (as it turned out) only Augusta Invitation event.

Jones did not like the idea of calling the Invitation event the Masters, deeming it presumptuous. However, as soon as the notion that the competition might have been called the Masters got out to the Press, they immediately adopted the name, though the official programme made no mention of "Masters". Many years went by before Jones joined the

general acceptance of the title, and indeed before entry became anything more than invitational. The other majors were never so restricted.

Jones finished ten shots behind the first winner, Horton Smith, one of the very few players who had beaten Jones in his climactic year of 1930.

The only leading player missing from the field in the first year was Gene Sarazen, who was playing on a tour of South America. He made up for his initial absence in a big way in 1935. He needed three birdies to catch Craig Wood, who had finished with 282. He got the three shots he needed in a flash by holing his four-wood second shot at the par-five 15th.

Sarazen made pars on 16, 17 and 18, and as usual when a player is

overtaken by such a cruel stroke as Sarazen's, Wood lost the play-off. Smith won again in 1936, by which time the title Masters was, for all but Jones, set in stone. More Masterly golf, with the new shafts of steel, came from Texan Byron Nelson, who set new standards in 1937 with a flying start of 66, hitting every green in regulation (except the par fives, which he reached in two). Still they poured out of Texas: stars like three-time winner Jimmy Demaret, Ralph Guldahl and Ben Hogan helped ticket sales soar, and yet another, Lloyd Mangrum, shook the Masters firmament, but not the eventual winner, Demaret, with a scintillating opening round of 64 in 1940.

Amazingly, even though Jones's golf was on the decline, the same could seldom be said right up to the Second World War of the space newspapers reserved for his rounds. All this finished after Nelson's second Masters in 1942, when the club was wound down for the duration, with cattle keeping the grass short, and profit made from turkey farming. Private contributions from rich members revived the club and course, improved the clubhouse, and got things rolling once Jones, Snead, Hogan and company got out of uniform.

The Masters was still far short of the riches it has attained in the television age, yet the strong flavour of exclusivity it has always had

began to work in its favour more and more, aided by the flowering of Ben Hogan as the first great post-war player. His astonishing recovery from dreadful injuries sustained in a road crash in 1949 added to the public sense of wonder at his achievements. He lost by a stroke to Herman Keiser in 1946, was within a stroke of the best four-round total in winning his first Masters in 1951, and beat it by five shots with 274 two years later, when he went on to win both the big Opens.

Hogan's quality was succeeded just at the right moment for Augusta by the irrepressible showmanship of a

player born to be a television star, for Arnold Palmer won his first Masters (1958) in the early days of sports coverage on the box.

The exclusive nature of the Masters has been enhanced by the outward symbol of success: the symbolic green jacket, made of a specially reserved cloth, that can only be worn by club members and Master golfers. Only the champions may wear it off the course, and only as long as they remain champion and provided it is not demeaned by its use for commercial purposes.

Entry is no longer solely a matter of invitation, and the highly

successful gain entry whether the club likes it or not. All the same, for the first 38 years no black player was admitted to the Masters, though such men as Charlie Sifford, in 1973, had performed as well as many white players who had gained a place. But he did not get enough points on a scale Roberts had developed and was excluded, despite grumbles from US congressmen. Next year Lee Elder won the Monsanto Open, and cut the Augustan knot for black players.

Palmer's four Masters triumphs were trumped by Jack Nicklaus's six, the last, in 1986, a tonic to every golfer over 40. Gary Player, thrice

Tiger Woods has become the master golfer of recent times and, with four victories already to his name, seems to have developed a particular liking for Augusta.

FALDO v. NORMAN, 1996 Masters

The 1996 Masters made a cold start on April 11, with the gates opening late to the public because of frost. The management wanted no footprints to mar Augusta's emerald perfection.

Temperatures soon soared into the 70s and 80s. Greg Norman, often an over-cautious starter here, was incandescent: out in 33 and back in 30 – with birdies on nine of the last 12 holes – he equalled Nick Price's course record 63, finishing with a 24ft birdie putt on the 18th for his best opening round at Augusta.

Phil Mickelson, who had already won twice on the '96 PGA Tour, also came home in 30, but was two shots behind the Australian. Nick Faldo's 69 was his best opening round since his first Masters victory in 1989. He said: "There's a long way to go yet."

He greatly improved his position with a second round of 67, Norman "slipping", so to speak, to a 69. He was still four ahead of Faldo, who joined him to make up the last pair out on Saturday and Sunday.

Norman had the better of it in their first 18 holes together: one-under par against one-over by the Englishman, extending his lead to six strokes. His gritty third-round performance on the ever-faster greens, after starting badly with a miss from 4ft at the second, and three-putting the third and fourth, was indeed heroic, especially the bogey putt he holed at the short 12th after hitting his approach into Rae's Creek. Faldo bogeyed from the back edge. The pair had been cautioned for slow play at the eighth, but nothing disturbed Norman's concentration for long. He drove with both passion and precision.

The last day's weather was at its Sunday best. Did Norman recall, as he and Faldo stood on the first tee, their third round together at St Andrews in the 1990 British Open? They had started level and Faldo had finished nine ahead. Ah, but he was six up now. Perhaps he did remember the Old Course horrors, for he immediately lost a shot to Faldo, after finding the sand by the first green. The speed at which he lost the other five strokes was astounding and was often received in paralysed silence by the galleries.

The second went when he overshot the 250-yard fourth. He regained it with a birdie at the fifth, lost it again to Faldo's 4ft birdie putt at the 180-yard sixth, and he was down to two ahead at the turn, for Faldo birdied the eighth and Norman bogeyed the ninth – out in 38 to Faldo's 34.

A pulled second by Norman at the tenth brought Faldo to within a shot; three putts at the 11th and they were all square. Faldo was implacable in his course management, notably at the 12th, where he resolutely turned away from risk at this little (155 yards) tester. and aimed left of the bunker just over the creek. Norman went "straight at it", but did not even clear the bunker. His ball bounced off the bank into the water. This time there was no bogey-saving putt: the Australian was two down.

Both men birdied the 15th, but was there a suggestion of a faster swing as Norman hooked straight into the lake at the 16th? He did not bother to watch the splash-down; four behind. Faldo's finishing touch was a reminder of Sandy Lyle's Masters – out of 18th fairway sand, a 20ft downhill putt for birdie, a 67, a five-shot victory and a sixth major title.

He had three-putted once in 72 holes and had achieved an 11-stroke swing in the last 18 holes. This was the tenth Masters won by European Ryder Cup men in 17 years.

Faldo believes that Norman's collapse will be remembered longer than his 67, the best on a day when the average score was fractionally over the par of 72. His body language over the last few holes was clear in its expression of sympathy for the Augustan fall of Norman.

1996 Masters at Augusta, Ga

Pos	Name	Score				
1	Nick Faldo	69	67	73	67	276
2	Greg Norman	63	69	71	78	281
3	Phil Mickelson	65	73	72	72	282

a winner, was, in 1961, the first non-American to succeed at Augusta. It was 19 years before another foreigner followed suit – the Spaniard Severiano Ballesteros, who began an unprecedented European domination of an American event. Five European wins in the 1980s (Ballesteros with two, Bernard Langer, Sandy Lyle and Nick Faldo) have been followed up in the 1990s by Faldo, completing a rare treble, Ian Woosnam, Langer (again), and José-Maria Olazabal.

Faldo's first two Masters were gained at the second extra hole, which is Augusta's 11th, against Scott Hoch in 1989 and Raymond Floyd the following year. Floyd had proved a most convincing champion in 1976 –

he was the outright leader after every round. His total of 271 equalled the record set in 1965 by Nicklaus.

A few weeks before Floyd's 271, Eldrick Woods first saw the light of day in Cypress, California: 21 years on, he shrugged off a first nine holes of 40 and lived up to his nickname "Tiger" by displacing Ballesteros (23 when he first donned the green jacket) as the youngest winner. So huge was this particularly aggressive young Tiger's hitting off the tee that most of his approaches were made with no more than a wedge. By these unprecedented methods, he posted a new low score of 270, 18-under par, and a record winning margin of 12 strokes over Tom

Kite. All this at his first attempt as a professional to win a "major".

For a nation riven by racialism, the most shattering aspect of his stunning victory was his status as the only black winner of a major.

His win silenced those who had ridiculed Nicklaus's predictions that Woods would win as many Masters as he and Palmer together – ten. Yet Woods had not managed another major by the time he returned to defend his Masters title. Moreover, Augusta 1998 was a triumph for the more mature player. Gary Player (aged 62) made the cut, Nicklaus, at 58, delighted the galleries with a last-day charge reminiscent of days gone by, to challenge for the lead

before falling back into a tie for sixth place. Woods, meanwhile, was eighth, at three-under par, while his friend, mentor and Florida neighbour, Mark O'Meara, birdied the final two holes to win his first major in what, for him, turned out to be a remarkable year.

In 1999, Greg Norman challenged once again for that elusive green jacket. In another final-round shoot-out, the crowds roared in appreciation as he vied for the lead with 1994 champion, José-Maria Olazabal. A year later, Vijay Singh surprised everybody as he found his touch on the Augusta greens to claim his first green jacket and his second major.

THE MASTERS: 2001

Tiger Woods held off the final-day challenge of David Duval and Phil Mickelson to win his fourth consecutive major – and complete the Tiger Slam.

Having won the US Open, the British Open and the US PGA Championship the previous year, all eyes were on Tiger Woods as he attempted to become the first player in the history of the game to hold all four major championships at the same time. His form going into the tournament could not be questioned: he had won the last two events he had entered – the Bay Hill Invitational and the Players' Championship.

Rain before the start of the tournament had left the Augusta greens softer and slower than usual and, as the first round got under way, the playing field was perhaps more level than it had been in previous years: 32 players out of 92 broke par in the first round. At the top of the pile stood 32-year-old Masters rookie, Chris DiMarco: his seven-under 65 giving him a two-shot lead over the likes of defending champion Vijay Singh, Phil Mickelson and John Huston. Tiger lurked in the background, opening up with a two-under 70.

As the players embarked on their second round, conditions for scoring were ideal for the second successive day: the sun shone, the greens were still soft and receptive and there was barely a hint of breeze. As a result, 41 players broke par – the second most of any round in Masters history – and the 36-hole cut fell at one-over 145 – the lowest ever in the tournament.

First-round leader DiMarco shot a solid 69 to retain his lead, but the major move of the day came from Woods. He shot a six-under 66 to move to within two shots of the halfway leader: his eight-under 36-hole total matched his 1997 effort – the year he went on to record a 12-stroke victory

– and he shot a veiled warning to DiMarco. "I've been there before. I've won majors and I've lost majors. But more than anything I've been there. If you haven't been there it's tough." Phil Mickelson, another player who has been there, but who had yet to add a major to his collection of 18 wins, joined Woods on six-under.

If the play through the first two days had been engaging, then Saturday was enthralling. Phil Mickelson and Tiger Woods were involved in wedge-to-wedge combat through Augusta's back nine to set up what would be a fascinating final day.

Woods shot a steady four-under 68 to move to the top of the leaderboard on 12-under. Mickelson, pulling out the stops, dashingly birdied the final two holes to record a three-under 69 and move into second place. The big left-hander was after his own place in the record books: "The way I look at it, the winner doesn't just win a major. He becomes a part of the history of the game and that's what excites me. History is made here, and I want to be a part of that."

Those who were fortunate to witness the final round did indeed see the making of history: Woods fired a final-round 68 to finish on 16-under par. It wasn't a stroll in the Augusta parklands, though. Woods had to be at his very best to fend off the challenges of David Duval and Phil Mickelson: in many ways the final 18 holes were reminiscent of the epic 1975 Masters, when Jack Nicklaus fought off Johnny Miller and Tom Weiskopf.

Duval posted eight birdies during a scintillating final round of 67 to

finish on 14-under. Mickelson also threatened, before falling away to a final total of 13-under. Try as they might, they could not knock Woods out of his stride: he shot a rock-steady 68 to finish two strokes ahead of Duval and three ahead of Mickelson – and crowned it with a near-perfect finish at the 18th: a 330-yard drive, a wedge to 15ft and a birdie putt into the centre of the cup.

For Duval it was the fourth time in the previous five years that he had finished in the top three at Augusta. "Been here before, huh? The first thing I'd like to say is congratulations to Tiger. Under these circumstances, to shoot a 68 and win the tournament in the manner that he did is outstanding... What happens as a player is you feel like you become invincible."

Mickelson was less reticent, left to rue a bogey four on the 16th that effectively put him out of contention:

"When I look back on this week, if I am going to win with Tiger in the field, I cannot make the mistakes I have been making."

The 2001 Masters was all about Woods, though. He had won six of the 17 major tournaments he had entered as a professional and become the first player in the history of the game to hold all four major titles simultaneously. The purists claimed that it was not a grand slam in the strictest sense because he had not won all four in the same year. That may be so, but it was still some achievement.

Tiger remained understated "I don't think I've ever accomplished anything this great." The chances are that no one else ever will.

THE 2001 MASTERS - The Top 5
1 Tiger Woods 70 66 68 68 272 -16
2 David Duval 71 66 70 67 274 -14
3 Phil Mickelson 67 69 69 70 275 -13
4 Toshi Izawa 71 66 74 67 278 -10
= Mark Calcavecchia 72 66 68 72 278 -10

It was smiles all round for Tiger Woods: victory at the 2001 Masters saw him become the first player in the history of the game to hold all four major championship trophies at the same time.

THE MASTERS: 2002

If 2001 was the year that Tiger Woods withstood all that was thrown before him, 2002 will go down as the year that the Masters was handed to him on a plate.

There were those who might have thought that Tiger Woods was going through a comparative slump in the major tournaments. Having won four in a row between the 2000 US Open and the 2001 Masters, he had then remained winless: he was going through a major crisis.

Those thoughts seemed confirmed when Tiger promptly carved his opening tee shot deep into the flower beds. Despite this poor start, the defending champion recovered to shoot a two-under 70.

At the top of the leaderboard after the first round was Davis Love III, who shot a bogey-free five-under 67 on the newly lengthened Augusta course. One stroke behind him was Spain's Sergio Garcia, with Garcia's fellow countrymen Miguel Angel Jimenez and two-time champion José-Maria Olazabal, plus Irishmen Darren Clarke and Padraig Harrington, all in contention.

In fact much of the day had been dominated by Harrington. He played the opening 12 holes in a scintillating six-under par before becoming unstuck around Amen Corner – he finished with a 69, two behind Love.

If day one was all about Love, then day two was all about 2000 Masters champion Vijay Singh. The Fijian took the second round by posting a seven-under 65 to surge into a four-shot lead. It was Singh's lowest ever round at Augusta. The unheralded South African, Retief Goosen, lay one stoke behind after shooting a faultless 67. Tiger Woods was still in contention, four strokes behind Singh, after a three-under round.

Major tournaments are rarely won over the first two days,

however, and Woods staked his claim for a second consecutive green jacket with a near-perfect round of 66 on the third day. He stood on top of a dream leaderboard that contained six of the world's seven top-ranked players, alongside Retief Goosen.

Woods was delighted as he has an incredible record at closing out tournaments. In the past he has won 22 of the 24 tournaments where he has led going into the final round. Goosen would have to play at his best if he wanted to collect his first major title.

He didn't, but then again neither did anyone else on a day that had promised so much but which ultimately petered out into one of the most anticlimactic finishes in recent Masters history: with so many of the world's top players in contention going into the final 18 holes, the tournament deserved more drama than it got.

In fairness to Woods he did all that he had to do to become only the third player, after Jack Nickalus and Nick Faldo, to win back-to-back Masters. He shot a one-under 71 to finish on 12-under for a three-stroke victory. He joined legendary figures such as Gary Player, Sam Snead and Nick Faldo as a three-time winner of the tournament. Only Arnold Palmer (4) and Jack Nicklaus (6) have won more times at Augusta.

A dogmatic, one-under 71 was enough to see Tiger to a three-stroke victory when no one stood up to the challenge: in fact, no one got close. To all intents and purposes the tournament was settled in the space of an unusual quarter of an hour.

It turned into an afternoon stroll in the park for Tiger as he became only the third back-to-back winner of the Masters, joining Jack Nicklaus and Nick Faldo.

A few moments after Woods had bogeyed the 11th to offer a glimmer of hope to the chasing pack, the first of his closest pursuers, Ernie Els, hooked his tee shot into the water hazard on the left side of the 13th fairway. The South African then put his next shot into Rae's Creek, visited the water once again and limped off the green with an eight. Any hopes that he might have had of winning the title were left in tatters. "I made a terrible swing on the 13th and it cost me the tournament," said Els.

It was a similarly watery story for Vijay Singh, who was lying in second when disaster struck. The galleries stood in stunned silence as the

Fijian knocked three consecutive pitches into the water on the 15th – and carded a nine.

Not that the failings of others should detract from Tiger Woods' achievement. Woods had now won six out of the last ten majors. The only question that remained, as Augusta chairman Hootie Johnson placed the green jacket on the young American's shoulders, was how many more was he going to win?

THE 2002 MASTERS - The Top 5
1 Tiger Woods 70 69 66 71 276 -12
2 Retief Goosen 69 67 69 74 279 -9
3 Phil Mickleson 69 72 68 71 280 -8
4 J-M Olazabal 70 69 71 71 281 -6
5 Padraig Harrington 69 70 72 71 282 -10
= Ernie Els 70 67 72 73 282 -10

THE MASTERS: 2003

There was a strange atmosphere surrounding the 2003 Masters: at the end of it Canada's Mike Weir was wearing the green jacket and had become the first left-hander to win a major for 40 years.

The unusual atmosphere that surrounded proceedings started some ten months before when Martha Burk wrote to Augusta chairman Hootie Johnson demanding that female members be admitted to the club. A controversy over membership erupted and the tournament was pushed through a rocky period during which sponsors were dropped. To make matters worse, Burk threatened a protest outside the gates during the tournament itself.

Things got worse when heavy rain soaked the course and caused the cancellation of the practice round. And the rain kept on coming: so much so that Thursday's first round was a washout. It led to the first 36-hole day in Masters history.

At the end of it all there was an unfamiliar look to the halfway leaderboard. Not everyone had completed their 36 holes, but standing at the top was Canadian Mike Weir on six-under. Phil Mickelson stood four back with Paul Lawrie and Jonathan Byrd was also in the hunt.

Among the names languishing in the middle of the pack were Ernie Els, Davis Love III and Tiger Woods. For Woods it was a scramble from the beginning as he was forced to chip in for a bogey on the first hole. Come the 18th, he had shot a first-round, birdie-free 76 and there was a distinct possibility that the defending champion could miss his first cut in 102 straight PGA tournaments.

If Friday's leaderboard had a somewhat unexpected look, you can assume that few would have picked the leading two names at the 54-hole stage. At the top of the pile was Jeff Maggert on five-under par. Two strokes behind him was Mike Weir, who had followed opening rounds of 70 and 68 with a disappointing 75.

Sitting behind the top two were Phil Mickelson, 2000 champion Vijay Singh, two-time Masters champion José-Maria Olazabal and, of course, Tiger Woods, who had put himself firmly back into contention with a best-of-the-day third-round 66. Surely the winner would have come from this bunch? History would suggest otherwise: the last time a winner had not come from the final day's final pair was way back in 1991, when Ian Woosnam triumphed.

Any of those who had their money on Jeff Maggert would have been left disappointed by events on the third hole of the final round. Having struck the ball, it hit a tree and bounced back and hit him: one of the most bizarre things to have happened to the leader of a major tournament.

Maggert hobbled off the green with a triple-bogey. He put himself right out of contention with a quadruple-bogey eight at the 12th.

So that left Weir. Not if Len Mattiace could do anything about it. The American was rolling in putts from all parts of the green, such as the 80-footer he holed on the tenth for a birdie. He eagled the 13th and then went on to birdie the 15th and the 16th. Mattiace closed with a 65 and a clubhouse total of 281: it was the best round of the day – by some stretch.

And nobody managed to get past it. How Mattiace must have rued his pulled tee shot on the 18th that led to his only bogey of the day. He would not have known it at the time, but the American had joined an elite group of three players who have had a chance to win the Masters with a par on the 18th but who have made a bogey or worse. It was only when Mike Weir completed his 72 holes with the same score that Mattiace would have realized his error.

And so the 2003 Masters would be decided by a sudden-death play-off.

Not for the first time during the day, it appeared that a par would have been enough to claim the green jacket. Neither player got one: Mike Weir became the first player in the history of the game to win a sudden-death play-off at a major championship with a bogey.

Mike Weir's bogey at the first hole of the play-off was enough to give him his first green jacket. His win confirmed the potential he had been showing on the PGA Tour for years.

THE 2003 MASTERS - The Top 5
1 Mike Weir* 70 68 75 68 281 -7
2 Len Mattiace 73 74 69 65 281 -7
3 Phil Mickelson 73 70 72 68 283 -5
4 Jim Furyk 73 72 71 68 284 -4
5 Jim Maggert 72 73 66 75 286 -2
*Won play-off at first extra hole

THE MASTERS: 2004

Phil Mickelson produced some scintillating golf to win his first major and finally shook the "best player never to win a major tag" firmly off his back.

It was only fitting that the Masters that signalled the end of the playing road for one of the game's greats should have been one of the most enervating and engaging tournaments for years. At the age of 74, four-time champion Arnold Palmer finally decided to say goodbye to the galleries who had adored him for half a century.

It was also fitting that the man who had assumed the moniker of the modern-day Palmer, with his attacking approach to the game, should have won his first major tournament. The script of the 2004 Masters was one of the most perfect in years. Well, almost ...

The headlines following the first round belonged to Justin Rose, the 23-year-old and the youngest professional in the field. The Englishman's five-under 67 propelled him into a two-shot lead over Chris DiMarco – whose hole-in-one at the sixth was the first ace at Augusta since 1996 – and Jay Haas.

Rose held firm in the second round with a 71 to leave him two shots ahead of Alex Cejka and two-time champion José-Maria Olazabal at the halfway stage. Korea's KJ Choi and Phil Mickelson lay a shot further back, with the American making his move over Augusta's inward nine, playing the final seven holes in three-under. It would be a portent of what was to come on the final day.

Meanwhile, Tiger Woods rebounded from a first-round 75 by shooting a 69 to ensure he made the cut.

One player to miss the cut, predictably one has to say, was Arnold Palmer. Forty years after his

final Masters win, Palmer, with tears in his eyes for most of the final round, was given a raucous send-off by the Augusta faithful.

If day two was all about Palmer, then day three was all about two close friends: Chris DiMarco and Phil Mickelson. The Americans who used to play against each other while they were at college, shared the lead going into the final round at six-under par. There was a lot of experience lurking behind the leaders, Bernhard Langer and Ernie Els among the chasing pack.

All eyes would be on Mickelson, though. He may have come closer than most to winning the major tournament that he so desired, but this year was a first. He had never led a major going into the final round. It was a sense of now or never for the big American.

He could take comfort from the fact that the previous 14 Masters champions had come from the final day's final pairing. He could also reassure himself in the knowledge that his final-round scoring average at Augusta, 71.70, was better than anyone else in the top five.

But Ernie Els nearly stole the show. The South African played beautifully, shooting two eagles on his way to a five-under 67 and a clubhouse total of eight-under. Mickelson needed to be at his very best if he wanted to beat him. He was. In a back-nine charge, Mickelson birdied five of the last seven holes to steal the green jacket from Ernie Els's back.

Only five players in the tournament's history had birdied the 18th hole to clinch the title but this wasn't a concern

A first major title for Phil Mickelson, but it did not come easily – the American had to be at his very best on the final day to see off the strong challenge of Ernie Els.

of Mickelson's as he drilled a perfect three-wood from the tee, struck an eight-iron to within 20ft and then agonizingly watched as his putt rolled in for the tournament-winning birdie.

THE 2004 MASTERS – The Top 5
1 Phil Mickelson 72 69 69 69 279 -9
2 Ernie Els 70 72 71 67 280 -8
3 K J Choi 71 70 72 69 282 -6
4 Sergio Garcia 72 72 75 66 285 -3
= Bernhard Langer 71 73 69 72 285 -3

THE MASTERS: 2005

It took a play-off and a nerveless putt before Tiger Woods finally saw off the determined challenge of Chris DiMarco to claim his fourth green jacket.

Tiger Woods was made to work a lot harder than he might have thought on his way to collecting a fourth green jacket and a ninth major title.

On a rain-shortened first day Vijay Singh plundered a four-under 68 and Phil Mickelson eased himself to two-under par after 11 holes. Ernie Els, who hit just four fairways in the 11 holes he played, struggled to three-over par.

The news was just as bad for all Tiger fans. After a bogey at the 11th, he was looking to get a shot back at the par-five 13th when he knocked a long iron to within 40ft of the flag. He had taken the water out of play with his approach and looked set to two-putt for his birdie. His eagle attempt kept picking up speed, rolled past the flag and carried on going until it came to rest in Rae's Creek – he left the hole with a bogey and stood on two-over par through 14 holes.

That left Chris DiMarco to lead the field on four-under (through 14 holes), one shot ahead of Mark Hensby and Luke Donald who, like DiMarco, still had four holes to play.

And play was cut short for the second consecutive day: at the end of it, three players were stuck out on the course on five-under par – DiMarco, Donald and David Howell. With so many players still to complete their rounds, the some-what confusing picture became clearer at the end of the third day – a day that had seen a tearful Jack Nicklaus bid an emotional farewell to the Augusta faithful who had cheered his every shot.

The 45-hole leader was Chris DiMarco – who had gone 44 holes without a bogey and who had made par-saving putts again and again to maintain his lead. He would have been looking grimly over his shoulder in the direction of Tiger Woods, though. The young American shot a second-round 66 and by completing nine holes of the third round in 31 shots the three-times Masters champion had shot himself right back into contention. DiMarco could take solace in the fact that Woods had never come from behind to win any of his eight majors.

But Woods wouldn't have to, when he picked up where he had left off the previous evening, reeling off four straight birdies to equal the Masters record of seven consecutive birdies. It meant that Woods would take a three-shot lead into the final 18 holes after DiMarco faltered with a third-round 76. Woods had never lost a lead when going into the final round of a major championship, but the big question was how would the slump affect DiMarco in the final 18 holes?

It would inspire him. Woods birdied the first hole of the final round to stretch his lead to four. Both made birdies at the second. The lead was down to three at the turn, but Woods bogeyed the tenth. DiMarco birdied the 11th, but promptly bogeyed the 12th. He responded with birdies at the 14th and 15th, with Woods also making a four at the latter. As the pair stood on the 16th tee, Woods's lead was down to one.

But after their tee shots, it was advantage DiMarco. Tiger shot through the green. But the advantage shifted quickly towards Woods after he produced a spectacular chip which broke some 25ft before trickling towards the hole: the ball hung momentarily on the hole's lip before falling. The place erupted. Woods was 2 up with two to play and it was game over.

Or so everyone thought. Woods bogeyed the final two holes, DiMarco made two pars, and the fascinating head-to-head would go to a play-off. The excitement was over almost as quickly as it had begun. A long drive, an eight-iron to 15ft and a nerveless putt later and Tiger Woods had won his fourth green jacket. He had been made to work for this one, though.

THE 2005 MASTERS - The Top 5
1 Tiger Woods* 74 66 65 71 276 -12
2 Chris Di Marco 67 67 74 68 276 -12
3 Luke Donald 68 77 69 69 283 -5
4 Retief Goosen 71 75 70 67 283 -5
5 Rod Pampling 73 71 70 72 284 -4
* Tiger Woods beat Chris Di Marco at the first extra hole of the play off

THE MASTERS: 2006

At one stage during the final round every member of golf's Big Five was in contention, but in the end Phil Mickelson claimed the title for the second time.

"They've ruined the course," said six-time winner Jack Nicklaus, "I can't compete on a course like this," said three-time champion Nick Faldo, but all the hubbub regarding the extra length added to the Augusta course (at 7,445 yards it was the second longest in major history) was soon forgotten after the completion of the first round and Augusta chairman Hootie Johnson's words, "We are comfortable with what we are doing with the golf course," seemed more than vindicated. On a windless first day, 18 of the field of 90 broke par, 12 eagles were posted (one short of the all-time record) and Vijay Singh, the 2000 Masters champion, stood on top of the leaderboard after posting a bogey-free, five-under round of 67, to leave him one shot ahead of Rocco Mediate. Arron Oberholser, winner of the AT&T Pebble Beach National Pro-Am earlier in the year, sat on three-under, with a group of four players – Tim Clark, Retief Goosen, Geoff Ogilvy and Phil Mickelson – all within sight of the top of the leaderboard on two-under par.

But, as the wind swirled on the second day, the revamped Augusta National found its bite. Only three players broke par, with Chad Campbell, who had only ever posted one top-ten finish in major championships, firing a best-of-the-day five-under 67 to propel him to a three-shot lead over Singh, Fred Couples and Rocco Mediate with Phil Mickelson, who had opted to carry two drivers in his bag, a shot further back, one ahead of defending champion Tiger Woods.

Rain and lightning on the third day meant only 140 minutes of play were possible, so, for the second successive year, the leaders would have to complete the third round and then, after a three-hour break, start the final round on the Sunday. By the time all the players had completed 54 holes, ten players were wwwithin three strokes of the lead (including five major winners with a combined 18 major victories between them). Leading the pack by a stoke, on four-under par, was Mickelson who would be partnered in the final round by Fred Couples, the 46-year-old seeking to become the oldest major winner and looking for a second Masters triumph after his popular win back in 1992. With Woods a further stroke behind, it promised to be a day to remember at Augusta.

But the drama was over by the time Mickelson had made birdies on the seventh and eighth holes. Woods could not buy a putt, Els imploded on the back nine, Singh and Goosen were steady if not spectacular, while Mickelson turned on the style, producing an error-free back nine with a level of precision many thought was beyond him to shoot a 69, with his only bogey of the day coming on the final hole when his second green jacket was already in the bag. Having won three of the last nine majors, and his second in a row following his victory at the 2005 US PGA Championship, the Californian left-hander was fast becoming a real threat to Tiger Woods's domination of the game.

THE 2006 MASTERS – The Top 5
1 Phil Mickelson 70 72 70 69 281 -7
2 Tim Clark 70 72 72 69 283 -5
3 Chad Campbell 71 67 75 71 284 -4
= Fred Couples 71 70 72 71 284 -4
= Retief Goosen 70 73 72 69 284 -4
= J M Olazabal 76 71 71 66 284 -4
= Tiger Woods 72 71 71 70 284 -4

Phil Mickelson produced a peerless performance in the final round to capture the 2006 Masters championship, his second green jacket and his second-successive major victory.

THE MASTERS: 2007

The battle for Augusta supremacy between Phil Mickelson and Tiger Woods may have dominated the pre-tournament headlines, but, little-heralded Zach Johnson emerged from the shell-shocked pack to become a most unlikely champion.

Zach Johnson kept his head in unseasonal Georgia weather over a desperately difficult course set-up to win the 2007 Masters by two.

From the moment Arnold Palmer hit the ceremonial opening tee shot, the un-seasonal Georgia weather was the talk of the galleries and it soon became clear that, aided by strong breezes, the oft-criticized and much-revamped Augusta course was going to provide an extreme examination of the players' skills. Battling tricky conditions, only ten of the field of 96 shot under-par in the first round, with England's Justin Rose and Brett Wetterich (a US Ryder Cup rookie in 2006) locked at the top of the leaderboard on three-under par (69). Woods was still in touch on one-over par, while, following an error-strewn 76, Mickelson's hopes of defending the title seemed dead and buried: no one has ever won the Masters after shooting higher than 75 in the first round.

Round two brought little respite from the elements and, at the end of a difficult day, only three players remained under-par: South Africa's Tim Clark and Wetterich on two-under and Augusta-raised Vaughn Taylor (on one-under). Rose, who shot 75 to return to level par, was just glad to stay in contention: "I'm happy. It was a hard, hard round, way harder than yesterday." As bad as the conditions had been, however, even worse was to follow.

Day three was brutal. The temperature dipped, the wind howled and swirled, the notorious greens had never played faster and player after player fell by the wayside. After a day that saw the highest third-round scoring average (77.35) since 1956 – and that yielded only one under-par score (Retief Goosen's 70), Stuart Appleby led the way and would carry a one-shot lead into the final round. Next to him in the final pairing would be Tiger Woods, with everyone expecting the world no.1, who had never lost a major championship after starting the final round in the final group, to surge through the field and claim a fifth green jacket. But the fourth and final round was far from business as usual.

Tamer conditions, well-watered, receptive greens (having overseen the carnage of the previous three days the Augusta committee finally decided to act) and ideal low-scoring conditions may have greeted them when they arrived at the course on Sunday, but the excitement had already been squeezed out of the tournament and the players, shell-shocked into playing conservative golf, seemed intent on not losing shots rather than gaining them. After a limp final round, Zach Johnson, a little-known 26-year-old from Iowa, led the field by two to claim an unexpected green jacket.

His score of one-over 289 matched the highest winning total in Masters history – equalling that of Sam Snead (in 1954) and Jack Burke (in 1956).

THE 2007 MASTERS - The Top 5

1 Zach Johnson 71 73 76 69 289 +1
2 Retief Goosen 76 76 70 69 291 +3
= Rory Sabbatini 73 76 73 69 291 +3
= Tiger Woods 73 74 72 72 291 +3
5 Jerry Kelly 75 69 78 70 292 +4
= Justin Rose 69 75 75 73 292 +4

THE MASTERS: 2008

At the end of a compelling four rounds where Augusta played relentlessly long, Trevor Immelman became the first South African to claim the green jacket for 30 years.

At the end of the first round the leaderboard possessed a distinctly English flavour: Justin Rose (along with Immelman) led the way after firing a four-under 68; Lee Westwood sat a shot further back on three-under; Ian Poulter, who recorded the 19th hole-in-one in Masters history (on the 16th), shot a two-under 70; and Paul Casey fired a one-under 71, the same score as two-time winner Phil Mickelson. Tiger Woods, who had set tongues wagging in the build-up to the tournament by suggesting a calendar grand slam was "easily within reason", opened with a level-par 72.

Inaccessible pin positions were the talk of the clubhouse following the second round. "I have to try and pick and choose the holes I can try and make birdie on," said Mickelson, whose 68 propelled him into a tie for third place on five-under, two shots behind Steve Flesch and Brandt Snedeker, and three shots behind halfway leader Immelman, who shot a second consecutive 68. "To shoot 68 the first two days is probably beyond my expectations," enthused the 28-year-old South African who, only four months previously, had undergone major surgery to remove a benign tumour from his diaphragm. With rain forecast for Saturday, however, the question was whether Immelman could maintain his impressive form of the opening two rounds.

The answer was a definitive yes. Taking advantage of the most favourable conditions at Augusta for three years, Immelman carded his third successive score in the 60s (a three-under 69) to stand on 11-under par, two shots clear of Snedeker and three ahead of Flesch. Woods, who had made a habit in previous years of making his move in the third round, shot a 68 and lay six shots behind the leader. Mickelson's hopes of winning a third green jacket went up in smoke after carding a three-over 75. With strong winds and plummeting temperatures forecast for the final round, Sunday was going to be all about managing mistakes on the golf course.

Nobody rose to the challenge. On a day that saw only four players break par, many of the leading contenders fell by the wayside: Snedeker shot a five-over 77; Flesch slipped out of contention after posting four bogeys in a six-hole stretch; Woods, yet again, could not buy a putt when it mattered; and Immelman, who shot a three-over 75 (the highest final round by a champion since Arnold Palmer's 75 in 1962), hung on to claim his first green jacket – and the first by a South African since Gary Player in 1978 – by three shots.

"Masters champion – it's the craziest thing I've ever heard of," purred a delighted Immelman. But the Masters was fast becoming renowned for its craziness: four of the last seven champions had been first-time major winners.

THE 2008 MASTERS - The Top 5
1 Trevor Immelman 68 68 69 75 280 -8
2 Tiger Woods 72 71 68 72 283 -5
3 Stewart Cink 72 69 71 72 284 -4
= Brandt Snedeker 69 68 70 77 284 -4
5 Steve Flesch 72 67 69 78 286 -2
= Padraig Harrington 74 71 69 72 286 -2
= Phil Mickelson 71 68 75 72 286 -2

A final round of three-over 75 was enough for South Africa's Trevor Immelman to see off the challenge of Tiger Woods to collect his first major.

THE MASTERS: 2009

After two disappointing, anti-climactic years in which a combination of bad weather and a brutal course set-up had reduced the tournament to a test of survival, the fun finally returned to the Masters in 2009.

Sunny skies, gentle breezes and friendly pin positions greeted the players as they teed off for the 2009 Masters and they responded to the perfect scoring conditions in style, shooting a host of red numbers. By the end of the first day's play a staggering 38 players had shot under-par scores (a Masters first-round record), with Chad Campbell grabbing the headlines: the Texan opened up with five straight birdies, accumulated four more on the back nine and stood on the 17th tee in with a chance of breaking Greg Norman's course-record 63. The pressure may have got to him as he bogeyed both 17 and 18, but he stood alone at the top of the leaderboard on seven-under, one shot clear of Hunter Mahan and Jim Furyk.

Aided by swirling winds, the course bit back on the second day. Campbell, who at one stage had stretched his lead to five, dropped three shots on the back nine to record a two-under 70 to take his score to nine-under, level with the day's big mover, Kenny Perry – the 48-year-old Kentuckian firing a bogey-free 67. The round of the day belonged to Anthony Kim, dubbed the "new Tiger Woods", who posted a Masters record 11 birdies en route to a 65 that hauled him up the leaderboard to seventh.

Despite a tornado passing through the area on Friday night, the third round, traditionally the round where the big moves are made, started on time. At the end of it, two players stood on 11-under par (the lowest 54-hole score at the Masters in seven years): Perry, who continued his resurgent form with a two-under 70, and Angel Cabrera, the big-hitting 2007 US Open champion, who shot 69 – his third straight round in the 60s. With 16 players (including Tiger Woods and Phil Mickelson) within seven shots of the lead, however, the fight for the green jacket was far from over.

The final round had it all and, with two holes to play, Perry, holding a two-stroke lead, seemed certain to become the oldest major winner in history. But the pressure got to him: bogeys on the last two holes – including a 15ft miss on the 18th for the championship – left him tied on 12-under par with Cabrera (who shot a 71) and Campbell (who fired a closing 69). The outcome of the 2009 Masters would be decided by a three-man play-off. A bogey on the first extra hole put paid to Campbell's title bid and then Perry faltered on the next hole, leaving Cabrera to become the first Argentine Masters winner in history.

"This is a great moment, the dream of any golfer to win the Masters" said Cabrera during the green jacket ceremony. "I'm so emotional I can barely talk." It had been some performance by Cabrera, who, after adding a Masters victory to his US Open triumph in 2007, could lay rightful claim to being the greatest South American golfer in history.

THE 2009 MASTERS – The Top 5
1 Ángel Cabrera* 68 68 69 71 276 -12
2 Chad Campbell 65 70 72 69 276 -12
= Kenny Perry 68 67 70 71 276 -12
4 Shingo Katayama 67 73 70 68 278 -10
5 Phil Mickelson 73 68 71 67 279 -9
*Won play-off at second extra hole

Angel Cabrera saw off Chad Campbell and Kenny Perry in a play-off to become the Masters' first-ever South American winner.

THE MASTERS: 2010

The most exciting US Masters for years, Phil Mickelson produced his best golf of the week in the final round, firing five birdies and no bogeys in a five-under 67, to see off the challenge of England's Lee Westwood, to collect his fourth major championship.

To the surprise of no one, the pre-tournament talk centred on Tiger Woods's return to golf for the first time since lurid revelations about his private life had dominated media coverage for weeks, seen sponsors distance themselves from him by the dozen and had sent his image crashing to an all-time low. More surprisingly was that the bookmakers installed him as favourite: the last time he had appeared at a major following a lengthy break – at the 2009 US Masters following surgery on his left knee – he finished in a tie for sixth place, but had barely threatened. Of the other contenders, it was Phil Mickelson who aroused the most interest: the week before, the two-time Masters champion had fired a 58 in a practice round and was in prime form.

Both Mickelson (67) and Woods (68) started well, but it was a couple of old-timers who stole the show on the first day. First Tom Watson, 60 years of age, rediscovered the form that had taken him to within a whisker of the 2009 British Open title by firing a five-under 67 to end the day in second, alongside Mickelson, Lee Westwood, YE Yang and KJ Choi. Then 1992 champion, Fred Couples, eased to a six-under 66.

The old boys – Couples (75) and Watson (74) – fell back to earth in round two. Instead, a pair of Englishmen basked in the Augusta limelight. Westwood followed up his first-round 67 with a solid three-under 69 to move to eight-under; and Ian Poulter fired a second-straight 68 to move into a share of the lead,

two ahead of a group of five players, including, menacingly, Mickelson (71) and Woods (70).

Westwood impressed once again on day three when he fired his third-straight round in the 60s (68) to move to 12-under to take a one-shot lead into the final round; Poulter posted a two-over 74 to slip out of contention. The charge of the day belonged to Mickelson: the Californian shot eagle, eagle, birdie on 13, 14 and 15 to post a 67 and move to within one of the lead. With Woods (70) in a tie for third, three behind Mickelson, the climax to the tournament threatened to be a magical one.

Westwood's Masters bid floundered as early as the first hole and, once behind, he could not find the birdies when it mattered. A second-place finish represented a good week's work, but yet another major had passed him by. Woods, clearly some way short of his A-game, finished fourth. Instead, the final round belonged to Mickelson, who, amid jubilant and emotional scenes, produced some outstanding golf to post a bogey-free 67 and win the green jacket for the third time.

"It's been such an incredible week, an emotional week," said Mickelson. "And to cap it off with a victory is something I can't put into words." He did not need to: those who had witnessed his performance in the final round knew they had seen a player at the top of their game.

THE 2010 MASTERS – The Top 5

1	Phil Mickelson	67 71 67 67	272	-16
2	Lee Westwood	67 69 68 71	275	-13
3	Anthony Kim	68 70 73 65	276	-12
4	K J Choi	67 71 70 69	277	-11
=	Tiger Woods	68 70 70 69	277	-11

Phil Mickelson produced a near-flawless final round to become one of only eight players to win the Masters on three or more occasions.

THE US OPEN

21st-century competitive golf is dominated by the professionals, but the amateurs of America were the fashionable end of the game as the US golf boom throbbed into action in the last decade of the 19th century. All the same, early attempts to stage both Amateur and Open Championships were a shambles. Neither the United States Golf Association (USGA) nor the US PGA recognize, as some record books do,

Ben Hogan dominated the tournament in a six-year stretch from 1948 to 1953, during which he picked up four victories. He also finished as runner-up in 1956.

US Open Championship Results

Year	Winner	Runner-up	Venue	Score
(36 holes till 1898)				
1895	H Rawlins	W Dunn	Newport, RI	173
1896	J Foulis	H Rawlins	Shinnecock Hills, NY	152
1897	J Lloyd	W Anderson	Chicago, Il	162
1898	F Herd	A Smith	Myopia, Ma	328
1899	W Smith	G Low, V Fitzjohn, W H. Way	Baltimore, Md	315
1900	H Vardon	J H Taylor	Chicago, Il	313
1901	W Anderson	A Smith	Myopia, Ma	331
	won 18-hole play-off 85 to 86			
1902	L Auchterlonie	S Gardner, W J Travis	Garden City, NY	307
1903	W Anderson	D Brown	Baltusrol, NJ	307
	won 18-hole play-off 82 to 84			
1904	W Anderson	G Nicholls	Glen View, Il	303
1905	W Anderson	A Smith	Myopia, Ma	314
1906	A Smith	W Smith	Onwentsia, Il	295
1907	A Ross	G Nicholls	Philadelphia CC, Pa	302
1908	F McLeod	W Smith	Myopia, Ma	322
	won 18-hole play-off 77 to 83			
1909	G Sargent	T McNamara	Englewood, NJ	290
1910	A Smith	J J McDermott, MacDonald Smith	Philadelphia CC, Pa	298
	won 18-hole play-off 71 to 75 to 77			
1911	J J McDermott	M J Brady, G O Simpson	Chicago, Il	307
	won 18-hole play-off 80 to 82 to 85			
1912	J J McDermott	T McNamara	Buffalo, NY	294
1913	F Ouimet	H Vardon, T Ray	Brookline, Ma	304
	won 18-hole play-off 72 to 77 to 78			
1914	W Hagen	C Evans Jr	Midlothian, Il	290
1915	J D Travers	T McNamara	Baltusrol, NJ	297
1916	C Evans Jnr	J Hutchison	Minikahda, Mn	286
1917–18	No championship			
1919	W Hagen	M J Brady	Brae Burn, Ma	301
	won 18-hole play-off 77 to 78			
1920	T Ray	H Vardon, J Burke, L Diegel, J Hutchison	Inverness, Oh	295
1921	J Barnes	W Hagen, F McLeod	Chevy Chase, Md	289
1922	G Sarazen	J L Black	Skokie, Glencoe, Il	288
1923	R T Jones Jr	R A Cruickshank	Inwood, NY	296
	won 18-hole play-off 76 to 78			
1924	C Walker	R T Jones Jr	Oakland Hills, Mi	297
1925	W Macfarlane	R T Jones Jr	Worcester, Ma	291
	won 18-hole play-off 147 to 148			
1926	R T Jones Jr	J Turnesa	Scioto, Oh	293
1927	T Armour	H Cooper	Oakmont, Pa	301
	won 18-hole play-off 76 to 79			
1928	J J Farrell	R T Jones Jr	Olympia Fields, Il	294
	won 36-hole play-off 143 to 144			
1929	R T Jones Jr	A Espinosa	Winged Foot, NY	294
	won 36-hole play-off 141 to 164			
1930	R T Jones Jr	MacDonald Smith	Interlachen, Mn	287

Year	Winner	Runner-up	Venue	Score
1931	B Burke	G Von Elm	Inverness, Oh	292
	won second 36-hole play-off 148 to 149: first tied at 149			
1932	G Sarazen	T P Perkins, R Cruickshank	Fresh Meadow, NY	286
1933	J Goodman	R Guldahl	N. Shore, Il	287
1934	O Dutra	G Sarazen	Merion CC, Pa	293
1935	S Parks	J Thomson	Oakmont, Pa	299
1936	T Manero	H Cooper	Baltusrol, NJ	282
1937	R Guldahl	S Snead	Oakland Hills, Mi	281
1938	R Guldahl	D Metz	Cherry Hills, Co	284
1939	B Nelson	C Wood, D Shute	W. Conshohocken, Pa	284
	won 36-hole play-off 138 to 141			
1940	W Lawson Little	G Sarazen	Canterbury, Oh	287
	won 18-hole play-off 70 to 73			
1941	C Wood	D Shute	Colonial, Ft Worth, Tx	284
1942–45	No championship			
1946	L Mangrum	B Nelson, V Ghezzi	Canterbury, Oh	284
	won 18-hole play-off 72 to 73			
1947	L Worsham	S Snead	St Louis, Clayton, Mo	282
	won 18-hole play-off 69 to 70			
1948	B Hogan	J Demaret	Riviera, L Angeles, Ca	276
1949	C Middlecoff	C Heafner, S Snead	Medinah, Chicago, Il	286
1950	B Hogan	L Mangrum, G Fazio	Merion, Pa	287
	won 18-hole play-off 69 to 73 to 75			
1951	B Hogan	C Heafner	Oakland Hills, Mi	287
1952	J Boros	P Oliver Jr	Northwood, Dallas, Tx	281
1953	B Hogan	S Snead	Oakmont, Pa	283
1954	E Furgol	G Littler	Baltusrol, NJ	284
1955	J Fleck	B Hogan	Olympic, Ca	287
	won 18-hole play-off 69 to 72			
1956	C Middlecoff	B Hogan, J Boros	Oak Hill, Rochester, NY	281
1957	R Mayer	C Middlecoff	Inverness, Oh	282
	won 18-hole play-off 72 to 79			
1958	T Bolt	G Player	Southern Hills, Ok	283
1959	W Casper	B Rosburg	Winged Foot, NY	282
1960	A Palmer	J Nicklaus	Cherry Hills, Co	280
1961	G Littler	R Goalby, D Sanders	Oakland Hills, Mi	281
1962	J Nicklaus	A Palmer	Oakmont, Pa	283
	won 18-hole play-off 71 to 74			
1963	J Boros	J D Cupit, A Palmer	Brookline, Ma	293
	won 18-hole play-off 70 to 73 to 76			
1964	K Venturi	T Jacobs	Congressional, Md	278
1965	G Player	K D G Nagle	Bellerive, Mo	282
	won 18-hole play-off 71 to 74			
1966	W Casper	A Palmer	Olympic, Ca	278
	won 18-hole play-off 69 to 73			
1967	J Nicklaus	A Palmer	Baltusrol, NJ	275
1968	L Trevino	J Nicklaus	Oak Hill, Rochester, NY	275
1969	O Moody	D Beman, A Geiberger, B Rosburg	Cypress Creek, Tx	281
1970	A Jacklin	D Hill	Hazeltine, Mn	281
1971	L Trevino	J Nicklaus	Merion, Pa	280
	won 18-hole play-off 68 to 71			
1972	J Nicklaus	B Crampton	Pebble Beach, Ca	290
1973	J Miller	J Schlee	Oakmont, Pa	279
1974	H Irwin	F Fezler	Winged Foot, NY	287
1975	L Graham	J Mahaffey	Medinah, Chicago, Il	287
	won 18-hole play-off 71 to 73			
1976	J Pate	A Geiberger, T Weiskopf	Duluth, Ga	277
1977	H Green	L Graham	Southern Hills, Ok	278
1978	A North	J C Snead, D Stockton	Cherry Hills, Co	285
1979	H Irwin	J Pate, G Player	Inverness, Oh	284
1980	J Nicklaus	I Aoki	Baltusrol, NJ	272
1981	D Graham	W Rogers, G Burns	Merion, Pa	273
1982	T Watson	J Nicklaus	Pebble Beach, Ca	282
1983	L Nelson	T Watson	Oakmont, Pa	280
1984	F Zoeller	G Norman	Winged Foot, NY	276
	won 18-hole play-off 67 to 75			
1985	A North,	D Watson, D Barr, T C Chen	Oakland Hills, Mi	279
1986	R Floyd	L Wadkins, C Beck	Shinnecock Hills, NY	279
1987	S Simpson	T Watson	Olympic, Ca	277
1988	C Strange	N Faldo	Brookline, Ma	278
	won 18-hole play-off 71 to 75			
1989	C Strange	I Woosnam, M McCumber, C Beck	Oak Hill, Rochester, NY	278
1990	H Irwin	M Donald	Medinah, Chicago, Il	280
	won play-off at first extra hole after tie (74) over 18 holes			
1991	P Stewart	S Simpson	Hazeltine, Mn	282
	won 18-hole play-off 75 to 77			
1992	T Kite	J Sluman	Pebble Beach, Ca	285
1993	L Janzen	P Stewart	Baltusrol, NJ	272
1994	E Els	L Roberts, C Montgomerie	Oakmont, Pa	279
	18-hole play-off scores: Els 74, Roberts 74, Montgomerie 78; Els beat Roberts at second extra hole of sudden-death play-off			
1995	C Pavin	G Norman	Shinnecock Hills, NY	280
1996	S Jones	T Lehman, D Love III	Oakland Hills, Mi	278
1997	E Els	C Montgomerie	Congressional, Md	276
1998	L Janzen	P Stewart	Olympic Club, Ca	280
1999	P Stewart	P Mickelson	Pinehurst CC, NC	279
2000	T Woods	M A Jimenez, E Els	Pebble Beach, Ca	272
2001	R Goosen	M Brooks	Southern Hills, Ok	276
	won 18-hole play-off 72 to 74			
2002	T Woods	P Mickelson	Bethpage Black, NY	277
2003	J Furyk	S Leaney	Olympia Fields, Il	272
2004	R Goosen	P Mickelson	Shinnecock Hills, NY	276
2005	M Campbell	T Woods	Pinehurst, NC	280
2006	G Ogilvy	P Mickelson, C Montgomerie	Winged Foot, NY	285
2007	A Cabrera	J Furyk, T Woods	Oakmont, Pa	285
2008	T Woods	R Mediate	Torrey Pines, Ca	283
	won at first sudden-death hole after both players shot 71 in 18-hole play-off			
2009	L Glover	R Barnes	Bethpage Black, NY	276

the 1894 affair at the St Andrew's Club, in New York City's Bronx, won by Willie Dunn from Musselburgh at matchplay against fellow Scot Willie Campbell by two holes. This is not surprising, because the USGA was not founded until the winter of 1894, by representatives of St Andrew's and four other clubs, Chicago, Newport, Shinnecock Hills and The Country Club, Brookline.

Their primary purpose was to decide when, where and on what basis the Amateur and Open titles were to be decided. For the first three years both were played at the same time and course; the USGA's first choice was Newport's nine-holer, in September, 1895, but the double-header was put off until the following month because of a clash with the America's Cup yacht races, which says a good deal about golf's standing at the time.

Moreover, the Open was relegated to a one-day, 36-hole affair to follow the three-day Amateur event, won from a field of 32 by Charles Macdonald, founder of the Chicago club. Most early American pros hailed from Scotland; their throaty accents were difficult to understand. Many had started out as caddies, and they had a reputation, deserved or not, as hard drinkers: they were not about to be admitted to the cream of East Coast society.

So Macdonald's victory was considered to be of far greater import than that gained on October 4 by Harold Rawlins, at 19 the youngest of all US Open champions. This Englishman, recently arrived to become assistant at the Newport club, scored 173 (91, 82) with a gutty ball, and won $150, a $50 gold medal and the Open Championship Cup for his club. He had beaten nine other pros and one amateur.

Though the US Open was dom-inated by Scottish and English pros until the 1911 victory of Johnny McDermott from Atlantic City, it quickly became the one to win for

paid or unpaid Americans, and there were some highly resourceful unpaid swingers about. The elevation of the pro to teacher, writer of instructional books and designer and endorser of all manner of golf gear and clothing made it, above all others, the crown that bestowed the Midas touch.

Modern pros have a true-blue amateur, Francis de Sales Ouimet from Boston, to thank for putting golf on the front page. His defeat of a formidable English pair in Harry Vardon and Ted Ray in a play-off for the 1913 Open lit the touch-paper of a further American golf explosion: and Ouimet was merely the scout, not the Seventh Cavalry.

It says much for the easy assumption of his prolonged status as American Sporting Hero number one, Ouimet's modern counterpart, Arnold Palmer, that although he won the US Open only once, with his most cavalier finish, he was the first of golf's major tycoons. Within ten years of his victory at Cherry Hills in 1960, Palmer's businesses had an annual turnover in excess of $15 million.

By contrast, Willie Anderson, four-time winner from North Berwick in Scotland, died at 31, some said because he drank too much. Anderson would strike a bizarre figure on the course today, for he deployed a flat swing with a bent left elbow. Although no one has equalled Anderson's feat of a hat-trick of Opens, from 1903 to 1905, his record of four victories is shared by an illustrious threesome in Bobby Jones, Ben Hogan and Jack Nicklaus, all giants of the game and all totally different from each other in style and temperament.

Jones, the southern gentleman, with degrees in mechanical eng-ineering, literature and law, and with more victories than any other amateur, added to his four US Opens two lost play-offs, a second place and (at 19 years of age) a joint fifth-place finish. Apart from his saving shot

Victory was sweet for Arnold Palmer at Cherry Hills in 1960 as he saw off the young pretender Jack Nicklaus, but it would be his only US Open title.

from the sand at Royal Lytham's 17th in 1926, the most remarkable of his career must surely have been at Interlachen, during the third leg of his 1930 grand slam, when he was five shots ahead with 18 holes to play. A miscue on the long ninth hole in the second round proved a godsend: although he almost topped his second shot, his ball, instead of diving into the lake guarding the green, skipped across it, ducks and drakes fashion, and was eventually holed for a birdie four.

OUIMET v. VARDON v. RAY, 1913 US Open

Francis de Sales Ouimet was the first amateur to become US Open champion, snatching the title in 1913 from the master golfer of the era, Harry Vardon, and another mature and powerful British professional, Ted Ray.

Ouimet's play-off victory got golf on to the front page, at least in Boston, where the US Open ended on September 20 at The Country Club, Brookline.

His triumph against all the odds had *Boys' Own Paper* romance about it, and sent the American golf juggernaut surging forward as the story of a slim young Yankee upsetting invading giants sank in with the US sporting public, who, like the English, love the underdog.

Besides, Ouimet was no rich country club member, and worked in a sports shop. He had started playing his golf in the fields around his home not far from Brookline's splendid clubhouse, and his credentials as the underdog were impeccable.

Though he lived close to The Country Club, he entered the US Open in 1913 as a Woodland club member. Shortly before it began, he had lost in the second round of the Amateur Championship to the eventual winner, Jerome Travers.

Vardon had done it all, winning the British Open five times, and the US Open in his only previous attempt. Ray had won the British Open the year before.

It was only as recently as 1911 that a native-born American, J J McDermott, had managed to end the British-born golfers' monopoly of the US Open. He won again in 1912, so was the main hope to repel the English experts.

Ouimet, with a 77, was six strokes behind the first-round leaders, both Scots, Macdonald Smith and Alec Ross, who fell from grace on the second day, when the English pair made their move. Ray returned 70, the lowest score of the entire championship, and Vardon, 72. Ouimet had a 74, but another 74 on the third day brought him level with Vardon and Ray, who did not fare well on the outward half of the final round.

Other players, notably Walter Hagen, had chances to catch Vardon and Ray, but only Ouimet did, playing the last four holes in one-under par. He chipped dead at the 15th to get his par four, chipped and putted for his par three at the next, and got the essential birdie at the 360-yard 16th, sinking a 12-footer across and down a slope: "a masterstroke", said Ray. Another good chip and a seven-footer at the 18th meant a total of 304, level with Vardon and Ray.

The crowd for the play-off was estimated at 10,000; they endured heavy rain gladly as an upset developed ... but a surprising one.

The local boy, using the less usual interlocking grip rather than the overlapping one that Vardon had made almost obligatory, most closely resembled the established pro, playing steadily from tee to green. His putting style also worked well: feet together, club swinging pendulum-style from the shoulder. His opponents fell into one error after another, the clincher coming one hole from home where Vardon bunkered his drive and took five. Ouimet birdied, as he had the day before, and finished in 72, beating Vardon by five and Ray by six.

The *New York Times* awarded Ouimet the title "World's Golf Champion". Hagen, who like Ouimet was 20, shared fourth place with Long Jim Barnes, Macdonald Smith and Louis Tellier, from France.

Ouimet's caddie, Eddie Lowery, aged ten, had fought off any suggestion that he should step down in favour of an older caddie in the play-off. The logo designed for the 100th US Open of 1995 at Brookline is based on a silhouette taken from a 1913 photograph of little Lowery standing beside Ouimet.

1913 US Open, Brookline, Ma

Pos.	Name	Score				
1	Francis Ouimet	77	74	74	79	304
2	Harry Vardon	75	72	78	79	304
3	Ted Ray	79	70	76	79	304

Ouimet won play-off 72 to 77 to 78

Hogan, almost universally re-cognized as the purest striker of the ball in golf history, gained all his Opens in a time span of only six years. He would certainly have earned a fifth and perhaps even a sixth US Open had his life at the top not been limited by the aftermath of the 1949 road crash injuries from which he recovered by a great effort of will to win his second Open in 1950, the Golden Jubilee of the championship. Even more remarkably, though every step of the extra 18 holes must have been a challenge, he triumphed in a play-off, scoring 69 against Lloyd Mangrum's 73 and George Fazio's 75. Mangrum would have come closer, with 71, had he not picked up his ball to blow a fly off it, incurring a two-stroke penalty.

Further Open successes followed in 1951 and 1953, when Hogan led after every round and finished (at Oakmont!) with three threes, a par and two birdies. He lost a play-off in 1955, and was joint second the following year.

Of the ones that got away, none would have caused him more regret than the 1960 Open, for it came close to his 48th birthday, and offered the juicy possibility of upstaging two young tigers in one

The great Bobby Jones triumphed in four US Opens, the greatest of which came in 1930 at Interlachen, when he completed the third leg of his grand slam.

Jack Nicklaus matched Willie Anderson's, Bobby Jones' and Ben Hogan's tally of four US Opens when he took the title at Baltusrol in 1980.

fell swoop, none other than Palmer and Nicklaus. Hogan required pars on the 71st and 72nd holes for 280, which would have equalled Palmer's winning score. He scored a six and a seven, four over. A fired-up Palmer ravenous for success might have been more than even Hogan could manage in a play-off, but the prospect of two generations in mortal combat is, to say the least, enticing.

Nicklaus, who had set an amateur scoring record of 282 in achieving second place at Cherry Hills, went one better in 1962, and won his fourth Open 18 years later. How typical of Nicklaus' career, high level from the first, that his first professional win should be in the 1962 Open at Oakmont. He was a little over 22; best of all, perhaps, it was gained at the expense of Arnold Palmer in a play-off.

Nicklaus was surely the best heeled as a youngster of all the professional giants of the US Open, for his father was a well-to-do owner of pharmacies. Financial security for Nicklaus did not mean security for his opponents: his single-minded pursuit of excellence and major titles has no parallel in golf's history.

While Nicklaus hit the target with his first professional attempt at the Open, Andy North has won only three titles, the first a PGA Tour event in 1977. The other two are US Opens, similar victories in that his final round in each case, at Cherry Hills in 1978 and Oakland Hills in 1985, was a nervous 74.

It seemed for some time at Oakland Hills that the first Open win by an Asian, Tze-Chung Chen from Taiwan, was about to burst on the world of golf. But a double hit at a crucial juncture led to a final 77, after rounds of 65, 66, 69. Even then he was only one shot away from a tie with North.

By contrast, David Graham played a final round to win in 1981 at Merion that was almost without flaw. He strode past George Burns to become the first Australian to win the title, and the first foreigner since Tony Jacklin 11 years earlier. He missed one fairway, the first, and that by not very much: he still birdied that hole, and his final 67 gave him a total of 273, one more than Nicklaus's record Open score, set at Baltusrol the previous year.

The round suited Graham's character: straight-backed, very correct in his manner.

His error-free round was succeeded 12 months later by a Tom Watson coup to rob Nicklaus of a coveted fifth Open. Watson's chip at Pebble Beach's short 17th recalls the defining moment of Sarazen's career, his double eagle to turn the 1935 Masters upside-down. Before long Watson was writing a book on the short game: how to get "up and down". He showed the world how on the Californian clifftops. Needing a birdie to get past Nicklaus, he overshot the 17th but, from dense semi-rough, he told his caddie he would hole a chip shot – and did hole, the ball running in downhill from a cuppy lie: a triumph of nerve and touch, for as Bobby Jones once wrote, "the delicate shot, if it fails, fails completely". Watson laid up at the long last hole, but still got a birdie to win by two.

Lack of a first British win since Jacklin's seven-stroke triumph has not been for want of trying by England's Nick Faldo and Scotland's Colin Montgomerie. Faldo lost by four shots in the 1988 play-off at Brookline to Curtis Strange, who won again in 1989 to land the first Open double since Hogan in 1950–51. Faldo also came close in 1990, sharing third place with Billy Ray Brown, a stroke behind the play-off pair of Hale Irwin and Mike Donald. Irwin won – it was his third title.

Since Graham's marvellous round, no foreigner had stormed the USGA's most closest guarded citadel

WATSON v. NICKLAUS, 1982 US OPEN

Tom Watson approached the US Open at Pebble Beach in 1982 with three British Opens and two Masters to his credit, but as yet no US Open title. Jack Nicklaus' thoughts were that his unmatched career record would touch even further heights of achievement if he could win a fifth Open and move one ahead of his fellow record-holders, Willie Anderson, Bobby Jones and Ben Hogan; and his hopes were high when he considered that he had won the only previous US Open held at Pebble Beach ten years earlier. Even for Nicklaus, now 42 years of age, time was running out.

Bruce Devlin shared the lead with the 1981 British Open champion, Bill Rogers, on the first day, but headed the field by two shots with a 69 for a 36-hole total of 139.

Watson and Nicklaus were like prudent mountaineers, quietly working themselves into position for a dart at the summit. Watson was the steadiest, though his putter had been his saviour in the first round, when his golf through the green had not been his best. But 72, 72, 68 for a 54-hole total of 212 earned him a share of the lead at 54 holes with Rogers. Devlin had faded to a 75 and stood on 214 along with George Burns, Scott Simpson and reigning champion David Graham.

Nicklaus was one-under par for the championship, a stroke behind this quartet. By the ninth hole in the final round on another gloomy day, only Rogers was ahead of him, by a stroke: and he had caught Watson. Nicklaus bogeyed the first and parred the second, then had five birdies in a row, including twos at the fifth and seventh, though another bogey at the eighth cut his advantage against par to four.

Behind him, Watson could make no impression on par over the first half of the course, even though the first six holes offer the best chance of birdies. He started back with a par that must have seemed like a birdie, for his second shot to the tenth might have bounced down on to the beach, but instead fell into spiky kikuyu grass below the green. His sand wedge left him a good eight paces from the hole, but down went the putt. A birdie

from more than 20ft at the 11th put him ahead, because his playing partner Rogers bogeyed it.

A poor bunker shot at the 12th cost him a shot, but for the moment he was one ahead of Nicklaus. Watson's birdie putt at the 13th missed by a fraction, while Nicklaus was saving a shot at the 15th, and they were level. A 35ft putt at the long 14th was, Watson considered, the putt that won him the title.

Rogers fell away, but Watson missed a birdie chance at the 15th, and was happy, in the circumstances, with a bogey at the next. There, thanks to falling foul of a newly fortified bunker, his fourth shot was perforce a 50ft putt with a 10ft break. Watson managed to get it stone dead.

Relieved, he went to the 17th level with Nicklaus, who was just coming off the last green with a round of 69 and a total of 284. When he saw Watson pull his tee shot at the 209-yard 17th into thick rough 20ft left of the flag, the odds against Nicklaus winning his fifth US Open were suddenly considerably shorter. Now Watson played the chip that won him the title. The sun came out, his ball was on top of the grass, and he easily sank his chip with a sand iron, landing it just on the green, a foot to the right to allow for the break.

He calmed down after a little jumping about and rejoicing, laid up cautiously at the long 18th, but pitched and putted for a final birdie for a 70, beating Nicklaus by two. No wonder Watson was the author of that definitive book on the short game, *Getting Up and Down*.

1982 US Open, Pebble Beach, Ca

Pos	Name	Score				
1	Tom Watson	72	72	68	70	282
2	Jack Nicklaus	74	70	71	69	284
3	Bobby Clampett	71	73	72	70	286
=	Dan Pohl	72	74	70	70	286
=	Bill Rogers	70	73	69	74	286

- until Ernie Els. The immensely powerful South African, at 24 years of age, beat off Loren Roberts and Montgomerie in a sweltering 1994 Oakmont at the second extra hole of a sudden-death play-off after a tie with Roberts in the 18-hole play-off round which is a feature of this championship.

Three years later, Els was champion again, shaking off Montgomerie with a daring iron close to the water at the back of the perilous 17th at Congressional - 480 yards, yet still a par four! Neither the Scot, nor the reigning British Open champion Tom Lehman, matched Els' decisive par. Indeed, Lehman's approach found the lake.

So Els and Montgomerie, watched by President Clinton, became the first non-Americans to lay claim to undisputed first and second places since the early years of the century. It was the Scot's third top-three finish in the event.

The 1997 Open dispelled the pipe-dreams of a grand slam for Masters champion, Tiger Woods, who finished ten shots adrift of the other "young gun" Ernie Els, who claimed his second Open title. Another player to collect his second victory was Lee Janzen when he fought off the challenge of Payne Stewart at the Olympic Club in 1998, but the effervescent Stewart went one better the following year - he

birdied the final hole to beat Phil Mickelson by a stroke at Pinehurst. Tragically, Stewart was killed in a plane crash later that year.

Over the years the championship has been given an added spice by the USGA's policy of setting courses that stretch nerves and (some say) exact undue punishment for off-line shots. Not every critic is in agreement with the way US Open greens are cut to lightning speed and the rough is encouraged to the extent that recoveries are a matter of damage-control. This, say the USGA's detractors, gives safety-first golfers an undue advantage. This view was widely expressed when Sam Parks, known only in the

immediate catchment area of the 1935 Open course, Oakmont in Pennsylvania, won with the only sub-300 score - 299.

Parks' stroke average of 74.75 rather bore out the cynical comment that Parks could score 75 on any course, but that that was about the sum of his abilities. For all that, Open courses, even justifiably feared Oakmont, have on occasion received rough treatment, notably Johnny Miller's final 63 at that very course in 1973. Still, the way that the USGA set up the courses nowadays means that the US Open remains the sternest test of a golfer's ability on the professional circuit.

THE US OPEN: 2000

Playing in his 100th tournament, Tiger Woods made one of the toughest tests in golf look like a stroll along the beach on the way to rewriting the record books.

It was to be a tournament of farewells. First of all to Jack Nicklaus, who declared that this would be his last visit to the championship that he had won four times. And then to Payne Stewart, the 1999 champion, who was tragically killed in a plane crash months after his victory.

On the eve of the tournament, some 40 of Stewart's peers hit golf balls into the ocean – the golfing equivalent of the 21-gun salute.

The tournament got under way in thick fog and one man dominated the headlines. Tiger Woods shot a six-under 65, the lowest ever score in the US Open at Pebble Beach, to take a one-stroke lead over Spain's Miguel Angel Jimenez and John Huston.

It wasn't such good news for John Daly: sitting on three-over par going into the par-five 18th hole, he shot a 14 – it included hitting one ball out of bounds and three further shots into the ocean. Daly stormed off the course and promptly withdrew from the tournament.

There were no such troubles for Woods during the second round. He shot a 69, containing six birdies and four bogeys, to leave him on eight-under par and with a six-stroke lead at the halfway stage. It was the largest 36-hole lead in the history of the US Open, beating Willie Anderson's mark of five strokes set in 1903. Behind Woods in second place were Jimenez and Thomas Bjorn.

Plenty of the game's biggest names fell by the wayside, however: among them Davis Love III (missing the cut at the US Open for only the third time in his career), Greg Norman (who went eight straight holes with a bogey or worse), 1995 champion

Corey Pavin and Jack Nicklaus. The Golden Bear shot an 11-over 81 in his final appearance at the tournament – his worst score in 160 rounds at the US Open – but he gave his adoring galleries one last thrill by lashing a three-wood into the Pacific breeze and reaching the 545-yard 18th in two shots – something that he had not tried to do in 20 years.

"It's been a great run of tournaments," said Nicklaus, holding back the tears as he said goodbye to the tournament that had treated him so well.

It was only after the third round that everyone started to realize that they were witnessing something special. Not only was Tiger Woods continuing his domination of the tournament, but records were starting to fall – records that had stood untouched for decades. He finished the third day with a lead of ten strokes, smashing the previous mark for the 54-hole lead (held by James Barnes and set in 1921) by three strokes. Woods also tied the biggest lead after 54 holes in a major tournament: set by Henry Cotton at the British Open at Royal St George's in 1934. The question was no longer who would win: it was how many records would Tiger Woods break?

And so while everyone else was busy playing for second place on the final day, Woods set about rewriting the history books. For the record, he shot a final-round, five-under par 67 – quite remarkable given that he was playing practically on his own: he was out of sight, playing against the tide of history. He had blown the rest of the field away.

When Woods sank his final putt on the 18th, he had collected his

The tournament brought the best out of Tiger Woods. His display during the four days at Pebble Beach was emphatic as he pushed long-standing records aside on his way to a stunning 15 stroke victory.

third major championship in only his fourth year as a professional. It had taken Jack Nicklaus four years to reach that goal. What's more, though, he had broken some of golf's longest established records.

He became the first player in the 106-year history of the US Open to finish the tournament at double digits under par – his 72-hole total was 12-under.

His 15-stroke victory not only shattered the previous US Open mark of 11, set by Willie Smith in 1899, but was the largest ever margin of victory in the history of major championship golf, beating the 13-stroke win by Old Tom Morris in the 1862 British Open – only the

third time the oldest tournament of them all had been played.

His 272 tied the lowest aggregate score at the US Open, first set by Jack Nicklaus in 1980 and later matched by Lee Janzen in 1993: both of these scores were recorded at Baltusrol, where par is 70.

But Woods seemed unfazed. "To perform the way I did, and on one of the greatest venues in golf, it doesn't get much better than that."

THE 2000 US OPEN – The Top 5

1 Tiger Woods 65 69 71 67 272 -12
2 Ernie Els 74 73 68 72 287 +3
= M A Jiménez 66 74 76 71 287 +3
4 John Huston 67 75 76 70 288 +4
5 Lee Westwood 71 71 76 71 289 +5
= Pádraig Harrington 73 71 72 73 289 +5

THE US OPEN: 2001

Retief Goosen could not hole a two-footer to win the championship on the 72nd hole, but when it came to the play-off, he could not miss.

Given that Tiger Woods had won the four previous major tournaments, it was perhaps only right to assume that he was favourite going into the 101st US Open. There was a feeling, however, that Southern Hills might not have been to his liking.

And so it proved following a rain-interrupted first round. Tiger Woods opened with a 74 and lay six shots behind South African Retief Goosen, who had taken control of the tournament in the first nine holes, going out in just 30 strokes, before finishing with a four-under 66.

Things got no better for the defending champion in the second round. Looking to make up shots on the leaders, he struggled his way to a 71, leaving him perilously close to missing the cut for the first time in 21 major tournaments. The best round of the day came from 40-year-old Texan Mark Brooks, who shot a 64 to give him a halfway share of the lead with Goosen, who had followed up his four-under first round with a rock-steady level-par 70.

It wasn't such easy going for the laidback South African the following day. He had to get up and down eight times during his round of 69, but it was enough to hold on to his lead after 54 holes. Joining him on five-under par was Stewart Cink, who had recorded his third consecutive round in the 60s. One stroke further back lay Spain's Sergio Garcia, Mark Brooks and Rocco Mediate: each one of the five was in contention.

Whoever the winner was going to be, one thing for certain was that it was not going to be Tiger Woods. The American finished with two consecutive 69s to leave him with a clubhouse score of three-over: it was the first time in 41 tournaments that he had failed to finish under par.

One player who finally got to grips with the course after having struggled for the first 54 holes was Vijay Singh, but his best-of-the-day round of 64 did nothing more than leave him in a tie for seventh place.

All eyes were on the five players still in contention. The five quickly became three. Sergio Garcia shot a final-round 77 – a disappointing nine strokes worse than his third-round effort – and Rocco Mediate a two-over 72 to leave him on two-under par.

As much as anything, this tournament will always be remembered for the manner in which the three leading players coped with the 18th hole. The 18th green had been labelled with criticism throughout the tournament. It would be fair to say that neither Brooks nor Cink nor Goosen coped well with it: all three stood on the 18th tee on five-under par.

First came Brooks, playing a couple of groups ahead of the final pair. A 263-yard drive was followed by a three-iron to the left side of the green. He was faced with a 40ft left-to-right putt for a birdie, which he left 8ft short. He left the straight downhill putt 2in short of the cup, tapped in for a bogey and retreated to the clubhouse and started to clear out his locker, convinced that his chance for title glory had gone.

Next came Cink. Following a 295-yard drive, he left his approach shot in thick rough over the back of the green. He chipped to within 15ft before fractionally missing his putt for par. Deciding to leave the stage clear for Goosen, he went to tap in

his 18in putt for par but missed. He tapped in for a double-bogey. And so it was left to Goosen. He was left with two putts from 12ft to collect his first US Open title after having played an immaculate approach shot to the heart of the green. His birdie attempt grazed the hole and finished 2ft away. An uphill gimme for the tournament: he missed and stood hands on hips before regaining his composure to make the putt he needed to put him into a play-off with Brooks the following day. Any psychological advantage must surely have been with Brooks: how would Goosen respond at the next days play-off after having thrown away the

tournament the day before? Goosen responded brilliantly and didn't miss a putt: indeed, he needed only seven putts to negotiate the first six holes and ran out a comfortable winner by two strokes – 72 to 74 – to become only the second foreign player to claim the US Open title in the last 20 years. He made hard work of it, though.

THE 2001 US OPEN - The Top 5
1 Retief Goosen* 66 70 69 71 276 -4
2 Mark Brooks 72 64 70 70 276 -4
3 Stewart Cink 69 69 67 72 277 -3
4 Rocco Mediate 71 68 67 72 278 -2
5 Tom Kite 73 72 72 64 281 +1
= Paul Azinger 74 67 69 71 281 +1
* Won play-off

The affable South African Retief Goosen put the nightmare of the previous day firmly behind him to win the play-off by two shots.

THE US OPEN: 2002

Staged in the shadow of New York, Tiger Woods followed his win at the Masters earlier in the year with a victory in the tournament billed as the "People's Open".

Whereas a year before the Southern Hills course had seemingly neutralized Tiger Woods's game – with its demands for accuracy off the tee as opposed to length – Bethpage, the first truly municipal course to host the US Open in its 108-year history, seemed ideally suited to the world number one's game.

Standing at 7,214 yards, it was the longest par-70 course in the history of the competition and featured the two longest par fours ever in the US Open – the 492-yard tenth and the 499-yard 12th.

To make matters worse for Woods's competitors, an already brutal course, with knee-high rough and fairways that seemed to stretch on as far as the eye could see, was made far worse by persistent rain that affected everything other than the greens, which remained lightning quick. And to the surprise of no one, Tiger Woods showed the way over the opening two rounds carding a 67 and a 68 to sit on five-under par.

The conditions may not have got to Tiger Woods, but they certainly got to plenty of others: among them Sergio Garcia. The young Spaniard slammed clubs and balls into the ground and made questionable gestures to a heckler in the galleries on his way to a second-round 74. After completing his round he suggested that play should have been halted after the course had become waterlogged. More controversially, he also suggested that USGA officials had displayed considerable favouritism towards Tiger Woods, who had played his round in the morning in steady rain, before

the course had deteriorated, and was, therefore, gaining advantages that other players were not. But, Woods apart, the weather certainly got the better of some of the players. Among them was Retief Goosen, the South African who again confirmed the curse of the defending champion when he carded 154 after two rounds and was forced to surrender his US Open title earlier than he might have hoped. Also heading home at the halfway stage was British Open champion David Duval. The American ended two rounds on 11-over 151 and missed the cut by one stroke – even though the cut mark had soared to its highest level since Shinnecock Hills in 1986 (also at ten-over par).

The bottom line, however, was that if anyone was going to catch Woods then they were going to have to make a considerable move on him. Tiger had made only four bogeys in the first two rounds and was showing no signs of letting up. At the halfway stage he was already three strokes ahead of his nearest competitor, Padraig Harrington.

Two players did make a move on Woods in the third round: first came Phil Mickelson – a favourite of the New York galleries – who posted a three-under 67 to leave him five strokes adrift; then came Garcia, putting his troublesome third round behind him to match Mickelson's score – it left the Spaniard on one-under, four strokes behind Woods who marched on oblivious of the moves of others and carded a rock-steady level-par 70.

The signs were ominous. Woods has an unbelievable record when it comes to closing out tournaments

when he either heads the field or has a share of the lead going into the final round. His record before the US Open stood at 23-2: what was worse for his pursuers, he had never relinquished a 54-hole lead in major tournaments.

He wobbled, bogeying the first two holes of the final round: his lead over Mickelson now stood at two – but it never got any closer. Mickelson, roared on by the galleries, could only shoot a 70. Woods's playing partner, Garcia, in the hunt for the second time in two years at the US Open, buckled under the pressure and once again blew his chance to notch up a first major tournament win – this time with a four-over round of 74.

But this tournament was all about Tiger Woods. He may have shot a two-over round of 72 on the final day, but he showed to the world why he should now be considered as one of the greatest players ever to have played the game. He made par

after par to show that he had the poise of Jack Nicklaus, Ben Hogan and Bobby Jones. Under the most extreme pressure, and on a course that was playing as hard as any in recent US Open history, he led the field in greens in regulation (53 out of 72) and was the only player in the field to finish the tournament under par.

Tiger's major tally now stood at eight: what's more, he had reached that mark faster than anyone else in the history of the game. It seemed as though that is all Woods was playing against – history – and even that appeared to be a mismatch.

THE 2002 US OPEN – The Top 5

1 Tiger Woods 67 68 70 72 277 -3
2 Phil Mickelson 70 73 67 70 280 E
3 Jeff Maggert 69 73 68 72 282 +2
4 Sergio García 68 74 67 74 283 +3
5 Nick Faldo 70 76 66 73 285 +5
= Scott Hoch 71 75 70 69 285 +5
= Billy Mayfair 69 74 68 74 285 +5

Tiger Woods was in a league of his own at Bethpage and a level-par final round was enough to see him to his eighth major title.

THE US OPEN: 2003

Jim Furyk may not be one of the prettiest players to watch, but his game was mighty effective over the Olympia Fields course as he notched up his first major.

The USGA might not have been able to control the weather, but it has made a concerted effort to shift away from the five-inch rough of recent years – rough that often made it impossible for players who found themselves in it to reach the green in two- to four-inch rough.

As a result, 24 players broke par in the first round and, against all expectations, none of the usual suspects were at the top of the leaderboard. It was left to the likes of Jim Furyk and Stephen Leaney, who both opened with a three-under 67, to bask in any first day headlines. Two-time champion Ernie Els was also in the hunt on one-under with Tiger Woods and Vijay Singh also in contention – although perhaps left slightly disappointed after shooting a level-par 70. The feeling around the course was that nobody had taken advantage of the benign conditions and shot a really low round.

That all changed on the second day and any disappointment that Vijay Singh might have felt after his opening round was swept firmly to one side as he recorded a blistering 63. It was the lowest round at the US Open for 23 years, equalling Jack Nicklaus's 63 in the first-round at Baltusrol in 1980.

The Fijian shared the halfway lead with Jim Furyk, who moved from three-under to seven-under with a round of 66: it had been an impressive start from the American. The pair's 36-hole total of 133 was a record for the tournament. Twenty-four other players joined them under par, the most since 1990 when the Open was played at Medinah – the last time that the championship had visited the Chicago area. Needless to say, the cut,

at three-over, was the lowest in the history of the tournament.

As the third day dawned, it was another ideal day for scoring. In the final 45 minutes of the round, Jim Furyk went from being in a head-to-head battle with Vijay Singh to holding a three-stroke lead over Stephen Leaney going into the final round. Singh stumbled badly on the inward nine to leave himself five strokes adrift of the American. Alongside him was Nick Price, who went five-under for his first six holes of the day only to go four-over for the final 12.

One player definitely not in contention going into the final round was Tiger Woods. The defending champion tumbled from three strokes back at the start of the day to 11 behind the leaders at the end of it after struggling to a 75.

So the destiny of the US Open lay in a head-to-head battle between Jim Furyk and Stephen Leaney, neither of whom are particularly long off the tee, but both of whom are straight hitters. The similarities end there. Going into this tournament, Furyk had recorded 12 top-ten finishes in the 31 majors he had played – with a best finish of fourth. Leaney, on the other hand, had only played in nine majors before Olympia Fields – and had only made the cut in two.

Even more so as dawn broke over Chicago on the final day as the sun shone for the first time at the US Open and the venue finally played like a US Open course. It was good news for someone trying to protect a three-stroke lead and, as a result, the final day was all about Jim Furyk.

His challengers stepped aside

quickly on a day where 19 players started the final round under par and only four remained there at the end. Starting the day five strokes behind, Vijay Singh birdied the second hole to lay down his challenge. Any aspirations that he might have had disappeared as quickly as they had arrived, however, as he double-bogeyed the next hole and was never in contention again: he made six straight bogeys at one point, recorded a 78 and finished in a lowly joint 20th. His playing partner, Nick Price, opened with three straight bogeys and was never a factor.

Any nerves that Furyk might have had were settled when he holed a 20ft putt to save par on the first hole. It maintained his three-stroke lead and no one would get any closer to him than that as he went on to win the US Open.

THE 2003 US OPEN – The Top 5
1 Jim Furyk 67 66 67 72 272 -8
2 Stephen Leaney 67 68 68 72 275 -5
3 Kenny Perry 72 71 69 67 279 -1
= Mike Weir 73 67 68 71 279 -1
5 Justin Rose 70 71 70 69 280 E
= Fredrik Jacobson 69 67 73 71 280 E
= David Toms 72 67 70 71 280 E
= Ernie Els 69 70 69 72 280 E
= Nick Price 71 65 69 75 280 E

Jim Furyk started the final round with a three-stroke lead: he never surrendered it and went on to post his first major championship title.

THE US OPEN: 2004

Retief Goosen outlasted Masters champion Phil Mickelson over a windswept Shinnecock Hills to collect his second US Open title.

Funny things happen when you return to a place full of good memories: such as going back to the place where you hit one of the greatest shots ever played in a major tournament – a four-wood to within 6ft to collect your first major championship. Such memories tend to inspire you.

That is exactly what happened to Corey Pavin over the course of the first two rounds when he returned to the scene of his one and only major triumph – he won the last time the US Open came to Shinnecock Hills in 1995. Pavin may not be the same player he was back then. His shot-making and scrambling skills seem to have been overpowered by the modern game, but he was still good enough over the first 36 holes to sit at two-under and firmly in contention at the halfway stage.

And during the second round, Phil Mickelson played the course to near perfection. The recently crowned Masters champion, roared on by the New York crowd who seem to love the left-hander as much as he loves New York, shot a four-under 66 to leave him in great shape to win the second leg of the grand slam.

Mickelson seemed a changed man following his win at Augusta earlier in the year: he was playing with a swagger normally associated with a multiple major winner. "After winning at Augusta I feel like the preparation I had, the style of shots I've worked on, seem to be allowing me to play and score well at the majors," said a confident Mickelson. He was joined on six-under by Japan's Shigeki Maruyama, who shot a two-under 68, despite a bogey on the final hole.

Jeff Maggert was a stroke further behind on five-under; at four-under stood Retief Goosen and Fred Funk.

Ernie Els shot four straight birdies in the course of a second-round 67 to lay a further stroke back, alongside Vijay Singh who was also still in contention at the halfway stage.

As was Tiger Woods, who had spent much of the second round flirting with the cut before easing thoughts of an early return home with back-to-back birdies and a round of 69: he was seven strokes behind the leaders, though, and would have to work hard over the weekend if he wanted to add to his two US Open titles.

After a topsy-turvy third day that had seen no less than five players take the sole lead of the tournament, Retief Goosen stood at the top of the leaderboard with a two-stroke lead after shooting 69. Two shots behind him were Ernie Els and Phil Mickelson, who recorded a 70 and a 73 respectively.

It would mean that Goosen and Els would be paired together for the final round – the first time that two former champions had played the final round together since Lee Trevino and Jack Nicklaus at Pebble Beach in 1972. Perhaps it would provide a chance to catch up on old times: the pair had played against each other in their homeland when they were children and had taken South Africa to success in the World Cup in 2002. Many thought that it would be a calming influence on the pair and would detract from the Mickelson-oriented galleries.

As the players arrived at the course on the final day they found weather conditions that were anything but calm: the wind had finally arrived at Shinnecock Hills.

Those with memories of the previous US Opens over the course – in 1986 and 1995 – would have known that when the wind picks up, the players have to muster all the skills they possess just to hang on to par.

Nobody did: the first time that this had happened in a US Open since 1963. The scoring average for the final round was 78.727 – the highest since Pebble Beach in 1972. Conditions were so tough that 28 players failed to break 80 – among them Ernie Els, playing in the final group.

With Els shooting himself out of the equation, the stage was set for Goosen and Mickelson. In an intriguing, see-saw final round that saw the players battling not only against each other but also against the conditions, the outcome of the tournament was settled in the space of a thrilling five minutes.

Mickelson stood on the 17th green holding a one-stroke lead over the South African and eyeing up an 8ft putt for par. In the background, the roar of the galleries indicated that Goosen had birdied the 16th. Mickelson missed the putt. It rolled 6ft past the hole. He missed the return putt as well and Goosen had a two-shot lead with two to play. The galleries were muted: more so when the South African finished par-par to become only the 21st multiple winner of the event.

Retief Goosen brought his best putting game to Shinnecock Hills on the final day to win the US Open for the second time.

THE 2004 US OPEN – The Top 5
1 Retief Goosen 70 66 69 71 276 -4
2 Phil Mickelson 68 66 73 71 278 -2
3 Jeff Maggert 68 67 74 72 281 +1
4 Shigeki Maruyama 66 68 74 76 284 +4
= Mike Weir 69-70-71 74 284 +4

THE US OPEN: 2005

After a dramatic final round qualifier Michael Campbell emerged to become the first New Zealander to win a major title since 1963.

The last time the US Open had been contested over the notoriously difficult Pinehurst No.2 course in North Carolina, Payne Stewart, the only player during the week to have broken par, saw off the challenge of Phil Mickelson to claim the last of his three major championships. Four months later, Stewart was dead: killed when the Learjet carrying him suffered a loss of cabin pressure and crashed after an uncontrolled descent. It is for this reason, perhaps, that the 1999 US Open was remembered more for Stewart's final major victory rather than for the devilishly difficult manner in which the course had played. It took only a few practice rounds for the course to re-establish its reputation among the players. The 2005 US Open, it seemed, would be about the survival of the fittest

After a first round blessed with bright skies and a gentle breeze, over a course that didn't play as tough as expected, two qualifiers – Olin Browne and Rocco Mediate – stood on top of the leaderboard at three-under par after shooting a 67. They were two of nine players to have recorded red figures, with Lee Westwood, defending champion Retief Goosen (following his two-shot win at Shinnecock Hills the previous year) and Brandt Jobe a shot behind. Masters winner Tiger Woods, seeking to become the first player since Ben Hogan in 1953 to win the year's first two majors, battled to an even-par 70.

In the second round, as the breeze stiffened and the tough pin positions on Pinehurst's notorious dome-shaped greens started to bite, the majority of the field began to struggle. But battling through the treacherous conditions, Goosen, confirming his reputation as a player capable of grinding out good scores on tough courses, dug out an even-par 70 to end the day on two-under, level with Browne and unheralded Jason Gore, the world no.818, who fired a round-of-the-day 67.

The punishing conditions continued in the third round, with Goosen picking up on Saturday where he had left off the previous day, posting a one-under 69 to establish a three-shot lead over Gore (72) and Browne (72) on even, with Michael Campbell (71) and Mark Hensby (72) a shot further back on one-over. Five other players, including Woods (on three-over) sat within six shots of the lead, but the smart money was on Goosen becoming the first player to defend the US Open crown since Curtis Strange (winner in 1988 and 1989). "I felt pretty relaxed on the golf course today, but you can lose three shots very quickly around here," said the 36-year-old South African. His words were prophetic.

In a fourth round dominated by strong winds and squandered shots, Goosen's grip on the title floundered when he dropped six shots in the opening nine holes; five more shots went on the back nine as the South African posted a sorry 81 and slipped to a disappointing 11th place. Gore shot an 84; Browne did little better (stumbling to 80); and the path was clear for Michael Campbell to hold off a charging Tiger Woods – who bogeyed two of the final three holes – to win his first major championship. "I can't believe I'm holding this trophy," an emotional Campbell told reporters. Neither could Goosen, for this, surely, was a major championship title the South African had thrown away.

THE 2005 US OPEN - The Top 5
1 Michael Campbell 71 69 71 69 280 E
2 Tiger Woods 70 71 72 69 282 +2
3 Sergio García 71 69 75 70 285 +5
= Tim Clark 76 69 70 70 285 +5
= Mark Hensby 71 68 72 74 285 +5

A final-round 69 was enough to secure New Zealand's Michael Campbell his first US Open victory.

THE US OPEN: 2006

The US Open returned to Winged Foot GC, and in a pulsating finale, Phil Mickelson threw away a two-shot lead over the final three holes to hand Geoff Ogilvy an unlikely victory.

Winged Foot GC served early notice of its reputation as being the sternest test in golf. In the first round only one player recorded a red number: Colin Montgomerie, who sat on top of the US Open leaderboard for the first time since 1997 after shooting an impressive one-under 69. Five players were a shot back on level par, including Phil Mickelson, seeking to become the second player in 50 years to win three straight majors. That accolade's other holder, Tiger Woods (playing his first tournament since the death of his father Earl), endured a difficult round, slipping to six-over par – his worst performance as a professional at the US Open.

Not much improved for Tiger on day two: the world no.1 shot a second consecutive 76 to miss the cut in a major for the first time in ten years as a professional. Not that he looked towards his father's death as an excuse: "When you don't execute, you're not going to be happy," said the world no.1. So, with Woods, heading home early for the weekend, the second-round headlines belonged to Steve Stricker, who posted a brilliant 69 to sit on one-under, a shot ahead of Montgomerie and two ahead of Geoff Ogilvy. Six other players, including Mickelson, sat within four strokes of the lead.

The tournament came to life in round three. To the delight of the galleries, Mickelson produced a magical 69 to grab a share of the 54-hole lead at two-over par. Little-known Englishman Kenneth Ferrie joined the world no.2 in the final group, one shot ahead of Ogilvy

and three shots ahead of a group of five players, including Montgomerie. It was still anyone's Open.

The main protagonists on a pulsating final day were Montgomerie, Ogilvy and Mickelson, and the outcome of the 106th US Open hinged on how the trio coped with the 450-yard par-four 18th. Montgomerie came first: standing on the tee in a share of the lead at four-over, he hit the perfect tee shot into the middle of the fairway and then, inexplicably, left his second short of the green; four shots and a double-bogey later, the Scot finished

on six-over par. Ogilvy was next: the Australian hit a superb drive, only to find his ball resting in a divot; a difficult second shot saw his ball fall short of the green, but a brilliant chip, followed by a nerveless 8ft putt for par, left him on five-over. Standing on the 18th tee holding a one-shot advantage, Mickelson imploded: he pushed his tee shot, his second shot hit a tree, his third left him plugged in a greenside bunker, his fourth overshot the green and two putts and a double-bogey later, the world no.2 had handed a stunned Ogilvy a first major title.

"As a kid, I dreamt of winning this tournament," said a distraught Mickelson. "I came out here and worked hard all four days and haven't made a bogey [on the 18th] all week. I can't believe I did that." Nor could anyone else, with the exception, perhaps, of Ogilvy. "I think I was the beneficiary of a little charity," said the 29-year-old Australian.

THE 2006 US OPEN - The Top 5
1 Geoff Ogilvy 71 70 72 72 285 +5
2 Phil Mickelson 70 73 69 74 286 +6
= Colin Montgomerie 69 71 75 71 286 +6
= Jim Furyk 70 72 74 70 286 +6
5 Pádraig Harrington 73 69 74- 71 287 +7

Geoff Ogilvy held his nerve while others around him faltered to collect his first major championship victory.

THE US OPEN: 2007

Oakmont Country Club, the scene of numerous history-making moments over the years served up yet another classic chapter when Argentina's Angel Cabrera played the golf of his life in the final round to win his first major title.

Much of the pre-tournament talk concerned the severity of the course. The greens were lightning fast, the fabled bunkers had been deepened, the fairways were narrow and the rough was penal. And although heavy overnight rain produced relatively tame conditions for the first round, only two players managed to break par: England's Nick Dougherty, with a round-of-the-day, two-under 68, and Argentina's Angel Cabrera, with a 69. Eighteen players, including Tiger Woods, sat within three shots of the lead. The overriding consensus, however, was that this was as placid as Oakmont could be, and the players had failed to take advantage.

Oakmont cranked up the challenge in round two. The wind whipped up, the sun shone, the greens regained their terrifying pace and the players faltered. After a day that saw an average round of 76.933, not one player remained under par – the first time that had happened at a US Open since Winged Foot in 1974. Out of a field of 156 players, only Cabrera, who shot a 71 to sit on level-par, had not yielded a shot to the course. Bubba Watson lay a shot further back, with four players tied on two-over.

Saturday saw heavily watered greens, the tamest conditions of the week and a trademark third-round move from Woods. Producing near-flawless golf – hitting 17 out of 18 greens in regulation – the world no.1 shot 69 to move to four-over par, two behind 54-hole leader Aaron Baddeley who, showing impressive poise, reeled off a second-successive 70. With 12 players within five shots of the lead, however, this US Open was still very much up for grabs.

The story of the final round was how the leaders failed to sustain a title challenge. Baddeley never recovered from a triple-bogey seven on the opening hole and eventually fired an 80 to slip to 13th place. Woods could not buy a birdie and finished with a 72 for six-over par and second place to continue his trend of never having won a major coming from behind in the final round. Jim Furyk, who hit three straight birdies on the back nine to take a share of the lead, paid the ultimate price for an errant tee shot on the 17th with a bogey and finished alongside Woods in second. Instead, the spoils went to Cabrera, who, having seemingly slipped out of contention following a 76 the previous day, shot a one-under 69 to finish on five-over par and become his country's first major champion for 40 years.

"I never thought I would be here at this moment," said an emotional Cabrera. "It is very difficult to describe. Probably tomorrow when I wake up with this trophy beside me in my bed, I will realize that I have won the U.S. Open." If he continued to play in the same manner, few doubted that more major championship trophies would be heading the Argentine's way.

THE 2007 US OPEN - The Top 5
1 Ángel Cabrera 69 71 76 69 285 +5
2 Jim Furyk 71 75 70 70 286 +6
= Tiger Woods 71 74 69 72 286 +6
4 Niclas Fasth 71 71 75 70 287 +7
5 David Toms 72 72 73 72 289 +9
= Bubba Watson 70 71 74 74 289 +9

Angel Cabrera fired a final-round 69 to see off the dual challenge of Jim Furyk and Tiger Woods to become the third first-time US Open winner in three years.

THE US OPEN: 2008

Torrey Pines, California, presented the players with the fairest US Open set-up for many years. And, after a pulsating five days, world no.1 Tiger Woods outlasted journeyman Rocco Mediate in a play-off to collect his third US Open crown.

The USGA's decision to pair the world's top-three ranked players – Tiger Woods, playing in his first round since the Masters after undergoing surgery on his left knee; hometown favourite Phil Mickelson; and Australia's Adam Scott – together for the first round may have provided a media and fan frenzy, but it did little to inspire the "Supergroup's" play. Mickelson shot a level-par 71, Woods 72 and Scott 73. Instead, the day's headlines belonged to two unknowns, Justin Hicks and Kevin Streelman, who held a joint lead at three-under par.

The first-round leaders' moment in the spotlight did not last long: Hicks shot a nine-over 80, Streelman a six-over 77 and the halfway lead belonged to Stuart Appleby, who added a 70 to an opening 69 to sit on three-under, one shot clear of Robert Karlsson, Rocco Mediate and Woods, who fired a three-under 68.

That Woods eventually signed for a one-under 70 after the third round to move to three-under and the 54-hole lead told only half the story. The world no.1 endured a rollercoaster of a round that started with three dropped shots on the opening four holes, before he chipped in for birdie on the 17th and closed out with a 30ft putt for eagle on the 18th to take a one-shot lead over Lee Westwood into the final round.

Mediate, two shots off the lead after 54 holes, was the final round's pacesetter. The 46-year-old, seeking to become the US Open's oldest-ever champion, took the lead as early

as the second hole and, with steely determination, did his level best to keep hold of it, closing with an even-par 71 to end on one-under. By the time Woods and Westwood arrived on the final hole, both needed a birdie to take the US Open into extra-time. They both found sand off the tee and then fired their approaches to within 15ft. Westwood putted first and missed. Then came Woods: in a moment of pure theatre, the world no.1 rapped in his 12ft birdie putt and fist-pumped the air in trademark fashion. The US Open would be decided by a play-off and Woods was the firm favourite to win.

For the majority of Monday's 18-hole play-off, however, it seemed the underdog would have his day. Woods, clearly hampered by his knee, could not put Mediate away. By the time the pair reached the 18th Woods trailed by one, but he rose to the occasion once again, digging out a birdie to force a sudden-death play-off, and then recording a par to Mediate's bogey on the first extra hole to collect a third US Open title.

"This is probably the greatest tournament I've ever had," enthused Woods. It had certainly been filled with some of his greatest moments, but at a price: following knee surgery, the world no.1 would not compete in a major championship again until the 2009 Masters.

THE 2008 US OPEN – The Top 5
1 Tiger Woods* 72 68 70 73 283 -1
2 Rocco Mediate 69 71 72 71 283
3 Lee Westwood 70 71 70 73 284 E
4 Robert Karlsson 70 70 75 71 286 +2
= D. J. Trahan 72 69 73 72 286 +2
* Won in play-off

Tiger Woods battled an injured knee and an inspired performance from Rocco Mediate before collecting his third US Open title and a 14th major championship victory.

THE US OPEN: 2009

The US Open returned to Bethpage Black and following a tournament blighted by inclement Long Island weather, 29-year-old Lucas Glover held his nerve to fight off the chasing pack in a dramatic final round to become a most unlikely champion.

Forecasts that the 109th US Open would be remembered as much for torrential rain as for the quality of play were realized as early as the first day as heavy rain left the course unplayable and play was suspended at 1.55pm. It was a similar story on day two, and by the time the players had completed 36 holes, in the middle of the third day, Saturday, the leaderboard had an upside-down feel to it, with Ricky Barnes, the 2002 US Amateur champion, leading the way after adding a five-under 65 to his opening round of 67 to sit on eight-under, one shot clear of Lucas Glover (who closed with a 64 to add to an opening 69). But there was plenty of golf left to play.

The hope on Sunday was that players would complete their third rounds by 4.30pm, turn around to start their final rounds and see how far they could get around the course before the light gave way. By the time the third round had come to a close, Barnes remained on top of the leaderboard after shooting an even-par 70 to remain on eight-under (although, at one stage, the Californian had reached 11-under par to become only the fourth player in history to reach double digits under par in a US Open). Barnes held a one shot lead over Glover (70) and a five-shot lead over David Duval, appearing at the sharp end of a major tournament for the first time since the 2001 British Open.

It may have been a frustrating US Open until now, but it was business as usual on Monday – only the third time, excluding play-offs, the tournament had been forced into overtime – as Bethpage conjured up a dramatic finale. Barnes faltered on the front nine, bogeying five of the first nine holes. He recovered on the back nine, but failed to apply pressure on the leaders and finished on two-under par. Phil Mickelson made a powerful final-round charge, making eagle on 13 to take a share of the lead, only to bogey two of the final four holes to end on two-under, tied for second at the US Open for the fifth time in his career. Duval threatened, before losing all momentum with a bogey on 17 and joining Barnes and Mickelson on two-under.

In the midst of this trio of almost-but-not-quite stories, Lucas Glover, handed the lead after Barnes's collapse, held his nerve, cancelling out a bogey on 15 with a birdie on 16 to close with a 73 and a winning four-under par total.

Clutching the US Open trophy that bears the names of Jack Nicklaus, Ben Hogan, Bobby Jones and Tiger Woods a reserved, almost embarrassed Glover told assembled journalists, "I hope I don't downgrade it or anything with my name on there." There was no fear of that: he may not have been a household name, but the tobacco-chewing 29-year-old from South Carolina had become a most unlikely, but most worthy, champion.

THE 2009 US OPEN – The Top 5
1 Lucas Glover 69 64 70 73 276 -4
2 Ricky Barnes 67 65 70 76 278 -2
= David Duval 67 70 70 71 278 -2
= Phil Mickelson 69 70 69 70 278 -2
5 Ross Fisher 70 68 69 72 279 -1

Lucas Glover held off the final-round challenges of Ricky Barnes, David Duval and Phil Mickelson to capture the 2009 US Open title, played over the Bethpage Black course in New York.

THE BRITISH OPEN

The British Open stems from the idea put forward by Prestwick Golf Club in 1860 to find a successor to the late, great Allan Robertson. Only eight players competed for the red morocco Championship Belt put up by Prestwick for competition over three rounds of the club's 12-hole course. Willie Park from Musselburgh won from seven rivals (all pros, so this was not technically an Open at all), but the early history of the Open, which involved amateurs from 1861 onwards, is dominated by Tom

Old and Young Tom Morris: between them, father and son won a total of eight British Open championships between 1861 and 1872.

British Open Results

Year	Winner	Runner-up	Venue	Score
(36 holes until 1892)				
1860	W Park	T Morris Sr	Prestwick	174
1861	T Morris Sr	W Park	Prestwick	163
1862	T Morris Sr	W Park	Prestwick	163
1863	W Park	T Morris Sr	Prestwick	168
1864	T Morris Sr	A Strath	Prestwick	167
1865	A Strath	W Park	Prestwick	162
1866	W Park	D Park	Prestwick	169
1867	T Morris Sr	W Park	Prestwick	167
1868	T Morris Jr	R Andrew	Prestwick	157
1869	T Morris Jr	T Morris Sr	Prestwick	154
1870	T Morris Jr	R Kirk, D Strath	Prestwick	149
1871	No championship			
1872	T Morris Jr	D Strath	Prestwick	166
1873	T Kidd	J Anderson	St Andrews	179
1874	M Park	T Morris Jr	Musselburgh	159
1875	W Park	B Martin	Prestwick	166
1876	R Martin	D Strath	St Andrews	176
	Strath refused to take part in the play-off			
1877	J Anderson	R Pringle	Musselburgh	160
1878	J Anderson	R Kirk	Prestwick	157
1879	J Anderson	J Allan, A Kirkaldy	St Andrews	169
1880	R Ferguson	P Paxton	Musselburgh	162
1881	R Ferguson	J Anderson	Prestwick	170
1882	R Ferguson	W Fernie	St Andrews	171
1883	W Fernie	R Ferguson	Musselburgh	159
	won 36-hole play-off 158 to 159			
1884	J Simpson	D Rolland, W Fernie	Prestwick	160
1885	R Martin	A Simpson	St Andrews	171
1886	D Brown	W Campbell	Musselburgh	157
1887	W Park Jr	R Martin	Prestwick	161
1888	J Burns	D Anderson, B Sayers	St Andrews	171
1889	W Park Jr	A Kirkaldy	Musselburgh	155
	won 36-hole play-off 158 to 163			
1890	J Ball	W Fernie	Prestwick	164
1891	H Kirkaldy	A Kirkaldy	St Andrews	166
1892	H H Hilton	J Ball, H Kirkaldy, A Herd	Muirfield	305
1893	W Auchterlonie	J E Laidlay	Prestwick	322
1894	J H Taylor	R Rolland	St George's	326
1895	J H Taylor	A Herd	St Andrews	322
1896	H Vardon	J H Taylor	Muirfield	316
	won 36-hole play-off 157 to 159			
1897	H H Hilton	J Braid	Hoylake	314
1898	H Vardon	W Park Jr	Prestwick	307
1899	H Vardon	J White	St George's	307
1900	J H Taylor	H Vardon	St Andrews	309
1901	J Braid	H Vardon	Muirfield	309
1902	A Herd	H Vardon, J Braid	Hoylake	307
1903	H Vardon	T Vardon	Prestwick	300
1904	J White	J H Taylor, J Braid	St George's	296
1905	J Braid	R Jones, JH Taylor	St Andrews	318
1906	J Braid	J H Taylor	Muirfield	300
1907	A Massy	J H Taylor	Hoylake	312
1908	J Braid	T Ball	Prestwick	291
1909	J H Taylor	J Braid, T Ball	Deal	295

Year	Winner	Runner-up	Venue	Score
1910	J Braid	A Herd	St Andrews	299
1911	H Vardon	A Massy	St George's	303
	won play-off at 35th hole			
1912	E Ray	H Vardon	Muirfield	295
1913	J H Taylor	E Ray	Hoylake	304
1914	H Vardon	J H Taylor	Prestwick	306
1915-19	No championship			
1920	G Duncan	A Herd	Deal	303
1921	J Hutchison	R H Wethered	St Andrews	296
	won 36-hole play-off 150 to 159			
1922	W Hagen	G Duncan, J Barnes	St George's	300
1923	A G Havers	W Hagen	Troon	295
1924	W Hagen	E R Whitcombe	Hoylake	301
1925	J Barnes	E Ray, A Compston	Prestwick	300
1926	R T Jones Jr	A Watrous	Lytham	291
1927	R T Jones Jr	A Boomer, F Robson	St Andrews	285
1928	W Hagen	G Sarazen	St George's	292
1929	W Hagen	J Farrell	Muirfield	292
1930	R T Jones Jr	Macdonald Smith	Hoylake	291
		L Diegel		
1931	T Armour	J Jurado	Carnoustie	296
1932	G Sarazen	Macdonald Smith	Prince's	283
1933	D Shute	C Wood	St Andrews	292
	won 36-hole play-off 149 to 154			
1934	T H Cotton	S F Brews	St George's	283
1935	A Perry	A H Padgham	Muirfield	283
1936	A H Padgham	J Adams	Hoylake	287
1937	T H Cotton	R A Whitcombe	Carnoustie	290
1938	R A Whitcombe	J Adams	St George's	285
1939	R Burton	J Bulla	St Andrews	290
1940-45	No championship			
1946	S Snead	A D Locke, J Bulla	St Andrews	290
1947	F Daly	R W Horne,	Hoylake	293
		F R Stranahan		
1948	T H Cotton	F Daly	Muirfield	284
1949	A D Locke	H Bradshaw	St George's	283
	won 36-hole play-off 136 to 147			
1950	A D Locke	R de Vicenzo	Troon	279
1951	M Faulkner	A Cerda	Portrush	285
1952	A D Locke	P W Thomson	Lytham	287
1953	B Hogan	F R Stranahan, A Cerda,	Carnoustie	282
		P W Thomson, DJ Rees		
1954	P W Thomson	A D Locke, S Scott,	Birkdale	283
		D J Rees		
1955	P W Thomson	J Fallon	St Andrews	281
1956	P W Thomson	F van Donck	Hoylake	286
1957	A D Locke	P W Thomson	St Andrews	279
1958	P W Thomson	D C Thomas	Lytham	278
	won 36-hole play-off 139 to 143			
1959	G Player	F van Donck,	Muirfield	284
		F Bullock		
1960	K D G Nagle	A Palmer	St Andrews	278
1961	A Palmer	D J Rees	Birkdale	284
1962	A Palmer	K D G Nagle	Troon	276
1963	R J Charles	P Rodgers	Lytham	277
	won 36-hole play-off 140 to 148			
1964	A Lema	J Nicklaus	St Andrews	279
1965	P W Thomson	B Huggett,	Birkdale	285
		C O'Connor		
1966	J Nicklaus	D C Thomas, D Sanders	Muirfield	282
1967	R de Vicenzo	J Nicklaus	Hoylake	278
1968	G Player	J Nicklaus,	Carnoustie	289
		R J Charles		

Year	Winner	Runner-up	Venue	Score
1969	A Jacklin	R J Charles	Lytham	280
1970	J Nicklaus	D Sanders	St Andrews	283
	won 18-hole play-off 72 to 73			
1971	L Trevino	Liang Huan Lu	Birkdale	278
1972	L Trevino	J Nicklaus	Muirfield	278
1973	T Weiskopf	N C Coles, J Miller	Troon	276
1974	G Player	P Oosterhuis	Lytham	282
1975	T Watson	J Newton	Carnoustie	279
	won 18-hole play-off 71 to 72			
1976	J Miller	J Nicklaus,	Birkdale	279
		S Ballesteros		
1977	T Watson	J Nicklaus	Turnberry	268
1978	J Nicklaus	S Owen, R Floyd,	St Andrews	281
		B Crenshaw, T Kite		
1979	S Ballesteros	B Crenshaw,	Lytham	283
		J Nicklaus		
1980	T Watson	L Trevino	Muirfield	271
1981	W Rogers	B Langer	St George's	276
1982	T Watson	P Oosterhuis,	Troon	284
		N Price		
1983	T Watson	H Irwin, A Bean	Birkdale	275
1984	S Ballesteros	B Langer, T Watson	St Andrews	276
1985	S Lyle	P Stewart	St George's	282
1986	G Norman	G J Brand	Turnberry	280
1987	N Faldo	R Davis, P Azinger	Muirfield	279
1988	S Ballesteros	N Price	Lytham	273
1989	M Calcavecchia	G Norman, W Grady	Troon	275
	won play-off over four holes			
1990	N Faldo	M McNulty,	St Andrews	270
		P Stewart		
1991	I Baker-Finch	M Harwood	Birkdale	272
1992	N Faldo	J Cook	Muirfield	272
1993	G Norman	N Faldo	St George's	267
1994	N Price	J Parnevik	Turnberry	268
1995	J Daly	C Rocca	St Andrews	272
	won play-off over four holes			
1996	T Lehman	M McCumber	Lytham	271
		E Els		
1997	J Leonard	D Clarke,	Troon	272
		J Parnevik		
1998	M O'Meara	B Watts	Birkdale	280
	won play-off over four holes			
1999	P Lawrie	J Van der Velde,	Carnoustie	290
		J Leonard		
	won play-off over four holes			
2000	T Woods	E Els, T Bjorn	St Andrews	269
2001	D Duval	N Fasth	Lytham	274
2002	E Els	T Levet, S Appleby,	Muirfield	278
		S Elkington		
	won play-off: E Els and T Levet even after four extra holes:			
	S Appleby (+1) and S Elkington (+2) eliminated;			
	Els wins at first sudden-death hole			
2003	B Curtis	T Bjorn, V Singh	St George's	283
2004	T Hamilton	E Els	Troon	274
	won play-off over four holes			
2005	T Woods	C Montgomerie	St Andrews	274
2006	T Woods	C DiMarco	Hoylake	270
2007	P Harrington	S Garcia	Carnoustie	277
	won play-off over four holes			
2008	P Harrington	I Poulter	Birkdale	283
2009	S Cink	T Watson	Turnberry	278
	won play-off over four holes			

Bobby Jones won back-to-back British Open titles in 1926 and 1927. He won again at Hoylake in 1930 on his way to a never-to-be-repeated grand slam – the British Open and Amateur championships as well as the US Open and Amateur championships.

Morris, runner-up in this first event, and his son, also called Tom, whose brilliant scoring in 1870 was not bettered until 1904.

After Old Tom won for the fourth time, Young Tom achieved a hat-trick of Opens, and so took the Belt outright before going on to win for the fourth time in succession, a record still, and becoming the first holder of the present trophy, a silver claret jug, in 1871.

Sport knows no more poignant story than the death of Young Tom in 1875, heartbroken after the death of his wife in childbirth while he and his father were playing Willie and Mungo Park in a challenge match at North Berwick across the Firth of Forth. Old Tom's assessment of his son's golf skills was that he could never

cope with young Tom, though he could with Robertson, which rather demolishes the legend of Robertson's invincibility.

Old Tom lived until 1908. "A legend in his own lifetime" could truly be said of Old Tom, for many years greenkeeper of the Old Course. He played in every Open until 1896, a year that linked two golfing eras ... the year of Harry Vardon's first victory.

Before the golfing giant of America was fully awake, three British champions (16 Opens between them) ruled the roost in the years before the First World War. Harry Vardon edged in 1914 to his record sixth Open, upstaging J H Taylor and James Braid (five each). Of the moderns, only Tom Watson has come closest to emulating Vardon.

Two names are inseparable from an account of the resurgence of the championship over the last 35 years: Keith MacKenzie, who officiated as Royal and Ancient Club secretary for the last time in 1983 before Michael Bonallack took over, and Arnold Palmer. The strength of US golf since the First World War has meant that when a representative entry has failed for whatever reason to cross the Atlantic, the British Open's significance has been much diminished.

The persistence of the Great Depression, fewer events on the PGA tour, and less prize money, meant that few Americans could afford to participate after the early 1930s, as evidence, the string of British winners following the almost-

unbroken run of American champions from 1921. In 1937, however, when the US Ryder Cup team was in Britain, Henry Cotton proved his world class.

Sam Snead, who won the first championship after the 1940-45 hiatus, found that the prize money (about $600) did not cover his expenses. The fact that he at first mistook the stark topography of St Andrews, the scene of his only major Open success on either side of the Atlantic, for an abandoned golf course may have put him in the right frame of mind to overcome any nerves.

South Africa and Australia provided the stars of the 1950s, in Bobby Locke and Peter Thomson respectively.

TREVINO v. JACKLIN, 1972 British Open

Lee Trevino's reputation as a joker and a miracle worker, especially in the pitching, chipping and putting departments, was well established when he arrived at Muirfield in 1972 for the Open. Yet only five years before he had drawn his first significant cheque, £6,000 for fifth place behind Jack Nicklaus in the US Open at Baltusrol.

Not only had he never won so much money, he had never seen so much, said Supermex: but then he had as many one-liners as any stand-up comedian about his family's poverty back in Dallas.

So Trevino knew "poor" and, after four years in the Marines, he also knew "tough". But, since 1967, he had been getting to know "rich", with two Open victories in America and one in Britain, by a whisker at Birkdale from the Taiwanese Mr Lu, and by two from the 1969 champion, Tony Jacklin.

The favourite at Muirfield was none of these, but the recent winner of both the Masters and the US Open, Jack Nicklaus. Like Arnold Palmer 12 years before, Nicklaus was burning to land the treble Ben Hogan had, uniquely, achieved in 1953. Besides, he knew how to win at Muirfield, having done so both as an amateur and in the 1966 Open, which he dominated with the length and accuracy of his iron play.

This deserted him on the first day, and the shape of things to come was heralded at the end of round two, when Trevino and Jacklin led, a stroke clear of Nicklaus, Johnny Miller, Peter Townsend and Peter Tupling.

Trevino's third round was slow to catch fire, but patience paid off with a quartet of birdies from the 14th to 17th. He holed lengthy putts for the first two. The third, at the short 16th, was a platinum-plated fluke. He thinned his shot from a greenside trap, and his ball was scooting speedily for no one knows where until it struck the flagstick, and vanished into the hole as quick as a wink.

His 66 gave him a one-stroke lead going into the final round over Jacklin, whose 67 had been distinguished by sterling play from tee to green. When Jacklin and Trevino set out last together on the final day, Nicklaus, struggling six strokes behind the leader, gambled with his driver and was out in 32, briefly disturbing the private duel the final pair were fighting out behind him, but faltering with a bogey at the 16th and with his failure to birdie the long 17th.

The Trevino-Jacklin plot did not so much thicken as curdle at the 17th, where a long, well-placed drive must be followed by a second shot of pin-point accuracy between the sandhills guarding the green. Jacklin was 20 yards short in two. Trevino wandered untidily from side to side, and the closest he could get with his fourth shot was on a bank of fluffy rough behind the pin. Jacklin chipped on, not very expertly.

Trevino's chip ran smartly into the hole. He compared it afterwards with the last straw that broke the camel's back ... and so it seemed as Jacklin three-putted. Another bogey on the last compounded British gloom, and gave Trevino his second British Open by a stroke from Nicklaus, who, like Arnold Palmer in 1960, missed his treble by a stroke, and with exactly the same total, 279.

Jacklin was third, a shattering descent after the security of 99 per cent of his play. "They" said of Jacklin's reverse, just as they had of Palmer's defeat at Olympic by Billy Casper, that he was never the same again.

The bottom line in Trevino's victory was the bottom line - 278 for four circuits of Muirfield, held by many to be a classic without peer. His total was a record, four shots fewer than Nicklaus had taken in 1966. No wonder Trevino reckoned Muirfield in particular, and Scottish links in general, his preferred golf terrain.

1972 British Open at Muirfield, Scotland

Pos.	Name	Score				
1	Lee Trevino	71	70	66	71	278
2	Jack Nicklaus	70	72	71	66	279
3	Tony Jacklin	69	72	67	72	280

The exception to this southern hemisphere to-ing and fro-ing provided one of the Open's defining moments: a player of legendary skill focusing his powers on a difficult course, and getting the better of it a little more each day.

This was Ben Hogan's one attempt on the Open. Not a man given to adulterating golf with sentiment, he had won the 1953 Masters and the US Open, and no one had ever won these two and the British Open in one season. The thought must also have occurred, as it did in times past to Walter Hagen and Bobby Jones, that he must prove his standing in the game's history by winning in Britain.

He could hardly have chosen a more difficult challenge. His preparations for Carnoustie were thorough; he spent a fortnight sizing up this longest of Open courses. His attitude may have been character-istically taciturn, but he was more forthcoming with the Press than his laconic legend suggested. His four rounds demonstrated that he could harness the accuracy of his striking to any course: his mastery of long, low shots controlled with a touch of fade was ideal for Carnoustie.

He scored 73, 71, 70, 68, and won by four shots. The only other notable American in the field, Lloyd Mangrum, was 19 behind Hogan. Mangrum was used to trailing the new Open champion by this time. He had been third to Hogan in the Masters - but eight strokes in arrears; and third in the US Open - nine behind. He cannot have enjoyed Carnoustie much, joking that the undulating fairways had made him feel seasick.

Hogan promised to come back to defend his title, but he never did. It would have been difficult to top his performance in any case: it was his last major success, and a date clash with the US PGA Championship meant he was ruled out of that. The clash demonstrates that the four modern majors were not yet seen as the four premier events in world golf. When Gary Player took his first major at Muirfield in 1959, the American challenge was non-existent.

The following year Arnold Palmer, who like Hogan in 1953 had already won the Masters and US Open, came, saw, but did not conquer, finishing second to Kel Nagle in the Centenary Open. Instead, he captivated the British public, and won the next Open at Birkdale, where his 73 in the worst of a gale in the second round fitted his publicity: heroic. He won again at Troon the next year, establishing a record aggregate of 276 and winning by six strokes.

The trickle of US participation did not immediately become a flood, but by the mid-1960s Palmer's initiative, followed by that of Jack Nicklaus, a winner at Muirfield in 1966, had ensured that the winner of the Open was again unarguably at the very top of his profession.

Thus the victory of Tony Jacklin in 1969 at Lytham by two shots

Just as Arnold Palmer had done before him, three-time British Open champion, Jack Nicklaus, helped make the tournament the truly representative championship that it has become today.

from Bob Charles, the first and only left-hander to win, in 1963, raised the British game as nothing else could. Jacklin's win had foreign players like Nicklaus, Orville Moody, Thomson, Nagle, Gay Brewer, Bert Yancey, Gary Player, Billy Casper, Ray Floyd and Lee Trevino all labouring in the Briton's wake.

His final drive to the tough-to-locate 18th fairway ("a corker", said Henry Longhurst, a favourite commentator in the United States just as in Britain) summed up the confidence and precision of his game as his greatest opportunity beckoned. He put his second shot just inside that of playing partner Charles as if to rubber-stamp his win.

Next year came the bitter disappointment of a thunder-and-lightning-interrupted first round at St Andrews, where Jacklin quickly holed three birdies plus an eagle two at the ninth. Starting home with another birdie, his luck ran out when a shout of "Fore" put him off his stroke, and he fired his ball into a gorse bush. Play was suspended, and next day

the magic had gone, Jacklin finishing in "no better" than 67.

His anguish was minor compared to that suffered at the climax of this championship by Doug Sanders, whose restricted swing still sent the ball a fair distance. On the 72nd hole came the moment every golfer both longs for and dreads: a down-hill four-footer for the Open. Disappointingly, he interrupted his routine to pick up some minute object. Instead of starting again, he putted, and the ball, as so often on the green named after Old Tom Morris, drifted marginally right.

More eyebrow-raising stuff came the next day in a play-off with Nicklaus, who drove through the 385-yard 18th, but still managed to chip back and hole his birdie putt to gain a second Open by a stroke from oh-so-nearly man Sanders.

Jacklin was in the same doleful situation in 1972, Lee Trevino's luck being thoroughly in at Muirfield when a series of iffy shots turned up trumps, notably his chip in for his par at the 71st hole after missing

the green with his fourth shot.

Turnberry 1977 is a popular choice as the most thrilling Open of all, as Tom Watson and Nicklaus both broke the aggregate record, and Watson took the title by a stroke. Spain's Severiano Ballesteros (even if his routes to Lytham's greens in 1979 tended to be circuitous) and Gary Player were the only players to break the American run of success that followed Jacklin's Open win and the trend persisted until a great sea change took place at the Open in the mid-1980s.

Willie Auchterlonie (1893) was the last home-based Scot to win the Open, but Sandy Lyle, a Scottish international, although living south of the border, redressed the balance a little in favour of the land that gave golf to the world by winning at Royal St George's in 1985.

Turnberry in 1986 was not about to provide the low-scoring conditions that the Watson-Nicklaus show had featured in 1977. The weather was brutal, the rough seemingly bottomless, and Greg

Norman needed every ounce of his strength and determination to keep afloat as his tee-off times condemned him to endure the worst of the weather on day three. A 69 as Turnberry relented on the last day gave him a five-shot margin.

More severe weather at Muirfield the following year brought the long-awaited Nick Faldo victory that seemed sure to follow his brilliant amateur career. Faldo was single-minded and brave enough to spend years remodelling his swing, and the fruits of this intense effort were a secure method that enabled him to par every hole of his fourth round and hold off Paul Azinger, who faltered at the last.

Faldo dominated the Open at St Andrews in 1990 with a record aggregate 270 and a five-shot win over Zimbabwe's Mark McNulty and the persistent Payne Stewart. Faldo's third Open, at Muirfield two years later, was a nerve-shredding affair after he started 64 ("best round of my life," said Faldo), 66 for a 36-hole total of 130 that equalled the record.

Yet he seemed to have thrown the title away as he started for home on the final day, and was overtaken by American John Cook, who, fatally, returned the compliment by missing a tiny birdie putt on the 17th, and dropping a shot at the 18th. Faldo, behind him, was carrying out his last-ditch task of "playing the best four holes of my life". In this critical situation, two birdies and two pars was a winning effort.

Scoring reached a new low - 267, 13-under par - at St George's in 1993 as Faldo chased Norman home, Stewart finished with a fruitless 63, and the Australian's final round of 64, a prodigy of accurate driving, earned a two-shot win from the Englishman.

A monstrous eagle putt on the 71st at Turnberry helped Nick Price edge out Jesper Parnevik for the 1994 title, and ease the pain of two earlier near-misses. Conversely, Costantino Rocca's 60-foot birdie putt,

WATSON v. NICKLAUS, 1977 BRITISH OPEN

The Royal and Ancient took a long time to move the British Open to the Ailsa course at Turnberry, and when at last they did, in 1977, this most scenic of courses on the west coast of Scotland rewarded them with a duel between the two leading players of the day, Jack Nicklaus and Tom Watson, that for persistent quality and tension is unlikely ever to be surpassed.

Over the last two rounds, the pair were playing partners, moving further and further away from any challengers. Hubert Green robbed Lee Trevino of third place with 279 - but Green was 12 shots short of victory. For the 1977 British Open produced the purest head-to-head that can be imagined in a strokeplay competition, the winner breaking the 72-hole record total by seven.

For the first three days the championship was played in hot, humid conditions, which followed more than a month of dry weather, so the rough was not up to usual Scottish standards. The wind died away at lunchtime on the first day, so scores were low, though not until well into the gloaming did the leader come in, with 66 ... John Schroeder, son of lawn tennis champion Ted. Much earlier, Nicklaus, Watson and Trevino had all gone round in 68 to share second place.

Mark Hayes, from Oklahoma, broke the British Open 18-hole record next day. His 63, 13 better than his first round, included a bogey at the 18th. But Roger Maltbie's 66 for a total of 139 gave him the lead, one ahead of Green, Trevino, Nicklaus and Watson.

This latter pair, aged 37 and 27 respectively, set off on their third rounds on what might be called Furious Friday, for they both gave the course, 6,875 yards, par 70 (35=35), a severe pounding. By the tenth, Nicklaus was two ahead with 31 strokes to 33 by Watson, who was level again by the long, but eminently reachable, 17th, where a birdie each was disappointing for Nicklaus. He had hit his second to 3ft. Six birdies and one bogey apiece left the duo level on 203 and all their rivals gasping. The Nicklaus-Watson scores were identical: 68, 70, 65.

The fourth round began with more assaults on par, Nicklaus finishing off, with a birdie from 10ft, a marvellous recovery from an awkward lie with the ball above his feet in the rough at the second.

Watson dropped a shot, and fell three behind when Nicklaus reduced the well-named Woe be Tide short hole to a two from ten yards. Watson came back at him, saving a shot at the fifth, another at the long seventh, with two drivers and two putts, and yet another at the eighth, only to reach the turn one behind when he could not get his par at Bruce's Castle, Turnberry's Lighthouse hole. Nicklaus out in 33, Watson 34.

Nicklaus stole two shots ahead on the 12th, with a sizeable putt. Watson pulled one back on the 13th, and the other with a two on the 15th from 20 yards: level again, and the form of both men holding up miraculously ... until Nicklaus hit his four-iron approach to the 17th (500 yards) fat. He pitched up to little over a yard, but missed the putt, a tiny nod expressing his frustration. Watson's birdie put him one up.

Still the Turnberry tale had a twist: Watson's drive at the last was a cautious, straight, one-iron. Nicklaus gambled, but his driver left him in gorse. Watson, playing first, pitched almost to gimme distance. Nicklaus ripped through the gorse and left himself, improbably, a birdie putt of about 12 yards. Even more improbably, he holed it.

Watson, brisk as ever in his tempo at this searching moment, tapped his ball underground for his second British Open triumph.

1977 British Open at Turnberry, Scotland

Pos	Name	Score				
1	Tom Watson	68	70	65	65	268
2	Jack Nicklaus	68	70	65	66	269
3	Hubert Green	72	66	74	67	279

improbably holed from the Valley of Sin on the 72nd at St Andrews in 1995, led only to a play-off defeat by John Daly. Tom Lehman's victory in 1996, founded on a 64 in the third round, continued American dominance, which continued at Troon in 1997 as Justin Leonard confirmed his great potential, running out the winner by three strokes from Darren Clarke and the hapless Jesper Parnevik.

A return to Royal Birkdale in 1998 saw part two of Mark O'Meara's annus mirabilis, as he fought off Brain Watts in a four-hole play-off. The story of the tournament, however, was the performance of the 17-year-old British amateur, Justin Rose, who finished in fourth place.

The biggest dramas of recent times were reserved for Carnoustie in 1999, and Jean Van de Velde in particular. Having played brilliantly through 71 holes, the Frenchman stood on the final tee with a three-shot advantage – and fell apart. A drive way right, a shot that rebounded off the stand, a shoes-and-socks-off visit to the burn and a long putt later, he was in a play-off ... which he lost. The beneficiary of Van de Velde's self-destruction was Paul Lawrie.

The greatest British Open clash of modern times saw Tom Watson get the better of Jack Nicklaus by one shot at Turnberry in 1977.

THE BRITISH OPEN: 2000

Continuing where he had left off at the US Open a month earlier, Tiger Woods brushed aside his competitors and continued his march towards golfing history.

The debate following Tiger Woods's 15-stroke rout in the US Open at Pebble Beach the previous month was whether the defences at the Old Course would be able to hold up to his game.

It was Ernie Els and not the American, however, who stole the headlines after the first day: the South African out-punched Woods by shooting a six-under 66 to the American's 67 on a course that was conducive to low scoring. Els stood on his own at the top of the leaderboard: joining Woods on 67 was Steve Flesch, with Tom Lehman and Dennis Paulson a further stroke behind.

If Tiger had managed to keep the assembled scribes quiet on the first day, then they were clamouring on the second. On a sun-baked Friday, Tiger made every shot on the Old Course look easy: he shot a six-under 66 to take the halfway lead.

It was an exceptional performance from Woods and he extended his major championship streak of holes without a bogey to 62 – the last had come on the tenth hole at Pebble Beach in the third round. He continued the streak here by avoiding every one of the Old Course's 112 bunkers.

There was one moment when he nearly wobbled, however. His approach shot to the 17th went through the green and came to rest on the grass by the side of the road. He chipped past the hole, using the bank of the Road Hole bunker as a backboard: the ball rolled back to within 8ft of the cup – it was still a tricky, two-break putt. He holed it and in a show of rare emotion punched the air. Tiger was on a roll

and he didn't want anything to break that momentum.

David Toms shot a 67 to lie three strokes behind Tiger. Behind him, a stroke further back, were Loren Roberts, Steve Flesch and Sergio Garcia – the last man to have challenged Woods in a major. First-round leader Els fell away with a level-par 72 to leave him five shots adrift.

Among the players who missed the cut were defending champion Paul Lawrie and John Daly, the last man to win the Open when it was staged at St Andrews. Another player not to make it into the weekend was Jack Nicklaus, who was playing in his last British Open.

The Golden Bear gave his adoring gallery one last thrill when he drilled his approach on the 18th to within yards of the flag: he missed the putt – and the cut for the first time in his seven British Open appearances at St Andrews.

But back to Woods: his 36-hole lead may not have been as large as at Pebble Beach (he led by six strokes at the halfway stage of the US Open), but the way he was playing you wouldn't have bet against him from running away with the tournament and taking another swipe at the record books.

And if that's the way you were thinking you would have been right to do so: Woods carried on where he had left off in the third round and fired a 67. The only player standing between him and the career grand slam – although at six strokes back he was perhaps only casting the slightest of shadows – was David Duval, the world number two. It did not promise to be the greatest of final-round shoot-outs, but if anyone

had the game to cast any doubts in Woods' mind it was Duval: and that was confirmed by his six-under third-round 66.

And Duval did his level best. Playing exhilarating golf through the front nine, he managed to add some drama to a British Open that was fast becoming the Tiger Woods Show. He made four birdies on the opening nine holes of the Old Course to pull within three.

But the wheels fell off at the par-four 12th. Woods had extended his lead to four by the time the pair arrived on the 12th tee: he drove at the green and found it. Duval followed suit and missed: a poor chip and a three putt later he had carded a double-bogey. Woods two putted for a birdie and a two-shot swing. Duval was back where he had started. He never recovered: he shot 43 on the back nine and finished with a 75.

But this Open was all about Tiger Woods. It was a coronation rather than a competition and confirmed not only his dominance over his fellow professionals, but also his status as one of the greatest players ever to have played the game. His eight-stroke victory saw him become the latest, and youngest, member of a quintet of players to have won the career grand slam. His 19-under par total was the second lowest score in relation to par and the lowest 72-hole total ever recorded in a major tournament.

THE 2000 BRITISH OPEN – The Top 5
1 Tiger Woods 67 66 67 69 269 -19
2 Thomas Bjørn 69 69 68 71 277 -11
= Ernie Els 66 72 70 69 277 -11
4 Tom Lehman 68 70 70 70 278 -10
= David Toms 69 67 71 71 278 -10

In victory, Woods became the latest, and youngest, member of players to have won all four of the major tournaments.

THE BRITISH OPEN: 2001

David Duval, the nearly man of recent years, emerged from both a congested final-round leaderboard and the shadow of Tiger Woods to win his first major.

The 130th British Open returned to Royal Lytham and St Anne's, the scene of Bobby Jones's triumph in 1926, of Seve Ballesteros out-duelling Nick Price in 1988 and where Tom Lehman came out on top in 1996 – the last time that the event had been played at the venue.

The talk of the previous Open had been of the manner in which Tiger Woods had negotiated 72 holes of the Old Course without finding a bunker. St Andrews had 112 of them; Lytham had a remarkable 197. And everyone suspected that Woods might not be able to repeat his 2000 romp to victory when he found the sand five times during his opening round of 73.

Instead, Colin Montgomerie gave the fans something to cheer about. The Scot headed the field after the first round having posted a six-under 65, including six birdies and an eagle. It was the first time that Monty had started with a round in the 60s in his 12 Open Championships and he clearly enjoyed the feeling, mouthing "thank you" to the fans who roared his every holed putt. The Scot was intent on keeping his feet on the ground, though. "I have set off well a couple of times and haven't held on to it."

He did his level, best with a second-round 70. It may not have been as impressive as his first-day efforts, but it was enough to see the seven-time winner of the European Order of Merit on top of the leaderboard at the halfway stage.

It was a great day for the European Tour, as seven of its players occupied the first eight places. Among them were Swede's Pierre Fulke, who shot a best-of-the-day 67, and

Jesper Parnevik – runner-up in the tournament in both 1994 and 1997). Tiger Woods lay four strokes behind the leader at the halfway stage after recording a battling 68.

Montgomerie failed to hold on to his lead after a third-round two-over 73, but he was still in contention to win his first major championship. As were a host of other players. In fact, rarely can any major championship have had so many players still in contention going into the final round: there were four players tied for the lead, with nine others just one stroke behind.

Of the 54-hole leaders, the man who stood out was David Duval. The American had started the third day in joint 36th, but he tore his way around the course with a scintillating 65 to take him to the top of the leaderboard. He was joined by two former Masters champions: Ian Woosnam and two-time champion Bernhard Langer. Also there was Alex Cejka, seemingly continuing his love affair with the Lytham course – he had finished in a tie for 11th when the Open last visited the course.

Among the players still in with a chance was defending champion Tiger Woods, who lay five strokes behind the leaders. That was as close as he got: he started the final round with a bogey and finished with an even-par 71 and a total of 283. It would leave him in a tie for 25th place: his lowest position in a major since the 1998 US PGA Championship. To cap a miserable week for the world number one, his 72-hole total was two strokes worse than when he had played Royal Lytham as an amateur in 1996.

The final day was all about David

Duval: although he shared some of the headlines with Ian Woosnam after disaster had struck the Welshman on the second hole. The American emerged from the congested leaderboard to fire a four-under 67 and take the championship by four strokes.

No one got close. His challengers fell out of contention one by one. The only threat came from Niclas Fasth, playing in his first major championship – he had previously failed to qualify for the British Open five times. The Swede matched Duval's final-round score of 67 and sat in the clubhouse with a total of seven-under 277. One sensed that it wasn't going to be enough. It wasn't.

Duval played with the poise and style that had graced his game when he emerged onto the world scene in 1997. Holding a three-stroke lead going into the 18th hole, he played it in championship style, splitting the fairway with his drive, pitching to within 10ft and then two-putting with ease. In a rare display of emotion, he took off his cap, removed the wraparound glasses that had been shielding his face for the whole week and acknowledged the applause of the crowd.

THE 2001 BRITISH OPEN - The Top 5
1 David Duval 69 73 65 67 274 -10
2 Niclas Fasth 69 69 72 67 277 -7
3 Darren Clarke 70 69 69 70 278 -6
= Ernie Els 71 71 67 69 278 -6
= M A Jiménez 69 72 67 70 278 -6
= Bernhard Langer 71 69 67 71 278 -6
= Billy Mayfair 69 72 67 70 278 -6
= Ian Woosnam 72 68 67 71 278 -6

In the final round, David Duval displayed the qualities that had taken him to the very top of the world game. His 67 was enough to hand him his first major victory.

THE BRITISH OPEN: 2002

Ernie Els survived the carnage of a stormy third round and emerged to win his third major title and joined an illustrious list of British Open winners at Muirfield.

It was a benign Muirfield that greeted the players on the first day, but slow greens saw few players able to take advantage of the benevolent conditions. Among those disappointed with their first-round display was Tiger Woods, seeking the third leg of a grand slam after having won the first two majors of the year.

Woods had to settle for a one-under 70, although he might have rued the fact that he missed six of the seven birdie chances to have come his way; particularly as the forecast for the weekend was less than encouraging.

Come the end of the second day, Ernie Els was one of five players at the top of the leaderboard at six-under. The biggest move of the day, though, came from Colin Montgomerie. After shooting a first-round 74 – after which he refused to talk to reporters – he cut a very different figure on day two as he carded a seven-under 64: it was the Scot's best-ever round at the British Open and moved him to within two of the lead.

On the third day the wind raged. As gales whipped off the Firth of Forth, the real 2002 British Open finally got under way. Coupled with cold, stinging rain, the course bit back – and there were plenty of casualties along the way. Among them was Tiger Woods: one of ten players who failed to break 80 during the course of the day. Woods shot an 81, his worst ever round as a professional, and any hopes that he might have had of completing the third leg of the grand slam were blown away on the Scottish breeze.

The previous day's hero, Colin Montgomerie came out of the third-round maelstrom in even worse shape. The Scot misfired an 84 – 20 shots worse than his effort on the previous day.

At the end of the gale-induced shake-up, Ernie Els still remained at the top of the leaderboard: he had succeeded where others had notably failed, surviving the horrendous conditions faced by those who played in the afternoon to shoot a one-over 72 and to hold a two-shot lead over Denmark's Soren Hansen going into the final round.

Sunday was one of the most intriguing days in recent major championship history. At the end of the regulation 72 holes, four men stood on top of the leaderboard with a six-under par total of 278. They had all embarked on an interesting journey to get there.

First there was Ernie Els, who squandered the three-stroke lead that he had built up by the ninth hole. The South African's rollercoaster ride began on the 13th, when he found the deepest of pot bunkers: he blasted out to 2ft and salvaged par on this occasion, but worse was to follow. On the next hole, as it happens, when he found another bunker from the tee and ended up with a bogey. Even worse was to follow: he missed the green on the par-three 16th and wound up with a double-bogey. He now needed a birdie-par finish to tie the leading clubhouse score: and did so.

Then there was Thomas Levet, whose final-round 67 included a dramatic eagle on the 17th. Stuart Appleby made six birdies in the last ten holes to record a joint-best-of-the-day 65. Then there was Steve Elkington who, compared to the others, shot a routine 66.

And so began the play-off.

After four holes they were down to two: Elkington bogeyed the first and the last of the play-off holes and Appleby bogeyed the last to leave Els and Levet to scrap it out for the Claret Jug. The trophy should already have been in the Frenchman's pocket. He birdied the second of the first four play-off holes and came down the 18th needing, essentially, a par for the tournament: the nerves got to him – he hit a poor drive and finished with a bogey. He hit another poor drive second time around and finished with another bogey. Els, meanwhile, found the greenside bunker with his approach shot, blasted the ball out to 5ft and holed the putt.

THE 2002 BRITISH OPEN - The Top 5
1 Ernie Els* 70 66 72 70 278 -6
2 Thomas Levet 72 66 74 66 278 -6
= Stuart Appleby 73 70 70 65 278 -6
= Steve Elkington 71 73 68 66 278 -6
5 Gary Evans 72 68 74 65 279 -5
= Pádraig Harrington 69 67 76 67 279 -5
= Shigeki Maruyama 68 68 75 68 279 -5
* Won play-off

Ernie Els capped an up-and-down final day to collect his third major championship win.

THE BRITISH OPEN: 2003

Little-known American Ben Curtis shocked the golfing world by claiming his first major trophy as Thomas Bjorn slipped up in dramatic style over the final holes.

You just knew that it was going to be one of the stranger British Open tournaments played in recent years from the moment that Tiger Woods had played his first tee shot. Despite the fact that there were 12 marshals hovering on the fairway and over 2,000 fans cheering on the world number one, nobody managed to find his ball after it had settled in the rough: Woods carded a triple-bogey on the first hole and ended up with a two-over 73.

And other big names seemed to take their cue from Woods. Defending champion Ernie Els carded a 78 – his worst ever score at the British Open – and Phil Mickelson scrambled his way round the course for a three-over 74. It was a day to forget for Denmark's Thomas Bjorn as well. After failing to get out of a bunker on the 17th, the Dane slammed his wedge into the sand in frustration – and picked up a two-shot penalty for his efforts for grounding his club.

Instead, it was left to a former Masters champion to hold the lead after the first round – although this one was won in Nashua, South Africa and not at the Augusta National. Hennie Otto, a little-known South African who had come through the qualifying tournament the previous week, headed the field after shooting a three-under 68.

The second day was all about Love – of the Davis III variety. The American was the only player to remain under par at the halfway stage of the tournament, although he had his luck on the way. His tee shot on the par-five 14th was heading for out-of-bounds territory before ricocheting off a boundary marker – which was all of three inches thick

– and bouncing back into play. A strange tournament, indeed.

When Henry Cotton had won the British Open on this course in 1934 using wooden-shafted equipment, he did so with a winning score of 283. As the players finished their third rounds, it seemed highly likely that anyone able to produce a similar score to Cotton's would almost certainly be holding aloft the Claret Jug at the end of proceedings. Given the advances in technology during the 69 years that had elapsed since Cotton's triumph, how could that be?

One man with an answer was Nick Faldo, who shot a best-of-the-day 67 in the third round. For him the reason was simple: the weather.

"This is the truest links we've played on for moons," said the three-time winner. "It's rock hard, the wind is blowing and you can see we are just under-prepared for this. You can't even really practise for these conditions – you wouldn't even try."

The conditions had rendered the tournament a trial of patience as much as anything. It was far removed from the target golf played week in week out by most of the European and PGA Tour regulars.

Two players who certainly had their patience tested were Mark Roe and Jesper Parnevik. Both players were disqualified from the tournament after signing for the wrong scores after they had failed to swap cards at the end of the third round. It was particularly galling for Mark Roe, who signed for Parnevik's 81 instead of his joint best-of-the-week 67: he was tied in third place at one-over par when news of his disqualification arrived.

The events of the final round

He may not have started the tournament as a household name, but come the end of it, everyone knew who Ben Curtis was.

will go down in golfing folklore: unfortunately for Thomas Bjorn he will appear towards the bottom end of the list of achievements alongside Jean Van de Velde, Doug Sanders and Scott Hoch – he will be remembered as one of the men who threw away his chance to win a major tournament.

Holding a two-stroke lead as he stood on the tee at the par-three 16th, the Dane watched as his tee shot faded into a bunker. He got the ball out of the hazard first time round and it pitched short of the flag: too short as it turned out – the ball rolled back agonizingly and ended up back at his feet. Take two: with identical results. Take three: the ball clung to the edge of the green. As Bjorn walked to the 17th tee he had carded a double-bogey and was level with Ben Curtis, who sat in the clubhouse on one-under par.

Bjorn bogeyed the 17th as well and his chances of winning the tournament had disappeared – no one had made a bogey on the 18th all day. The Dane made a par.

And so it fell to Ben Curtis, the world's 396th ranked player, competing in his first major tournament to hold aloft the oldest trophy in the sport. The American earned his place in golf's rich history by being the only player to break par. In winning, he became the first player to win a major tournament at his first attempt since Francis Ouimet had shaken golf's foundations to its very roots by beating the best names of the day and taking the 1913 US Open.

THE 2003 BRITISH OPEN - The Top 5
1 Ben Curtis 72 72 70 69 283 -1
2 Thomas Bjørn 73 70 69 72 284 E
= Vijay Singh 75 70 69 70 284 E
4 Davis Love III 69 72 72 72 285 +1
= Tiger Woods 73 72 69 71 285 +1

THE BRITISH OPEN: 2004

Todd Hamilton became the tenth different player to win the last ten major tournaments, outlasting South Africa's Ernie Els to lift the Claret Jug.

For the first time in 59 years, not one American featured on the leaderboard after a calm first day at Troon. It was a strange fact, considering that seven of the last nine winners of the tournament had hailed from the United States.

Heading the leaderboard was France's Thomas Levet and Paul Casey, the Englishman who lived in America and who attended Arizona State University and who had failed to survive the cut on his previous two visits to the championship. They both fired five-under opening rounds of 66. A stroke further behind was New Zealand's Michael Campbell.

Phil Mickelson did his level best to arouse American interest on the second day. The reigning Masters champion stood on the first tee on Friday seven strokes behind the leaders and in serious danger of missing the cut. He was aggressive from that moment onwards and mounted an Arnold Palmer-like charge to produce the best round of the day – a five-under 66 that brought him back to within four strokes of the leaders with two rounds still to play.

But the American was not the leader after 54 holes. Instead it was Todd Hamilton, the ultimate journeyman professional who strolled around a breezy Troon course in 67

Nobody can say that Todd Hamilton did not deserve his victory at the 2004 British Open: he made only two bogeys during the whole week.

shots to take a one-shot lead into the final round. Hamilton had spent 12 years plying his trade on the Japan Tour trying to keep his hopes of playing on the PGA Tour alive before becoming a PGA Tour rookie in 2004 at the age of 38 after securing his card at the eighth attempt. He played his third round with great poise and with the air of a man who had been there before.

Behind him stood Ernie Els, the 2002 champion, who birdied three of the last six holes to find himself in the last round's final pairing for a second successive major. Ten other players stood within five shots of the lead – among them were five former major winners. Another of the players in that group was Colin Montgomerie. The Scot was playing on the course where he grew up and his support had never been louder. He produced the comedy moment of the day on the 15th, when he hit his bunker shot with such force that he tumbled out of the back of the hazard.

As Els stood on the 18th green after completing his 72 holes, he had the look of a man who knew that he had blown his chance – he had just missed a birdie putt that would have brought him his fourth major title and capped one of the greatest back-nine comebacks in history: it would also have brought him his second British Open title in three years.

The South African was seemingly out of the tournament after he had come unstuck on the tenth: he double-bogeyed the hole to fall two strokes behind the leader. He then drilled his drive on the following hole deep into the rough – it seemed as though it was all over. The ball ended up waist high in a gorse bush. He could have taken a drop for an unplayable lie, but he would also have had to take the one-stroke penalty that came with it, a stroke that at this stage of proceedings he could ill afford to throw away. So he took a baseball-style swing at it and moved his ball 20 yards up the fairway: he hit his approach to 20ft and holed his putt to salvage par.

He was still behind by two, but the tide had turned. He matched leader Todd Hamilton with two birdies on the next five holes and then drew to within one shot after holing a birdie putt on the devilishly difficult par-three 17th. Hamilton bogeyed the 18th: Els missed a 12ft birdie attempt for the championship – the pair were in a play-off.

The South African missed his birdie attempt on the first extra hole and a ten-footer for par on the third, the 17th. Hamilton made a par. On the 18th, the American played a miraculous chip-and-run shot from 40ft stone dead. Els had to hole a 15ft putt for birdie to keep the tournament alive: he missed.

And so Hamilton became the second long-shot winner of the British Open in two years. This was no fluke, though: he had played impressive golf and earned the title, and his reward was the most time-honoured trophy in golf.

THE 2004 BRITISH OPEN – The Top 5
1 Todd Hamilton* 71 67 67 69 274 -10
= Ernie Els 69 69 68 68 274 -10
3 Phil Mickelson 73 66 68 68 275 -9
4 Lee Westwood 72 71 68 67 278 -6
5 Thomas Levet 66 70 71 72 279 -5
= Davis Love III 72 69 71 67 279 -5
* Won play-off

THE BRITISH OPEN: 2005

The last time the British Open had been held at St Andrews, Tiger Woods famously romped to an eight-shot victory. 2005 would see another a peerless performance.

The first day's headlines belonged to Woods. His bid to repeat his sand-free experiences of 2000 may have come to an end as early as the seventh hole (where he found a greenside bunker and still made birdie), but his form was unflappable and impressive. Seven birdies in a nine-hole stretch saw him shoot a six-under 66 – one better than his St Andrews start in 2000 and his best start in a major championship since his opening-round 66 at the 2000 US PGA Championship – to grab the lead, one shot ahead of Mark Hensby. A group of ten players sat on four-under par. Woods had sent a clear message to the rest of the field. "It's ominous who's on top of the leaderboard, ominous," opined Colin Montgomerie. "If there's a course built for him, it's this one. He won by eight shots last time here, and who says he won't do the same again."

The second round was about champions past and present. First came Jack Nicklaus. After 164 majors, the 18-time winner was finally calling it a day. Amid great roars, he closed out with a birdie on the 18th for a level-par 72, missed the cut by two and gave the raucous crowds a final farewell. The tears had barely dried before the modern game's torchbearer reached the final hole. Woods, continuing his blistering form, fired a bogey-free 67 to move to 11-under and establish his largest 36-hole lead in a major since his magical run in 2000. The second loudest cheers of the day (after Nicklaus) were reserved for Colin Montgomerie, who birdied three of the final five holes for a 67 to move into second, four shots behind Woods. The last time the pair had

appeared together in the final group at a major – at the 1997 US Masters, Woods's first as a pro – Montgomerie had confidently predicted experience would triumph. Instead, the young Woods shot 65, nine shots better than the Scot, to win the tournament by 12. Montgomerie could only hope for a better outcome on this occasion.

After two relatively placid days, Saturday brought blustery winds to the Old Course, and Woods struggled. Rallying over the final holes, he battled to a one-under 71 to leave him on 12-under, two shots clear of José-Maria Olazabal and three ahead of Montgomerie (70).

Woods's march to a second British Open title continued unabated in the final round. Battling stiff winds, the world No.1 was never threatened, closing out with a two-under 70 – the only sub-par score in the final seven groups – to finish on 14-under par, five strokes clear of Montgomerie. Clutching the coveted Claret Jug, he rounded sharply on those who had criticized him for re-vamping his swing: "Why would I change my game? This is why. First, second and first in the last three majors. That's why." With a tenth major championship title in the bag, few would have argued against Tiger's prospects of claiming a handful more.

THE 2005 BRITISH OPEN - The Top 5
1 Tiger Woods 66 67 71 70 274 -14
2 Colin Montgomerie 71 66 70 72 279 -9
3 Fred Couples 68 71 73 68 280 -8
= J M Olazábal 68 70 68 74 280 -8
5 Michael Campbell 69 72 68 72 281 -7
Sergio García 70 69 69 73 281 -7
Retief Goosen 68 73 66 74 281 -7
Bernhard Langer 71 69 70 71 281 -7
Geoff Ogilvy 71 74 67 69 281 -7
Vijay Singh 69 69 71 72 281 -7

Tiger Woods' love affair with St Andrews continued in 2005 when he collected his second British Open championship with a five-stroke victory.

THE BRITISH OPEN: 2006

It was business as usual: Tiger Woods produced a memorable final round to record his 11th major victory and become the first back-to-back British Open champion since Tom Watson in 1982-83.

Overnight rain, that delayed the start of the first round by half an hour, tamed the brown, fast-running Royal Liverpool course on the first day and, in ideal scoring conditions (that prompted an all-time major record 67 sub-par rounds), Northern Ireland's Graeme McDowell stole the limelight, firing a bogey-free round of six-under 66 to lie in the lead, one shot ahead of a group of five players on five-under, including defending champion Tiger Woods. The world No.1, who started day one of his defence of the Claret Jug by missing a 30cm par putt on the first and ended it by rolling in a 25ft putt for eagle on 18, cast a looming presence on the leaderboard.

And Woods produced a golfing clinic in the second round, hitting a succession of piercing long irons – his strategy for the week – to record a seven-under 65, to match his best-ever round in a major championship. It moved him to 12-under par, one shot ahead of South Africa's Ernie Els, who matched Woods's score late in the day to take him to 11-under. Chris DiMarco's 65 moved him to third on the leaderboard. The 135th British Open had only reached the halfway stage, but, for many, its outcome had already been decided.

By the end of the third round, Woods was exactly where he wanted to be: on top of the leaderboard. But it had been a relatively pedestrian and far from convincing performance from the defending champion: he misfired with his long irons and three-putted three times over the

final eight holes to grind out a one-under 71. As a result, Woods would go into the final round holding the slenderest of leads: one shot over Sergio Garcia, whose round-of-the-day 65 propelled him to 12-under and into a share of second, alongside Els (71) and DiMarco (69). Thanks to an uncharacteristic stumbling performance from Woods, the 2006 British Open was still wide open.

But not for long: the final round found Woods in imperious form. Back to his blazing best with the long irons, the world No.1 cruised to a five-under 67, a final total

of 18-under par and an 11th major title. It marked Woods's first major victory since the death of his father Earl two months previously and, after tapping in his final putt to secure a two-shot victory over DiMarco, he buried his head in caddie Steve Williams' shoulder and sobbed uncontrollably.

The champion's first words to the assembled media were about the lasting influence his father had on his game: "He was always on my case about thinking my way around the golf course and not letting emotions get the better of you. Just use your

mind to plot your way around the golf course and if you had to deviate away from the gameplan, make sure it is the right decision to do that. He was adamant that I play like that my entire career." His father would have been proud: Woods Jr had produced yet another masterful performance when it mattered.

THE 2006 BRITISH OPEN - The Top 5
1 Tiger Woods 67 65 71 67 270 -18
2 Chris DiMarco 70 65 69 68 272 -16
3 Ernie Els 68 65 71 71 275 -13
4 Jim Furyk 68 71 66 71 276 -12
5 Sergio García 68 71 65 73 277 -11
= Hideto Tanihara 72 68 66 71 277 -11

Tiger Woods produced a golf masterclass at Hoylake to retain the British Open title he had won at St Andrews in 2005.

THE BRITISH OPEN: 2007

The British Open returned to Carnoustie in 2007 and saw a European triumph with Padraig Harrington beating Sergio Garcia in a four-hole play-off to collect his first major championship.

The last time Sergio Garcia had played Carnoustie in a British Open he posted rounds of 89 and 82 – his worst two rounds in majors – and missed the cut. This time, however, it was all smiles as the Spaniard fired a six-under 65 – his best ever start in a major – to take a two-shot lead after the opening round over Paul McGinley. Five players sat on three-under par, with defending champion Tiger Woods a shot further back after posting a 69.

A solid even-par 71 by Garcia in round two saw his lead grow to two strokes over second-placed KJ Choi, who posted a two-under 69. The round of the day belonged to Mike Weir, whose three-under 68 put him in third on three-under, alongside Miguel Angel Jimenez. Woods, in his quest to become the first player in 51 years to win three consecutive British Opens, shot 74 and sat seven off the lead.

By the end of the third round, Garcia's odds of winning a major championship had never been better. A commanding three-under 68 saw him move to nine-under and extend his lead to three, over Steve Stricker, who posted 64. A group of seven players sat in a tie for third on three-under.

The final round evoked memories of Carnoustie 1999 because, yet again, the par-four 499-yard 18th served up moments of pure theatre. It was fast becoming a tournament nobody wanted to win. First came Andres Romero, who made ten birdies – including four in a row to take the lead – before losing three shots on the

final two holes to finish on six-under. Then came Padraig Harrington. By the time the Irishman arrived on the 18th, he held a two-shot lead. But then disaster struck: he miscued his tee shot and, agonizingly, watched the ball bounce over a bridge before falling into a hazard a mere yard from safety. He hit his third into the burn, pitched his fifth to within 5ft and holed out for a double bogey to end on seven-under. It left Garcia needing a par on 18 to win: using an iron off the tee for safety, the Spaniard found the middle of the fairway. Then, after a 15-minute wait, he pushed his approach into a greenside bunker; he chipped out to 10ft, but missed the par putt. Garcia joined Harrington on seven-under.

The pair headed out for their four-hole play-off, Harrington took charge from the off, making birdie to the Spaniard's bogey, and never looked back. When Garcia missed a 25ft birdie putt on 18, Harrington had become the first Irishman for 60 years to win the Claret Jug.

And with one major championship now in the bag, Harrington was eager to win more: "My goal was always to win more than one major," said the delighted Irishman. "If I ever crossed that threshold to win one, I wouldn't feel like that was the end of my road... I'll try to win another."

THE 2007 BRITISH OPEN – The Top 5
1 Pádraig Harrington* 69 73 68 67 277 -7
= Sergio García 65 71 68 73 277 -7
3 Andrés Romero 71 70 70 67=278 -6
4 Ernie Els 72 70 68 69 279 -5
= Richard Green 72 73 70 64 279 -5
* Won play-off

It was all smiles for Padraig Harrington after he overcame disaster on the 72nd hole to beat Sergio Garcia in a playoff to claim his first major.

THE BRITISH OPEN: 2008

Tiger Woods may have been missing but the tournament barely noticed his absence as Royal Birkdale served up yet another spellbinding classic before Padraig Harrington emerged to make a successful defence of his title.

The first round was a tale of two halves: the morning, that saw a brutal Royal Birkdale, ably assisted by gusting winds; and the afternoon, when the wind and the scoring conditions eased. Not that conditions became much easier, however. Of the field of 156 players, only three of them broke par: Robert Allenby, Graeme McDowell and Rocco Mediate, who posted late-afternoon 69s. Bart Bryant, a resurgent Greg Norman and fellow Australian Adam Scott sat on level-par. Defending champion Padraig Harrington, nursing a sore wrist, remained in contention after posting a four-over 74.

The clouds threatened on Friday, but the rain stayed away and 53-year-old Norman's dream start continued. Rolling back the years, the two-time winner (1986 and 1993) shot a second consecutive 70 and temporarily took the clubhouse lead on level-par, before South Korea's KJ Choi posted 67 to move to the top of the leaderboard on one-under. The round of the day belonged to Colombia's Camilo Villegas, who closed with five consecutive birdies for a 65 to move to third on one-over, a shot ahead of a group of seven players that included Harrington, who shot an impressive 68.

The winds returned with gusto for the third round on Saturday, but the inclement conditions did little to perturb Norman. On a day when no player broke par, the Great White Shark recorded a two-over 72 to take a two-shot lead into the final round. Harrington matched Norman's 72 to move to second alongside Choi, who struggled to a 75. Who would triumph: Norman, seeking to become the oldest major champion in history; or Harrington, looking to become the tournament's 15th back-to-back winner?

Norman maintained a one-shot lead after the first nine holes of the final round, and then the shots started to tumble away and the dream went with it. The disappointed Australian closed with a seven-over 77 to finish on nine-over in a tie for third with Henrik Stenson. The charge of the day belonged to Ian Poulter, who closed with an impressive 69 to move to seven-over. But then Harrington took centre stage: he first took the lead on the 12th and extended it with a birdie on 15 and an eagle on 17. By the time he stood on the 18th tee, his lead stood at four and when his tee shot found the fairway the tournament was effectively won; the Irishman closed with a one-under 69. For Norman, the 2008 British Open was yet another case of what could have been; for Harrington, a successful title defence had propelled him into an exclusive club.

Victory at Royal Birkdale saw Padraig Harrington become the British Open's 15th back-to-back winner.

THE 2008 BRITISH OPEN - The Top 5
1 Pádraig Harrington 74 68 72 69 283 +3
2 Ian Poulter 72 71 75 69 287 +7
3 Greg Norman 70 70 72 77 289 +9
= Henrik Stenson 76 72 70 71 289 +9
5 Jim Furyk 71 71 77 71 290 +10
= Chris Wood 75 70 73 72 290 +10

THE BRITISH OPEN: 2009

Tom Watson rolled back the years in exhilarating fashion to produce the most compelling golf story in years. But Watson's Turnberry fairytale turned sour and 36-year-old Stewart Cink celebrated his first victory in a major championship.

After an opening round played in surprisingly placid conditions over the Ailsa Craig course at Turnberry, Miguel Angel Jimenez took the overnight lead by firing a six-under 64 that included a 66ft birdie putt on 18. But the day's headlines belonged to Tom Watson, and Jimenez knew it. The 59-year-old, a five-time winner at the British Open, evoked memories of his glory years, posting a five-under 65 – matching his famous, championship-winning round when he overcame Jack Nicklaus in the "Duel in the Sun" over the same course in 1977 – to sit in second, alongside 2003 champion Ben Curtis and Japan's Kenichi Kuboya.

The rain and wind swept in for the second round and, at the end of a day that tested every one of the players' skills, Tom Watson, the oldest player in the tournament, was still leading it. Producing some vintage golf, a mere nine months after hip surgery, he posted an even-par 70 to sit on top of the leaderboard on five-under with British Open rookie Steve Marino, who posted a two-under 68.

Watson's fairytale continued into the third round. By the time he closed out on 18 for a one-over 71, he looked across to see his name on top of the leaderboard on four-under par, one shot ahead of Ross Fisher and Matt Goggin, and two ahead of Lee Westwood and Retief Goosen. The entire golfing world hoped he could conjure up the perfect denouement to what, thus far, had been a compelling plot.

And, for all but the final moments of the final round, the world watched on with fascination as what could have been the greatest story in the game's history reached its climax. Playing with admirable control, Watson reached the 18th with a one-shot lead over Stewart Cink who, moments earlier, holed a 12ft birdie putt on the last to close with a 69 and sat in the clubhouse on two-under. To great cheers, Watson found the middle of the 18th fairway, then nailed an eight-iron, only to see the ball bound over the back of the green. Taking a putter from the fringe, he raced his ball past the hole, but still had an 8ft putt for par, the championship and a unique place in history. He missed and faced a four-hole play-off with Cink.

Watson's moment had gone. Demonstrably fatigued and emotionally spent, he posted four-over par in the play-off to Cink's two-under. History will record that Cink, who, until Watson's missed putt on 18, had not sat on top of the leaderboard all week, won the 2009 British Open, but this tournament was all about Tom Watson and what could have been.

"It would have been a hell of a story, wouldn't it?" said Watson afterwards. And it was, almost. Almost. The dream almost came true." Few who saw it would ever forget: this had been the most fascinating major in recent history.

THE 2009 BRITISH OPEN – The Top 5
1 Stewart Cink* 66 72 71 69 278 +2
Tom Watson 65 70 71 72 278 +2
3 Lee Westwood 68 70 70 71 279 +1
Chris Wood 70 70 72 67 279 +1
5 Luke Donald 71 72 70 67 280 E
Mathew Goggin 66 72 69 73 280 E
Retief Goosen 67 70 71 72 280 E
* Won play-off

Stewart Cink came through a four-hole playoff against a fatigued Tom Watson to win the 2009 British Open at Turnberry, the American's first major championship.

US PGA CHAMPIONSHIP

Rodman Wanamaker is a name that does not loom large in the minds of most followers of golf, yet he set in motion the championship which is today the fourth "major" in the world game ... not only fourth in the golfing calendar (except for an unpopular and short-lived February experiment in Florida in 1971) but also ranked fourth in most people's estimation behind the two Opens and the Masters.

This does not mean it is the easiest to win, since the ranking US professionals are involved. While Australians and South Africans have done the trick, Europe-based players have found the going tough, though moves have been made in recent years to make the US PGA and US Open more accessible to leading foreign players and so more representative of the world game.

The genesis of the US PGA Championship stemmed from attempts to better the lot of club professionals who, during the first years of the 20th century, were about as far removed from the millionaire status of today's tour stars as were most operators of small retail businesses of the time.

Rodman Wanamaker was himself in the business of selling, in New York, and a keen golfer. It did not take a genius to see that the professionals needed organizing, and, slowly, regional groups were formed, leading to a national Professional Golfers' Association, to whom Wanamaker presented a trophy for a national professional championship. The name Wanamaker is still there on the trophy.

The first winner was born in Britain, as were most of the early winners of the US Open. Long Jim Barnes, whose nickname "Long" was

on account of his great length off the tee, came from Lelant, in Cornwall. He beat a Scot, Jock Hutchison, at Siwanoy Country Club, Bronxville, New York, by one hole in the final of what was, for many years, a matchplay event.

Owing to the war, the second US PGA Championship was not played until 1919, when Barnes won again against Fred McLeod at the Engineers Club, Long Island. McLeod was Scottish also, from North Berwick, and already a US Open winner. For many years, and long after the Second World War, McLeod, who was as short in stature as Barnes was tall, formed the traditional starting twosome in the Masters with Hutchison, who was from St Andrews, and finally got his hands on the Wanamaker Cup in 1920. He defeated a talented English pro, John Douglas Edgar, from Newcastle-upon-Tyne, in the first US PGA played outside New York, at Flossmoor, Illinois.

Three of American golf's big "names" now took over, for Walter Hagen (for five years), Gene Sarazen (two) and Leo Diegel (two) won the right to look after Wanamaker's gift throughout the rest of the 1920s (and Sarazen won again in 1933).

To tell the truth, Hagen did not look after the trophy all that well. He could not recall where he had left it ("In a taxi?" he pondered), after Diegel's 1928 victory at Baltimore Country Club. It was not located until 1930, parcelled up in a Detroit factory.

Hagen's record in Open championships either side of the Atlantic attests to his strokeplay ability, but he was surely of all golfers who ever lived the most richly endowed with every

US PGA Results

Year	Winner	Runner-up	Venue	Score
(matchplay until 1958)				
1916	J Barnes	J Hutchison	Siwanoy, NY	1 hole
1917-18	No championship			
1919	J Barnes	F McLeod	Engineers, NY	6&5
1920	J Hutchison	JD Edgar	Flossmoor, Il	1 hole
1921	W Hagen	J Barnes	Inwood, NY	3&2
1922	G Sarazen	E French	Oakmont, Pa	4&3
1923	G Sarazen	W Hagen	Pelham, NY	38th hole
1924	W Hagen	J Barnes	French Lick, In	6&4
1925	W Hagen	WE Mehlhorn	Olympic Fields, Il	6&5
1926	W Hagen	L Diegel	Salisbury, NY	4&3
1927	W Hagen	J Turnesa	Dallas, Tx	1 hole
1928	L Diegel	A Espinosa	Five Farms, Md	6&5
1929	L Diegel	J Farrell	Hillcrest, Ca	6&4
1930	T Armour	G Sarazen	Fresh Meadow, NY	1 hole
1931	T Creavy	D Shute	Wannamoisett, RI	2&1
1932	O Dutra	F Walsh	St Paul, Mn	4&3
1933	G Sarazen	W Goggin	Blue Mound, Wi	5&4
1934	P Runyan	C Wood	Buffalo, NY	38th hole
1935	J Revolta	T Armour	Twin Hills, Ok	5&4
1936	D Shute	J Thomson	Pinehurst, NC	3&2
1937	D Shute	H McSpaden	Oakmont, Pa	37th hole
1938	P Runyan	S Snead	Shawnee, Pa	8&7
1939	H Picard	B Nelson	Pomonok, NY	37th hole
1940	B Nelson	S Snead	Hershey, Pa	1 hole
1941	V Ghezzie	B Nelson	Cherry Hills, Co	38th hole
1942	S Snead	J Turnesa	Atlantic City, NJ	2&1
1943	No championship			
1944	R Hamilton	B Nelson	Manito, Spokane, Wa	1 hole
1945	B Nelson	S Byrd	Morraine, Dayton, Oh	4&3
1946	B Hogan	E Oliver	Portland, Or	6&4
1947	J Ferrier	C Harbert	Plum Hollow, Mi	2&1
1948	B Hogan	M Turnesa	Norwood Hills, Mo	7&6
1949	S Snead	J Palmer	Hermitage, Va	3&2
1950	C Harper	H Williams Jr	Scioto, Columbus, Oh	4&3
1951	S Snead	W Burkemo	Oakmont, Pa	7&6
1952	J Turnesa	C Harbert	Big Spring, Ky	2&1
1953	W Burkemo	F Torza	Birmingham CC, Mi	2&1
1954	C Harbert	W Burkemo	Keller, St Paul, Mi	4&3
1955	D Ford	C Middlecoff	Meadowbrook, Mi	4&3
1956	J Burke	T Kroll	Blue Hill, Boston, Ma	3&2
1957	L Hebert	D Finsterwald	Miami Val., Dayton Oh	2&1
1958	D Finsterwald	W Casper	Llanerch, Pa	276
1959	B Rosburg	J Barber, D Sanders	St Louis Pk, Mi	277
1960	J Hebert	J Ferrier	Firestone, Akron, Oh	281
1961	J Barber	D January	Olympia Fields, Il	277
	won 18-hole play-off 67 to 68			
1962	G Player	B Goalby	Aronimink, Pa	278
1963	J Nicklaus	D Ragan	Dallas Athletic, Tx	279
1964	B Nichols	A Palmer, J Nicklaus	Columbus, Oh	271
1965	D Marr	W Casper, J Nicklaus	Laurel Valley, Pa	280
1966	A Geiberger	D Wysong	Firestone, Akron, Oh	280

Year	Winner	Runner-up	Venue	Score
1967	D January	D Massengale	Columbine, Denver, Co	281
	won 18-hole play-off 69 to 71			
1968	J Boros	RJ Charles, A Palmer	Pecan Valley, Tx	281
1969	R Floyd	G Player	NCR, Dayton, Oh	276
1970	D Stockton	R Murphy, A Palmer	Southern Hills, Ok	279
1971	J Nicklaus	W Casper	PGA National, Fl	281
1972	G Player	T Aaron, J Jamieson	Oakland Hills, Mi	281
1973	J Nicklaus	B Crampton	Canterbury, Oh	277
1974	L Trevino	J Nicklaus	Tanglewood, NC	276
1975	J Nicklaus	B Crampton	Firestone, Akron, Oh	276
1976	D Stockton	R Floyd, D January	Congressional, Md	281
1977	L Wadkins	G Littler	Pebble Beach, Ca	282
	won play-off at first extra hole			
1978	J Mahaffey	J Pate, T Watson	Oakmont, Pa	276
	won play-off at second extra hole			
1979	D Graham	B Crenshaw	Oakland Hills, Mi	272
	won play-off at third extra hole			
1980	J Nicklaus	A Bean	Oak Hill, NY	274
1981	L Nelson	F Zoeller	Atlantic Ath Club, Ga	273
1982	R Floyd	L Wadkins	Southern Hills, Ok	272
1983	H Sutton	J Nicklaus	Riviera, Los Angeles, Ca	274
1984	L Trevino	L Wadkins, G Player	Shoal Creek Al	273
1985	H Green	L Trevino	Cherry Hills, Co	278
1986	R Tway	G Norman	Inverness, Toledo, Oh	276
1987	L Nelson	L Wadkins	PGA National, Fl	287
	won play-off at first extra hole			
1988	J Sluman	P Azinger	Oak Tree, Edmond, Ok	272
1989	P Stewart	A Bean, M Reid, C Strange	Kemper Lakes, Il	276
1990	W Grady	F Couples	Shoal Creek, Al	282
1991	J Daly	B Lietzke	Crooked Stick, In	276
1992	N Price	J Cook, N Faldo, G Sauers, J Gallagher Jr	Bellerive, St Louis, Mo	278
1993	P Azinger	G Norman	Inverness, Toledo, Oh	272
	won play-off at second extra hole			
1994	N Price	C Pavin	Southern Hills, Ok	269
1995	S Elkington	C Montgomerie	Riviera, Los Angeles, Ca	267
	won play-off at first extra hole			
1996	M Brooks	K Perry	Valhalla, Ky	277
	won play-off at first extra hole			
1997	D Love III	J Leonard	Winged Foot, NY	269
1998	V Singh	S Stricker	Sahalee CC, Wa	271
1999	T Woods	S Garcia	Medinah, Il	277
2000	T Woods	B May	Valhalla, Ky	270
	won three-hole play-off			
2001	D Toms	P Mickelson	Atlanta AC, Ga	265
2002	R Beem	T Woods	Hazeltine National, Mn	278
2003	S Micheel	C Campbell	Oak Hill, NY	276
2004	V Singh	J Leonard, C DiMarco	Whistling Straits, Wi	280
	won three-hole play-off			
2005	P Mickelson	T Bjorn	Baltusrol, NJ	276
2006	T Woods	S Micheel	Medinah, Il	270
2007	T Woods	W Austin	Southern Hills, Ok	272
2008	P Harrington	S Garcia	Oakland Hills, Mi	277
2009	YE Yang	T Woods	Hazeltine National, Mn	280

Denny Shute won back-to-back US PGA Championships in 1936 and 1937 in the days when the event was still played as a matchplay tournament.

matchplay talent. Having become champion at the expense of the inaugural winner, Barnes, in 1921, Hagen did not defend in 1922, but from the time he lost the 1923 final (at the 38th hole) to Sarazen, Hagen was unbeaten till Leo Diegel gained revenge in the third round in 1928 for many Hagen defeats.

One of Hagen's victims, Wild Bill Mehlhorn, must have feared the worst after Hagen's first tee shot against him in the 1925 final, for it went into the hole. Mehlhorn went down 6&5.

In addition to self-confidence, and the ability to scrape a way out of trouble and slot the most daunting putt, Hagen's armoury included a smile that must have seemed crocodile-like to his opponents.

It didn't always work: before getting down to a 20ft putt at a critical moment in the third round of the US PGA in 1928, he turned and directed the full force of one of these smiles at Diegel, a frequent victim of his match-playing ability. Hagen holed the putt, but Diegel, though he had lost an early four-hole lead and was clearly shaken, managed to survive. He

No player has won the US PGA Championship on more occasions than Jack Nicklaus; the American's first title came in 1963 - his last win, in 1980, silenced the critics who had said that he was past his best.

went on to record a crushing final win against Al Espinosa (6&5), and followed up the following season with a 6&4 victory over Johnny Farrell, one of the few to have beaten Bobby Jones over 36 holes ... for the US Open, too.

There was no suggestion at first that the US PGA was a "major" title. The leading amateurs of the day were still to be reckoned with as the elite of golf. Between 1913 and 1933 the two big Opens were won by an amateur on 11 occasions.

Tom Creavy, like John Daly in 1991, was among the most surprising winners of a national championship. He won the US PGA in 1931, aged 20, beating Denny Shute at Wannamoisett, Rhode Island, in the final, and two other US Open champions on the way to it. He lived until 1979, but illness restricted his golf after he reached the last four in 1932 and the last eight in 1933, and finished eighth in the US Open of 1934.

The US PGA Championship remained a matchplay event until 1958, providing in 1942, soon after Pearl Harbor, Sam Snead's first national title. He was able to play only because he persuaded his recruiting officer to let him enlist a few days late so that he could compete at Seaview, Atlantic City, where he beat Jim Turnesa 2&1.

The Second World War caused only one year's inaction, for Bob Hamilton beat Byron Nelson at Spokane, Washington, in 1944, and the following year Nelson was back to regain the title he first won in 1940, at Snead's expense. The US PGA was also Ben Hogan's first national title, and with the growth of the PGA Tour, and the absence of amateurs good enough to beat the pros, the event grew in importance.

Americans love the pencil and card game, and in its new guise as a medal competition (from 1958) the US PGA gained more and more attention. It also caused agonized disappointment as Arnold Palmer took the place of Hogan in the nation's high regard, for this is the one major Palmer did not win. He certainly tried hard, finishing joint second in 1964, 1968 and 1970.

Discounting early immigrant winners like Barnes, Hutchison, Tommy Armour and (in 1947) the Australian Jim Ferrier, long based in the United States and a heavy money-winner on the PGA Tour, the first foreign winner was Gary Player in 1962. Three years later, by winning the US Open, Player became, along with Sarazen and Hogan, the third golfer to have won the modern quartet of majors. Australia's David Graham beat Ben Crenshaw in a play-off only after an excruciating 72nd hole at the difficult Oakland Hills course near Detroit in 1979.

He began with a misplaced drive, and an over-strong approach. Two indifferent chips and a missed putt left him needing a downhill putt to equal Crenshaw's 272. He holed it, and then made two lengthy putts to keep the sudden-death play-off going to the third hole, which he birdied for victory.

The suspense attached to John Daly's 1991 triumph, his first on the PGA Tour, started for this Californian-born long hitter from Arkansas before he even reached Crooked Stick, Indiana. He was ninth "reserve" in line for a place in the event, and got in because Nick Price departed to be with his wife, who shortly afterwards gave birth to Gregory, their first child. Daly, 25, decided to take a chance and make the seven-hour drive to Crooked Stick

RUNYAN v. SNEAD, 1938 US PGA Championship

If ever there was a tale of two contrasting styles going head-to-head in the world of golf then this was it. Sam Snead was the new kid on the block as the US PGA Championship wound its way to the Shawnee Country Club, and the 26-year-old had taken the tournament by storm, breezing his way into the matchplay final. The only blip – following 4&3 victories in the rounds of 32 and 16 over Terl Johnson and Felix Serafin and a crushing 8&7 victory over Jim Foulis in the quarter-final – came in his semi-final clash against Jimmy Hines. It required four consecutive threes to see Snead into the final by the slenderest of margins, 1up.

And the bookies saw it as a one-horse race: they gave odds of 10-1 on Snead – some odds in a two-man shoot-out.

But even before the start of the final there were those who thought that too many were underestimating the powers of his opponent. Paul Runyan, the diminutive 28-year-old had won the tournament only four years earlier and was a proven performer in matchplay. A glance at how he had reached the final proved as much: he had taken some notable scalps along the way to securing his final berth, including 1936 US Open winner Lloyd Mangrum (1up), double Masters champion Horton Smith (1up) and the reigning Masters champion Henry Picard (4&3). The man could definitely play.

But he was too short off the tee, cried the Snead fans. He'll be overpowered by Slammin' Sam's game. That proved to be the case, but Runyan wasn't given the moniker "Little Poison" for nothing. He possessed a short-game of Ballesteros-like genius. From 80 yards in, Runyan had few equals.

In the golfing equivalent of the hare and the tortoise, Runyan sat back and watched Snead march on down the fairways – sometimes as much as 70 yards ahead of him. It was here that the contest started, however. And how... In the morning's 18 holes, Runyan went round in 67 to take a 5-up lead into the afternoon. Snead was starting to fume...

And things got no better for him in the afternoon either. Runyan reached the turn in one-under 35 to extend his lead to seven holes. By the 28th hole of the final it was all over and Runyan had won by 8&7 – the largest winning margin in all the years that the event had been played as a matchplay competition.

If it had been played as a strokeplay competition he would probably have come out on top as well. Runyan completed the 196 holes he had played during the course of the week in 24-under par – and made only one bogey in the last 70 holes he had played.

Snead had not fared so badly either: he finished the 147 holes of matchplay in 21-under par, but it had been a demoralizing introduction to the tournament that he would go on to win three times: in 1942, 1949 and 1951.

This was the last major that Runyan would win, but he had proved above all else that in golf, as in all things, size isn't everything. After his mauling on the Shawnee Country Club fairways, Sam Snead would have been the first to agree with that.

Quarter-finals:
Jimmy Hines bt Byron Nelson 2&1
Paul Runyan bt Horton Smith 4&3
Sam Snead bt Jim Foulis 8&7
Henry Picard bt Gene Sarazen 3&2

Semi-finals:
Sam Snead bt Jimmy Hines 1up
Paul Runyan bt Henry Picard 4&3

Final:
Paul Runyan bt Sam Snead 8&7

Gary Player became the first foreign plater to win the tournament when he captured the title in 1962- a success he would emulate ten years later.

before he knew of Price's decision.

His gamble paid off. After two rounds he led on a 7,289-yard course he had never seen before. Daly, known to about one golf fan in a million, was a huge hit with the media, gaining instant fame as "Wild Thing" with his fulsome swing and 300-yard plus drives, not to mention sand wedges that flew 150 yards. His winning total of 276, three strokes ahead of Bruce Lietzke, also owed a good deal to a sharp short game. He received a ten-year exemption on the tour, lifetime US PGA exemption,

and a $230,000 (£137,000) start towards finishing 17th on the 1991 money list. Naturally, he was also voted Rookie of the Year.

Price was back for the 1992 US PGA at Bellerive, with his caddie Jess "Squeaky" Medlen, whom Daly had taken over the previous year in Price's absence. Price, a Zimbabwean who come close to "major" fame in the British Opens of 1982 and 1988, won by three shots, and repeated the dose, this time by six shots, two years later at Southern Hills, Tulsa, a month after

John Daly, the ninth reserve for the tournament, profited from Nick Price's absence to spring a major surprise in 1991.

WOODS v. GARCIA, 1999 US PGA CHAMPIONSHIP

The line-up for the 81st US PGA Championship was the strongest in the history of the event. Ninety-two of the world's top-100 players took their places for the tournament at the Medinah Country Club. And during the fourth round, it was the two youngest members of the field who took centre stage and who enthralled the galleries and television audiences around the world.

After the third round, it seemed as though the final day would all be about Tiger Woods, seeking his second major win, and Canada's Mike Weir. The pair stood two shots ahead of the chasing pack with just 18 holes left to play. The situation got the better of the left-handed Weir, however, and he fell away with a final round of 80 to leave Tiger Woods on a solitary march to the title. Or so everybody thought.

Sergio Garcia, the 19-year-old who led after the first round and who was the youngest player to appear in the US PGA since Gene Sarazen in 1921, had other ideas, though. But he had to wait his turn.

The first nine holes were all about the poise of Tiger Woods. He holed a 15ft putt for a birdie on the second hole and by the time he turned for home held a five-shot lead over the young Spaniard. It was a lead he maintained as he stood on the 12th green facing a 60ft birdie putt.

Then came the Spaniard. Standing on the 13th tee, Garcia ripped a six-iron to within 15ft on the 219-yard par three. He skipped off the tee and bounded along the fairway. Woods missed his birdie attempt and then missed the follow-up par-saver. He recorded his first bogey of the day and his lead was down to four.

Moments later it was down to three, as the Spaniard charged his putt into the centre of the cup for a birdie. He plucked his ball from the hole, glared back down towards the 13th tee and tipped his hat to the waiting Woods. It was game on.

In response, Woods ripped a six-iron from the tee – too hard as it happened. The ball flew over the back of the green and landed in thick rough. He stabbed the ball out ... and on and on it rolled down the slope before coming to rest in more rough. He chipped back to 6ft and missed the putt. A double-bogey and the lead was down to one.

Perhaps the pressure started to get to the 19-year-old. He bogeyed the 15th to fall two behind and produced a wild tee shot on the 16th which saw his ball roll through the fairway and come to rest in the exposed roots of one of Medinah's 4,161 trees. The only sensible course of action was to chip the ball back out into the fairway and hope to get up and down. Someone forgot to tell Garcia.

He pulled a six-iron from his bag, opened the blade of his club, closed his eyes and let rip. The ball arced on a high left-to-right flight and came to rest some 60ft away from the flag, but on the green. To the roars of "Sergio, Sergio", the Spaniard scissor-kicked his way along the fairway pounding his chest. He two-putted to save his par.

It will be remembered as one of the best, and bravest, shots in the history of major championship golf. The Spanish say "seurte o muerte", luck or death. On this occasion Garcia had been lucky, but that's where his luck ran out.

He missed two birdie attempts on the last two holes to allow Woods to come through. When the American two-putted on the 18th, he had become the youngest player since Seve Ballesteros in 1980 to win two major tournaments and had regained his world number one spot.

But the trophy was the only thing that belonged to Tiger Woods that day: everything else, including the hearts of the Medinah galleries and the millions watching on television, belonged to Sergio Garcia. Everyone now hoped that golf had discovered a rivalry that mattered as the game drifted into the 21st century.

1999 US PGA Championship, Medinah CC, III

Pos	Name	Score				
1	Tiger Woods (US)	72	75	68	72	277
2	Sergio Garcia (Sp)	66	73	68	71	278

his British Open at Turnberry. At Tulsa, at the age of 37, Price set new US PGA scoring standards. His 269 (11-under par) beat Bobby Nichols's 1964 record by two shots.

Price's first nine in the final round ruled out much chance of excitement later on, as he reached the turn in 32, but three birdies on the back nine were cancelled out by three bogeys, which cost Price his chance of taking Nicklaus's championship record winning margin which stands at seven shots. Despite these blemishes, no one got to within three shots of him. Proof of Arnold Palmer's lasting popularity came on the eve of the championship, when

Palmer, making his 37th and final appearance in the US PGA, which he never won, was presented with the PGA of America Distinguished Service Award.

Between Price's twin triumphs, which meant that "Squeaky" had carried for three winners in four years, came a most popular win by Paul Azinger. The New Englander beat Greg Norman in a play-off at Toledo, making the Australian the unhappy owner of a unique record: he has lost play-offs for all four majors. In the 1986 event (also at Toledo), he lost the championship when playing partner Bob Tway birdied the 72nd hole out of a bunker.

An American full-house looked likely in 1995, as Ben Crenshaw, Corey Pavin and John Daly won the first three majors. But the US PGA champion Steve Elkington, although a Houston resident was born in Australia. His play-off birdie cost Scotland's Colin Montgomerie his first major; their 72-hole totals of 267 were the lowest in a major championship played in the United States.

Mark Brooks scored another first-hole sudden-death win in 1996, as local hero Kenny Perry suffered one disaster after another at the long and difficult 18th at Valhalla.

British Open champion Justin

Leonard tried hard but could not part Davis Love III from his first major at Winged Foot in 1997. It was a case of practice makes perfect in 1998, when Vijay Singh's relentless work on the practice ground finally paid off as he romped to his first major by two strokes.

A year later, at Medinah, it was the turn of two young guns to thrill the galleries. Spain's teenage sensation, Sergio Garcia, played every shot in the book and leaped around the fairways – winning an army of fans in the process with his exuberance – but he could not stop Tiger Woods from collecting his second major title.

THE US PGA CHAMPIONSHIP: 2000

In a thrilling finale, Tiger Woods held off the dogged challenge of Bob May to retain his US PGA title and claimed his third consecutive major title.

It only seemed appropriate that Tiger Woods, in his bid to become the first man since Ben Hogan to win three major tournaments in a season, should have been paired with the legendary Jack Nicklaus in his opening two rounds in the defence of his US PGA title at Valhalla Country Club.

Nicklaus must have been impressed with what he saw. The defending champion went round the course in six-under par, a round which included four straight birdies between the seventh and the tenth.

Woods hit 16 out of 18 greens in regulation and only missed three fairways: it was his 12th consecutive round of par or better in the majors since his first-round 75 back at Augusta.

The world number one continued his march on a second day that had been delayed because of a waterlogged course. The softer conditions seemed to be to his liking, as he shot a five-under 67 to hold a one-shot lead at the halfway stage.

The 18th hole signalled the end of the road at the US PGA Championship for Jack Nicklaus. The moment he walked off the final green with Tiger Woods by his side was a significant one: you got the sense that the torch had been passed from the best player of one generation to the man who was fast becoming the best player of the next.

There was a sense of relief following the end of the third day's play. Woods had been ten strokes ahead after 54 holes at the US Open and six strokes ahead at the same stage at the British Open: this time his lead stood at just one, and for the first time in a while it looked as though we would have a major championship that lasted for 72 holes. Woods included a double-bogey in his round of two-under: his first in 153 holes of major championship golf.

One stroke behind Woods was Bob May. The man who had finally secured his PGA Tour card after plying his trade on the European Tour for the previous four years shot a six-under 66 to keep alive his hopes of becoming the first rookie to win this event since John Daly shocked the golfing world at Crooked Stick in 1991. Joining May on 204 was Scott Dunlap.

It was also a day when the course record was broken twice. First veteran Tom Watson rolled back the years with a 65. Then came José-Maria Olazabal, who became the 18th player in history of major championship golf to shoot a 63 - a round in which he narrowly missed a 15ft birdie chance on the 17th hole.

It had been 42 years since this tournament switched to a strokeplay format, but during the course of a thrilling final afternoon it was like a throwback to yesteryear as Woods and May slugged it out, shot for shot, hole for hole: it felt like matchplay at its very best.

And, through to the 17th hole, it was May who looked the most likely player to emerge as the winner. He outplayed Woods through the first nine, taking the lead as early as the second hole of the day, capitalizing on a rare Tiger bogey with a birdie of his own.

And May remained in front, before Woods began to turn things around on the back nine: the world number one needed just 12 putts to negotiate the last nine greens. As the pair approached the 17th, May was 17-under and Woods 16-under. May scrambled a par five; Woods holed a 6ft birdie to go all square with one to play. They both birdied the 18th: May holed a difficult downhill putt from 20ft for a birdie - shortly after, Woods held his nerve to hole his birdie putt from 6ft and to take the tournament into a play-off. Any momentum, you felt, was back with the world number one.

The play-off was contested over the last three holes. Woods decisively birdied the 16th with a putt from 25ft. Both players showed signs of nerves but the clinching shot for Woods came on the 18th: his ball lay in a tricky lie in a greenside bunker - he chipped out to 18 inches from the flag. May had to hole a 40ft birdie attempt to keep the tournament alive: he missed.

"The fireworks started on the back nine," said Woods. "This is probably one of the greatest duels I've had in my life. Hats off to Bob. He played his heart out."

Hats off indeed. Tiger Woods would go to the Masters with a chance of becoming the first player to hold all four major trophies simultaneously, but at least this time he had to work for it.

THE 2000 US PGA CHAMP - The Top 5

1 Tiger Woods* 66 67 70 67 270 -18
2 Bob May 72 66 66 66 270 -18
3 Thomas Bjørn 72 68 67 68 275 -13
4 Stuart Appleby70 69 68 69 276 -12
= Greg Chalmers 71 69 66 70 276 -12
= J M Olazábal 76 68 63 69 276 -12
* Won three-hole play-off

After romping to victory in his last two majors, Tiger Woods was made to work hard for his second US PGA title ... the unheralded Bob May pushed the world number one all the way.

THE US PGA CHAMPIONSHIP: 2001

Phil Mickelson was the bridesmaid once again as David Toms outlasted the lefthander over the final holes to win his first major championship.

The 83rd US PGA Championship returned to the Atlanta Athletic Club for the first time since 1981 with Tiger Woods looking to become the first player since Walter Hagen in the 1920s to complete a hat-trick of wins.

But the first-day headlines belonged to Grant Waite, a little-known New Zealander who broke the course record by two strokes with a six-under 64. The 37-year-old held a two-shot lead over a pack of nine players at four-under. Among them was British Open champion David Duval, who birdied the first three holes of the day, and Phil Mickelson, who took sole possession of the first-round lead on the 13th, but then bogeyed the final hole of the day.

It was a difficult day for defending champion Woods, who got off to the worst possible start. He bogeyed his first hole, the tenth, had two double-bogeys and finished up with a three-over score of 73: it left him nine strokes off the lead.

And things didn't improve for the world number one on the second day: he spent most of his round flirting with the cut mark before producing two birdies late on to secure his spot for the weekend to keep what hopes that remained of retaining his title alive. Before plucking the birdies out of the bag, he was in real danger of missing only his second cut as a professional.

It left David Toms and Shingo Katayama in the joint lead at the halfway stage on a nine-under total of 131: a tournament record for 36-holes. Toms, a five-time winner on the PGA Tour had a chance to go

one better, but missed a 10ft putt for a birdie on the final hole.

Phil Mickelson shot a second-consecutive 66 to remain in the hunt, one shot off the pace, but the round of the day belonged to Mark O'Meara. The 44-year-old American had remained winless since his double-major year at the Masters and the British Open in 1998, but he rolled back the years with a flawless round of 63, becoming the 18th player to do so in a major championship.

David Toms stood at the top of the leaderboard with a round to play, helped by a hole-in-one on the 15th. He would go into the final round with a two-shot lead over Phil Mickelson, who shot his third successive round of 66 to lie on 12-under. Toms was one stroke behind Mickelson when he stood on the 15th tee: he was in the lead moments later, though, as he watched his five-wood shot at the 227-yard par-three bounce twice, hit the flag and drop into the hole.

It was a nip and tuck day on Sunday, but when David Toms rolled in an 8ft putt for par he had secured his first major championship. His victory came at the expense of Phil Mickelson, who for the second time in three years was foiled by an opponent's putt on the final green in a major – he had watched on agonizingly as Payne Stewart won the 1999 US Open at Pinehurst with a par putt on the 72nd hole.

Toms went round in 69 to end on a 15-under total 268: the lowest 72-hole score in the history of the US PGA Championship. Mickelson also broke the previous mark, but once again it

was not enough to see him win the major championship that the golfing world thinks is so overdue.

But Mickelson did not let this one slip away without a fight: he dragged himself level with Toms three times during the final round. The third time came at the par-three 15th – the scene of Toms' ace the previous day. This time Toms found a bunker off the tee and made a bogey: Mickelson chipped in from 35ft to bring the scores level. The lefthander hit a tree off the tee on the 16th, but the golfing gods seemed to be with him as the ball bounced back onto the fairway. They weren't moments later, as a 7ft par putt slid by the hole.

Toms made a par and his lead was back to one.

They both made pars on 17, but then came Mickelson's chance. Toms was forced to lay up after finding the rough on the 18th, the 490-yard par four. Mickelson lay 30ft from the flag after two. Toms had to get down in two from 90 yards to win. He hit a wedge to 8ft. Mickelson's birdie attempt stopped just short of the hole. Toms held his nerve and holed his putt.

THE 2001 US PGA CHAMP - The Top 5
1 David Toms 66 65 65 69 265 -15
2 Phil Mickelson 66 66 66 68 266 -14
3 Steve Lowery 67 67 66 68 268 -12
4 Mark Calcavecchia 71 68 66 65 270 -10
= Shingo Katayama 67 64 69 70 270 -10

David Tom's sixth PGA Tour success was his sweetest – it was his first major championship.

THE US PGA CHAMPIONSHIP: 2002

Hollywood could not have come up with a better script as a former mobile phone salesman went head-to-head with Tiger Woods and came out on top.

You just knew that it was going to be one of those strange tournaments moments after Tiger Woods bisected the fairway with his opening tee shot. As the world number one was walking towards his ball, sirens sang out signalling that thunderstorms were approaching the area. Play was halted. At the end of an oft-interrupted day, 37 players would need an early alarm call the following day to come and complete their first rounds. In the clubhouse, Jim Furyk, who had missed the cut in the season's three previous majors, and Fred Funk, who had failed to qualify for any of them, stood on top of the leaderboard at four-under par.

It wasn't such good news for 1991 champion John Daly who posted a 77 that included an 11 on the tricky par-four 16th. Joining him on five-over par was defending champion David Toms.

Tiger Woods was also faced with an uphill struggle. After getting to within two strokes of the lead after three birdies in four holes on the front nine, his putting stroke deserted him. He made one bogey and no birdies on the back nine to leave him four shots out of the lead. With strong winds forecast for the next day, Woods knew that he might well have missed a good opportunity to have made a move.

The weather forecasters got it spot on. As 35mph winds gusted around the tree-lined fairways of Hazeltine National, only four players managed to break par: and only one player managed to break 70. That was Justin Leonard, who would take a three-stroke lead over Rich Beem into the final round.

It might not have been that way if the unheralded Beem had managed to keep his game together over the final five holes of the day. He found himself in the unusual position of leading a major tournament, but two bogeys in the closing holes saw a one-shot lead turn into a three-shot deficit.

One man who has forged a reputation during his career as a comeback king is Leonard. He rallied from five strokes down to take the British Open at Troon in 1997, did the same to collect the Players' Championship the following year and came from four down with seven to play against José-Maria Olazabal to win the Ryder Cup for the Americans at Brookline. This time he was ahead, though. How would he cope?

Badly, as it turned out. His lead had gone by the third hole and he never recovered, winding up up in fourth place.

That left the man who didn't think that he had what it took to lead the championship, but Tiger Woods was doing his level best to chase him down. The world number one was just a single shot back after the front nine. Then he stood on the 13th green, eyeing up a putt for a birdie. He was disturbed by the uproar from the galleries surrounding the 12th green. Beem had hit a three-wood 263 yards to within 6ft of the flag – he then holed the putt for an eagle. Tiger's birdie putt became that little bit longer: he missed; then he missed again for a bogey. He bogeyed the next as well and a one-shot deficit had become five. It seemed as though the tournament was over.

The next passage of play was tournament golf at its very best as Tiger Woods rediscovered his old form and returned to his fist-pumping, birdie-blitzing best: he made birdies on the last four holes to the appreciation of the frenzied galleries and finished on nine-under par. How would Beem cope?

He would cope like a man who had been there before. The tournament was won on the 16th, when Beem holed a 35ft putt for a birdie and a two-shot lead. He parred the 17th and by the time he had found the 18th green in two, even Woods conceded defeat. Beem had the luxury of three-putting – his only three-putt of the week – to win his first major tournament.

Rich Beem used to sell mobile phones for $7 an hour in Seattle. Seven years later he stood up to the world's best player and won. It was the stuff of Hollywood dreams and even Beem could not quite believe what he had achieved.

It was the stuff that dreams are made of, but Rich Beem did an awful lot more than just hold his nerve on the way to the US PGA crown.

THE 2002 US PGA CHAMP – The Top 5

1 Rich Beem 72 66 72 68 278 -10
2 Tiger Woods 71 69 72 67 279 -9
3 Chris Riley 71 70 72 70 283 -5
4 Fred Funk 68 70 73 73 284 -4
= Justin Leonard 72 66 69 77 284 -4

THE US PGA CHAMPIONSHIP: 2003

Shaun Micheel held his nerve and produced one of the finest shots in major tournament history to see off the challenge of Chad Campbell on the final day.

With fairways averaging just 23 yards wide and with six-inch rough to punish any errant tee shot, only the best, it was thought could prosper here.

And that feeling was maintained after the first round, as Phil Mickelson fashioned a four-under par 66 to take the joint lead at the end of the first day. It could have been better, too, had the man looking to become the second lefthander of the year to win a major not missed a 10ft par putt on the final hole.

Mickelson was joined at the top of the leaderboard by Australian Rod Pampling. The 34-year-old former greenkeeper had been in this position before, at the 1999 British Open over the equally tough Carnoustie course, but he would have been hoping that history didn't repeat itself. He went out the next day to shoot an 86 and missed the cut.

Both had prospered on a difficult day when only 12 players had managed to break par. Tiger Woods, looking to avoid his first grand slam shutout since 1998, only managed to hit a total of five fairways during his opening round of 74. It was the sixth consecutive time that he had failed to break par in his first round at the majors.

It could have been worse. Nineteen members of the field failed to break 80, among them defending champion Rich Beem, whose 82 was the highest round by a defending champion since the tournament reverted to a strokeplay format in 1958.

On a course that was claiming its casualties, there was a surprise leader at the end of day two. Shaun Micheel, a man who had entered 163 tournaments on the PGA Tour but who had never one won, birdied four of the final five holes to post a two-under 68 to take a two-shot lead at the halfway stage of the 85th US PGA Championship. His halfway total was the highest total in relation to par for 23 years – the last time the tournament had been played over this venue.

Plenty of big names failed to make the cut, set at eight-over par. Among them were Davis Love III, British Open champion Ben Curtis, Rich Beem, Greg Norman, Colin Montgomerie and Tom Watson, seeking to add the US PGA title to his resumé of majors – he would have to wait another year.

True, 12 of the last 15 winners of this tournament claimed their first major titles with that victory, but few would have predicted that the final pairing for the final day would consist of Shaun Micheel – who held on to his halfway lead – and Chad Campbell – considered by many as a rising star of the PGA Tour and recently voted by his peers as the most likely player to be the game's next big thing.

Micheel, perhaps showing the nerves of a man not used to leading a major tournament, bogeyed the final three holes of the day to shoot a one-under 69. Campbell shot a best-of-the-day 65 to join him in the final pair – three strokes ahead of Masters champion Mike Weir. On a course that was playing as tough as Oak Hill, that lead might not have been as large as you might think – particularly as these were uncharted waters for both players.

Nobody seemed to tell them, though, and the pair seemingly put their situations behind them and produced a level of golf that was as good, and as captivating, as anything golf audiences had witnessed in recent years.

They started off level. Micheel birdied the first, Campbell bogeyed it and they would never be level again during the 18 holes. By the 14th hole, Campbell had managed to reduce the deficit to one: Micheel birdied it, Campbell bogeyed it – the lead stood at three. They reversed roles on the 15th when Campbell holed his 35ft birdie putt. The lead was back to one and so it remained as the pair stood on the final tee. Could Micheel hold his nerve?

You bet he could. There are few more memorable shots in golf than the must-make shot on the final hole of a tournament. Micheel produced one that will go into golfing lore. Micheel hit a seven-iron from the first cut off the rough and 165 yards away to within two inches of the flag. The galleries erupted, Micheel, with a rare display of emotion, pumped his fists on the fairway and the tournament was over.

THE 2003 US PGA CHAMP - The Top 5
1 Shaun Micheel 69 68 69 70 276 -4
2 Chad Campbell 69 72 65 72 278 -2
3 Tim Clark 72 70 68 69 279 -1
4 Alex Dejka 74 69 68 69 280 E
5 Ernie Els 71 70 70 71 282 +2
= Jay Haas 70 74 69 69 282 +2

Shaun Micheel led the field throughout the final round and sealed his first major victory with a spectacular shot on the final hole.

THE US PGA CHAMPIONSHIP: 2004

Vijay Singh continued his hot run of form in 2004 to see off Justin Leonard and Chris DiMarco to win the title as the US PGA found a new venue at Whistling Straits.

Few knew what to expect as the players made their way to the 86th US PGA Championship. They were heading for a course that was the longest in the history of the tournament and also the newest to stage a major championship. Whistling Straits, possessed an incredible 1,400 bunkers, and would be the nearest that you could get to a links-style environment in the United States.

With strong winds predicted for the first day, the officials brought three of the tees forward and placed the flags in slightly generous positions. The expected wind never arrived.

Darren Clarke was one of many to take advantage of the favourable conditions, firing a course-record seven-under par. Any talk of a brutally difficult course became a hushed whisper as the Northern Irishman reeled off four straight birdies on

his opening four holes to forge clear of the field: his 65 was the lowest opening round in a major since Chris DiMarco shot a 65 on the first day of the Masters in 2001.

A shot behind Clarke stood Ernie Els and Justin Leonard. Among the group a further shot down was the man who had been in the hottest form all year, Vijay Singh. The Fijian had switched from using a broomhandle putter to a conventional one just two weeks before the start of the tournament: the change seemed to be working for him.

It was hard to see which part of Tiger Woods's game was working. The world number one shot a three-over 75 on day one to leave him nine shots off the pace and in serious danger of missing the cut.

The Whistling Straits course failed to find its bite on the second day

as well, despite being back to its full length. At the end of it all, Vijay Singh and Justin Leonard stood on top of the leaderboard. Singh, the champion in 1998, carded a 68, one better than Leonard – they both sat on nine-under at the halfway stage. Els, who had led the field through nine holes, was a shot further back.

It was a day of triumph for Woods, as well. Not so long ago the golfing world was wondering what it would take to stop him from winning everything. These days he seems to spend most of his time having a personal competition with the cut mark: he managed to win this battle, but only after making birdies on three of the last six holes. At nine strokes off the lead, it seemed as though Tiger would have to wait until 2005 for a ninth major victory.

Saturday, just as had been the case on Friday, was all about Singh and Leonard. As the final round dawned, the Fijian would hold a one-stroke lead over the American after posting a 69 to the latter's 70. Phil Mickelson, aided by a red-hot putter, brought himself back into contention with a best-of-the-day 67, but at four strokes off the pace he would have to have a repeat performance if he wanted to win his second major of the year.

The early momentum on the final day quickly switched to Justin Leonard. The American had caught up with Singh as early as the third hole, when he holed a birdie attempt from 15ft. He moved clear at the fourth when the Fijian made a double-bogey, but the lead became

one when Leonard missed a short putt to save par on the seventh. Pars followed on the eighth and the ninth.

But while the focus of attention was on the leading group, someone was starting to make his move: not Mickelson or Els, but Chris Di Marco. The American made birdies on nine, 11 and 12 to move to ten-under – a score that he would finish on to set the clubhouse target.

When Leonard birdied the 13th it took him two shots clear once more, but he bogeyed the 14th. When the American arrived on the 18th tee, he had a one-shot lead over DiMarco and Singh who both stood on ten-under. Leonard missed his approach to the green and faced a 12ft, par-saving putt for the tournament. He missed: the three were in a play-off.

And something happened in the first hole of the three-hole play-off that had not happened all day: Vijay Singh rolled in a putt from 10ft to make birdie. Two pars over the next two holes were enough to see him to a second US PGA title. For Leonard it was the second time in two years that he had had a shot at the title, and the second time in two years that he had blown it. For Singh it was a sweet victory, he had claimed his third major title.

Whistling Straits, set on the shores of Lake Michigan, was a welcome addition as a US PGA Championship venue.

THE US PGA CHAMPIONSHIP: 2005

Phil Mickelson stole the limelight at Baltusrol Golf Club, New Jersey, leading the tournament from wire to wire to collect his second major.

After a first round played in sweltering heat, the leaderboard had a congested feel to it, with six players sitting on three-under 67, including Phil Mickelson, whose back-nine charge (including three birdies) sent a surge of electricity through the galleries. However, in what had been a year to remember for Tiger Woods, the first round turned out to be a day to forget. The world No.1 got off to a stumbling start and posted a five-over 75 – his worst-ever start in a major as a professional.

In the second round, Mickelson tore through the front nine and scrambled on the back nine to post a five-under 65 and establish a three-stroke lead on eight-under par. American Jerry Kelly matched Mickelson's score to move to second on five-under. Woods made a late charge, holing a do-or-die birdie putt on 18 to sit right on the cut line at four-over.

The relentless heat continued on day three. Mickelson recovered from a nervous start to post a two-over 72 that left him on six-under for the tournament and in a tie for the lead with Love III (68). The round of the day belonged to Denmark's Thomas Björn, whose seven-under 63 – matching the best-ever round in a major – moved him to five-under and into third place. Four players sat a shot back in fourth. Woods posted his best round of the week (66) to move to level par, six shots off the lead.

When lightning brought play to a premature halt on Sunday, meaning the climax would have to wait for Monday morning, the tournament had been given an unexpected twist: Woods, who birdied the final two holes for a closing 68, was the clubhouse leader on two-under, but with several players still to complete their rounds – Mickelson, on the 14th hole when the sirens sounded, had slipped to four-under, a single stroke ahead of Steve Elkington – few expected the world No.1 to be

celebrating his 11th major victory the following day.

And so it proved. Elkington (71) and Björn (72) finished on three-under – although both missed birdie attempts on the final hole. By the time Mickelson arrived at the par-five 18th on the same score, he knew he needed a birdie for victory. He found the middle of the fairway off the tee and left his second in deep rough, but then produced the shot of

a champion, pitching to 3ft to leave a straightforward putt for the title. The man dubbed the best player never to win a major had now won two of them – and, in this form, it seemed certain more would follow.

THE 2005 US PGA CHAMP – The Top 5
1 Phil Mickelson 67 65 72 72 276 -4
2 Thomas Björn 71 71 63 72 277 -3
= Steve Elkington 68 70 68 71 277 -3
4 Davis Love III 68 68 68 74 278 -2
= Tiger Woods 75 69 66 68 278 -2

American Phil Mickelson was the class act of the field at Baltusrol, thrilling the vocal New Jersey galleries en route to claiming his second major.

THE US PGA CHAMPIONSHIP: 2006

World number one Tiger Woods was the class act of the field, producing a dominant performance in the final round to coast to a five-shot victory to collect his 12th major.

The pairing together of the year's three major winners – Phil Mickelson (US Masters), Geoff Ogilvy (US Open) and Tiger Woods (British Open) – may have attracted the majority of the crowds and a huge media scrum, but, on a day that yielded 60 under-par rounds (a record for any round in the US PGA Championship), all three of them would have been disappointed with their opening rounds of three-under par. Instead, the first-round headlines belonged to two lesser highlights: Lucas Glover and Chris Riley, who both shot six-under 66 to sit on top of the leaderboard.

A surprisingly generous course greeted the players for the second day running on Friday and, yet again, the field took full advantage. Following a day that saw 61 sub-par rounds and the tournament's lowest cut mark in relation to par since Riviera in 1995 (even-par), the 88th US PGA Championship was loaded with possibilities and subplots as a mere four shots separated the top 24 players. There were four joint leaders (on eight-under): Luke Donald and Henrik Stenson (seeking to become the first Europeans for 76 years to win the tournament – following Tommy Armour's victory at Fresh Meadows in 1930), Tim Herron and Billy Andrade. But it was the presence of Tiger Woods that loomed largest over the leaderboard: the world No.1 fired a four-under 68 to sit a single shot off the lead, alongside Ogilvy and Davis Love III.

Eleven-time major-winner Woods was in red-hot form in the third round, playing supreme golf to post a seven-under 65, equalling the course record, to move to 14-under par for the tournament and into a share of the lead with Donald (66). Woods, with an 11-0 record in majors when he had at least a share of the 54-hole lead, remained the firm favourite, but, over a forgiving course that was throwing up birdie opportunities by the dozen, and with six players within four shots of the lead, the tournament was still wide open.

Not for long, as, yet again, Woods overwhelmed the competition. He started with a birdie on the first hole of the day to take the outright lead and no one caught him the rest of the day. He established a four-shot lead by the turn, added a solitary birdie to seven ground-out pars by the time he reached the 18th to stretch the lead to five and tapped in for a routine par at the last to win his 12th major championship. Few of them had come more easily.

"I just had one of those magical days on the greens today," said the world no.1. "I just felt like if I got the ball anywhere on the green, I could make it. It's not too often you get days like that, and I happened to have it on the final round of a major championship."

Tiger Woods was in imperious form at Medinah, shooting four sub-70 rounds and easing to a third US PGA title (and 12th major) by five shots.

THE 2006 US PGA CHAMP – The Top 5
1 Tiger Woods 69 68 65 68 270 -18
2 Shaun Micheel 69 70 67 69 275 -13
3 Luke Donald 68 68 66 74 276 -12
= Sergio García 69 70 67 70 276 -12
= Adam Scott 71 69 69 67 276 -12

THE US PGA CHAMPIONSHIP: 2007

In blistering heat, Tiger Woods, defending the title he had won the previous year at Medinah, outlasted the rest of the field to win by two shots and collect his 13th major.

After a first round played out in sweltering heat and gusting winds, the US PGA leaderboard was headed by some unusual names. England's Graeme Storm posted a bogey-free, round-of-the-day, five-under 65 to lead a major tournament for the first time. Two strokes back, remarkably, lay John Daly. The two-time major winner took to the course he had not seen for 13 years without playing a practice round and shot an improbable three-under 67 – his best round at the US PGA for ten years. Defending champion Tiger Woods, in last-chance saloon for a major victory in 2007, had to settle for a 71.

The second round belonged to Woods. The world No.1 fired one of the greatest rounds of his career, a seven-under 63, and came within a whisker of recording the lowest-ever round in a major championship. Going for a birdie on 18 for a 62, Woods watched on as the ball, agonizingly, lipped out of the hole in horseshoe fashion before he tapped in for par. The chance for the outright record may have gone, but Woods would have been delighted to take a two-shot lead over Scott Verplank (who shot a bogey-free 66) into the third round.

The world No.1's third-round efforts may not have been as spectacular as those in the second, but, in torrid conditions, Woods produced a notably measured round and shot a one-under 69, to move to seven-under for the tournament and extend his lead from two shots to three. Stephen Ames, who shot his third consecutive round in the 60s (69), sat in second on four-under. However, given that Woods had never lost a major when holding at least a share of the 54-hole lead – or any tournament anywhere in the world when leading by more than one shot going into the final round – the signs were ominous. Someone would have to produce something special to prevent Woods from collecting his 13th major.

And, during a final round that saw temperatures hit 102 degrees Fahrenheit (the day saw 264 people at the course treated for heat stroke), nobody did, even though Woods failed to produce the dominant display many expected of him. It looked like business as usual when the world No.1 made birdies on 7 and 8 to extend his lead to five shots. But as others began their last-gasp charge – notably Ernie Els and Woody Austin – Woods faltered.

When he made bogey on 14, his lead was down to one. He responded in style, making a birdie on 15 and, minor wobble over, closed out with three straight pars for a one-under 69 and, in the end, a comfortable two-shot victory.

THE 2007 US PGA CHAMP – The Top 5
1 Tiger Woods 71 63 69 69 272 -8
2 Woody Austin 68 70 69 67 274 -6
3 Ernie Els 72 68 69 66 275 -5
4 John Senden 69 70 69 71 279 -1
= Arron Oberholser 68 72 70 69 279 -1

A second-round 63 (equalling the lowest-ever round in a major championship) proved the catalyst for Tiger Woods as he eased to a two-stroke victory and a 13th major title.

THE US PGA CHAMPIONSHIP: 2008

The outcome of the 2008 US PGA Championship came down to a 36-hole shootout on the final day that saw Sergio Garcia squander yet another opportunity to win and Padraig Harrington take full advantage of the Spaniard's slip.

The free-scoring course set-ups of the previous two US PGA Championships fast became a distant memory when the players arrived at notorious Oakland Hills, with the greens in particular rated the hardest anyone had seen all year, Augusta National included. As a result, only seven of the field of 156 players remained under par when darkness brought the first round to a premature halt with 18 players unable to finish their rounds. Sweden's Robert Karlsson and India's Jeev Milkha Singh held the clubhouse lead on two-under par (68).

The second day's headlines belonged to big-hitting American JB Holmes, who fired a two-under 68 to take the halfway lead on one-under, one shot ahead of compatriot Ben Curtis, South Korea's Charlie Wi and England's Justin Rose. With 20 players within four shots of the lead going into the weekend, however, this tournament was still very much up for grabs.

Before thunderstorms brought the third round to a premature halt, Andres Romero fired a five-under 65 – the joint lowest round in a major at Oakland Hills – to move to two-over for the tournament. But the Argentine was one of only 25 players (of the 73 left in the field) to have finished their round: with 36-hole leader Holmes yet to start his third round, Sunday promised to be the first 36-hole final day of a major for 40 years – on a course that would have been considerably subdued by the rain.

When play resumed on Sunday morning, Curtis fired a two-under 66 to take a one-shot lead into the final round which would be played in threesomes. Overnight leader Holmes and Sweden's Henrik Stenson (both on one-under for the tournament) would make up the final group. Sergio Garcia and British Open champion Padraig Harrington were also still very much in contention on one-over par.

Garcia got off to a blistering start in the final round, making a birdie and an eagle in the first two holes to take the outright lead. Playing flawless, bogey-free golf through the first 15 holes, the Spaniard seemed set to end his major tournament famine, but then, on the 16th, disaster struck. Holding a slender one-stroke lead over Harrington and Curtis, Garcia fired at the pin and watched in despair as his ball trickled into the pond. A bogey left him in a three-way tie for the lead with two to play. On the par-three 17th, moments after Harrington rolled in a 10ft putt for birdie and the lead, Garcia missed a four-foot birdie attempt of his own. The Irishman never looked back, sealing a two-stroke victory with a nerveless 15ft putt for par on 18.

THE 2008 US PGA CHAMP - The Top 5
1 Pádraig Harrington 71 74 66 66 277 -3
2 Sergio García 69 73 69 68 279 -1
= Ben Curtis 73 67 68 71 279 -1
4 Camilo Villegas 74 72 67 68 281 +1
= Henrik Stenson 71 70 68 72 281 +1

Victory by two strokes over Sergio Garcia and Ben Curtis in the 2008 US PGA Championship at Oakland Hills meant that Padraig Harrington had won three of the previous seven majors.

THE US PGA CHAMPIONSHIP: 2009

In a dramatic final-round South Korea's YE Yang first chased down and then passed the world No.1 Tiger Woods to become the first Asian-born winner of a major championship in history.

Pre-tournament favourite Tiger Woods started his quest for a 15th Major title in blistering fashion, firing a five-under 65 over a stretched Hazeltine National – at 7,674 yards it was the longest in major championship history – to build a one-shot lead over defending champion Padraig Harrington. It was only the third time in his career that Woods had opened a major with a bogey-free round: on the other two occasions – at the US and British Opens in 2000 – he had gone to win by a combined 23 shots. The omens for the rest of the field were not good.

Woods's seemingly uncontested march to a fifth US PGA title continued unabated in the second round. The world No.1 reeled off three straight birdies on 16, 17 and 18 for a two-under 70 that handed him a four-shot lead over a group of five players at the halfway stage. The 84th US PGA Championship was fast becoming a coronation, and, for the rest of the field, there were some startling figures to back it up: Woods had an 8-0 record in majors when leading after 36 holes and had never lost a tournament anywhere in the world when leading going into the weekend.

But on Saturday, that coronation turned into a contest. While Woods played conservatively, grinding out a one-under 71 to move to eight-under, others made their charge. Harrington, who made his only bogey of the day on 18, posted a three-under 69 to move within two shots of Woods. The round

of the day, however, belonged to South Korea's YE Yang, whose five-under 67 propelled him to second alongside Harrington and into Sunday's final group with Woods – something that would be an entirely new experience for the 37-year-old world No.1 10.

It inspired him. In a pulsating final round, Yang did something no other player had achieved before him: he chased down Tiger Woods in the final round of a major and beat him. The South Korean matched the world No.1 stroke for stroke over the opening holes and finally caught him by the turn. Still tied with five holes to play, Yang chipped in from 60ft for eagle on 14 to take the lead. Just when a three-putt bogey on 17 seemed to indicate nerves were getting the better of him, he nailed his approach on 18 to within 12ft and closed out for a two-stroke

win. Woods's remarkable streak when leading a major going into the final round was over and Yang had become the first-ever Asian-born player to capture a major title.

THE 2009 US PGA CHAMP – The Top 5
1 Yang Yong-eun 73-70-67-70 280 +8
2 Tiger Woods 67-70-71-75=283 +5
3 Rory McIlroy 71-73-71-70=285 +3
4 Lee Westwood 70-72-73-70 285 +3
5 Lucas Glover 71-70-71-74=286 +2

Y.E. Yang made history at Hazeltine when he outlasted Tiger Woods over the back nine to collect the 2009 US PGA Championship title to become the first Asian-born major winner.

THE RYDER CUP

Year	Venue	United States	GB and I
1927	Worcester, Ma	9½: W Hagen	2½: T Ray
1929	Moortown, Leeds	5: W Hagen	7: G Duncan
1931	Scioto, Columbus, Oh	9: W Hagen	3: C A Whitcombe
1933	Southport and Ainsdale, Lancashire	5½: W Hagen	6½: J H Taylor*
1935	Ridgewood, NJ	9: W Hagen	3: C A Whitcombe
1937	Southport and Ainsdale	8: W Hagen*	4: C A Whitcombe
1939–45	No matches		
1947	Portland, Or	11: B Hogan	1: T H Cotton
1949	Ganton, Yorkshire	7: B Hogan*	5: C A Whitcombe*
1951	Pinehurst, NC	9½: S Snead	2½: A J Lacey*
1953	Wentworth, Surrey	6½: L Mangrum	5½: T H Cotton*
1955	Thunderbird Club, Ca	8: C Harbert	4: D J Rees
1957	Lindrick, Notts	4½: J Burke	7½: D J Rees
1959	Eldorado CC, Ca	8½: S Snead	3½: D J Rees
1961	Lytham, Lancs	14½: J Barber	9½: D J Rees
1963	Atlanta, Ga	23: A Palmer	9: J Fallon*
1965	Royal Birkdale, Southport	19½: B Nelson*	12½: H Weetman*
1967	Houston, Tx	23½: B Hogan*	8½: D J Rees*
1969	Royal Birkdale, Southport	16: S Snead*	16: E C Brown*
1971	St Louis, Mo	19: J Hebert*	13: E C Brown*
1973	Muirfield, Scotland	19: J Burke*	13: B J Hunt*
1975	Laurel Valley, Pa	21: A Palmer*	11: B J Hunt*
1977	Lytham, Lancs	12½: D Finsterwald*	7½: B Huggett*
1979	The Greenbrier, WV	17: W Casper*	11: J Jacobs*

(* = non-playing)

Year	Venue	United States	Europe
1981	Walton Heath, Surrey	18½: D Marr*	9½: J Jacobs*
1983	PGA National, Fl	14½: J Nicklaus*	13½: T Jacklin*
1985	The Belfry, West Midlands	11½: L Trevino*	16½: T Jacklin*
1987	Muirfield Village, Columbus, Oh	13: J Nicklaus*	15: T Jacklin*
1989	The Belfry, West Midlands	14: R Floyd*	14: T Jacklin*
1991	Kiawah Island, SC	14½: D Stockton*	13½: B Gallacher*
1993	The Belfry, West Midlands	15: T Watson*	13: B Gallacher*
1995	Rochester, NY	13½: L Wadkins*	14½: B Gallacher*
1997	Valderrama, Spain	13½: T Kite*	14½: S Ballesteros*
1999	Brookline CC, Ma	14½: B Crenshaw*	13½: M James*
2002	The Belfy, West Midlands	12½: C Strange*	15½: S Torrance*
2004	Oakland Hills CC, Mi	9½: H Sutton*	18½: B Langer*
2006	The K Club, Ireland	9½: Tom Lehman*	18½: Ian Woosnam*
2008	Valhalla, Louisville, Ky	16½: Paul Azinger*	11½: Nick Faldo

(* = non-playing)

From the first Ryder Cup match between the United States and Britain up to the first between the US and Europe, the American advantage in points scored, in 22 matches, surpassed three figures. In the first eight US v. Europe cup meetings, total American advantage was 12 points. The improvement was not immediate.

Even the most rock-ribbed Euro sceptic could not discount the value to the Ryder Cup and golf in general of the European connection, which was first mooted seriously at the last "old-style" cup match at Lytham. The late Earl of Derby, who was President of the PGA, discussed the idea with Jack Nicklaus, Henry Poe, Lord Derby's opposite number at the US PGA, and senior British professional Neil Coles.

In 1979, at The Greenbrier, West Virginia, with Severiano Ballesteros and Antonio Garrido of Spain in the team led by John Jacobs, the new series began – not too well, as it turned out, for the brand new team of Europe.

Europe's "banker", Ballesteros, ran into a jinx, in the smooth-swinging shape of Larry Nelson, to whom he lost in singles and three times in partnership with Garrido, though the Spaniards did beat Fuzzy Zoeller and Hubert Green. All told, the result was dustier than the usual one.

The second European match, at Walton Heath, was dominated by an American side which many good judges believe to have been the equal of any sent forth by the US PGA. Moreover Europe, again led by Jacobs, were handicapped by the absence of Ballesteros and Tony Jacklin, who was less than pleased that Mark James had been chosen in his stead.

Non-selection of the two players, who alone in the European ranks had won major championships in Britain and the United States, was an even bigger mistake in hindsight than it seemed at the time. This was the team in which Bernhard Langer, Scotland's Sam Torrance, José-Maria Canizares and Manuel Pinero were all making their first appearances. All were to play a part in European victories, and the missing pair's experience might have inspired these new boys to even greater heights. Five points behind entering the singles, Europe wound up losing by nine.

At the PGA National, Palm Beach Gardens, Florida, in 1983, Europe came within a putt or two of beating the US on their own soil. Even in the days when there were only 12 points at stake, Britain and Ireland had never got closer than a four-point deficit in America. To start with, strength in depth and depth of experience were at last approaching American standards … but not yet quite close enough, it transpired.

There was certainly experience at the helm, where non-playing captain Jacklin was getting powerful support from his top-of-the-draw men. Nick Faldo was fulfilling his early promise, and won three times out of four in company with Langer. He also beat Jay Haas. After an initial stumble, Masters champion Seve Ballesteros partnered new boy Paul Way to two wins and a half. Then, after being three up against Fuzzy Zoeller, he had to claw his way back to a half, notably with a wood shot from a bunker that impressed many witnesses as the best shot they had ever seen.

Hearts pounded faster on both sides as, in the last three matches, Brown easily beat Raymond Floyd, but Lanny Wadkins was relentlessly cutting back Canizares's three-hole lead, and Gallacher was in a pressure

Walter Hagen (right) led the United States into their first six Ryder Cup matches, winning four and losing two of them.

cooker of a match against Watson. Wadkins' pitch almost to "gimme" range at the 18th squeezed a half out of Canizares, and Gallacher said later of his four-footer for a half against Watson: "I still think to this day that I hit a good putt. There was a subtle break but I missed and that was it, two and one." And that was it, 14½ to 13½ for the United States, a score that sold any number of tickets for the 1985 battle at British PGA HQ, The Belfry.

This new course had several holes that were, in the view of some critics, not good enough for a cup match. Moreover the flat terrain restricted spectators' view of play. Nevertheless some 27,000 of them celebrated a victory for Europe, with Concorde flying over the course in a roaring celebration of European togetherness.

A five-point win for Europe was promise of giant gates for future cup matches, and total vindication

for the words of Jack Nicklaus almost a decade earlier: "It is vital to widen the selection procedures if the Ryder Cup is to continue to enjoy its past prestige."

In the British Isles the cup had never lost its prestige, even when the US were handing out hidings every two years. This was because opportunities to see the leading American players were limited, and for the most part eagerly taken up. Interest in the United States, however, was dwindling. Europe's victory at The Belfry, though, had elevated the status of the Ryder Cup to Open Championship standards and, in the opinion of some, even beyond.

Dispossessing the American team, led by non-playing Lee Trevino, of the cup for the first time since Dai Rees scored his greatest triumph as player and leader in 1957 at Lindrick was achieved, at last, with gratifying ease at The Belfry. Here, Europe performed

the rare feat of winning the singles by three points after finishing fourballs and foursomes two ahead. Ironically, the two leading European players of the era barely contributed in singles, Faldo losing to Hubert Green and Ballesteros halving with Tom Kite.

It was now that the new-found strength in depth came to the aid of Jacklin in his second stint as captain, for Pinero gave Europe a flying start on the final day by beating Lanny Wadkins, and Lyle, Langer, Torrance and Clark made a clean sweep of the middle four matches in the singles order.

To Sam Torrance fell the great moment: his opponent Andy North put his drive into the water at the 18th, Sam Torrance hit his ball a vast distance into position A, and sank the birdie putt offered by his accurate approach.

Concorde took the British team to Ohio for the 1987 match, Jacklin having insisted that all of the

European planning for the defence of the cup should be top bracket.

The excitement around Muirfield Village was not merely intense over the last couple of hours; it was almost insupportable. The Ryder Cup, 1980s style, had been given the imprimatur of live coverage by US television, a complete reversal of previous media disinterest. An all-ticket crowd of 25,000 was another reward for the success of the Nicklaus European initiative.

Seve Ballesteros and José-Maria Olazabal netted three points out of four, and Faldo and Woosnam dropped only half a point out of four, in the process beating Wadkins and Masters champion Larry Mize after falling four holes behind. Lyle and Langer also contributed three points. So Europe led by five as the singles began; but the match was far from decided.

America won five and halved one of the top eight singles matches,

Jack Nicklaus and Tony Jacklin have provided many memorable Ryder Cup moments - none more so than at Birkdale in 1969.

Andy Bean beginning the rally with a last-hole victory over the previously unbeaten Ian Woosnam. It was with considerable relief that Jacklin took in the sight of what looked like the world's happiest golfer, Eamonn Darcy, repeatedly shaking his fist after holing a testing downhill putt to beat Crenshaw by one hole. On the American side, Nelson suffered his first defeats, three of them, in 13 starts, and Nicklauss' score as captain was now one win, one defeat. This was the first time America had lost a home Ryder Cup match.

The Ryder Cup fortunes of the two captains had never lacked dramatic qualities, notably in 1969 at Birkdale, where 16-16 was the result under the ruling 32-match format. After getting his four on the final green

from 3ft, Nicklaus gave an 18-inch putt to Jacklin which brought up the tied score, saying that he was sure Jacklin would have holed it, "but I was not prepared to see you miss". Jacklin, the Open champion, was not to see Nicklaus and Co. beaten for many years. The 32-match format gave Jacklin two singles against Nicklaus, and he had halved one and won the other.

The next Ryder Cup extravaganza at The Belfry in 1989 went all the way through hours of tension to a final cliff-hanging and decisive moment: a cup-saving long-iron shot across the lake at The Belfry's finishing hole that Christy O'Connor Jr will never forget, nor the multitudes who saw him ... the television audience was estimated at 200 million.

Europe, without Sandy Lyle at his own request owing to lack of form, were two clear as the singles began. Paul Azinger and Chip Beck, both making their first cup appearances, rapidly evened the score against the seasoned Ballesteros and Langer. They had already gained two points in two starts as partners. Prospects now began to look bleak, with Mark James the only leader lower down the order. He beat Mark O'Meara at the 16th, and Olazabal and Ronan Rafferty fought back to right the ship. The crux of the matter came with that O'Connor shot to foil Fred Couples, and Canizares's cool long putt on the last, where, as it turned out, Ken Green three-putted the cup away.

A draw at 14 each fired the Americans to prepare a hot welcome in 1991 for the team led by Jacklin's successor, Bernard Gallacher, at a new layout on Kiawah Island, South Carolina. The media hyped the match as "The War on the Shore", a phrase which was anathema to traditionalists and not too well received by the players.

Again the tension was almost beyond bearing, especially as this

time the reckoning was 8-8 with the singles to come, which had so often produced a final-day bonanza for the Americans. Only 11 singles were to be played, since Steve Pate, bruised in a car crash the previous Wednesday, had played in one fourball, with Corey Pavin, and lost, and now withdrew. So a half was agreed with David Gilford. Originally Pate had been due to play Ballesteros, who had dropped only half a point throughout - a good switch for US captain Dave Stockton.

Azinger and Beck were again the US singles heroes, as were Pavin,

Couples and Wadkins, though an effective first appearance was made by Paul Broadhurst for Europe, and Colin Montgomerie too, for he got a half against Mark Calcavecchia by winning all of the last four holes. This time the clincher was not a long iron, but a not very long putt. Langer, who had come back from behind against Hale Irwin, faced it for par and a win and a tied match, for Irwin had already bogeyed. He missed, right edge, and - to a mighty roar - the Ryder Cup was held aloft by Stockton.

The 1993 meeting was again at

Tom Watson and Jack Nicklaus formed part of the United States team at Walton Heath in 1981 which is considered by many to be the strongest ever to have been assembled.

José-Maria Olazabal and Severiano Ballesteros formed an almost impregnable pairing: the Spaniards' contribution to the Cup was rewarded when the 1997 event was played at Valderrama.

The Belfry, but the 1997 European staging was earmarked for Spain, whose players had done so much to bring a new vitality to Ryder Cup play. Tom Watson took up the American leadership with Raymond Floyd, captain when they were beaten in 1989, in the team; for Europe, Bernard Gallacher led again, and had problems. Ballesteros asked to be dropped from his partnership with Olazabal on the grounds of loss of form, though the pair had won twice in three starts. Gallacher, controversially, conceded to him. Joakim Haeggman joined Olazabal, and they lost. Sam Torrance was sidelined by a poisoned toe.

Gallacher was buoyed up by a wonderful display by new cup selection, Midlander Peter Baker, who had little sleep, because of his daughter's illness, before he beat Corey Pavin on the final day. But elsewhere in singles, the old American magic worked again, despite a stunning hole-in-one by Faldo in holding Azinger. The upshot was that the Americans eased to a two-point victory. All attention turned towards 1995 and the next meeting of the Ryder Cup at Oak Hill.

RYDER CUP: 1995

The Europeans rallied on the final day to take the singles series and win back the Ryder Cup. It was a particularly special moment for their captain, Bernard Gallacher.

There was an unusual air of pessimism surrounding the European team as they made their way to play on US Open-style course Oak Hill.

But the pessimism was unusual as, on paper, the American team sheet seemed as though it was one of the weakest US teams for a long time.

This sense was exacerbated when captain Lanny Wadkins inexplicably selected the horribly out of form Curtis Strange as his wild-card pick, ahead of reigning US Open champion Lee Janzen. It all suggested that this would be a lot closer than those in the European ranks seemed to think.

And so it proved on an overcast, rainy opening day. There was nothing to choose between the two teams after the opening series of foursomes. Davis Love III and Jeff Maggert (4&3) defeated Mark James and Howard Clark and Corey Pavin and Tom Lehman (1 up) got the better of Nick Faldo and Colin Mongomerie, but the Europeans evened things up with wins for Sam Torrance and Costantino Rocca, 3&2 over Jay Haas and Fred Couples and Bernhard Langer and Per-Ulrik Johannson won the last hole of the morning to beat Ben Crenshaw and Curtis Strange.

It was a different story in the afternoon fourballs, though. The Americans won the series 3-1: and their three victories oozed comfort. The only bright note for the Europeans was a victory for David Gilford and Seve Ballesteros - an inspired pairing by captain Bernard Gallacher. The pair ran out 4&3 winners over Peter Jacobsen and Brad Faxon.

The Europeans bounced back the following morning, reversing the 3-1 deficit of the previous afternoon to bring the tie back to 6-6. Costantino Rocca showed his true ball-striking abilities with a hole-in-one to partner Sam Torrance to a crushing 6&5 victory over Love and Maggert.

The momentum continued as Faldo and Montgomerie (4&2) beat Strange and Haas and Langer and Gilford (4&3) put away Pavin and Lehman.

Any cheers ringing around the Oak Hill course in the afternoon were American, though. They turned the tables once more to take a 9-7 advantage into the final day. The climax came when Corey Pavin chipped in from 20ft to gain the win over Faldo and Langer - in a match that had taken the best part of six hours: it may have been slow, but it was gripping stuff.

The advantage lay with the Americans: they only needed to win five out of the 12 singles matches to retain the cup. History would suggest otherwise. The Europeans had only won the singles series once, in 1985.

There was an air of defiance about the European team as the singles matches got underway. It was the Americans who got off to the better start, though. Lehman beat a struggling Ballesteros 4&3 and Love III beat Rocca 3&2 to give the Americans an 11-8 advantage: the home side only needed another three points to retain the cup.

But things started to change. Inspired perhaps by Howard Clark's hole-in-one on the 14th, the Europeans began to claw their way back into the match. Five singles matches would make their way to the final hole: tellingly, perhaps, Europe would emerge with four-and-a-half points out of those five ties.

First came Howard Clark, who held his nerve to emerge victorious over Peter Jacobsen. Then Ian Woosnam and Fred Couples shared the spoils. Then David Gilford got the better of Brad Faxon to gain a vital point, but most of all, then came Nick Faldo and Philip Walton.

All eyes were on the Faldo-Strange match: notably because of the latter's controversial selection. The American was 1 up with two to play: he bogeyed the 17th and Faldo's par brought the match back to all-square. Faldo then pitched to within feet of the flag from 90 yards and holed the putt for par. Strange made another bogey: the man who had been brought into the US team because of his "grit and tenacity" had played the last three holes bogey-bogey-bogey - and handed the Europeans a vital point. Europe only needed one more for victory, though.

And Philip Walton made them sweat. Three up with three to play, it was 1 up with one to play as he stood on the 18th tee with Jay Haas. The American pulled his drive and the Irishman could afford to take a bogey on the final hole to hand the Europeans victory. That's exactly what he took and the celebrations started.

It was a sweet moment for captain Bernard Gallacher: in his previous nine times as a player and captain he had always been on the losing side. On this occasion, it was tenth time lucky.

1995 RYDER CUP
OAK HILL COUNTRY CLUB, NEW YORK, UNITED STATES
Captains: L Wadkins (United States)
B Gallacher (Europe)

Friday Fourballs: 2-2
Friday Foursomes: United States 3- 1
Saturday Foursomes: Europe 3-1
Saturday Fourballs: United States 3-1
Sunday Singles: Europe 7½-4½

Overall: Europe 14½ United States 13½
Europe win the Ryder Cup

It was a victory to savour for European captain Bernard Gallacher - it was his first success in ten attempts over the United States as either a player or captain.

RYDER CUP: 1997

When the Ryder Cup moved to Spain there was only one man who could possibly have led the European challenge - and Seve Ballesteros proved an inspirational leader.

On paper, at least, it looked like an uneven contest as the Ryder Cup. The United States team boasted seven of the world's top-12 players and had three of the year's four major winners among their ranks.

As dark clouds gathered over the Valderrama course, the golfing world was reminded why the Ryder Cup remains the brightest jewel in the game's crown. There were two matches still to be decided as darkness fell, but of the six completed on the first day, four of them had gone all the way to the 18th hole: the outcome of the final-hole deciders was 2-2.

The only two completed matches that did not go all the way both involved Tiger Woods. Playing with his close friend Mark O'Meara, the pair saw off Colin Montgomerie and Bernhard Langer in the morning fourballs 3&2. The European pair turned the tables in the afternoon foursomes match, trouncing the good friends 5&3. Europe ended the day all-square and had dampened any talk of an American rout.

That talk became the faintest of whispers on a Saturday when captain Seve started to weave his magic. As darkness brought a premature halt to proceedings for the second successive day, the Europeans had claimed an unlikely six points out of the seven on offer.

Having mustered only half a point from the two matches still left out on the course from the previous day - Faldo's win saw him become the leading points winner in the history of the Ryder Cup - US captain Tom Kite sent out his big guns for the morning's fourball matches. They were duly silenced. The Love-Couples,

Leonard-Faxon, Woods-O'Meara and Mickelson-Lehman pairings managed only half a point between them.

They didn't play badly, far from it, it's just that the Europeans played, and in particular putted, better. With Seve haring around the course in his golf buggy, offering advice here, cajoling there - one wit suggested that there must have been several Seve-clones on the course, such was his omnipresence - the Europeans were inspired, rolling in putts all over.

When the only afternoon match completed saw Montgomerie and Langer defeat Janzen and Furyk on the final hole, the Americans were left with a mountain to climb of Everest proportions. They trailed by 9-4: equalling the largest margin in the history of the event after two days. No team has ever trailed by more than two points going into the singles matches and emerged victorious in the 70-year history of the event.

That five-point lead was maintained after the completion of the three unfinished matches early on Sunday morning. The Europeans led 10½-5½ and needed only three-and-a-half points to retain the cup.

But when Fred Couples trounced Ian Woosnam 8&7 in the first of the singles matches - it equalled the record margin of victory in the event and left the Welshman still searching for a singles win after eight attempts - it looked as though the win had galvanized the Americans.

And then came the hammer blows. First Per-Ulrik Johannson saw off Davis Love III, 3&2, and then came the biggest body blow of them all. Tiger Woods's game crumbled in the face of some inspired golf from

Victory was sweet for the European side as they withstood a last-day fightback from the United States to claim a one-point victory.

Costantino Rocca, and the Italian emerged victorious (4&2) to take the biggest scalp in the game. It was a huge win for the Europeans.

Thomas Bjorn mounted the comeback of the week, rallying from four down after four to squeeze a half out of Justin Leonard, but wins for Mickelson and O'Meara kept the American ball rolling ...

Indeed, they started to mount a challenge. Lee Janzen, one down on the 17th, drilled an iron to within 15ft and holed the putt to take his match with José-Maria Olazabal to the wire. He won the next as well to take the tie. Moments later, Brad Faxon fired his wedge to 12ft to keep his match with Bernhard Langer alive. Maggert holed a putt to defeat Lee Westwood 3&2 ... the score had closed to 13-11.

But the rally died almost as quickly as it had begun. Faxon missed the putt, Langer had won 2&1 and Europe had reached the 14 points that they needed to retain the cup.

As the rain started to pour and as darkness started to envelop the course, Colin Montgomerie gained the extra half point that the Europeans so badly wanted for an outright win. The Scot's approach shot on 18 nestled next to the cup: he conceded Scott Hoch's long par putt, the American did the same and the Europeans had won the cup outright.

The United States had taken eight out of a possible 12 points in the singles matches: it had not been enough. And so thousands of rain-soaked European fans who celebrated their team's fifth victory in the last seven Ryder Cups.

1997 RYDER CUP
VALDERRAMA, ANDALUCIA, SPAIN
Captains: S Ballesteros (Europe)
T Kite (United States)
Friday Fourballs: 2-2
Friday Foursomes: Europe 2½- 1½
Saturday Foursomes: Europe 3½-0½
Saturday Fourballs: Europe 2½- 1½
Sunday Singles: United States 8-4
Overall: Europe 14½ United States 13½
Europe retain the Ryder Cup

RYDER CUP: 1999

Justin Leonard's 45ft birdie on the 17th hole completed an amazing comeback by the Americans, but the scenes that followed it sent shockwaves through the golfing world.

After two successive defeats, the United States felt as though they had a point to prove. If the home team wanted to rekindle a sense of American pride, then they could not have chosen a better venue. Brookline Country Club was the spiritual home of American golf.

The American team was strong once again: no player in the line-up was ranked lower than 28th in the world. In contrast, the Europeans were a blend of experience and youth: there were seven rookies among their ranks.

But the European rookies took to the Ryder Cup like ducks to water on the first day: they contributed to the scoring in every match they played. Indeed, the only rookie not to register a point was American, not European – David Duval coming up short in both of his encounters.

At the end of the first day the European's had eased into a 6-2 lead.

Perhaps it was the fact that the strongly fancied US team were floundering against their inexperienced European counterparts, but the atmosphere started to turn sour on the second day. Twice during the course of his matches, Colin Montgomerie had to back off putts. In the morning, after being heckled on the sixth green, the Scot holed a 6ft putt and turned with clenched fist towards the galleries: it may have been an act of defiance, but it certainly did not do anything to settle the disquiet among the home fans.

The tension continued to mount. On the 18th green, in his match with Justin Leonard and Hal Sutton, Miguel Angel Jimenez had to back away from his crucial to-win-the-match putt as someone yelled from the side of the green. He took aim again ... and

missed: the match was halved. It was no coincidence that Hal Sutton had been playing in both the Montgomerie and the Jimenez matches.

At the end of it all, Europe had maintained their four-point advantage and would go into the final day 10-6 ahead. The Americans had a mountain to climb.

When Ben Crenshaw announced his line-up for the singles matches, though, there was a sense that something unexpected could happen. The US captain loaded the top order with his big guns. He knew that if the home side were to stand any chance, they would have to gain the early momentum.

During the first two days, Mark James had relied heavily on his best players. It had paid dividends, but rookies Jarmo Sandelin, Jean Van de Velde and Andrew Coltart had not yet played a game. A glance at the singles line-up saw that they would be making their Ryder Cup debuts in a charged atmosphere against Phil Mickelson, Davis Love III and Tiger Woods respectively. It would be some baptism of fire.

"I'm a big believer in fate," said Crenshaw. "I have a good feeling about this."

By the time that Tiger Woods had closed out his match against an unexpectedly defiant Andrew Coltart we were all believers. As chants of "U-S-A, U-S-A" echoed around the course, the Americans had won the first six singles matches – none of them had reached the 17th green. Unbelievably, the score now read: United States 12 Europe 10.

When Jim Furyk and Steve Pate also won their matches, the excitement had

reached fever pitch. The Americans now needed only a further half point to win back the cup.

Europe stopped the rot as Padraig Harrington closed out Mark O'Meara and Europe were back to within a point. With Colin Montgomerie and British Open champion Paul Lawrie in control of their games the destiny of the cup lay in the hands of José-Maria Olazabal and Justin Leonard.

And what a battle that was proving to be. Leonard had been four down with seven to play before winning four straight holes to tie the match by the 17th. The American stood over a 45ft birdie putt. It went in: the place erupted. This time, though, the extent of American celebrations crossed the line – literally. As wives, girlfriends, caddies and players charged across the green to celebrate with Leonard, they had forgotten one very important fact. Olazabal still had a 25ft putt of his own to halve the match. When the furore finally died down, the Spaniard took aim ... and missed.

The events on the 17th over-shadowed what had been a truly amazing achievement by the US. They had done what no side had done before, but as the dust settled, golf fans knew that the Ryder Cup had a lot of growing up to do before the next event, at The Belfry in 2001.

1999 RYDER CUP
THE COUNTRY CLUB, BROOKLINE,
MASSACHUSETTS, UNITED STATES
Captains: B Crenshaw (US)
Mark James (Europe)
Friday Foursomes: Europe 2½- 1½
Friday Fourballs: Europe 3½-0½
Saturday Foursomes: 2-2
Saturday Fourballs: 2-2
Sunday Singles: United States 8½-3½

Overall: Europe 13½ United States 14½
United States win the Ryder Cup

The media hype follwing the scenes that acompanied Justin Leonard's miracle putt overshadowed what had been a remarkable American comeback.

RYDER CUP: 2002

Europe came out storming in the final-day singles to snatch the Ryder Cup back from the US in a week that did much to restore the respectability and honour of the event.

The players reassembled at The Belfry for the 34th edition of the Ryder Cup a year later than had been planned. The 2001 Ryder Cup had been cancelled following events in New York on September 11: that, coupled with the air of bad feeling following the stampede on the green at Brookline, placed the Ryder Cup under a greater focus than usual.

The Europeans took the opening fourball series 3-1. It was a morning capped by spectacular golf and Europe, in particular, had their putting boots on. Thomas Bjorn and Darren Clarke made six putts of over 18ft on their way to defeating Tiger Woods and Paul Azinger, making his first appearance in the cup since 1993, 1 up – their victory, fittingly was secured by a 25ft birdie putt from the Dane.

Lee Westwood and Sergio Garcia beat Davis Love III and David Duval 4&3, and Colin Montgomerie and Bernhard Langer beat Scott Hoch and Jim Furyk by the same margin. Phil Mickelson and David Toms prevented a clean sweep by seeing off Padraig Harrington and Niclas Fasth on the final hole to get the Americans onto the scoreboard.

The Americans clawed their way back in the afternoon foursomes, taking the series 2½ to 1½, but the lightened mood in the US camp wouldn't have been shared by Tiger Woods. A second defeat of the day, this time paired with Mark Calcavecchia, against Lee Westwood and Sergio Garcia, meant that the world number one was the only American player not to have registered a point on the opening day.

He put that right the following morning. Paired with close friend Davis Love III, Woods tasted victory at last with a thumping 4&3 victory over Clark and Bjorn. The Saturday foursomes were shared, but the US pulled the tie level by taking the fourballs in the afternoon. At the end of the second day the scores stood level at Europe 8 United States 8. It was the first time that the teams had been level going into the final day since Kiawah Island in 1991. The scales were certainly tipped in the Americans' favour: since 1981, they had won the singles series six out of eight times.

Final-day line-ups had provided plenty of scope for discussion in recent years and the 2002 event was no exception. Sam Torrance raised a few eyebrows by stacking the top order with his best players, hoping no doubt to excite and involve the crowd by swinging the early momentum in the home side's favour.

The highest eyebrow of them all belonged to American captain Curtis Strange. He had placed his best three players at the bottom end of the order. There was a danger that if Torrance's strategy worked, then the contributions of Love III, Mickelson and Woods would be rendered meaningless.

And that's exactly what happened. Europe flew out of the blocks in the singles and gathered an early momentum that they never relinquished.

They were led off by the man who has become their talisman in the event. Colin Montgomery ran out a 5&4 winner over Scott Hoch to cap a great week for him: he amassed four-

and-a-half points out of a possible five. David Duval and David Toms did their level best to stem the tide of blue that was appearing on the leaderboard with a half against Clarke and a win against Garcia, but wins for Langer, Harrington and Bjorn maintained the European charge. The home side had won four and halved one of the opening six singles matches.

Paul Azinger kept the slimmest of American hopes alive when he continued his 18th-hole heroics by holing out from a greenside bunker to halve his match with Niclas Fasth, but in the end it was Europe – and in particular their rookies – who brought the cup home.

The moment that the home side had been waiting for arrived a few moments after Azinger and Fasth had left the 18th green. Paul McGinley had fought back from two down with six to play against Jim Furyk and the match went to the final hole. Furyk almost

"did an Azinger" with his bunker shot … it didn't drop this time, though, and the Irishman was left with the opportunity to fulfil what must be the dream of every childhood golfer – he had an 8ft putt to halve his match and win the Ryder Cup. It went in.

The home team charged onto the green after the putt had dropped and the match was over. They threw McGinley into the lake edging the 18th green for good measure. He emerged, soaked, holding an Irish flag and wearing a smile that would not fade for some time.

2002 RYDER CUP
THE BELFRY, WARWICKSHIRE, ENGLAND
Captains: S Torrance (Europe)
C Strange (US)
Friday Fourballs: Europe 3-1
Friday Foursomes: United States 2½ - 1½
Saturday Foursomes: 2-2
Saturday Fourballs: United States 2½- 1½
Sunday Singles: Europe 7½ - 4½

Overall: Europe 15½ United States 12½
Europe win the Ryder Cup

Paul McGinley's 8ft putt on the 18th gave the Europeans the half point that they needed.

RYDER CUP: 2004

A record victory for a young European team confirmed their new-found status as the leaders of world team golf and left the Americans looking desperately for answers.

The worst kept secret in golf was revealed on the eve of the tournament when American captain Hal Sutton announced his fourball pairings for the first morning. Tiger Woods would have his ninth different partner in Ryder Cup matches: this time it would be the Dream Team – the world number one would be paired with the world number two, Phil Mickelson. They would be unbeatable, thought the US captain.

The trouble was Woods and Mickelson aren't, to put it bluntly, the best of friends. Sutton also overlooked the implications of

2004 RYDER CUP, Oakland Hills CC, Mi, USA

Europe		United States	
Captain: B Langer		Captain: H Sutton	
Friday Fourballs			
C Montgomerie & P Harrington (5&4)	1	T Woods & P Mickelson	0
D Clarke & M A Jimenez (5&4)	1	D Love III & C Campbell	0
P McGinley & L Donald	½	C Riley & S Cink	½
S Garcia & L Westwood (5&3)	1	D Toms & J Furyk	0
Friday Foursomes			
M A Jimenez & T Levet	0	J Haas & C DiMarco (3&2)	1
C Montgomerie & P Harrington (4&2)	1	D Love III & F Funk	0
D Clarke & L Westwood (1 up)	1	T Woods & P Mickelson	0
S Garcia & L Donald (2&1)	1	K Perry & S Cink	0
Saturday Fourballs			
S Garcia & L Westwood	½	J Haas & C DiMarco	½
D Clarke & I Poulter	0	T Woods & C Riley (4&3)	1
P Casey & D Howell (1 up)	1	J Furyk & C Campbell	0
C Montgomerie & P Harrington	0	S Cink & D Love (3&2)	1
Saturday Foursomes			
D Clarke & L Westwood (5&4)	1	J Haas & C DiMarco	0
M A Jimenez & T Levet	0	P Mickelson & D Toms (4&3)	1
S Garcia & L Donald (1 up)	1	J Furyk & F Funk	0
P Harrington & P McGinley (4&3)	1	D Love III & T Woods	0
Sunday Singles			
P Casey	0	T Woods (3&2)	1
S Garcia (3&2)	1	P Mickelson	0
D Clarke	½	D Love III	½
D Howell	0	J Furyk (6&4)	1
L Westwood (1 up)	1	F Funk	0
C Montgomerie (1 up)	1	D Toms	0
L Donald	0	C Campbell (5&3)	1
M A Jimenez	0	C DiMarco (1 up)	1
T Levet (1 up)	1	F Funk	0
I Poulter (3&2)	1	C Riley	0
P Harrington (1 up)	1	J Haas	0
P McGinley (3&2)	1	S Cink	0
Europe	**18½**	**United States**	**9½**

Bernhard Langer did not put a foot wrong during the course of the three days: his reward was to lead his side to a crushing victory.

what would happen if, inconceivable as though its might seem, the invincible duo lost. And that it exactly what happened: they didn't just lose, they were hammered – 5&3 by Colin Montgomerie and Padraig Harrington.

It sparked an unprecedented bout of European confidence, and if Luke Donald had holed his 20ft putt on the final hole, then the visitors would have claimed a clean sweep of the morning's series of matches. As it was, they still edged into a 3½ -1½ lead.

Things only improved slightly for the home side in the afternoon. Jay Haas and Chris DiMarco registered the Americans' first win of the campaign with a 3&2 victory over Miguel Angel Jimenez and Thomas Levet, but that was all they could cheer about on day one. Montgomerie and Harrington picked up where they had left off in the morning to record a 4&2 win over Davis Love III and Fred Funk, and Sergio Garcia and Donald beat Kenny Perry and Stewart Cink 2&1.

The coup de grâce for the European team came when the Dream Team went down for the second time of the day. All square standing on the 18th tee, Mickelson carved his tee shot way right and into an unplayable lie: the pair could only manage a six and Darren Clarke and Lee Westwood reaped the rewards with a 1-up victory and inflicted a huge psychological blow on the American camp. The Europeans held a 6½-1½ advantage after the first day and the home side already had a huge mountain to climb in their attempt to regain the cup.

They took the fourball series 2½-1½, with Woods (now partnered by Chris Riley) the dependable partnership of Stewart Cink and Davis Love both recording comfortable wins. It could have been even better for the Americans. Rookies David Howell and Paul Casey came back from one down with two to play to win the final two holes and secure a crucial European

The European team celebrate their record-breaking victory at the 2004 Ryder Cup.

win – their only one of the morning.

It certainly galvanized the European team and they came out firing once again in the afternoon series of foursomes. Clarke and Westwood, buoyed by their performance the day before, crushed the previously unbeaten pairing of Haas and DiMarco 5&4. Garcia and Donald combined for a 1-up win over Jim Furyk and Funk, and the Irishmen, McGinley and Harrington added to Tiger Woods's woes (he was paired with Davis Love III this time) for a telling 4&3 victory.

It left the Europeans with a massive 11-5 advantage. What could the American team do? Not a lot, seemed to be Hal Sutton's answer when he announced his line-up for the following day's singles. It may have lacked imagination, but he simply announced his line-up in the order that the players had qualified for the event: "Seems as good a way as any," said Sutton. It smacked of the golfing equivalent of a raised white flag.

Not that Tiger Woods seemed to notice. Showing the form and touch that have made him the best player

in the world, he did his level best to ignite some passion into both the crowds and his colleagues. Back to fist-pumping best, he put away Paul Casey 3&2 to give the Americans their first point of the day. After an hour's play, the home side were leading in the first five matches and, all of a sudden, anything seemed possible.

All of which went a long way to making Sergio Garcia's match with Phil Mickelson such a crucial encounter. The American got off to a quick start, going 2 up through eight holes. It was at that point that the Spaniard showed why he is such a crucial member of the European side. He birdied the next three holes to turn the match around. After Mickelson found the water on the 16th, the match was over – as were any dreams of an American fightback.

It capped a miserable week for the world number two: he had registered only one point. For the Spaniard, it was his first win in Ryder Cup singles matches, and he ended the week with four and a half points out of a possible five: it also pushed his team-mates that much closer to the finishing line.

Darren Clarke came back from two down with three to play to earn a half with Davis Love III. Then Lee Westwood closed out Fred Funk to take Europe to within half a point of retaining the cup. In doing so, the Englishman became the second member of the European team to acquire four and a half points during the week.

You could not have written a more fitting finale. Colin Montgomerie, the man who had endured such a difficult year both on and off the course, and who was only there as a result of a captain's pick, had the putt to win the cup. No one would have denied him his moment as he holed from 4ft and put his hands to his head. The week had been a huge turnaround for the Scot: from fans chanting his name, to more inspirational play, he confirmed his status as one of the greatest Ryder Cup players of all time.

That the Europeans won the last four singles matches was the icing on the cake. They had trounced their American counterparts by a record score – 18½-9½ – and dismissed any further talk of Europe being the underdogs in the event.

RYDER CUP: 2006

Europe continued their domination of the Ryder Cup with a crushing and record-equalling 18½-9½ victory over the United States at the K Club in Ireland.

Having won seven of the last ten events, Europe started the 36th Ryder Cup – played in Ireland (at the K Club in County Kildare) for the first time – as firm favourites, with many thinking this was their best-ever side.

In the opening Friday fourballs, over a rain-saturated course, Tiger Woods may have managed to end his unwanted streak of losing seven consecutive opening matches (dating back to 1997) when he partnered Jim Furyk to a 1-up victory over Europe's marquee pairing of Colin Montgomerie and Padraig Harrington, but that was as good as it got for Team USA on day one. First Paul Casey and Robert Karlsson halved their match with Stewart Cink and JJ Henry to register Europe's first points of the week; then

Sergio Garcia and José-Maria Olazabal recorded a 3&2 victory over David Toms and Brett Wetterich; and a fine morning was completed when Darren Clarke, playing a little over a month after the death of his wife Heather from cancer, partnered old friend and fellow captain's pick Lee Westwood to a 1-up win over Phil Mickelson and Chris DiMarco. It had been a fine morning for the Europeans.

The home side's good play continued in the afternoon foursomes. The pairings may have

2006 RYDER CUP, The K Club, County Kildare, Ireland

EUROPE		UNITED STATES	
Captain: Ian Woosnam		**Captain: Tom Lehman**	
Friday Fourballs			
C Montgomerie & P Harrington	0	T Woods & J Furyk (1 up)	1
P Casey & R Karlsson	½	S Cink & JJ Henry	½
S Garcia & JM Olazabal (3&2)	1	D Toms & B Wetterich	0
D Clarke & L Westwood (1 up)	1	P Mickelson & C DiMarco	0
Friday Foursomes			
P McGinley & P Harrington	½	C Campbell & Z Johnson	½
D Howell & H Stenson	½	S Cink & D Toms	½
L Westwood & C Montgomerie	½	P Mickelson & C DiMarco	½
L Donald & S Garcia (2 up)	1	T Woods & J Furyk	0
Saturday Fourballs			
P Casey & R Karlsson	½	S Cink & JJ Henry	½
S Garcia & JM Olazabal (3&2)	1	P Mickelson & C DiMarco	0
L Westwood & D Clarke (3&2)	1	T Woods & J Furyk	0
H Stenson & P Harrington	0	Z Johnson & S Verplank (2&1)	1
Saturday Foursomes			
S Garcia & L Donald (2&1)	1	P Mickelson & D Toms	0
C Montgomerie & L Westwood	½	C Campbell & V Taylor	½
P Casey & D Howell (6&4)	1	S Cink & Z Johnson	0
P Harrington & P McGinley	0	T Woods & J Furyk (3&2)	1
Sunday Singles			
C Montgomerie (1 up)	1	D Toms	0
S Garcia	0	S Cink (4&3)	1
P Casey (2&1)	1	J Furyk	0
R Karlsson	0	T Woods (3&2)	1
L Donald (2&1)	1	C Campbell	0
P McGinley	½	JJ Henry	½
D Clarke (3&2)	1	Z Johnson	0
H Stenson (4&3)	1	V Taylor	0
D Howell (5&4)	1	B Wetterich	0
JM Olazabal (2&1)	1	P Mickelson	0
L Westwood (2 up)	1	C DiMarco	0
P Harrington	0	S Verplank (4&3)	1
EUROPE	**18½**	**UNITED STATES**	**9½**

Playing barely a month after his wife's death, the emotions finally got to Darren Clarke after he secured a 3&2 Sunday singles victory over Zach Johnson.

been different - Europe's captain Ian Woosnam had, admirably, opted to give every member of his team a run-out on the opening day (unlike his American counterpart Tom Lehman - but the results were just the same. Europe did not lose a single match in the afternoon - halving three and winning one of them - and held a 5-3 lead at the end of the first day. With all but one of the day's matches having gone to the final hole, however, Woosnam was quick to warn against complacency: "Any one of the games could have changed and gone the other way," said the European captain. For Lehman, however, it had been a day of what-could-have-beens: "Both teams played well but we could have done with a little more luck on the greens... I feel a little frustrated." That frustration would only get worse.

It was more of the same for Europe on the second day. In the morning's fourballs, Garcia and Karlsson resumed their battle with Cink and Henry and the match ended in a half for the second consecutive day. But then wins for Garcia and Olazabal (3&2 over Mickelson and DiMarco) and Clarke and Westwood (by the same scoreline over an out-of-touch Woods and Furyk) extended the European lead to four (7½-3½). Zach Johnson and Scott Verplank may have prevented complete disaster by beating Henrik Stenson and Harrington 2&1 in the morning's final fourball match to leave the score on 7½-4½, but the Americans needed some afternoon to pull themselves back into contention.

That magical afternoon failed to materialize. Garcia and Donald beat Mickelson and Toms (2&1); Montgomerie and Westwood grabbed a half against Chad Campbell and Vaughn Taylor; and Casey (who fired a hole-in-one on the par-three 14th - only the fifth ace in Ryder Cup history) and playing partner David Howell proved too strong for Cink and Johnson and romped to a 6&4 victory. Woods and Furyk may have

taken some of the gloss off it all - with a 3&2 victory in the final match of the day against local favourites Paul McGinley and Harrington - but it had been another commanding day for Europe and, with just the singles to play, they led 10-6. Seven years earlier, at Brookline, Europe had taken a 10-6 lead into the final day and lost and captain Woosnam still refused to take anything for granted: "The Americans have always been strong in singles... We've got to take every day individually and we start another day tomorrow."

And Colin Montgomerie, leading from the front as has become his fashion in recent Ryder Cups, ensured Europe began the final day in style when he beat David Toms 1 up in the opening encounter to extend his remarkable unbeaten record in singles matches to eight.

Moments later, Paul Casey added the home side's second point of the day when he completed a 2&1 victory over Jim Furyk. American victories for Cink (4&3 over Garcia - the Spaniard's only defeat of the week) and Woods (3&2 over Karlsson) redressed the balance momentarily, before an emphatic mid-afternoon surge saw Europe coast to victory. Howell outclassed Wetterich (5&3); then Donald produced a late surge to see off Chad Campbell (2&1); which left Henrik Stenson with the honour of confirming Europe's third consecutive Ryder Cup win when he completed a 4&3 victory over Vaughn Taylor. The loudest cheer of the week was reserved for Darren Clarke, who secured a tearful 3&2 victory over Zach Johnson. The wins did not end there: Olazabal beat Mickelson 2&1 (the American's return for the week

had been half a point in five matches) and Westwood beat DiMarco (2up) to confirm a crushing 18½-9½ victory.

"Very emotional," European captain Ian Woosnam told reporters after seeing his team match the record-winning margin achieved over the United States at Oakland Hills two years earlier to make it three European wins in a row for the first time. "I just can't say enough about my team. They have played fantastic."

"I need to tip my hat completely to the European team," added a disappointed US captain Tom Lehmann. "They played incredibly well... I just don't know if there has ever been a European team that has played better." Few who had seen Europe's comprehensive and effortless destruction of a talented American team would have disagreed with those sentiments.

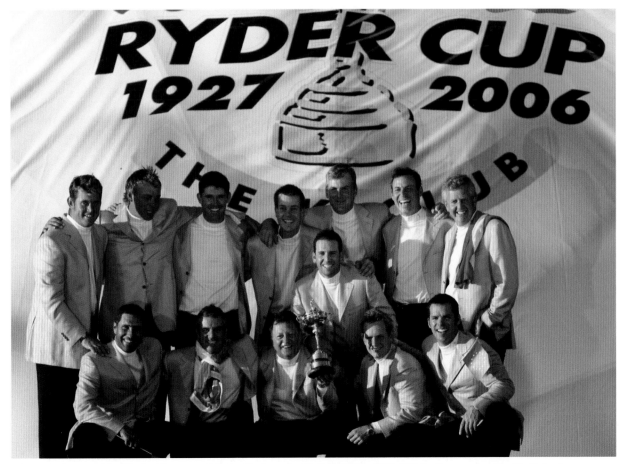

The Europe team, captained by Ian Woosnam, celebrate after trouncing the United States 18½-9½ for the second consecutive Ryder Cup.

RYDER CUP: 2008

A resurgent United States team led the 37th Ryder Cup from wire to wire to record their first victory over Europe for eight years.

The contrast between the two captains before events got underway was as stark as it was noticeable. For Europe, an emotional and edgy Nick Faldo knew his team – every member of which was ranked inside the world's top-50 players – was aiming for an unprecedented fourth consecutive victory and, for the first time in history, would start a Ryder Cup contest on American soil as firm favourites. Faldo's counterpart, Paul Azinger, on the other hand, exuded poise and self-belief: with his team (containing six Ryder Cup rookies) considered major underdogs – and missing Tiger Woods (through injury) for the first time since 1997 – they simply had nothing to lose. "We have everything to gain in this situation," said the American captain. "Not a lot of people expect us to pull this off, minus Tiger Woods. Everybody feels pressure, but hopefully they [my players] will be freewheeling out there. That's my hope."

The American team handed their captain the perfect start in the Friday foursomes – well, almost perfect. After Europe had surged into an early lead in all four matches it appeared to be Ryder Cup business as usual, but then the US pairings struck back. Justin Leonard (playing in the event for the first time since 1999) and Hunter Mahan claimed their side's first point when they saw off Paul Casey and Henrik Stenson 3&2; then Phil Mickelson and Anthony Kim rallied over the final holes to halve their match against Padraig Harrington and Robert Karlsson; a European three-putt on 18 then handed the US another point, with Chad Campbell and Stewart Cink benefiting from Ian Poulter and Justin Rose's slip-up to win 1 up (it was the first match the Americans had won on the 18th in 11 attempts). And a fine morning for the home side was complete when Jim Furyk and home-crowd favourite Kenny Perry held on to claim a half against Europe's most

2008 RYDER CUP, Valhalla GC, Louisville, KY

EUROPE		UNITED STATES	
Captain: Nick Faldo		**Captain: Paul Azinger**	
Friday Foursomes			
P Harrington & R Karlsson	½	P Mickelson & A Kim	½
P Casey & H Stenson	0	J Leonard & H Mahan (3&2)	1
J Rose & I Poulter	0	C Campbell & S Cink (1 up)	1
L Westwood & S Garcia	½	J Furyk & K Perry	½
Friday Fourballs			
P Harrington & G McDowell	0	A Kim & P Mickelson (2 up)	1
I Poulter & J Rose (4&2)	1	B Curtis & S Stricker	0
S Garcia & MA Jimenez	0	J Leonard & H Mahan (4&3)	1
S Hansen & L Westwood	½	JB Holmes & B Weekley	½
Saturday Foursomes			
J Rose & I Poulter (4&3)	1	C Campbell & S Cink	0
G McDowell & MA Jimenez	½	J Leonard & H Mahan	½
O Wilson & H Stenson (2&1)	1	P Mickelson & A Kim	0
P Harrington & R Karlsson	0	J Furyk & K Perry (3&1)	1
Saturday Fourballs			
S Hansen & L Westwood	0	JB Holmes & B Weekley (2&1)	1
P Casey & S Garcia	½	B Curtis & S Stricker	½
G McDowell & I Poulter (1 up)	1	J Furyk & K Perry	0
R Karlsson & H Stenson	½	H Mahan & P Mickelson	½
Sunday Singles			
S Garcia	0	A Kim (5&4)	1
P Casey	½	H Mahan	½
R Karlsson (5&3)	1	J Leonard	0
J Rose (3&2)	1	P Mickelson	0
H Stenson	0	K Perry (3&2)	1
O Wilson	0	B Weekley (4&2)	1
S Hansen	0	JB Holmes (2&1)	1
MA Jimenez	0	J Furyk (2&1)	1
G McDowell (2&1)	1	S Cink	0
I Poulter (3&2)	1	S Stricker	0
L Westwood	0	B Curtis (2&1)	1
P Harrington	0	C Campbell (2&1)	1
EUROPE	**11½**	**UNITED STATES**	**16½**

Phil Mickelson and Anthony Kim formed an impressive partnership on the opening day, winning 1½ out of two points.

imposing pairing, Sergio Garcia and Lee Westwood. A 3-1 lead for the Americans represented a fine morning's work: it was the first time the Americans had held the lead in the Ryder Cup since the "Miracle of Brookline" in 1999.

The American's fun continued in the afternoon fourballs. Mickelson and Kim rallied from three holes down with six to play to beat Harrington and Graeme McDowell 2 up - the one-and-a-half points Mickelson had gathered on the first day were more than he had mustered in the previous two Ryder Cups. Poulter and Rose may then have steadied the European ship with a commanding 4&2 victory over Ben Curtis and Steve Stricker, but the respite was brief and it wasn't long before the boisterous home crowds had reason to cheer again. Leonard and Mahan completed their second victory of the day with a comprehensive 4&3 win over Garcia and Miguel Angel Jimenez - pointedly, it was the first time in his Ryder Cup career that Garcia had failed to register a win on the opening day. A fantastic start to Team USA was confirmed when rookies JB Holmes and Boo Weekley mustered a half against Westwood and Soren Hansen. The 5½-2½ lead the home side took into the second day was the largest since continental Europe was first included in the Ryder Cup in 1979. "We're in a good place," gushed Azinger. "Who'd have thought it?"

The European fightback started in earnest on the second day. With Garcia and Westwood (Europe's two longest-serving players) controversially omitted from the Saturday morning foursomes pairings and watching on from the sidelines, Rose and Poulter notched up their second victory of the week (easing past Campbell and Cink 4&3) to reduce the overall deficit to two points. McDowell and Jimenez held unbeaten duo Leonard and Mahan to a half, before Stenson and rookie Oliver Wilson (who had

It was champagne-soaked smiles all round for JB Holmes (left) and captain Paul Azinger (right) after the United States eased to a 16½-11½ victory at Valhalla.

been the only player on both sides to miss out in both sessions on Friday) rallied from four down after six to beat Mickelson and Kim 2&1. The deficit was now down to one. Only briefly, however, as Furyk and Perry lead from start to finish to see off Harrington and Karlsson 3&1. The Americans led 7-5, and Europe needed to make further inroads in the afternoon fourballs.

It did not happen. The birdies flew in from all angles during a scintillating afternoon session that was squared at 2-2, with a European win for McDowell and Poulter (1 up over Furyk and Perry), an American win for Holmes and Weekley (2&1 over Hansen and Westwood - the Englishman's first Ryder Cup defeat in six years and 13 matches) and two matches were halved. It left

the Americans holding a two-point lead going into the Sunday singles - the first time that had happened since 1995.

US rookie Anthony Kim set the American ball rolling in the opening match of the final day, finishing off a sensational week that confirmed his status as one of the game's brightest new stars, by shooting 30 on the front nine and easing to a comprehensive 5&4 win over Garcia. Europe rallied briefly with wins for Karlsson (5&3 over Leonard) and Rose (3&2 over Mickelson), but successive US victories for Perry (3&2 over Stenson), Weekley (4&2 over Wilson), Holmes (2&1 over Hansen) and Furyk (2&1 over Jimenez) took the Americans over the winning line. By the time the singles were over, the final score

stood at 16½-11½ - the Americans biggest victory margin over Europe for 27 years.

"I'm disappointed for the guys. We've all given 100 percent" said Nick Faldo, whose captaincy was roundly criticized by the European press. In contrast, an emotional Azinger was ecstatic: "The crowd energised our players for the whole week - the 13th man really made the difference." Of his own efforts Azinger said "I poured my heart and soul into this for two years. The players poured their heart and soul into this for one week. They deserved it." He went on to say "." Few observers would have disagreed: in previous Ryder Cups, the Americans had been criticized for their individual approach to the event; this time round, they had been the ultimate team.

BRITISH AMATEUR CHAMPIONSHIP

Allan MacFie was the first British Amateur champion, but never attained the fame of Horace Hutchinson (more properly Horatio Gordon Hutchinson), whom he beat in the inaugural final at Royal Liverpool's course, Hoylake. Hutchinson won the second and third finals, the third against John Ball. The Hoylake-bred Ball was accounted the greatest of them all long before 1912, when he won his eighth title, which is still a record.

In any case the first championship,

organized by the Royal Liverpool, was not recognized as official until 1920, when the Royal and Ancient finally took over full control of the event.

In 1995, the R&A, who like the USGA have a well-developed sense of tradition, marked the 100th Amateur by bringing the event back to its Hoylake birthplace. Besides, Michael Bonallack, then secretary of the R&A, is the most successful living competitor in the Amateur, with five titles, including a hat-trick in 1968-70.

Before the turn of the century the entry had reached 100, and by 1958 almost 500. Lower and lower handicaps were demanded to keep down the flood of would-be competitors. In 1983, 36-hole qualifying was introduced, the leading 64 reverting to matchplay over four days.

Bonallack's feat in the days of greatly increased competition from a worldwide entry is at least the equal of John Ball's achievements. From 1887 to 1895 either Johnny Laidlay

or Ball or both figured in every final. At the same time, Ball was the first Englishman (in 1890) and another amateur, Harold Hilton, two years later, the second, to win the British Open.

Freddie Tait, a long hitter who managed to play golf with an extraordinary regularity considering his position as an officer in the Black Watch, might well have emulated Hilton, but in 1900, aged 30, he was killed leading his men against the Boers at Koodoosberg.

Year	Winner	Venue	Year	Winner	Venue	Year	Winner	Venue
1885	A F McFie	Hoylake	1928	T P Perkins	Prestwick	1972	T Homer	St George's
1886	H G Hutchinson	St Andrews	1929	C Tolley	St George's	1973	R Siderowf	Porthcawl
1887	H G Hutchinson	Hoylake	1930	R T Jones Jr	St Andrews	1974	T Homer	Muirfield
1888	J Ball	Prestwick	1931	E Martin Smith	Westward Ho!	1975	M M Giles	Hoylake
1889	J E Laidlay	St Andrews	1932	J De Forest	Muirfield	1976	R Siderowf	St Andrews
1890	J Ball	Hoylake	1933	Hon. M Scott	Hoylake	1977	P McEvoy	Ganton
1891	J E Laidlay	St Andrews	1934	W Lawson Little	Prestwick	1978	P McEvoy	Troon
1892	J Ball	St George's	1935	W Lawson Little	Lytham	1979	J Sigel	Hillside
1893	P C Anderson	Prestwick	1936	H Thomson	St Andrews	1980	D Evans	Porthcawl
1894	J Ball	Hoylake	1937	R Sweeney Jr	St George's	1981	P Ploujoux	St Andrews
1895	L M B Melville	St Andrews	1938	C R Yates	Troon	1982	M Thompson	Deal
1896	F G Tait	St George's	1939	A T Kyle	Hoylake	1983	AP Parkin	Turnberry
1897	A J T Allan	Muirfield	1940-45	No championship		1984	J-M Olazabal	Formby
1898	F G Tait	Hoylake	1946	J Bruen	Birkdale	1985	G McGimpsey	Dornoch
1899	J Ball	Prestwick	1947	W P Turnesa	Carnoustie	1986	D Curry	Lytham
1900	H H Hilton	St George's	1948	F R Stranahan	St George's	1987	P M Mayo	Prestwick
1901	H H Hilton	St Andrews	1949	S M McCready	Portmarnock	1988	C Hardin	Porthcawl
1902	C Hutchings	Hoylake	1950	F R Stranahan	St Andrews	1989	S Dodd	Birkdale
1903	R Maxwell	Muirfield	1951	R D Chapman	Porthcawl	1990	R Muntz	Muirfield
1904	W J Travis	St George's	1952	E Harvie Ward	Prestwick	1991	G Wolstenholme	Ganton
1905	A G Barry	Prestwick	1953	J B Carr	Hoylake	1992	S Dundas	Carnoustie
1906	J Robb	Hoylake	1954	D W Bachli	Muirfield	1993	I Pyman	Portrush
1907	J Ball	St Andrews	1955	J W Conrad	Lytham	1994	L James	Nairn
1908	E A Lassen	St George's	1956	J C Beharrell	Troon	1995	G Sherry	Hoylake
1909	R Maxwell	Muirfield	1957	R Reid Jack	Formby	1996	W Bladon	Turnberry
1910	J Ball	Hoylake	1958	J B Carr	St Andrews	1997	C Watson	St George's
1911	H H Hilton	Prestwick	1959	D R Beman	St George's	1998	S Garcia	Muirfield
1912	J Ball	Westward Ho!	1960	J B Carr	Portrush	1999	G Storm	Royal Co. Down
1913	H H Hilton	St Andrews	1961	M F Bonallack	Turnberry	2000	M Ilonen	Hoylake
1914	J L C Jenkins	St George's	1962	R D Davies	Hoylake	2001	M Hoey	Prestwick
1915-19	No championship		1963	M S R Lunt	St Andrews	2002	A Larrazabal	Porthcawl
1920	C Tolley	Muirfield	1964	G J Clark	Ganton	2003	G Wolstenholme	Troon
1921	W I Hunter	Hoylake	1965	M F Bonallack	Porthcawl	2004	S Wilson	St Andrews
1922	E Holderness	Prestwick	1966	R E Cole	Carnoustie	2005	B McElhinney	Birkdale
1923	R H Wethered	Deal	1967	R B Dickson	Formby	2006	J Guerrier	St George's
1924	E Holderness	St Andrews	1968	M F Bonallack	Troon	2007	D Weaver	Lytham
1925	R Harris	Westward Ho!	1969	M F Bonallack	Hoylake	2008	R Saxton	Turnberry
1926	J Sweetser	Muirfield	1970	M F Bonallack	Newcastle, Co. Down	2009	M Manassero	Formby
1927	Dr W Tweddell	Hoylake	1971	SN Melnyk	Carnoustie			

Bobby Jones's only victory in the event came during his year of years, 1930.

The British Amateur was to attract a growing number of Americans, but the first to win, Walter Travis, in 1904, did not improve transatlantic golf relations. Ironically, the cause of the rift was that Travis, a triple US Amateur champion, won with a brand new putter, adopted in desperation for the Amateur at Royal St George's because, during his preparations for the event, his putting, his greatest strength, suddenly "went off".

But the instrument he chose was looked upon by the British establishment as unfair. It was called a Schenectady putter, invented and patented by Arthur Knight of New York, and had its shaft attached to the middle of a mallet-shaped head.

No one had ever seen putting such as Travis now deployed against one opponent after another, beating Hilton and Hutchinson in turn to reach the final, where he won at the 33rd against Ted Blackwell. Travis relished a victory which was received with a minimum of applause, which cannot have surprised him, for he felt he had not been accorded the usual courtesies, particularly in the matter of clubhouse facilities and an effective caddie.

The Travis Schenectady, centre-shafted wand of victory, though approved by the USGA, was banned by the R&A, though not, contrary to popular legend, directly as a result of Travis's 1904 victory. The ban was imposed in 1910, and even then only after Nga Motu GC, in New Zealand, asked if a small croquet mallet was legal. No, said the R&A. Not until mid-century was such a weapon unbanned.

From 1920, when the championship resumed after the war, it became far more difficult to put together even as few as two wins, and Ball's eight began to look unrepeatable. Cyril Tolley, an England international for a quarter of a century, managed two wins. He and Robert Gardner relaunched the Amateur with a 37-hole cliff-hanger of a final at Muirfield. Both men had survived war service (Tolley, who won the Military Cross, was a POW).

Three thousand cheered as Tolley birdied the extra hole, for amateur golf was thoroughly fashionable, and was to become even more so with the advent of Bobby Jones, though he won the Amateur only once, in his grand slam year of 1930, at St Andrews. His closest call came against Tolley, whose extra-hole luck was out this time, Jones going through with the aid of a stymie which was, as Jones himself said, "a cruel way to lose".

William Lawson Little followed Jones' grand slam with two "Little Slams" in 1934 and 1935, capturing both the US and British Amateurs twice. Six American victories in the British Amateur between the wars were succeeded by five more in seven years immediately following the Second World War. Even when James Bruen, the Irish Ryder Cup player, won in 1946, he had to beat an American, Bob Sweeney, to do it. So did Sam McCready, another Belfast golfer, in 1949, holding off Willie Turnesa, the 1947 champion, 2&1 at Portmarnock.

Joe Carr carried on the Irish tradition with three wins, but since the war there has been an even stronger American tradition, which lasted until 1983 and was unbroken except in 1963: that is, whenever the US Walker Cup team was, at four-year intervals, visiting Britain, there was an American winner of the Amateur.

On six occasions – 1947, 1951, 1959, 1967, 1971 and 1979 – both finalists were American. None of Bonallack's five wins came in years of American visits, but he did win the English Championship five times, shooting a 61 at Ganton, in Yorkshire in 1968.

Since Jay Sigel's win over Scott Hoch in 1979, another change has come over the Amateur, for continental invaders from France (1981), Spain (1984), Sweden (1988) and Holland (1990) have replaced US winners. That trend continued in 1998, when Europe's answer to Tiger Woods, Spain's Sergio Garcia, followed in his compatriot José-Maria Olazabal's footsteps to win the title. Finland added its own unique European flavour when Miko Ilonen won in 2000 and Alejandro Larrazabal became Spain's latest winner in 2002. British golfers took the title over the next three years before, in 2006, Julien Guerrier became the event's second French winner. Italy's Matteo Manassero won in 2009.

José-Maria Olazabal is the only recent winner of the British Amateur championship to have gone on to win a major tournament.

THE US AMATEUR CHAMPIONSHIP

The first United States Amateur Championship started three days before the nation's first Open, and play lasted three times as long. Across the Atlantic the Open pre-dated the Amateur by a quarter of a century, and rapidly became the Holy Grail for all golfers.

There is a direct personal link between the US Amateur and the British Open. Old Tom Morris, winner of four British Opens, coached the first winner of the American

Amateur, a well-built, self-willed Chicagoan named Charles Blair Macdonald. He had first fallen in love with golf in Scotland as a student at St Andrews in the 1870s, and in the early 1890s built the Chicago club, then a much-improved 18 holes at Wheaton, a Chicago suburb.

Macdonald had first come to the public's notice in his campaign to become American Amateur champion. Since golf lacked a national authority, the clubs of Newport,

Rhode Island, and St Andrew's, New York, put on "Championships" in 1893 and 1894.

Macdonald came second in both, but discounted the quality both of the venues and of his opponents. He was an influential man, a stockbroker on the New York exchange, but the game was clearly in need of leadership a little less egotistical than his. So the US Golf Association came into being at the end of 1894, and the first president, Theodore Havemeyer, a

sugar baron, gave an extra veneer of authority to the inaugural Amateur starting on September 1, 1895, by donating a championship trophy.

Macdonald won it, easily. His victim in the final, by 12&11, at Newport, was Charles Sands. Although Macdonald went on to perform great service as a USGA committee man and (unpaid) course designer, his fame was as nothing compared to that of Walter J. Travis, the champion in 1900, 1901 and 1903.

Year	Winner	Venue	Year	Winner	Venue	Year	Winner	Venue
1895	C B Macdonald	Newport, RI	1934	W Lawson Little	Brookline, Ma	1973	C Stadler	Inverness, Oh
1896	H J Whigham	Shinnecock Hills, NY	1935	W Lawson Little	Cleveland, Oh	1974	J Pate	Ridgewood, NJ
1897	H J Whigham	Chicago, Il	1936	J W Fischer	Garden City, NY	1975	F Ridley	Richmond, Va
1898	F S Douglas	Morris County, NJ	1937	J Goodman	Portland, Or	1976	B Sander	Bel-Air, Ca
1899	H M Harriman	Onwentsia, Il	1938	W P Turnesa	Oakmont, Pa	1977	J Fought	Aronomink, Pa
1900	W J Travis	Garden City, NY	1939	M H Ward	Glen View, Il	1978	J Cook	Plainfield, NJ
1901	W J Travis	Atlantic City, NJ	1940	R Chapman	Winged Foot, NY	1979	M O'Meara	Canterbury, Oh
1902	L N James	Glen View, Il	1941	M H Ward	Omaha, Ne	1980	H Sutton	Pinehurst, NC
1903	W J Travis	Nassau, NY	1942-45	No championship		1981	N Crosby	Olympic, Ca
1904	H Chandler Egan	Baltusrol, NJ	1946	S E Bishop	Baltusrol, NJ	1982	J Sigel	Brookline, Ma
1905	H Chandler Egan	Wheaton, Il	1947	R H Riegel	Pebble Beach, Ca	1983	J Sigel	North Shore, Il
1906	E M Byers	Englewood, NJ	1948	W P Turnesa	Memphis, Tn	1984	S Verplank	Oak Tree, Ok
1907	J D Travers	Cleveland, Oh	1949	C R Coe	Rochester, NY	1985	S Randolph	Montclair, NJ
1908	J D Travers	Garden City, NJ	1950	S Urzetta	Minneapolis, Mn	1986	S Alexander	Shoal Creek, Al
1909	R Gardner	Wheaton, Il	1951	W J Maxwell	Saucon Valley, Pa	1987	W Mayfair	Jupiter Hills, Fl
1910	W C Fownes Jr	Brookline, Ma	1952	J Westland	Seattle, Wa	1988	E Meeks	Hot Springs, Va
1911	H H Hilton	Apawamis, NY	1953	G Littler	Oklahoma City, Ok	1989	C Patton	Merion, Pa
1912	J D Travers	Wheaton, Il	1954	A Palmer	Detroit, Mi	1990	P Mickelson	Cherry Hills, Co
1913	J D Travers	Garden City, NY	1955	E Harvie Ward	Richmond, Va	1991	M Voges	Honours Course, Tn
1914	F Ouimet	Ekwanok, Vt	1956	E Harvie Ward	Lake Forest, Il	1992	J Leonard	Muirfield Village, Oh
1915	R Gardner	Detroit, Mi	1957	H Robbins	Brookline, Ma	1993	J Harris	Houston, Tx
1916	C Evans	Merion, Pa	1958	C R Coe	San Francisco, Ca	1994	T Woods	Sawgrass, Fl
1917-18	No championship		1959	J Nicklaus	Broadmoor, Co	1995	T Woods	Newport, RI
1919	S D Herron	Oakmont, Pa	1960	D R Beman	St Louis, Mo	1996	T Woods	Portland, Or
1920	C Evans	Engineers Club, NY	1961	J Nicklaus	Pebble Beach, Ca	1997	M Kuchar	Cog Hill, Il
1921	J Guilford	Clayton, Mo	1962	L E Harris Jr	Pinehurst No. 2, NC	1998	H Kuehne	Oak Hill, NY
1922	J Sweetser	Brookline, Ma	1963	D R Beman	Des Moines, Io	1999	D Gossett	Pebble Beach, Ca
1923	M R Marston	Flossmoor, Il	1964	W C Campbell	Canterbury, Oh	2000	J Quinney	Baltusrol, NJ
1924	R T Jones Jr	Merion, Pa	1965-72	Decided by strokeplay		2001	B Dickerson	Eastlake GC,
1925	R T Jones Jr	Oakmont, Pa	1965	R Murphy	Southern Hills, Ok	2002	R Barnes	Oakland Hills, Mi
1926	G von Elm	Baltusrol, NJ	1966	G Cowan	Merion, Pa	2003	N Flanagan	Oakmont, Pa
1927	R T Jones Jr	Minikahda, Mn	1967	R Dickson	Broadmoor, Co	2004	R Moore	Winged Foot, NY
1928	R T Jones Jr	Brae Burn, Ma	1968	B Fleisher	Columbus, Oh	2005	E Molinari	Merion, Pa
1929	H R Johnson	Del Monte, Ca	1969	S N Melnyk	Oakmont, Pa	2006	R Ramsay	Hazeltine, Mn
1930	R T Jones Jr	Merion, Pa	1970	L Wadkins	Portland, Or	2007	C Knost	Olympic, Ca
1931	F Ouimet	Beverley, Il	1971	G Cowan	Wilmington, De	2008	D Lee	Pinehurst, NC
1932	C R Somerville	Baltimore, NJ	1972	M M Giles	Charlotte, NC	2009	A Byeong-hun	Southern Hills, Ok
1933	G T Dunlap	Kenwood, Oh		The Championship reverted to matchplay				

The great Bobby Jones took the US Amateur Championship crown on five occasions.

by virtue of a 5&3 victory over a 14-year-old from Georgia playing in his first USGA championship. This was R T (Bobby) Jones Jr, five times a winner between 1924 and 1930.

Only one man had two wins in the 1930s, William Lawson Little, but he added the novelty of winning the British Amateur in the same years, 1934 and 1935.

With Jones's retirement, and the fitful but sure growth of the professional tour, the fascination of the amateur game began to fade.

Gene Littler, Arnold Palmer and Jack Nicklaus used the Amateur as a stepping-stone to wealth, yet the continuing high standards of the amateur game in the US were never more clearly demonstrated than at Broadmoor, Colorado, in 1959, when Charles Coe, at 35 twice a winner, took Jack Nicklaus, then a student at Ohio State University, to the 36th hole of the final. The winner was about to begin a run of second, fourth and first in the US Open. At 19 years and eight months, Nicklaus was the second youngest Amateur champion being three months older than Robert Gardner when he won half a century earlier.

Eight years of strokeplay format, begun with Bob Murphy's win at Southern Hills, Oklahoma, in 1968, were abandoned in 1973, when more future PGA stars began to take the title, notably Craig Stadler, Jerry Pate, John Cook, Mark O'Meara and Hal Sutton.

In 1981, a stir was caused by a famous name from quite another sphere: Crosby. The singer's son Nathaniel, aged 19, won at Olympic, San Francisco, close to his home.

But 1981 was Nathaniel Crosby's sole moment of glory: Jay Sigel, champion for the next two years, was far more consistent. When he won in 1982 at Brookline, he was 38, twice as old as Crosby had been the previous year.

A hand injury 20 years earlier dissuaded Sigel from a professional career and, in any case, he earned a living in insurance. His services to US golf are legion, and recently took a new turn when he began to coin money on the Senior Tour.

Phil Mickelson, a left-hander who hits long and chips with a velvet touch from the tightest lies, was 1990 champion and within a year, still an amateur, won a PGA tournament at Tucson. Even cynics were ready to believe that here at last was the next great American player.

Mickelson was soon supplanted as "the next great" by a tall, slim Californian of mainly Afro-American and Thai blood, Eldrick Woods, nicknamed "Tiger" by his father Earl. Young Tiger, the first black to win the US Amateur title in the 94 years of the event, was also the youngest champion at 18 in 1994. He won again the next two years to complete a unique hat-trick.

In the last 50 years, eight former US Amateur champions have gone on to win major tournaments (as opposed to just one in the British Amateur) – no wonder, then, that the winners of the championship nowadays are scrutinized to such an extent.

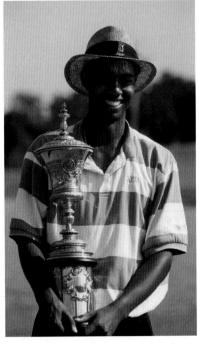

Tiger Woods became the youngest champion (aged 18) when he won in 1994.

Travis came from Australia as a child and did not take up golf until he was 35. At 37, he reached the semi-final of the US Amateur, and the following year, 1900, he won it.

Travis was a short hitter but a devastating putter. His most celeb-rated single feat was his British Amateur title, his last major win, in 1904. His "trademark" was his eternal black cigar.

Travis's victory on foreign soil, for the British title, was answered seven years later by Harold Hilton, who had two British Opens to his credit. Having won the British Amateur in 1911, he went for the transatlantic double at the age of 42. He strolled through the early rounds, but Fred Herreshoff took Hilton to the 37th hole in the final before surrendering.

Ouimet's Amateur title in 1914 sounds pallid after his 1913 giant-killing in the US Open, but it had been the great ambition of his life to lift the Amateur.

Chick Evans followed recovery-expert Jerome Travers' record fourth Amateur success with a unique double in 1916. First he recorded a total of 286 to win the US Open at Minikahda, Minnesota, a figure not beaten for 22 years. Three months later, he beat Bob Gardner in the Amateur final.

Gardner had got into the last four

WOMEN'S CHAMPIONSHIPS

Writing in April, 1893, to Blanche Martin, who was to become Ladies' Golf Union treasurer, Horace Hutchinson, one of the leading amateurs of late Victorian times, issued what might today be termed a triple whammy. Women were, he pontificated, incapable of pushing any scheme to success: they would soon quarrel. Secondly, they would never get through a single ladies' championship with credit. Thirdly, they were unfit for golf because they were incapable of lasting through two rounds of a long course in a day.

Regardless, within a few weeks of the receipt of his letter the LGU was formed and the first British Women's Amateur Championship completed at St Anne's. Lady Margaret Scott, aged 18, won, and did so again twice. Contrary to Hutchinson's expectations, Lady Margaret could not only propel the gutty ball close to 150 yards, despite the long skirts she wore, but also excite the admiration of seasoned male pros at the graceful way in which she did so. Her third win was followed by the first women's international, in which England beat Ireland.

Ninety-five years later, in November 1990, the Solheim Cup match between the US and Europe at Lake Nona, in Florida, the inaugural US v. Europe professional international, demonstrated that the women's game was entering its most sophisticated era. The trophy is named after Karsten Solheim, the engineer who built a club-making empire, most famously with his distinctive Ping putter.

The US won it 11-4, with one match halved, but fears that this was to become another one-sided series like the Walker Cup were dispelled by Europe's 10-5 victory, with three matches halved, at Dalmahoy in Scotland in 1992.

The Cup had speedily become a compelling contest. There was some hand-wringing over the fact that Dalmahoy had received such poor media coverage, particularly on television, but it was clear to officials that the fixture would be a money-making event which would become a magnet to the media in the future, and to sponsors. And so it has proved.

Persistent is an inadequate term to describe America's pioneer of international team golf for women,

Margaret Curtis. The game was in her blood, and that of her sister, Harriot: they were nieces of Lawrence Curtis, who had much to do with the formation of The Country Club at Brookline, Massachusetts, who was present at the meeting that formed the USGA in 1894, and became the second USGA president.

Margaret, a woman of great energy, compassion and considerable organizing skill, was engaged before the First World War in social service and relief work. During the war, and for six years afterwards, she worked in France for refugees under the banner of the Red Cross.

The idea of a US v. GB match had been born, in the mind of the British LGU secretary, Issette Pearson, as early as 1898. The visits of Margaret, Harriot and several other prominent US women golfers to British events in 1905 and 1907 (the year when Margaret beat Harriot in the US Amateur final) brought the first international closer, but the 1909 offer from the USGA of a cup for such a match was not

US Women's Open Results

Year	Winner	Year	Winner
1946	Patty Berg	1979	Jerilyn Britz
1947	Betty Jameson	1980	Amy Alcott
1948	Babe Zaharias	1981	Pat Bradley
1949	Louise Suggs	1982	Janet Anderson
1950	Babe Zaharias	1983	Jan Stephenson
1951	Betsy Rawls	1984	Hollis Stacy
1952	Louise Suggs	1985	Kathy Baker
1953	Betsy Rawls	1986	Jane Geddes
1954	Babe Zaharias	1987	Laura Davies
1955	Fay Crocker	1988	Liselotte Neumann
1956	Kathy Cornelius	1989	Betsy King
1957	Betsy Rawls	1990	Betsy King
1958	Mickey Wright	1991	Meg Mallon
1959	Mickey Wright	1992	Patty Sheehan
1960	Betsy Rawls	1993	Lauri Merten
1961	Mickey Wright	1994	Patty Sheehan
1962	Murle Breer	1995	Annika Sorenstam
1963	Mary Mills	1996	Annika Sorenstam
1964	Mickey Wright	1997	Alison Nicholas
1965	Carol Mann	1998	Se Ri Pak
1966	Sandra Spuzich	1999	Juli Inkster
1967	Catherine Lacoste	2000	Karrie Webb
1968	Susie Berning	2001	Karrie Webb
1969	Donna Caponi	2002	Juli Inkster
1970	Donna Caponi	2003	Hilary Lanke
1971	JoAnne Carner	2004	Meg Mallon
1972	Susie Berning	2005	B Kim
1973	Susie Berning	2006	A Sorenstam
1974	Sandra Haynie	2007	C Kerr
1975	Sandra Palmer	2008	I Park
1976	JoAnne Carner	2009	Eun-Hee Ji
1977	Hollis Stacy		
1978	Hollis Stacy		

British Women's Open

Year	Winner	Year	Winner
Recognized as a major championship since 2001		1992	Patty Sheehan
		1993	Karen Lunn
		1994	Liselotte Neumann
1976	Jenny Lee Smith	1995	Karrie Webb
1977	Vivien Saunders	1996	Emilee Klein
1978	Janet Melville	1997	Karrie Webb
1979	Alison Sheard	1998	Sherri Steinhauer
1980	Debbie Massey	1999	Sherri Steinhauer
1981	Debbie Massey	2000	Sophie Gustafson
1982	Marta Figueras-Dotti	2001	Se Ri Pak
1983	No competition	2002	Karrie Webb
1984	Ayako Okamoto	2003	Annika Sorenstam
1985	Betsy King	2004	Karen Stupples
1986	Laura Davies	2005	J Jang
1987	Alison Nicholas	2006	S Steinhauer
1988	Corinne Dibnah	2007	L Ochoa
1989	Janet Geddes	2008	J Shin
1990	Helen Alfredsson	2009	C Matthew
1991	Penny Grice-Whittaker		

Two-time US Women's Open winner Babe Zaharias was one of the foremost women players of her day and did much to raise the profile of the game.

taken up by the LGU. Nor were two unofficial matches followed up: in 1907 England beat America 6-1, and in 1911 Britain won 7-2 against "American and Colonial".

Financial considerations defeated initiatives for an international series in the 1920s. A guarantee of $5,000 per match by Margaret Curtis in 1928, and a third unofficial match in 1930 were not in themselves enough to start the transatlantic golf ball rolling, but perhaps they gave officialdom the necessary nudge ... for in 1931, the year of the first official women's international (between Britain and France for the Vagliano Cup), the LGU and USGA agreed to biennial matches. The idea was to involve France – all comers if possible – but that option was never adopted.

Fifteen thousand turned up on May 21, 1932, at Wentworth, south-west of London, to see the American tourists, who were led by Marion Hollins and included the outstanding US golfer of the era, Glenna Collett Vare. She and Opal Hill beat the British captain, Joyce Wethered, and Wanda Morgan in foursomes, all of which the US won.

Wethered beat Collett Vare 6&4 in singles, but despite further victories by Enid Wilson over Helen Hicks and Diana Fishwick over Maureen Orcutt, the Curtis Cup, a silver Revere bowl donated by the Curtis family, went back to the US, by 5-3, with one match halved.

Collett Vare captained a successful defence at Chevy Chase in 1934, and the whole match was halved four years later, thanks to a huge putt by Jessie Valentine on her debut for Britain and Ireland.

The US kept defeat at bay until 1952 at Muirfield, where Elizabeth Price, a diabetes sufferer, took the deciding match.

Polly Riley was the inspiration of the US team that wrested back the Cup at Merion, Pennsylvania, two years later. Then Britain and Ireland managed a four-year tenure of the

Perhaps graced with the best swing that the game has ever seen, Mickey Wright captured four US Women's Open titles in a distinguished career.

Cup by winning 5-4 at Prince's in Kent in 1956 and halving the 1958 event at Brae Burn, Massachusetts.

There followed 26 years of US domination, the longest one-sided run yet, but suggestions that European players should be brought in to redress the balance have fallen on stony ground, certainly as far as the Americans are concerned. A resounding 13-5 victory by the Great Britain and Ireland side so meticulously prepared for the Cup match of 1986 by their captain, Diane Bailey, put an end to the run of 13 US victories. The win, achieved at Prairie Dunes, Kansas, was another first against the US, who in more than 60 years had never lost a home match to a visiting international side, male or female, pro or amateur.

Bailey completed an unprecedented double by leading Britain and Ireland to another win at Royal St George's in 1988, but the US replied in some style in 1990 with a 14-4 trouncing at Somerset Hills, New Jersey.

Caroline Hall's fine four-iron to the last hole of the last match at Royal Liverpool against Goetze was the key for the 1992 repatriation of the Cup for Britain and Ireland, who brought the Cup back with them in 1994. Another US defeat – still only the sixth against 20 wins – followed in 1996 at Killarney.

Men pros had long since outclassed the amateurs when American women were struggling to set up a professional circuit in the late 1940s. In the women's game, the amateurs were not only dominant, but fashionable, indeed glamorous. The "bewitching blonde" Edith Cummings, winner of the 1923 Amateur, was reputed to be the model for one of F. Scott Fitzgerald's beautiful high-society women in his novel *The Great Gatsby*.

There was no better amateur than Polly Riley, who played six Curtis Cup matches from 1948 to 1958, and beat Babe Zaharias 10&9 in the 36-hole final of the 1948 Texas Open. When the LPGA got started in 1950 after the fade-out of the WPGA, Riley won their first tournament, the Tampa Open.

All the same, Zaharias was the glittering star of the early years of the LPGA. The tour, with such players as Patty Berg to back her up, would doubtless have become prosperous without her, eventually, but she was the catalyst to its more rapid development.

Fame followed Zaharias around, starting from her two 1932 Olympic gold medals and one silver in athletics. At 16, she could reputedly drive a golf ball more than 250 yards, but she did not take the game at all seriously until she was 23. The range of her skills, from baseball to ballroom dancing and playing the harmonica, is scarcely credible. Yet as a golfer there were few tournaments and little money

Zaharias could try for after she had been reported for breaking the amateur status rules and designated a pro by the USGA, a decision which Jack Burke termed "the dirtiest deal I've heard of in a long time".

Her strength was her strength, and after taking a raft of amateur titles when her status was restored, Zaharias turned pro again (voluntarily, upon accepting an offer of $300,000 to make golf films), and proceeded to outhit every rival.

She tended to be a prima donna, using her fame to get her own way, which irritated rivals, but they had much to thank her for as sponsors, especially makers of products that interested women, recognized the attractions of women's golf. At the same time the emerging talents of Louise Suggs, Betsy Rawls and Peggy Kirk enlivened competition. A decade after that amateur victory by Polly Riley in the LPGA's first event, the tour prize money was $200,000, and events numbered 26.

The supreme stylist Mickey Wright and then Nancy Lopez, were the next dominating figures.

Though Kathy Whitworth achieved a career record of 88 tournament wins between 1959 and 1991, the immediate and lasting impact of Lopez had a publicity value second only perhaps to that of Zaharias. Lopez, second in the Open as an amateur, took nine events in 1978, her first full year on the tour, including five in a row. This galvanized the golfing public and sent gate receipts soaring.

The professional women's set of majors has varied over the years with the nature of sponsorship. There have not always been four. Two players have managed a seasonal sweep of the available majors, Zaharias with the three available in 1950 (US Open, Titleholders and Western Open), Sandra Haynie with the two on offer in 1974, the US Open and LPGA title.

Pat Bradley came closest to the current feminine version of Bobby Jones' Impregnable Quadrilateral.

She won the 1986 LPGA title, the du Maurier Classic, and the Nabisco Dinah Shore, but finished third in the US Open to Jane Geddes.

The late Dinah Shore added to her fame as a singer by becoming the Bing Crosby, so to speak, of women's professional golf. Her tournament, richly sponsored by Colgate, who also owned the Ram golf company, began in 1972 at Palm Springs, California, and attracted plenty of Shore's Hollywood and music-business friends. Like the Masters, this major is always played at the same venue, Mission Hills in California, at which the 1991 winner Amy Alcott jumped into the lake with Dinah.

The success of Chako Higuchi, an LPGA champion, and Ayako Okamoto, 1987 Player of the Year, gained the attention of Japanese sponsors: these and other supporters swelled average tournament purses from $30,000 in the early 1970s until it was nudging $700,000 in 1997 when the total purse offered by the LPGA reached $30 million.

And the LPGA Tour has continued to attract golfers from all over the globe. Following the success of Japanese players came a European invasion, which started when Laura Davies captured the US Open in dramatic style in 1987. It set a trend: Alison Nicholas deprived Nancy Lopez of an Open win in 1997, the year that Swede Annika Sorenstam failed in her attempt to capture the event for the third year in a row. In recent times, prompted by Se Ri Pak's sensational arrival onto the world scene in the late 1990s, it has been players from South Korea who have stolen the limelight – three of the last five US Women's Open winners have been Korean-born.

The European women's tour was a good deal slower achieving rich and piping times than the American. Total prize money, nearly £3 million ($4.5 million) is still only about one-eighth of the US figure. The first British Women's Open in 1972, won by Jenny Lee Smith,

In recent years, Annika Sorentsam has taken the game to new levels of performance: she has even been invited to play events on the men's tour.

Laura Davies' 1987 US Women's Open success kickstarted the game's popularity in Europe – but the women's European Tour is still playing catch-up with its American counterpart.

post-dated the American version by a quarter of a century. It was not played at all in 1983, for lack of a sponsor. Since 1987 it has been safe-guarded under the banner of Weetabix and since 2001 has become one of the women's game's four majors.

Sponsorship has generally been hard to come by from the inception of the European tour, when prize money totalled £80,000. Cathy Lewis, the first winner of the tour's inaugural Order of Merit, earned £2,494.50. These relatively meagre pickings did not suggest to the best amateurs that turning pro would make their fortunes. Early standards of play were patchy, and helped depress the number of tournaments from an initial 18 to ten in 1982.

But things have changed – and considerably for the better. By 2009, the schedule consisted of 28 tournaments in 21 countries with players competing for a total purse of Ð11.65 million. Other signs of prosperity were Amex "headline" sponsorship, the need for a qualifying school, and live coverage of the Solheim Cup – on both sides of the Atlantic.

THE US PGA TOUR

Now the powerhouse of world golf, the American PGA Tour in its early, cash-strapped, play-it-by-ear days had need of the spirit of the frontiersman. There were huge distances to cover, usually by automobile, cheap lodgings to find if prize money had been elusive, and even in most cases if it hadn't. Tournaments were loosely organized and players had to have other sources of income because prize money was short, and the available cash did not go far down the list of also-rans.

Since the tour began as a winter event in Florida, Texas and other southern states, the players could combine playing for prize money with a club job in the north during the months when play was difficult or impossible, and custom at professional shops correspondingly light. The tournaments, often at tourist resorts, were usually sponsored by the local chamber of commerce, as the results were reported in the great cities of the north-eastern seaboard and the middle west, and it was a cheap way of gaining publicity.

There was a touch of the western gunslinger about the early tour pro, travelling from town to town chancing his luck. Wild Bill Mehlhorn, whose father had left Germany rather than join the ranks of Kaiser Wilhelm's army, kept dollars in his pocket by giving lessons en route to the winter tour venues and selling magazine subscriptions.

Besides, the living from a pro's shop was not all that magnificent. Ability to teach the game was not always accompanied by marketing skills, which were the forte of the suppliers of golf clubs, clothing and the like. These middlemen made it a hard life for many club pros, and clubs were wont to command profits on ball sales, the pro's main stock-in-trade.

Hence the establishment in 1916 of the US Professional Golfers' Association, which was and is basically an organization to protect the interests of the club pro.

A good many British prejudices still ruled in America, inimical to professional golf, for the amateur was still king, and the paid man was looked down upon. Pros in England commanded a good deal more respect thanks perhaps to the mighty reputations, in technique and competitive drive, of players such as Harry Vardon and J H Taylor, first and second in the 1900 US Open, and the excitement of watching money matches. What a treat for the Scottish islanders of Islay to watch Vardon and Taylor v. James Braid and Alex Herd in an international fourball on the newly consecrated Machrie course.

Tournament life took a different route in the United States. The PGA gave the pros a peg to hang their season on (Open Championship apart) with the US PGA Championship, for which the first (1916) winner, Jim Barnes, received $500 – about what Vardon would get in a big money challenge match in the old country. The US PGA and Open were far from becoming the central events in a well-ordered tour, the growth of which began haphazardly in the Sunbelt of the south immediately around the turn of the 20th century, with prize money reaching three figures in Florida resorts. No detailed chronology exists of how it began, except to say that winter tournaments in California, Texas and Florida in the early 1920s were crucial elements.

Amateur events were held at the resorts long before the First World

Leading US Tour money-winners

Year	Winner	$	Year	Winner	$	Year	Winner	$
1934	Paul Runyan	6,767	1960	Arnold Palmer	75,262	1986	Greg Norman	653,296
1935	Johnny Revolta	9,543	1961	Gary Player	64,540	1987	Curtis Strange	925,941
1936	Horton Smith	7,682	1962	Arnold Palmer	81,448	1988	Curtis Strange	1,147,644
1937	Harry Cooper	14,138	1963	Arnold Palmer	128,230	1989	Tom Kite	1,395,278
1938	Sam Snead	19,534	1964	Jack Nicklaus	113,284	1990	Greg Norman	1,165,477
1939	Henry Picard	10,303	1965	Jack Nicklaus	140,752	1991	Corey Pavin	979,430
1940	Ben Hogan	10,655	1966	Billy Casper	121,944	1992	Fred Couples	1,344,188
1941	Ben Hogan	18,358	1967	Jack Nicklaus	188,998	1993	Nick Price	1,478,557
1942	Ben Hogan	13,143	1968	Billy Casper	205,168	1994	Nick Price	1,499,927
1943	no statistics compiled		1969	Frank Beard	164,707	1995	Greg Norman	1,654,959
1944	Byron Nelson	*37,967	1970	Lee Trevino	157,037	1996	Tom Lehman	1,780,159
1945	Byron Nelson	*63,335	1971	Jack Nicklaus	244,490	1997	Tiger Woods	2,066,833
1946	Ben Hogan	42,556	1972	Jack Nicklaus	320,542	1998	David Duval	2,591,031
1947	Jimmy Demaret	27,936	1973	Jack Nicklaus	308,362	1999	Tiger Woods	6,616,585
1948	Ben Hogan	32,112	1974	Johnny Miller	353,021	2000	Tiger Woods	9,188,321
1949	Sam Snead	31,593	1975	Jack Nicklaus	298,149	2001	Tiger Woods	5,687,777
1950	Sam Snead	35,758	1976	Jack Nicklaus	266,438	2002	Tiger Woods	6,912,625
1951	Lloyd Mangrum	26,088	1977	Tom Watson	310,653	2003	Vijay Singh	7,573,907
1952	Julius Boros	37,032	1978	Tom Watson	362,428	2004	Vijay Singh	10,905,166
1953	Lew Worsham	34,002	1979	Tom Watson	462,636	2005	Tiger Woods	10,628,024
1954	Bob Toski	65,819	1980	Tom Watson	530,808	2006	Tiger Woods	9,941,563
1955	Julius Boros	63,121	1981	Tom Kite	375,698	2007	Tiger Woods	10,867,052
1956	Ted Kroll	72,835	1982	Craig Stadler	446,462	2008	Vijay Singh	6,601,094
1957	Dick Mayer	65,835	1983	Hal Sutton	426,668	2009	Tiger Woods	10,508,163
1958	Arnold Palmer	42,607	1984	Tom Watson	476,260			
1959	Art Wall	53,167	1985	Curtis Strange	542,321			

* War bonds

Before the establishment of the professional tour, Walter Hagen did much to spread the golfing gospel with a series of money-spinning exhibition matches around the United States.

War, and pro events grew up alongside them, although the Press usually granted them fewer column inches.

What the pro game needed was a hero. Amateurs in particular and US golf in general certainly found a hero at the 1913 US Open in Francis Ouimet. Walter Hagen almost achieved that status in the same championship, but fell just short of the epoch-making play-off in which Ouimet beat Ted Ray and Vardon. Such was his confidence that he might well have surprised all three; 12 months later Hagen was US Open champion, and became leader in the considerable task of transforming the golf pro into an envied, though not

always prosperous pillar of society.

There is little difference between Hagen's role and that of the touring pro of today, except that he depended less on prize money and more on exhibition matches. He played such a match rather than defend his first US PGA title, and attracted thousands of spectators to hundreds of his one-day appearances at a dollar or so admission when a dollar was a dollar. He had the happy knack of being able not only to impress the galleries with his golf but also to entertain them.

This stroll-around comedian created his own lucrative theatre of the open air, aided by players such as

Gene Sarazen, just out of his teens and winner of the US Open and US PGA titles in 1922. This was the US PGA Hagen had passed up to play in an exhibition, so another exhibition, a challenge match between the pair, was set up, expansively billed as being for the Golf Championship of the World.

Sarazen, two down after the first two rounds at Oakmont, Pennsylvania, was in pain before the final holes at the palatial Westchester-Biltmore Country Club in New York. In wind and rain Sarazen struggled on, overtook Hagen, and next day had an emergency operation to have his appendix removed. His prize was $2,000, Hagen's

$1,000: winning the US Open was not worth $1,000 until 1929.

One rock upon which the PGA Tour was founded was the Texas Open, founded in 1923 by businessmen in San Antonio. The total purse was a record at $5,000. Another tour foundation stone was laid three years later by the Los Angeles Junior Chamber of Commerce: this one worth $10,000. A year later, other Californian cities organized pro events. The tour was now getting into some kind of order, the players starting in the west early in the New Year, moving east to Texas and Florida, then up the east coast to spring and summer events.

The advent of television, coupled with the emergence of Arnold Palmer, changed the face of the game in the United States.

Total prize money of $77,000 was available in 1928. This supported a growing band of men who depended almost entirely on their playing, rather than pro-shopkeeping, skills. Walter Hagen was no longer the one and only touring pro. But there was no central organization, until a succession of newspapermen, who had every reason to want the tour to expand, took a

hand. Of these the most influential was Bob Harlow, son of a Congregationalist minister. Unsurprisingly, he was also Hagen's manager.

No man has a better claim than Harlow to be the chief begetter of the PGA Tour, though his main difficulty was ... the PGA. Like those before him who had tried to bring order to the tour, he wanted to supplement his income from

newspaper articles, and as an agent for Hagen and other leading players, with a salary or commission for putting tournaments together and persuading sponsors to part with cash.

At length he got a $100 a week salary, but was sacked in 1932 by the PGA, some of whose officials looked upon touring pros as a pampered, footloose gang of opportunists, who

unjustly commanded too many choice club pro jobs on the basis of their playing prowess. Ostensibly he was dismissed because he was spending too much time on his extra-tour activities.

When the PGA re-employed Harlow in 1933, the economy had become chronically sick, yet he invented the minimum purse and worked out a system by which the best players were exempted from qualifying. Already the players, avid for more cash and freedom from the PGA and its club-pro fixation, were looking at ways to set up a rival organizational shop of their own.

Another journalist, Fred Corcoran, was next to ride the tour tiger, beginning in 1936 at $5,000 a year ... golf had moved on quite a way. A born publicist, he improved information services for the public, with coloured scoreboards, and brought a greater range of sponsors into play.

The final rift between the PGA and the players widened to involve threats of boycott in the 1960s. Though the sums pocketed by the leading performer on tour had declined radically at times in the depressed 1930s, better times, looser corporate purse-strings and the sheer quality of pros, such as Ben Hogan, Sam Snead and Byron Nelson, made life easier for tour managers as peace broke out in 1945. The advent of the greatest crowd pleaser since Hagen, Arnold Palmer, together with the advent of televised golf, changed many things. Television started with local coverage of the 1947 US Open at St Louis, Missouri, and soon progressed under the influence of George S. May's tournament, the Tam O'Shanter National Open. Golf in general had a golden stroke of luck in 1953. May was not present when ABC television offered national coverage for $32,000. Chet Posson, May's assistant, took a chance and accepted. When he heard what Posson had done, May, a management consultant in a big way, said: "I don't care if it costs us a million. Do it!"

An estimated two million saw the Tam O'Shanter live on television: lo and behold, Lew Worsham won it with a 135-yard wedge approach shot to the final green. It went in ... it was quite a television debut.

Television gave golf the Midas touch. It enabled prize money to double in ten years. The leading post-war players would soon be thinking airplane instead of automobile. The younger ones, many of them not long out of college, had no knowledge of mending clubs. Once television rights began to swell, tour pros could not see why the PGA should get much of what their skill alone, as they saw it, was channelling into the prize pot.

Boycott threats by the touring pros in 1967 were followed by an overt move for independence ... an announcement that the breakaway American Professional Golfers' Association had a $3.5 million tour programme for 1969. In this particular poker game the PGA held two pairs, the touring pros held a royal flush, and a gun to the head of the PGA. Without the leading players, which now included Jack Nicklaus, a prime mover in the negotiations with Gardner Dickinson, television and sponsors didn't fancy PGA golf at all: only Sam Snead stuck by the old regime.

So the players became free men, their Magna Carta granted uncondi-tionally under what was no more than a convenient fiction, the creation of a new PGA division. Golf is still the only sport where the professionals run their own events.

There was a lasting bitterness between the club pros and tour players after the split. Club-makers MacGregor, it was reported, got requests from club pros to remove Jack Nicklaus's name from their products. They perhaps forgot that Nicklaus, Palmer and Co. have enticed battalions of their fans to buy golf gear in pro shops across the world.

Tiger Woods' spectacular arrival on the PGA Tour in 1996, and his subsequent success, changed everything. For the first time in its history, golf suddenly had a broad appeal and, in the 24-7 age in which media exposure is everything, money from sponsors and television companies started to pour into the game. And the main beneficiaries of Tiger's crowd- and sponsor-pulling capabilities were the players. In 1995, a year before Woods' arrival, South Africa's David Frost finished 50th on the money list and earned $357,548; in 2009, young American John Mallinger finished in the same end-of-year position but took home $1.72 million. The PGA Tour, even for journeymen golfers it seemed, had become big, big business.

American star Jack Nicklaus played a major part in the negotiations that saw the players take control of the running of the game.

THE EUROPEAN PGA TOUR

The European Tour is the second most powerful tour in the world after America, although these days the name has become something of a misnomer: the tour is now several months old before it even touches down in Europe. By that stage play has been conducted in three other continents, by way of tournaments co-sanctioned with other tours.

Its extraordinary development was overseen by Ken Schofield, its executive director from 1975 to 2004. Schofield was once the youngest bank manager in Scotland, and he applied a keen mind to the task of getting the best possible deal for European professionals. Schofield's mantra was to "maximize opportunity and incentive". If that meant treading on the toes of some of the game's traditionalist views, then so be it.

The European Tour evolved in much the same way as the PGA Tour, with touring professionals becoming increasingly restless at being under the umbrella of the Professional Golfers' Association, which looked after the interests of the club pros. On October 1, 1971, the breakaway was finally made. John Jacobs was made tournament director-general of the PGA, and the European Tour was born.

When Schofield took over in 1975, there were 17 tournaments on the schedule with total prize money of £42,917. It was his brief both to increase the number of tournaments and the amounts that the players were playing for, and in both tasks he succeeded spectacularly. Eight years later there were ten more tournaments and prize money had shot up to a shade under £2.5 million.

Schofield would be the first to admit that he was helped in his task by an extraordinary stroke of luck. Soon after he took over it became clear that European golf was heading for some exciting times. In 1976, a 19-year-old Spaniard called Severiano Ballesteros finished runner-up in the British Open at Birkdale and went on to win the Dutch Open in his next outing. And there was not just Ballesteros. Bernhard Langer also emerged from Germany. Two countries that had never considered golf as anything other than a game for the bourgeoisie suddenly had modern, working-class heroes.

There was more. From Wales came Ian Woosnam, from Scotland came Sandy Lyle and from England, Nick Faldo. All not only combined an innate skill for the game with a champion's touch, they were all photogenic, too. Here were five players upon whom you could hang any tour.

And soon they started to win major championships. It was Ballesteros who set the ball rolling with the 1979 British Open. Then Langer won the Masters. Then Lyle won the British Open. Now Schofield could go to every potential sponsor in the land and say legitimately: we have some of the best players in the world here in Europe – where's the money?

These five players quickly captured the public's imagination. Their images started to hang from bedroom walls in places where before there had only been footballers. And there were not only the major championships: there were also their performances on the European Tour – and then came the 1985 Ryder Cup.

That performance put the lid on the best ever year for European golf. Wins in the Masters for Langer and the British Open for Sandy Lyle were accompanied by the first win over the Americans for 28 years. And a win in Europe to boot.

When Europe repeated the trick at Muirfield Village two years later, golf was riding an amazing wave of popularity. Courses were springing up all over the continent to satisfy a new audience. Most of all, though, people wanted to see their new heroes in the flesh.

Leading European Tour money-winners

Year	Winner	£	Year	Winner	£	Year	Winner	
1962	Peter Thomson	5,764	1981	Bernhard Langer	95,991	From 1999, prize money was in Euros		
1963	Bernard Hunt	7,209	1982	Sandy Lyle	86,141			
1964	Neil Coles	7,890	1983	Nick Faldo	140,761	1999	Colin Montgomerie	1,822,880
1965	Peter Thomson	7,011	1984	Bernhard Langer	160,883	2000	Lee Westwood	3,125,147
1966	Bruce Devlin	13,205	1985	Sandy Lyle	254,711	2001	Retief Goosen	2,862,806
1967	Gay Brewer	20,235	1986	Seve Ballesteros	259,275	2002	Retief Goosen	2,360,128
1968	Gay Brewer	23,107	1987	Ian Woosnam	439,075	2003	Ernie Els	2,975,374
1969	Billy Casper	23,483	1988	Seve Ballesteros	502,000	2004	Ernie Els	4,061,905
1970	Christy O'Connor	31,532	1989	Ronan Rafferty	465,981	2005	Colin Montgomerie	2,794,223
1971	Gary Player	11,281	1990	Ian Woosnam	737,977	2006	Padraig Harrington	2,489,337
1972	Bob Charles	18,538	1991	Seve Ballesteros	790,811	2007	Justin Rose	2,944,945
1973	Tony Jacklin	24,839	1992	Nick Faldo	1,220,540	2008	Robert Karlsson	2,732,748
1974	Peter Oosterhuis	32,127	1993	Colin Montgomerie	798,145	The Order of Merit then became the Race to Dubai		
1975	Dale Hayes	20,507	1994	Colin Montgomerie	877,135	2009	Lee Westwood	4,237,762
1976	Seve Ballesteros	39,504	1995	Colin Montgomerie	1,038,718			
1977	Seve Ballesteros	46,436	1996	Colin Montgomerie	875,146			
1978	Seve Ballesteros	54,348	1997	Colin Montgomerie	798,947			
1979	Sandy Lyle	49,233	1998	Colin Montgomerie	933,077			
1980	Greg Norman	74,829						

Countries like Germany, France and Spain, instead of having just one event, now had two, three or even more. Now, instead of going to sponsors, Schofield found them coming to him. He was in the wonderful position of having more potential benefactors than there were slots in the calendar. He could drive up the price.

The best deal he ever signed came in 1988 when he was approached by Volvo. The car manufacturer was fed up with the brattish behaviour of some tennis players and wished to switch their sponsorship funds to a sport with a more pristine image. The deal still goes on and has been worth well over £100 million to the European Tour.

One of the major problems faced by Schofield was that the Ryder Cup was still owned by the PGA. It irked him. As it began to rake in huge profits - with his members, the people who were actually playing in it not receiving a cent - he got hotter and hotter under the collar.

The problem was that the PGA refused to budge, even when they were faced with the threat of players withdrawing from the event. The drama was played out in front of the Press - something that threatened to damage the hitherto pristine image of the game.

The arguments from the two sides were clear. Schofield argued that the Ryder Cup was nothing without the players, so why should their organization not be entitled to some of the rewards. The PGA claimed that they had stuck with the tournament through thick and thin.

Something had to give. It did. The chief executive of the PGA, John Lindsay, was forced out by his board of directors and was replaced by Sandy Jones - a Scot and an old friend of Schofield. The pair had no trouble brokering an agreement and the ownership of the Ryder Cup was split between the two bodies: every time it came to Europe, they would be entitled to choose the venue on an alternate basis and keep the profits.

All was well for a few years. The players continued to win the trophies at the highest level. Europe's record at the Masters became a thing of beauty, with seven wins in ten years from 1985. The schedule took on a settled, prestigious look and the prize money continued to rise.

Then something happened. The boom came to an end in the early 1990s and Schofield found that he would have to go in search of sponsorship deals once again: as it cost more than £1 million to stage a tournament, the takers were few and far between.

That is where the Ryder Cup slush fund came in handy. Tournaments with no title sponsor were supported. In return for the Ryder Cup going to Spain in 1997, the European Tour got an agreement from the Spanish Tourist Board that they would run a number of events. The same agreement was found with De Vere Hotels, who own The Belfry, and the Irish Tourist Board - in return for bringing the Ryder Cup to Ireland in 2005. The number of tournaments on the schedule may have reduced slightly, but the European Tour was still alive and kicking.

Another short-sighted decision was made during this period that has caused the game as a whole to repent at leisure. In 1995, Sky Television agreed to pay the tour an undisclosed sum for the right to televise the Ryder Cup exclusively plus 26 European Tour events, including a number that had hitherto been the preserve of the BBC.

It comes as little surprise that the European Tour's increased profile coincided with the arrival on the golfing stage of Severiano Ballesteros.

Sandy Lyle's British Open success in 1985 triggered an unprecedented period of European domination in the world game.

should never have been played: holding events in Spain in February, when the weather was unpredictable to say the least, was never a good idea.

The tour rightly abandoned the practice and has sought fresher pastures. The Dubai Desert Classic, for example, has been a wonderful step in the right direction and the Emirates Course, its venue for all but one year, is literally a classic

Nick Faldo continued the trend of European success – in an eight-year period, the Englishman won the British Open three times and the Masters on three occasions.

Schofield, more than anyone, knew how many people had taken up the game after watching the heroics at the 1985 and 1987 events. Now that contest would be confined to a smaller audience – most of whom were golf fanatics anyway.

It was a decision that has had catastrophic effects on the game: the number of people playing has fallen dramatically. Since the fall in people playing can be traced back

to the time when events were taken away from the BBC, it can hardly be seen as a coincidence.

And so we come to the present. The drop in the number of tournaments played might be seen by some as a negative, but on the plus side the events played are all of a better standard. The venues are better and so is their conditioning. Only a decade ago, some of the tournaments place to play golf. The tour also visits Australia and South Africa, and while this provokes a mixed reaction among the membership, no one can dispute the fact that the courses are in a better condition than their European counterparts would be at that time of the year.

As the tour has grown so, naturally, has the number of players who wish to be members. Aping the PGA Tour, a challenge circuit was created to give non-members an arena in which to hone their skills.

It is a hard circuit to play: it costs a lot and the rewards are small, but the incentive is there, and the message from the tour's survivors is that if you can make it there you can make it on the regular tour. Two notable graduates are Thomas Bjorn and Costantino Rocca, both of whom, of course, have gone on to achieve a considerable measure of success in the Ryder Cup arena.

Another initiative taken from the other side of the Atlantic has been the setting up of the Senior Tour. Although not as big as its American counterpart, the European Seniors Tour has grown in stature since its foundation in 1992. In 2008, players contested 18 tournaments for a total purse of Ð7.3 million.

With over 100 tournaments spread over three tours, Schofield can rightly be proud of his 30 years at the helm (he retired at the end of 2004). The foundations he helped develop have played a significant role in European golfers' steady rise to the top of the world game: they have won five of the last seven Ryder Cups and by May 2010 had six players inside the top 20 of the world rankings.

Nobody has had more success on the European Tour than Colin Montgomerie. The Scot headed the Order of Merit for seven consecutive years from 1993 to 1999.

OTHER PRINCIPAL GOLF EVENTS

Amazingly, not only junior extensions have been grafted on to the organization of the two major tours: even greater success has been achieved by the return of senior players to regular competition in their own tour. Fred Raphael, producer of the popular "Shell's Wonderful World of Golf" series, was mustard keen to make Sam Snead's idea of an old timers' circuit work. Some players were fearful that they would not look good in their (relative) old age. This did not apply to Snead, of whom Raphael said: "He knew he was going to play well." Snead did, and, partnered by Gardner Dickinson, won the inaugural event in 1978.

This celebration of mature talents was made into a smash hit by Roberto de Vicenzo and Julius Boros the following year, when they scored in an event named "Legends of Golf". They beat Art Wall and Tommy Bolt in a spectacular low-scoring six-hole play-off that suggested that old golfers do not fade away; they just get more cunning.

Besides, Arnold Palmer, still the darling of the galleries, reached 50 in 1979, his fourth year without a win on the main tour. A four-event Senior Tour was organized in 1980, and the age limit later dropped to 50, and Senior success was assured. Its practitioners are earning far more money than they ever did on the PGA Tour itself 30 years or more ago. Lee Trevino earned $3.4 million on the regular tour in 20 years, $7.5 million in his first five years with the Seniors.

Significantly, the great players of the post-war period have cleaned up most prize money on the Senior Tour, their nerve and the security of their technique overcoming the penalties of age. Jack Nicklaus won six times in his first three Senior years, including two US Senior Opens. Trevino won seven events and more than $1 million in his first year. Ray Floyd put one over on young and old with a victory on the regular tour and the Senior in the same season.

And the Senior Tour – or the Champions Tour as it is now known – has gone from strength to strength. What was once perhaps seen as an arena in which ageing professionals could showcase their talent and add a few dollars to their retirement funds has become a second, and extremely lucrative, leg of a player's career. Bernhard Langer, the leading winner on the Champions Tour in 2009, earned $2.16 million from the 21 events he played – only 35 players on the regular tour finished with more money in the bank that season. Hale Irwin, the all-time career money winner on the tour has amassed a staggering $31.39 million in prize money during his Senior career. It's all about money ...

Talking about which, back in 2001, officials were starting to talk about the possibility of a Senior Ryder Cup.

"We would like to get a match up sooner rather than later and negotiations with our counterparts are ongoing," said Andy Stubbs, the managing director of the European Senior Tour. "But there is a complicated television schedule we would have to fit into and there would be pressure in America for the match to be an immediate success."

What works for television works for American golf. Given that the likes of Langer, Woosnam and Couples – not to mention a revitalized Tom Watson – are all flourishing on the Champions Tour, youn can rest assured that the Senior Ryder Cup will be up and running in the not too distant future. It would be too good a money-making opportunity to miss. Sponsors would clamour to be involved in it.

President's Cup results

Year	Venue	United States	International
1994	Robert Trent Jones GC, Va	20: H Irwin	12: D Graham
1996	Robert Trent Jones GC, Va	16$\frac{1}{2}$: A Palmer	15$\frac{1}{2}$: P Thomson
1998	Royal Melbourne, Australia	11$\frac{1}{2}$: J Nicklaus	20$\frac{1}{2}$: P Thomson
2000	Robert Trent Jones GC, Va	21$\frac{1}{2}$: K Venturi	10$\frac{1}{2}$: P Thomson
2003	George, South Africa	17: J Nicklaus	17: G Player
2005	Robert Trent Jones GC, Va	18$\frac{1}{2}$: J Nicklaus	15$\frac{1}{2}$: G Player
2007	Royal Montreal, Canada	19$\frac{1}{2}$: J Nicklaus	14$\frac{1}{2}$: G Player
2009	Harding Park, Ca	19$\frac{1}{2}$: F Couples	14$\frac{1}{2}$: G Norman

Shigeki Maruyama shone when the President's Cup travelled outside the United States for the first time in 1998 ... it was staged at the Royal Melbourne club in Australia.

And it is the increase in sponsorship money that has led to such a long season. After a full ten months of weekly chances to win "official money" in PGA tournaments, plus further cash and glory on offer in the Masters and the US Open, PGA Tour players and their peers from other tours look forward to an unbroken series of extra earning opportunities reaching all the way to Christmas and beyond.

Some brave spirits, like José-Maria Olazabal of Spain, prefer family pursuits and will not play as the holiday approaches; others head for an international event such as the Kapalua International, Hawaii, and there are special events for the superstars, such as the Skins Game, and the Grand Slam. Skins are played by four golfers, with prizes available on every hole, which can be won by one of the quartet outscoring the other three. If the hole is halved, the players progress hole by hole, with the eventual prize money increasing hole by hole, until someone does come out on top. Six-figure sums can rest on one hole.

And if winning a major tournament during the season, with the financial reward that goes with it isn't enough, a tournament was established in 1994 to get the four major winners together (or the runners-up if someone had won more than one major) and have them play against each other for a winner-takes-all prize of $1 million. The main beneficiary has been Tiger Woods, who has won the tournament seven times – including five in a row between 1998 and 2002.

Sun City, near Johannesburg, was the first to dangle a $1 million prize carrot, though the so-called "World Championship" in Jamaica just before Christmas, was not to be sniffed at: prizes totalled $2.5 million. The event was strictly for the successful – winners of specified events through the year – and was terminated in 1995.

Various events over the years

have carried the word "world" in their title in an attempt to add more weight to an already weighty cash purse. In 1999, however, four events were brought together under the World Golf Championship moniker. Three of these were new events – one matchplay, the other two 72-hole strokeplay – open to only the top-64 players in the world rankings. The prize money was huge: Ian Poulter, the winner of the 2010 WGC-Accenture Matchplay Championship, took home a winner's cheque of $1.4 million.

The fourth of these events, the World Cup, was given a new lease of life under the WCG umbrella. Formerly one of the most prestigious events in the game, it had fallen significantly in stature by the mid-1990s. It became caught out in an increasingly tight tournament schedule and the world's best players chose to give it a miss – this was highlighted in 1998 when the United States were represented by Scott Verplank and John Daly: both good players, but not the best that America has on offer. It wasn't always the case. Once upon a time the tournament was welcomed by players with open arms. It was founded by American industrialist Jay John Hopkins, who felt that the golfing world was ready for a team competition involving all nations. In 1953, he launched the Canada Cup and countries were invited to send two-man teams to represent them. The first winners were the formidable Argentine pairing of Antonio Cerda and Roberto de Vicenzo. Twelve months on, Peter Thomson and Kel Nagle won the tournament, now the World Cup, for Australia.

The format has always been the same: 72 holes of strokeplay with all scores counting. An individual prize is awarded, but it is the team trophy that everyone is playing for.

An indication of the event's former stature came in 1956 when it was staged at Wentworth: both Ben Hogan and Sam Snead travelled to take part. Predictably they won, with Hogan also taking the individual prize.

It set a tone for the Americans, who have won the World Cup on more occasions than any other nations (22). Their best players have all represented them: Arnold Palmer and Jack Nicklaus combined to win the event on four occasions, and Tiger Woods has won it twice, partnered by Mark O'Meara in 1999 and David Duval in 2000.

There was room for another team event as well. Never shy of capitalizing on a commercial opportunity, the marketing men of the PGA Tour were keen to jump on the newfound popularity of the Ryder Cup: the problem for them was what to do in the years that the cup did not take place?

The answer was staring them in the face and in 1994 the President's Cup was born: featuring a United

States team against a non-European International team. The format of the competition is similar to that of the Ryder Cup except that five fourball matches are played instead of the four.

And despite their poor recent showing in the Ryder Cup – in which they have lost five of the last seven contests – the Americans have performed strongly in this event, winning six of the eight editions played and losing only once, when the tournament moved overseas for the first time and was staged at the splendid Royal Melbourne course in Australia. The 2003 event, held in South Africa for the first time, ended in a 17-17 draw.

For the individual professional, there is money to be had in other

World Golf Championships Recent Winners

Matchplay Championship

Year	Winner	Score
2004	T Woods by D Love III	3&2
2005	D Toms bt C DiMarco	6&5
2006	G Ogilvy bt D Love III	3&2
2007	H Stenson bt G Ogilvy	2&1
2008	T Woods bt S Cink	8&7
2009	G Ogilvy bt P Casey	4&3
2010	I Poulter bt P Casey	4&2

NEC Invitational

Year	Winner
2004	S Cink
2005	T Woods
2006	T Woods
2007	T Woods
2008	V Singh
2009	T Woods

American Express Championships

Year	Winner
2005	T Woods
2006	T Woods
2007	T Woods
2008	G Ogilvy
2009	P Mickelson
2010	E Els

Following on from their successful debuts in the Ryder Cup, Luke Donald and Paul Casey took England to only their second World Cup success in 2004.

World Cup of Golf

Year	Country	Winners	Year	Country	Winners	Year	Country	Winners
1953	Argentina	A Cerda, R de Vicenzo	1972	Taiwan	Hsieh Min Nan, Lu Liang Huan	1991	Sweden	A Forsbrand, P-U Johannson
1954	Australia	P Thomson, K Nagle						
1955	United States	C Harbert, E Furgol	1973	United States	J Nicklaus, J Miller	1992	United States	D Love III, F Couples
1956	United States	B Hogan, S Snead	1974	South Africa	B Cole, D Hayes	1993	United States	D Love III, F Couples
1957	Japan	T Nakamura, K Ono	1975	United States	J Miller, L Graham	1994	United States	D Love III, F Couples
1958	Ireland	H Bradshaw, C O'Connor	1976	Spain	S Ballesteros, M Pinero	1995	United States	D Love III, F Couples
1959	Australia	P Thomson, K Nagle	1977	Spain	S Ballesteros, A Garrido	1996	South Africa	E Els, W Westner
1960	United States	S Snead, A Palmer	1978	United States	J Mahaffey, A North	1997	Ireland	P Harrington, P McGinley
1961	United States	S Snead, J Demaret	1979	United States	J Mahaffey, H Irwin	1998	England	N Faldo, D Carter
1962	United States	S Snead, A Palmer	1980	Canada	D Halldorson, J Nelford	1999	United States	T Woods, M O'Meara
1963	United States	A Palmer, J Nicklaus	1981	Not played		2000	United States	T Woods, D Duval
1964	United States	A Palmer, J Nicklaus	1982	Spain	M Pinero, J-M Canizares	2001	South Africa	E Els, R Goosen
1965	South Africa	G Player, H Henning	1983	United States	R Caldwell, J Cook	2002	Japan	S Maruyama, T Izawa
1966	United States	A Palmer, J Nicklaus	1984	Spain	J-M Canizares, J Rivero	2003	South Africa	R Sabbatini, T Immelman
1967	United States	A Palmer, J Nicklaus	1985	Canada	D Halldorson, D Barr	2004	England	L Donald, P Casey
1968	Canada	A Balding, G Knudson	1986	Not played		2005	Wales	S Dodd, B Dredge
1969	United States	O Moody, L Trevino	1987	Wales	I Woosnam, D Llewellyn	2006	Germany	B Langer, M Siem
1970	Australia	B Devlin, D Graham	1988	United States	B Crenshaw, M McCumber	2007	Scotland	C Montgomerie, M Warren
1971	United States	J Nicklaus, L Trevino	1989	Australia	W Grady, P Fowler	2008	Sweden	R Karlsson, H Stenson
			1990	Germany	B Langer, T Gideon	2009	Italy	E Molinari, F Molinari

World MatchPlay Championship Results

Year	Winner	Result	Year	Winner	Result	Year	Winner	Result
Played at Wentworth, Surrey, England until 2007			1979	Bill Rogers bt Isao Aoki	1 hole	1996	Ernie Els bt Vijay Singh	3&2
			1980	Greg Norman bt Sandy Lyle	1 hole	1997	Vijay Singh bt Ernie Els	1 hole
1964	Arnold Palmer bt Neil Coles	2&1	1981	Seve Ballesteros bt Ben Crenshaw	1 hole	1998	Mark O'Meara bt Tiger Woods	1 hole
1965	Gary Player bt Peter Thomson	3&2	1982	Seve Ballesteros bt Sandy Lyle	37th	1999	Colin Montgomerie bt Mark O'Meara	3&2
1966	Gary Player bt Jack Nicklaus	6&4	1983	Greg Norman bt Nick Faldo	3&2	2000	Lee Westwood bt Colin Montgomerie	38th hole
1967	Arnold Palmer bt Peter Thomson	1 hole	1984	Seve Ballesteros bt Bernhard Langer	2&1			
1968	Gary Player bt Bob Charles	1 hole	1985	Seve Ballesteros bt Bernhard Langer	6&5	2001	Ian Woosnam bt Padraig Harrington	2&1
1969	Bob Charles bt Gene Littler	37th	1986	Greg Norman bt Sandy Lyle	2&1	2002	Ernie Els bt Sergio Garcia	2&1
1970	Jack Nicklaus bt Lee Trevino	2&1	1987	Ian Woosnam bt Sandy Lyle	1 hole	2003	Ernie Els bt Thomas Bjorn	4&3
1971	Gary Player bt Jack Nicklaus	5&4	1988	Sandy Lyle bt Nick Faldo	2&1	2004	Ernie Els bt Lee Westwood	2&1
1972	Tom Weiskopf bt Lee Trevino	4&3	1989	Nick Faldo bt Ian Woosnam	1 hole	2005	Michael Campbell bt Paul McGinley	2&1
1973	Gary Player bt Graham Marsh	40th	1990	Ian Woosnam bt Mark McNulty	4&2	2006	Paul Casey bt Shaun Micheel	10&8
1974	Hale Irwin bt Gary Player	3&1	1991	Seve Ballesteros bt Nick Price	3&2	2007	Ernie Els bt Angel Cabrera	6&4
1975	Hale Irwin bt Al Geiberger	4&2	1992	Nick Faldo bt Jeff Sluman	8&7	2008	No tournament	
1976	David Graham bt Hale Irwin	38th	1993	Corey Pavin bt Nick Faldo	1 hole	2009	R Fisher bt Anthony Kim	4&3
1977	Graham Marsh bt Ray Floyd	5&3	1994	Ernie Els bt Colin Montgomerie	4&2			
1978	Isao Aoki bt Simon Owen	3&2	1995	Ernie Els bt Steve Elkington	3&1			

parts of the world apart from the United States and Europe. The lords of the links can jet off to Japan, where the action gets underway with the $1.5 million Token Cup and culminates in the $2 million Dunlop Phoenix, Japan's richest event. Johnny Miller won it first, in 1974, since when 12 other Americans have triumphed, but only two Japanese – Tommy Nakajima in 1985 and the ruler of the Japanese circuit, Jumbo Osaki, with a record last round of 65 to beat Tom Watson by a stroke in 1994. The Japanese Open has seldom been won by a foreigner. Seve Ballesteros did so twice (1977 and 1978).

Then there are the Australasian and Asian honey-pots to think about. The Australian Open (which Jack Nicklaus has won six times, Gary Player seven) dates back to 1904, but the depression years of the late 1980s hit the Australian circuit harder than most.

The South African Open, first played in 1903, is older than that of Canada, Australia or New Zealand. Brothers Sid and Jock Brews had dominated South African golf for many years until Bobby Locke won the Amateur and Open in the space of a few days in 1935. He won the Open eight times more – twice as an amateur – and Gary Player has

triumphed on 13 occasions. Another to have enjoyed success there is South Africa's most recent addition to world superstardom, Ernie Els.

And then there is tradition. The World Matchplay Championship used to be seen by golf fans as the bookend to the season. That is hardly the case given the number of tournaments played nowadays, but it is a fine testament to the competition that was staged over the Wentworth course every year between 1964 and 2007. The idea arose when Mark McCormack, the head of the IMG management group, thought that it would be a good idea to bring together the best eight players in golf and have them battle it out over 36 holes of matchplay. Given that McCormack managed the best three players in the world at the time – Arnold Palmer, Jack Nicklaus and Gary Player – he had no problem putting together a top-class field.

But times changed ... By the mid-1990s the event was struggling to live up to its reputation. The four major champions were always invited, but one or more seemed to have a prior commitment. Just as the event looked as though it was going to die a death, Tiger Woods came along – he didn't win, he left that privilege to his close friend and neighbour Mark

O'Meara, but the crowds flocked to the Surrey course to see the world number one in action. It gave the tournament a new lease of life. The changes made to the event in 2009 – it is now staged in Malaga, Spain, with players competing in a four-group round-robin format, with the group winners progressing to the semi-finals – were intended to extend the event's legacy still further into the 21st century.

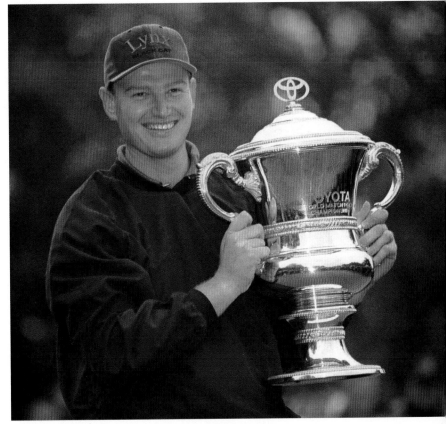

South African Ernie Els has achieved the unique feat of completing two separate hat-tricks in the World Matchplay tournament – the first in 1994-96 and the second in 2002-04.

PART THREE:
THE GREAT GOLFERS

Every era produces its great golfers. These are the men and women who have captivated the galleries down the years, not only with their play but also through their charisma. They drew spectators who may personally have had only the most rudimentary golfing talent, but who were awe-struck by the skills of their idols. Here is a selection of the greatest of them all.

South African Ernie Els takes in the view from the seventeenth green at Loch Lomond.

Thomas Aaron

Born: February 22, 1937
Gainesville, Ga, USA

His name may well mean that he heads an alphabetical list of any of the great players, but his playing record also stands up against the members of this group. Aaron's name will forever be associated with the Masters. In 1968, he marked down a four instead of a three for Roberto De Vicenzo at the par-three 17th; it was a shot that cost the Argentine a place in the play-offs because he failed to see the error before signing the card. Five years later, Aaron shot a final-round 68 to win the title himself by one stroke over J C Snead.

Amy Alcott

Born: February 22, 1956
Kansas City, Mo, USA

At club level many women golfers take the club back much too far and then have to waste effort in lifting it back again to a horizontal position. Alcott is the reverse. The club goes back little beyond shoulder height and she then delivers a very firm blow indeed. The short backswing, if not taken to extremes, can be an aid to consistency, and over a long professional career she has been one of the most consistent performers week-in week-out, though her career may now be on the wane. In her first 15 years on the LPGA Tour, she was never worse than 18th on the money list and often did a great deal better than that, finishing in the top five five times. Her tournament wins are also impressive. Between 1975 and 1991 she amassed 29 wins, of which five rank as majors: three Dinah Shores, one Peter Jackson plus the 1980 US Women's Open. Her best years were 1979, 1980 and 1984, when she won four times. Perhaps her outstanding achievement was her US Women's Open victory. Her 280 aggregate was then a record for the event and saw her home by a remarkable nine-stroke margin.

Robert Allenby

Born: July 12, 1971
Melbourne, Australia

If ever there was a player to avoid in a play-off, then it's Robert Allenby. When he came through a play-off at the Nissan Open in 2001 to secure the third of his four PGA Tour titles he took his career play-off record to 8-0: it would be hard to question his nerve. Following an impressive amateur career in his native Australia, Allenby gained his first European Tour success at the Heineken Classic, again on home ground. His next season was his best, and almost his last. Facial injuries and a broken sternum sustained in a car accident in Spain brought the curtain down on a season that had seen three wins and a climb to third place in the Order of Merit. A switch to the PGA Tour and the States finally came good in 2000 when he defeated Craig Stadler in the first of those play-offs to secure the Houston Open; he defeated Nick Price in another play-off at the Western Open to secure his second title of the year. Further successes on the PGA tour may have eluded him, but he has rediscovered winning ways back in Australia. In 2003, he won the Australian Masters; two years later he completed a stunning hat-trick by winning the Australian Masters, the Australian Open, and the Australian PGA in consecutive weeks to become the only player in history to win Australia's Triple Crown. His best finish in a major came at the 2004 US Open, where he came home tied for seventh place. Allenby has represented the Rest of the World in the President's Cup on five occasions.

Peter Alliss

Born: February 28, 1931
Berlin, Germany

This is a man who likes talking, and does it incomparably well. Apparently it all began when a BBC producer heard him keeping his fellow tour players in uproar on a journey back to England from Ireland. An invitation followed for him to make a few comments on the air about a tournament round he had just completed and how the course was playing. In due course this led on to television commentary, immediately after his main playing career ended in 1969. Peter is now regarded as comfortably the world's best golf commentator and has been voted, in Britain, the best sports commentator. As a professional golfer, he never quite fulfilled his potential, though he was very good indeed, winning some 20 important events during the 1950s and 1960s, including three successive events in Europe in 1958. He was selected for every Ryder Cup team bar one between 1953 and 1969, and also

THOMAS AARON His legacy will always be linked with the Masters tournament at Augusta.

played ten times for England in the World Cup. Alliss was one of the longest and most consistent hitters in the game and was also very tidy around the green, but his putting became his Achilles heel. He had begun with a highly unorthodox grip - but it worked. He was advised to change it, and did, never to be the same player again.

Willie **Anderson**
Born: October 21, 1879
North Berwick, Scotland

In the US Open, Anderson set two records that have still to be surpassed. In 1905, he won his fourth championship, a record since equalled only by Bobby Jones, Ben Hogan and Jack Nicklaus - but even they couldn't go on to a fifth title. Anderson also won three of his titles in a row, an achievement which might have been matched by Ben Hogan - winner in 1948, 1950 and 1951 - but for his severe car accident early in 1949. Anderson had a very high performance level in the US Open, for besides his victories he had one second place, one third, two fourths and three fifths. In a relatively short career - he died at the age of 30 - Anderson was nearly always in contention in this championship. He had numerous successes in local tournaments, as well as a remarkable four wins in the Western Open, which in those days ranked second only to the US Open. Anderson is unusual in that his victories came with two different kinds of ball, the gutta percha and the rubber core. He had a flat swing, with a good deal of bend in the left arm, and opponents thought his greatest strength was an unflappable temperament.

Isao **Aoki**
Born: August 31, 1942
Abiko, Chiba, Japan

Aoki is one of the most unlikely looking great players, for he uses a remarkable - now unfashionably

wristy - technique for both full shots and the short game. In his putting stroke, where he is one of the best ever performers, he uses a centre-shaft putter with the toe of the club cocked high in the air - and raps it into the hole. He is one of the rare Japanese golfers to come close to winning a major championship. This is because the Japan Tour is very lucrative indeed and so few trouble themselves to play on other tours. Aoki does, and in 1994 he won well over $500,000 on the Senior Tour. He has been the leading money winner in Japan five times and has won more than 50 times in both his home country and worldwide. He is the only Japanese player to have won on four different tours - Japan, Australia, Europe and the USA. His greatest international success came in the 1980 US Open, where he broke the scoring record with rounds of 68, 68, 68, 70 and still finished a couple of strokes behind Jack Nicklaus. He won the 1978 World Matchplay title at Wentworth and the 1983 European Open, while his third-round 63 in the 1980 Open Championship at Muirfield equalled the lowest ever shot in the event. He has won nine times on the Senior Tour and ranks in the top 30, all-time money winners - in 18th with $9.8 million.

George **Archer**
Born: October 1, 1939
San Francisco, Ca, USA

Archer was one of the players who must have rejoiced that the Senior Tour had become such a great commercial success. In the 1990-94 period, he averaged over $750,000 per year and got very near to the million mark on two occasions. In just a few years he piled up 15 victories, surpassing his achievements on the main tour when he collected 12 wins between 1965 and 1984. One of these was a major, the 1969 Masters, where he began with a very good first round

Robert Allenby One of a growing number of Australians to have achieved success on the PGA Tour.

of 67 and held on to win by a single stroke. The greatest strength of his game was his putting, where he must surely be ranked in, say, the top half dozen of modern times. From his great height of 6ft 5in, he crouched low over the ball and then got himself even nearer by gripping well down the handle of his putter. Besides his highly unusual set-up to the ball for putting, Archer liked to feel that he was guiding the putter with his left hand, while his right hand gave him a feel for the pace. Playing in the 1980 Heritage Classic, he set a tour record by taking only 94 putts for the four rounds.

Tommy **Armour**
Born: September 24, 1895
Edinburgh, Scotland

Tommy Armour won three major championships. First came the US Open of 1927, when he holed a putt of 10ft or so on the last hole to tie Harry Cooper and then beat him in a close-fought play-off. Armour's effort had been particularly fine because he had scattered shots in

his fourth round and needed an excellent last four holes to draw level. His next win was in the 1930 US PGA, where he had a narrow victory in the final over Gene Sarazen. But the prize he really sought was the British Open, and he won it, against the odds, at Carnoustie in 1931, producing a very good final round while others threw it away. By this time Armour was already on his way out, suffering from the putting "yips", a term he himself invented. When he retired from the game, he became a very highly paid teacher and author. Armour was known as a superb iron player, but considered himself a better wooden club player and claimed it was his tee positioning which gave him easier shots into the greens. Perhaps that is why the woods he is said to have originally designed are much sought after today. Tommy is also remembered for the immortal reply he gave when challenged about his notoriously slow play: "Whoever said golf was supposed to be played fast?"

Paul Azinger

Born: January 6, 1960
Holyoke, Ma, USA

"When you're 33 you don't expect anybody to tell you that you've got cancer. I was in my prime. I felt bullet-proof." Before 1993, Azinger was possibly the man in American golf and the one who was thought most likely to become a superstar. In a seven-year winning run from 1987 on the PGA Tour he had been in the top four money winners four times and had never finished lower than 11th. In 1993, he took the US PGA Championship. Then, following the best season of his professional career, Azinger was informed that a troublesome problem in the shoulders was in fact lymphoma in the right shoulder-blade. Happily, good performances from late 1994 onwards indicated both recovery from the disease and a return to golf form. However, he is not the dominant figure he once was and that may be influenced by the memory of his failure in the British Open at Muirfield in 1987. That is the one Nick Faldo won because Azinger dropped shots at both of the last two holes. However, he has also had plenty of successes. The most dramatic came in the 1993 Memorial Tournament, when he holed out from a greenside bunker to win by a stroke from Corey Pavin. He has won once since his return from illness, the 2000 Sony Open in Hawaii, and made the last of his four Ryder Cup appearances in 2002 at The Belfry, halving his singles match with Niclas Fasth by, you've guessed it, holing out from the greenside bunker on the 18th. In recent years, his appearances on the PGA tour have been limited by an ailing back, although he did find himself back in the limelight in 2008, when he captained the US team to its first victory over Europe since 1999.

Ian Baker-Finch

Born: October 24, 1960
Nambour, Australia

At Birkdale in the 1991 British Open, all the talk centred on whether or not Seve Ballesteros could perform in the final round and win. Meanwhile, no one was paying much attention to Baker-Finch. They soon were, after he birdied five of the first seven holes and played the first nine in 29, a very rare feat indeed. He finished with a 66, to win by two strokes. He had looked a champion seven years earlier – at St Andrews in 1984, when rounds of 68 and 66 gave him a three-stroke lead. A 71 then left him tied for the lead with Tom Watson, but a disaster at the first hole in the final round damaged his confidence. Playing to the green, his ball twisted back into the Swilcan Burn which fronts it. And that was that. He managed to break 80, but only by a single stroke. His next real attempt at a British Open title came in 1990 when a third-round 64 took him into a tie for second place, with Nick Faldo five strokes ahead. Faldo did not falter. Baker-Finch won a PGA Tour event in 1989 (the Southwestern Bell Colonial) and was consistently successful in his homeland, Japan and Europe, until back and shoulder injuries and eye surgery in 1994 led to years of missed cuts. He announced his retirement from tournament golf following an opening-round 92 at the 1997 British Open. He now works as a commentator for CBS in the United States.

John Ball

Born: December 24, 1861
Hoylake, England

This player has a very strong claim to be considered the greatest amateur of all time – as long as one excludes Bobby Jones. But even Jones did not win as many amateur championship titles in Britain and the United States as Ball, who totalled eight in Britain between 1888 and 1912 and was also the beaten finalist twice. He did not compete at all in America. During his peak years, in the 1890s, he was fully capable of competing with the very best professionals. In 1890, he became the first Englishman to win the British Open, which he achieved at Prestwick as a result of extremely consistent play. In the next few years, he was a man to watch out for, but it is highly likely that he was far more interested in the Amateur Championship, as he may well have preferred the matchplay format and also the camaraderie of those he knew best. Ball was not renowned as a putter, and his great strength was the accuracy of his long shots up to the flag. In this respect, he was a revolutionary player for the game. Before his great days, all had been content to aim for the green. Ball, however, wanted to be close to the flag.

Severiano Ballesteros

SEE PAGE 141

Miller Barber

Born: March 31, 1931
Shreveport, La, USA

Barber's money-winning achievements show just how important the Senior Tour can be. He has won over $4 million as one of the more effective performers, with 24 victories between 1982 and 1989. He twice led the money list and finished inside the top ten on eight occasions. Barber was also extremely effective on the main PGA Tour, which he joined in 1959, going on to win 11 times. He played in two Ryder Cup matches, in 1969 and 1971. During the period from 1963 to 1978 he was never out of the top-40 money winners and finished in the top 25 12 times. Barber seldom featured strongly in the major championships, though he did equal the Masters then-record low round with a 64 in 1979. His best chance of victory in a major came in the 1969 US Open, which he led by three going into the final round. However, he then fell away with a round of 78 to finish in sixth position. Barber's swing is highly unorthodox, but it has worked well for him. Indeed, he has flourished in Senior golf and has gone on to win the US Senior Open three times.

IAN BAKER-FINCH A final-round 66 handed him the 1991 British Open title.

SEVERIANO BALLESTEROS
The Natural

For long periods, Severiano Ballesteros made the rest of a golf field look like a collection of cart-horses. The glory of his game was his golf swing and the poise and rhythm of the follow-through.

But there was a contradiction. If you watched the man on a practice ground or playing a competitive round, he was all worry and rehearsal. With the driver, in particular, he was often crooked but long; but he showed real genius around the greens to get out of the awkward positions his frequently wayward driving put him in.

After learning to play the game on the beaches of Redreña, his home in northern Spain, he burst onto the world scene in 1976, at the age of 19, when he challenged for the British Open at Royal Birkdale. Few paid much attention when he tied for the first-round lead with a 69. Who was he? How did you pronounce his name? Interviewed in the Press tent afterwards, Seve declared he might take 80 if the wind got up the next day. That remark may have been the beginning of the love affair that the Press have had with Ballesteros – particularly in Britain – throughout his career.

The next day, another 69 gave him a two-stroke lead. Could this very young unknown win? It was not to be, though he held the same margin over Miller after the third day's play. On the last day, however, Miller took the lead quickly, while Ballesteros had more than his usual ration of wild tee shots. A late burst allowed him to finish second and he knew he was on his way.

It was only a matter of time before he won the British Open, which he did at Lytham in 1979 three years after his stunning debut, cementing his growing fame for wild play in his final round by carving his drive into BBC vehicles and, of course, recording a birdie on the hole. When it was all over, his playing partner, Hale Irwin, remarked bemusedly that he could not understand how anyone could finish as British Open champion after so much bad driving.

Seve had still to prove himself in the US. It didn't take him long: in the 1980 Masters his start of 66, 69, 68 gave him a seven-stroke lead going into the final round. At one point he increased that to ten before some embarrassing play from the 11th to the 13th. Easing up, he ran out a comfortable four-stroke winner.

There was the same four-stroke margin in 1983, this time largely because of a blistering start in his final round – birdie, eagle, par, birdie and out in 31. There were no real alarms and he finished by chipping in for a par on the last after roaring through the green with his second and then misjudging his third.

The following year came his second British Open title, at St Andrews. It saw some of the steadiest play the Spaniard has produced. Par followed par through the rounds, but birdies were few. By generally choosing to go left from the tee to avoid trouble, he was leaving himself more difficult lines into the greens. On the 71st hole, he again went well left into the rough, giving himself little chance of hitting, let alone holding, the green. But that is what he did. A birdie putt at the relatively easy last hole then saw him home by two from Watson and Langer.

As well as his five majors, Ballesteros also carried Europe in the Ryder Cup for many years and his heroics were rewarded with the captaincy at Valderrama in 1997. Loss of form ruled him out as a player for the tournament; although his game seldom faltered, his tee shots often did. His joy in victory over the old enemy – on Spanish soil, too – was almost unconfined.

SEVE BALLESTEROS **A genius around the greens.**

From 2000 onwards, appearances in tournaments became scarce and Ballesteros announced his retirement from the game in July 2006. Two years later, in October 2008, news emerged from Spain that the five-time major winner was "gravely ill" in a Madrid hospital. Over the course of the next few weeks, as the golfing world held its breath, Ballesteros underwent several operations to remove a brain tumour. Thankfully, he appears to be making a steady recovery, and delighted everybody by announcing his intention to play in the 150th British Open at St Andrews in July 2010. The entire golfing world will be glad to see him there.

1957	1976	1979	1980	1983
Born on April 9, Pedrena, northern Spain	Wins first Tour event, Dutch Open, aged 19	First Spaniard to win the British Open and first Continental European since Arnaud Massy in 1907	First European to win the Masters and, at 23, the youngest champion	A second Masters title

1984	1988	1997	2008
His second British Open title, distinguished by steady play	Third British Open title, defeating Nick Faldo and Nick Price with a final-round 65 – "the best round of my life"	Captained Europe to Ryder Cup success on home soil at Valderrama	Undergoes treatment and surgery for a brain tumour

Brian Barnes

Born: June 3, 1945
Addington, England

Regarded as one of golf's eccentrics, Barnes has been known to wear shorts, smoke a pipe and drink copious quantities of canned beer when out playing a tournament. Some would say that this player's greatest achievements came in the Ryder Cup, where he was in every team from 1969 to 1979. In the 1975 event, he beat Jack Nicklaus twice in singles in one day. He has also made many appearances for Scotland in both the World Cup and the Double Diamond event. The winner of nearly 29 professional tournaments, he probably had his finest hour in the 1981 Tournament Players' Championship: a last-round 62 took him into a play-off, which he then won. He is a powerful player using a short backswing, followed by a lunge at the ball. He might have become a great player if he had won a British Open early in his career, as he certainly had the potential to do so. He made a sensational start to his Seniors career by winning the 1995 Senior British Open and defended his title the following year. He also won on the US Senior Tour. Injury brought his career to a premature end. He is now a familiar voice on British television.

Jim Barnes

Born: 1887
Lelant, England

Nicknamed "Long Jim" because of his 6ft 3in height, Barnes emigrated from his native Cornwall in 1906 to San Francisco. In 1913, he tied for fourth place in the US Open and the following year achieved the first of three victories in the then very important Western Open. Even more significant was his victory in the first ever US PGA Championship of 1916. He also won the first post-war event in 1919, and was to reach two more finals, in 1921 and 1924, losing on both occasions to Walter Hagen. His greatest triumph came in the 1921 US Open. His opening-round 69 gave him the lead and he drew away round by round, eventually finishing with a nine-stroke winning margin. Though Barnes became an American citizen, he still liked to return to Britain, where he tied for second place in the 1922 British Open and won in 1925 in the infamous Prestwick event. It was thought that Macdonald Smith had been cheated of victory because of crowd disturbances during his final round. Barnes played in what some consider the first Ryder Cup in 1926, but was ruled out afterwards because he was not a native-born American.

Chip Beck

Born: September 12, 1956
Fayetteville, NC, USA

Undoubtedly the highlight of Beck's career is the 59 he scored in the third round of the Las Vegas Invitational at Sunrise Golf Club in October 1991. That made him only the second player, after Al Geiberger, to break the magic 60 in a PGA Tour event. He went out in 29, starting at the tenth, with seven birdies, and the other nine holes were just as eventful. The birdies continued to flow in, and at the 18th he fired in an eight-iron shot to about 3ft and then completed the job. That meant a total of 13 birdies and no dropped shots – and a reward of $500,000. Beck had a quiet start to his PGA Tour career in 1979 and did not begin to make any real money until 1983. His first big year came in 1987, though he had still failed to record a win. He rectified that in 1988 with two victories. His closest approach to a major came in the 1993 Masters, when he finished in second place, four strokes behind Bernhard Langer. Some observers considered that he had been mentally ready to settle for second place. However, in the Ryder Cup that same year he came from three down with five to play to defeat Barry Lane by one up. He switched to the Senior Tour in 2006 and has enjoyed considerable success, making the cut in 70 of the 71 events he has played (recording three

RICH BEEM He saw off the challenge of Tiger Woods to win the 2002 US PGA Championship.

top-three finishes) and amassing a further $1.3 million in prize money.

Rich Beem

Born: August 24, 1970
Phoenix, Tx, USA

Disillusioned by the game and selling mobile phones and car stereos in Seattle, a chance visit to the 1998 Buick Classic – where fellow El Paso resident, J P Hayes, won the tournament – rekindled Rich Beem's interest in the game. Giving up the job in Seattle, he worked in a pro shop in Texas, played on the mini tour and secured his tour card for the 1999 season with an eighth-place finish at qualifying school: since then the Texan has not looked back. Victory at the Kemper Open in only his 12th start on tour secured him a pay cheque of $450,000 and went some way to earning him the Rookie of the Year accolade. His best year on tour to date came in 2002. He won The International tournament to gain his second tour title and held off the challenge of Tiger Woods with a final-round 66 in his next start – the US PGA Championship – to secure a first major championship. An eagle at the 13th and a 35ft birdie putt on the 16th saw him become the first player to come from behind on the final day to win a major since Paul Lawrie at the 1999 British Open. Beem ended the season in seventh place on the money list with season's earnings of $2,938,365: not bad for a mobile phone salesman. He has not hit such dizzy heights since, but remains aa regular feature on the PGA tour.

Patty **Berg**
Born: February 13, 1918
Minneapolis, Mn, USA
Berg reached the final of the US Women's Amateur on her first entry in 1935. She was there again two years later, but had to wait until 1938 for her first victory. A hugely successful amateur golfer, she won in the region of 40 events before turning professional just before the Second World War. Together with Babe Zaharias and Betty Jameson, she was one of the three founder members of the fledgling US Women's Tour, which took off properly in 1948 and in which she became a dominant force. In 1946, she had won the first US Women's Open, then matchplay, and went on to win what was billed as the World Championship in 1953, 1954, 1955 and 1957. She was also the leading money winner in 1954, 1955 and 1957. This meant that she was the first woman to pass $100,000 in career money winnings. Berg also set the low round record, 64, in 1952 which stood for 12 years until it was beaten by Mickey Wright. Having first won a professional tournament in 1941, she won her last more than 20 years later, in 1962, bringing her total to 57.

Thomas **Bjorn**
Born: February 17, 1971
Silkeborg, Denmark
The best player to have come out of Scandinavia? You don't have to look much further than Thomas Bjorn. After a record-breaking season on the Challenge Tour in 1995, the Dane claimed his first European Tour win at the Loch Lomond World Invitational and went on to collect the tour's

Rookie of the Year title. A year later, he became the first player from his country to play in the Ryder Cup. Nine other tournament victories have followed, but none as yet in the major championships: although he has come close. He has reserved his best performances in the majors for the British Open. He tied for second behind a runaway Tiger Woods at St Andrews in 2000, but his biggest disappointment came in 2003 at Royal St George's. A double bogey on the par-three 16th and then a bogey at the 17th saw him fall one stroke behind eventual winner Ben Curtis: it may have been his fourth consecutive top ten at the British Open, but it must surely have left a sour taste in the big Dane's mouth. He suffered more major championship heartbreak at the 2005 US PGA, when he lost out to Phil Mickelson by a single stroke.

Tommy **Bolt**
Born: March 31, 1918
Haworth, Ok, USA
Bolt was a sublime striker of a golf ball and, in his peak years, was thought to have the most fluid golf swing in the game. However, he was a rather poor putter – the worst, he was known to claim, among his playing contemporaries. Temperamentally he could handle his bad putting, believing that the good putters were inferior players who didn't appreciate what the game of golf was all about – excellence in the shots through the green. Here Bolt excelled, but earned his "Thunderbolt" nickname as a result of his quite frequent losses of temper when such a shot didn't come off. Although he had already been a professional for a few years, Bolt did not join the PGA Tour until 1950, at the age of 32. He went on to win 11 tour events between 1953 and 1961, and four others of significance, but not then regarded as official. His most important victory came in the 1958 US Open, which he took by four strokes from the very young Gary Player. Bolt also had a run at the

THOMAS BJORN A huge talent who had a near-miss at the 2003 British Open.

Masters, in 1952, but his putting let him down – he three-putted three of the last four and came in third.

Michael **Bonallack**
Born: December 31, 1934
Chigwell, England
Bonallack is one of just three candidates for the title of "Greatest British Amateur Ever", the others being John Ball and Harold Hilton. However, with his consecutive wins in 1968, 1969 and 1970, he achieved something that even they had not managed in the British Amateur Championship. Bonallack had also won this event in both 1961 and 1965. Sometimes uncertain regarding his long shots, Bonallack was unsurpassed even by his professional contemporaries at

the short game in general and, particularly, at putting. Asked about his method in this department, he declared that he simply "willed the ball into the hole". A more obvious feature was the way he spread his feet wide and crouched over the ball, a style that may not be seen so much nowadays, but which was common in the earlier parts of the 20th century. Bonallack was indeed a master of the short game. During one of his five wins in the British Amateur Championship, one final came his way despite the fact that he missed 22 greens and still managed to get down in two. Later, he went into golf administration, and, after serving as secretary of the R&A for 16 years, he retired in 1999.

Julius **Boros**

Born: March 3, 1920
Fairfield, USA

Boros was one of those golfers who look more relaxed than they really are. Fearful of becoming locked over the ball, he evolved a method to prevent such a situation from occurring. He would walk casually up to his ball, shuffle his feet into his stance – and then swing. It worked so well that people thought that this was the way the game should be played. Boros was a late developer, not giving up his accountancy work for professional tournament play until the age of 30. He then immediately contended for the US Open in 1950 and was fourth the following year. In 1952, he comfortably beat the great Hogan, having trailed him by four strokes after 36 holes. If this was a surprise victory, his win in 1963 came as something of a shock to Boros himself. His 76 in the third round did his chances little good, and a 72 in the afternoon round, leaving him nine-over par, merely suggested he would get a reasonable pay cheque in a very high-scoring event. But no one beat that score, and in the 18-hole play-off the following day, Boros's 70 was good enough to beat Arnold Palmer by six strokes and Jacky Cupit by three. His other major success came at the 1968 US PGA at the impressive age of 48, making him the oldest ever winner of a major championship. He died in May 1994 at the age of 74.

Pat **Bradley**

Born: March 24, 1951
Westford, Ma, USA

Pat Bradley was one of the very top players on the LPGA Tour for a long time. She first won in 1976, and her 31st victory came in 1995. From 1976 to 1991 she recorded 12 placings in the top-six money winners and had just one bad year, the result primarily of hyperthyroidism. She has won six LPGA events which count as majors. Her family's neighbours are by now well used to the sound of the bell her mother rings – at all hours – on the back porch every time Bradley wins. Her greatest money-winning year came in 1991, when she took home more than $750,000 and was first on the money list. She had the same placing in 1986, but 1991 was easily her best year. She had four victories, increasing her total to 30, and thus earning her a place in the LPGA Hall of Fame. That same year she also won the Rolex Player of the Year award and the Vare Trophy (for best scoring average) for the second time in her career. Aided by yearly increases in prize money, Bradley was the first woman golfer to surpass, in turn, career winnings of $2 million, $3 million, $4 million and then the $5-million mark. She has been playing on the US Women's Senior Tour since 2002.

Harry **Bradshaw**

Born: October 9, 1913
Delgany, Ireland

In 1949, Bradshaw was playing in the British Open at Sandwich and in contention after a first-round 68 and at the peak of his form. Playing the fifth hole in the second round, he found his ball resting against broken glass. He thought he was very likely entitled to a free drop, but was unsure. Nowadays any professional would automatically call for an official ruling. Bradshaw, however, decided to play the ball as it lay, was hit by flying glass and moved the ball less than 20 yards. He took six instead of the par four which had been likely. Worse, he was upset and his normally superb putting stroke was far less sure for the rest of his round of 77. The next day he had recovered his composure, and with rounds of 68 and 70 he went on to tie with South African Bobby Locke – only to be totally outplayed in the play-off. Bradshaw was never again to be in real contention for the British Open. His greatest achievement, in partnership with Christie O'Connor, was to win the World Cup, in which, despite being affected by the high altitude, he was individually second. He made a total of three Ryder Cup appearances, and amongst his other successes recorded two wins in one of the most important tournaments of the day, the Dunlop Masters.

James **Braid**

SEE PAGE 145

Gay **Brewer**

Born: March 19, 1932
Middletown, Oh, USA

His name may well conjure up a host of images in one's mind, but the fact remains that Gay Brewer was a very useful golf player; good enough to win the Masters in 1967. Just a year earlier, he had been involved in a three-way play-off for the green jacket with Jack Nicklaus and Tommy Jacobs, but he was never a factor, scoring a 78 that left him eight shots behind the eventual winner, Nicklaus. He bounced back the following year, however, fighting tooth and nail with Bobby Nichols over the closing holes before coming out on top by a single stroke, courtesy of a marvellous last-round 67. Brewer collected 11 tour titles during the course of his career and was a member of the US Ryder Cup team in both 1967 and 1971.

GAY BREWER He tamed the Augusta greens in 1967 to pick up the green jacket - his only major.

JAMES BRAID
The Great Scot

James Braid's legacy is considerable. He was a founding member of the Professional Golfers' Association; he was also a notable course architect, with perhaps the King's Course at Gleneagles his most well-known design. He also helped enhance and develop the reputation of the two marvellous courses at the club that became his first love, Walton Heath.

First and foremost, however, he was one of the greatest golfers who ever lived. Braid won the British Open five times in the space of just ten years, from 1901 to 1910: during the course of the 20th century, nobody won the British Open more times.

Even in retirement he remained a considerable golfer. "This tall, stoop-ing, ruddy-complexioned Scot is one of the wonders of the golfing world," wrote Henry Cotton. "I write in 1948 and he still plays a round every day if it is fine, on occasions going round twice – and he was born in 1870."

As the last sentence indicates, Braid devoted his life completely to his sport. In childhood, he never spent any time playing football like his peers, because that was time wasted from the links. In his biography of Braid, Bernard Darwin wrote: "Some readers may complain that there is too much golf in this book. To them I must reply that this is inevitable, since golf is James' life."

Braid showed early promise on the links in Elie. He was a joiner by trade and used to practise every evening, despite a walk of several miles. Braid was a long hitter, but, like his great rival Harry Vardon, it was on the greens that he betrayed any weaknesses that he had.

Still, word about his prowess spread, and his apprenticeship as a joiner stood him in good stead when he was offered the post as clubmaker in the Army and Navy Stores in London in 1893.

He found time to practise his golf and, in 1894, entered for the British Open at Royal St George's, finishing tenth. Two years later, at Muirfield, he finished sixth. One year on, and he was runner-up to Harold Hilton over the latter's home course, Hoylake.

In the early years of the 20th century, it was Braid who dominated as J H Taylor's powers waned and Vardon struggled with tuberculosis.

The first of his five British Open titles came at Muirfield. Having finished third behind runaway champion J H Taylor and Harry Vardon the previous year, Braid turned the tables on the duo as he ran out a three-stroke winner over Vardon with Taylor a further stroke behind – all this despite shooting a final-round 80.

Four years later he triumphed again, this time at St Andrews. The Great Triumvirate dominated proceedings when the Open returned to Muirfield the following year – and once again Braid finished on top of the pile.

Any disappointment that may have followed his fifth-place finish in 1907 was brushed to one side when the Scot romped to an eight-stroke victory the following year – at Prestwick. It was the third time that he had lifted the famous Claret Jug in four years. His fifth and final triumph came at St Andrews in 1910, when, in the course of a four-stroke victory, he became the first player to break the 300-mark over the Old Course.

He finished fifth the following year and was third in 1912 when the championship returned to his favourite hunting ground, Muirfield. Braid's final appearance in the British Open came in 1914 at Prestwick: Vardon won a record sixth title; Braid lay ten strokes behind in tenth place. It would be the Scot's final appearance in the tournament as the First World War brought a six-year halt to proceedings.

JAMES BRAID A five-time British Open winner.

In summing up this most worthy of lives, Darwin, as ever, found the right words: "I think everyone recognized in him modesty, dignity, reticence, wisdom, and a deep and essential kindliness," he wrote. "They would also call him almost instinctively a great man. Great is one of those adjectives which we are unable to define, and if we are wise, we shall resolutely decline to try. We know what we mean by it; we naturally and unhesitatingly apply it to some people, and James was one of them."

1870	1901	1905	1906
Born on February 6 in Elie, Fife, Scotland	Wins British Open for the first time	Collects second British Open title, this time at St Andrews	Successfully defends British Open crown, his second triumph at Muirfield

	1908	1910	
	Wins his fourth British Open	Wins the British Open for the fifth and final time and is the first to break the 300-mark over the Old Course at St Andrews	

JOANNE CARNER She compiled an enviable amateur career before turning professional.

Eric Brown

Born: February 15, 1926
Edinburgh, Scotland

If they ever selected an all-time European Ryder Cup team from all the players who have ever participated in the contest, then a place would have to be found for this combative Scot. He may not have collected the major championships of some of his peers, but he possessed a grit and determination that was seen at its best in the rough and tumble of matchplay. Perhaps his finest moment came in Great Britain and Ireland's glorious victory in the 1957 contest at Lindrick. The captain, Dai Rees, put Brown out first in the singles in the hope that he would meet the ever-erupting volcano that was Tommy Bolt. Rees guessed right and Brown duly beat him 4&3. His great times were not just confined to beating Americans. He won a host of tournaments all over Europe and

was second in the Los Angeles Open in 1960. He always came up short in the British Open, however, finishing third in both 1957 and 1958. The latter was particularly hard to bear, since he took a six at the last when a four would have given him the title. Brown's final act in the spotlight was as Ryder Cup captain of the Great Britain and Ireland side that shared the spoils in the famous halved match at Birkdale in 1969.

Walter Burkemo

Born: October 9, 1918
Birmingham, Mi, USA

Here's a terrific quiz question: name two golfers who won major championships in 1953. Ben Hogan, who won three majors that year, is one. But who won the US PGA, the one that Hogan did not enter because it finished the day before the British Open started? The answer is Walter Burkemo, who, over several years,

established a reputation for himself as an accomplished matchplay golfer. In addition to winning the US PGA, he was a beaten finalist on two occasions (1951 and 1954). His victory was a popular one, as it was played in his hometown of Birmingham, MI.

Dick Burton

Born: October 11, 1907
Darwen, England

Burton's greatest achievement came in the last British Open to be played before the Second World War. At St Andrews he had rounds of 70, 72, 77 and 71 to win by two strokes from the American Johnny Bulla. Burton's play on the final hole particularly impressed all who witnessed it. The 350-yard 18th on the Old Course must be one of the easiest climaxes in championship golf. The only real danger for the tee shot is to hit a hotel or golf clubhouse along the right and go out of bounds. Most players, in conditions where they think they have no chance of reaching the green, play safe and aim left. Burton, however, hit his drive tight along the railings to the right. Though dangerous, this gives the best line into the green. It was almost all over. He flicked a short iron to a holeable distance and then, as his putt went on line, casually tossed the club to his caddie. Because of the war, he was British Open champion for the longest spell of anyone – seven years. Alas, again because of the war, he made little money from his win. Burton had two other high placings in the championship, and set a record for tournament scoring with rounds of 68, 66, 64 and 68 – 266.

Angel Cabrera

Born: September 12, 1969
Cordoba, Argentina

Nicknamed "El Pato" (The Duck), this big-hitting Argentine, a former caddie at the Cordoba Golf Club, was encouraged to take up the game

more seriously at the age of 15 by his friend and mentor Eduardo Romero. Turning professional at the age of 22, he shot a 61 in the Argentine Open, but it took four attempts before he finally secured his card on the European Tour in 1995. He came to the attention of the wider golfing public with a runner-up finish in the Irish Open in 1999 and had a putt on the final hole of the British Open the same year to join a play-off with Mark O'Meara and Brian Watts. Cabrera joined forces with Romero to guide Argentina to second place in the World Cup in 2000 in his native country, behind a US team represented by Tiger Woods and David Duval, and he secured his breakthrough win on tour by taking the Argentine Open the following year, 2001. He finished in the top ten in both the Masters and the US Open the same year before winning the Benson and Hedges Open, his first win on European soil. It is in more recent times, however, that he has achieved the plaudits his game warrants. At the 2007 US Open at Oakmont, he overturned a four-stroke deficit in the final round to win by one; two years later, at Augusta, he held off Chad Campbell and Kenny Perry in a playoff to win the Masters. The Duck has become a force to be reckoned with.

Mark Calcavecchia

Born: June 12, 1960
Laurel, USA

Mark Calcavecchia's best years to date came between 1987 and 1990, when he was always in the top ten on the US money list. He also claimed five of his 11 wins on that tour during that period. However, a greater claim to fame is his victory in the 1989 British Open at Royal Troon. Here, he was always in touch with the leaders but never looked a likely winner until, in his final round, he first holed a long putt on the 11th and then lobbed a shot from a bank into the hole on the next. His round took him into a play-off with

Wayne Grady and Greg Norman, who had come storming through the field. In the four-hole play-off, Norman took an early lead, but dropped a shot on the penultimate hole. The last was a disaster for him as he first drove into a fairway bunker he believed he could not reach, and then went out of bounds through the green. Calcavecchia, on the other hand, hit a much poorer drive, but into a reasonable position and then ripped a five-iron to about 7ft and birdied for victory. Calcavecchia has represented America in four Ryder Cups, most famously perhaps in 1991, when he squandered a four-up lead over Colin Montgomerie with four to play, halved the match and broke down in tears. In July 2009 he set a PGA tour record by posting nine consecutive birdies in the second round of the Canadian Open.

Chad **Campbell**
Born: May 31, 1974
Andrews, Tx, USA

Some players emerge on the professional scene with a bang; others make their way to the upper echelons of the game the hard way. One such player is Chad Campbell. The Texan ground his way around the lesser Hooters Tour for five years before earning his card for the top flight. He set records on his way, though: he won the Player of the Year title for three consecutive seasons from 1998; set a tour record by hitting 66 greens in regulation at the Parmian Basin Open and set the mark for the highest single-season earnings. Three tournament victories during 2001 secured his PGA Tour card for the 2002 season. Campbell's best year on tour came in 2003. He became the first player in tour history to record his first victory at the end-of-season Tour Championship, a performance that included a course-record 61 in the third round. Earlier that season, he had pushed Shaun Micheel all the way at the US PGA Championship: tied for the lead going into the final round, he was outdone on the final hole as Micheel struck a seven-iron

from 175 yards to within inches of the hole to run out winner by two strokes. Campbell won his second tour title in 2004 at the Bay Hill Invitational and added further victories in 2006 (at the Bob Hope Chrysler Classic) and 2007 (at the Viking Classic). He came close to winning his first major in 2009, only to lose in a play-off to Angel Cabrera at the US Masters.

Michael **Campbell**
Born: February 23, 1969
Hawera, New Zealand

A proud Maori by descent on both sides, with Scottish ancestry, Michael Campbell started playing golf at the age of eight and by the age of 12 was playing to a handicap of 11. A third-place finish on the Challenge Tour in 1994 was enough for the 1992 Australian Amateur champion to earn his European Tour card. The following year saw him hit the media spotlight when he led the British Open, at St Andrews, after three rounds, only to fall away to a tie for third – one shot behind eventual winner John Daly – following a disappointing final round of 76. His failure on the game's biggest stage knocked the stuffing out of him; he finished outside the top 40 of the European Tour money list in the next four seasons. And then came a return to form that saw him win five times between 2000 and 2003 to establish himself as one of the world's best players. His year of years came in 2005, and began at Pinehurst in the US Open, where he held off the considerable challenge of Tiger Woods to become the first New Zealander to win a major since Bob Charles in 1963, before rounding off a stellar season by winning the World Matchplay Championship at Wentworth. He has failed to reach the same heady heights since, but, on his day, there are few more naturally talented golfers.

JoAnne **Carner**
Born: April 4, 1939
Kirkland, Wa, USA

Nicknamed today "Big Momma" and earlier "The Great Gundy" (which referred to her maiden name of Gunderson), Carner compiled one of the great records in amateur golf. Starting with the USGA Girls title in 1956, she went on to win the US Amateur five times – 1957, 1960, 1962, 1966 and 1968 – and then turned professional after winning an LPGA event as an amateur in 1969. She was immediately successful, but her best years came in the period from 1974 to 1984, when she never finished worse than ninth on the

money list, headed it three times and was second or third on another four occasions. She added the US Women's Open to her list of majors in 1971 and had a repeat victory in 1976. The first of those wins meant that she became – and still remains – the only woman to win the USGA Girls title, the US Amateur and the US Women's Open. On the LPGA Tour, she won a massive 42 times between the years of 1970 and 1985. In 1994, she was a very popular captain of the US Solheim Cup team – and a victorious one.

MICHAEL CAMPBELL He held off a final-round charge by Tiger Woods to win the 2005 US Open.

Joe Carr

Born: February 18, 1922
Dublin, Ireland

Carr is one of the greatest amateurs ever to have hailed from the British Isles. With his vast hitting and tremendous recovery powers, he is also one of the few British players to have prospered in the US Amateur, where he reached the semi-final stage in 1961. In his native Ireland his record was outstanding. Besides a host of regional successes, he also won the Irish Closed Amateur Championship on six occasions and the Irish Open Amateur four times – 1946, 1950, 1954 and 1956. Even more significant were his performances in Britain and abroad. In the British Amateur he had a formidable record, winning in 1953, 1958 and 1960. On two occasions he beat leading American amateurs in the final at a time when they were normally superior. He played in every Walker Cup team from 1947 to 1965, captaining the side on the last occasion. He was then non-playing captain for the next match. Carr made a limited number of entries in professional tournaments and was second in the 1959 Dunlop Masters, which was then one of the most prestigious events in Europe. He also came quite close in the centenary British Open, entering the final round just two strokes behind the leader.

Paul Casey

Born: July 21, 1977
Cheltenham, England

Paul Casey, nicknamed "Popeye" because of his forearms, made his mark on the amateur game in the 1999 Walker Cup when he became one of only three players in the 77-year history of the competition to record four victories without defeat. He won back-to-back British Amateur and Pac-10 Championships in 1999 and 2000: his victory in the latter in 2000 saw him break the tournament's 72-hole record (held by Tiger Woods) by five strokes. Success in the professional game came

slowly, but he broke his tournament duck in the ANZ Championship in 2003 and secured a second title when he walked away with the B&H International Open. The following season saw Casey make his Ryder Cup debut and the young Englishman made a promising contribution during Europe's crushing victory. He added three European Tour victories in 2006, remained unbeaten in Europe's defence of the Ryder Cup and ended a spectacular season by claiming the World Matchplay title at Wentworth to end a memorable campaign second in the Order of Merit. The good form continued into 2007, with a season-opening win in Abu Dhabi. He was consistent but winless in 2008, but in 2009 produced a remarkable surge of form that brought him a maiden PGA tour victory, at the Houston Open. His best performance in a major was a tie for sixth at the 2004 US Masters.

Billy Casper

Born: June 24, 1931
San Diego, Ca, USA

Casper was a phenomenally successful golfer on the PGA Tour, though he was somewhat prosaic in style compared with his charismatic contemporary Arnold Palmer. Casper's aim was to get his ball onto the fairway and then find the green. Thereafter, he knew he was just about the best putter around, albeit an unusually wristy one. As a competitor in the majors, his most dramatic moments came in the 1966 US Open. With nine holes to play, Arnold Palmer held a seven-stroke lead. It was all over, it seemed; Billy Casper was merely playing for second place. But Palmer then began to cast strokes to the wind while Casper plodded methodically on. In the end Palmer had to hole a testing putt just to tie with Casper. It was a similar story in the 18-hole play-off. At the halfway point Palmer led by four, but again collapsed, handing Casper his second US Open.

Bob Charles The 1963 British Open winner's strengths came to the fore on the greens.

His first, in 1959, had also been remarkable: he used only 112 putts in his four rounds. Casper's other major victory came in the 1970 Masters, and he also took a total of 51 events on the PGA Tour. Only five players have won more. Moving on to the Senior Tour, he notched up nine more wins.

Bob Charles

Born: March 14, 1936
Carterton, New Zealand

It is an oddity of golf history that the greatest left-handed golfer ever is naturally right-handed. He began playing left-handed purely because his parents played that way round and had some spare clubs. It took Bob Charles a long time to make up his mind to become a professional –

six years after he won the 1954 New Zealand Open. Thereafter he was soon winning in both Europe and in America. On the main PGA Tour he won five times and had eight wins in Europe. Putting excellence was central to his success and led to his greatest triumph, the 1963 British Open, when he averaged 30 putts per round. He then went on to destroy American Phil Rodgers in the 36-hole play-off. However, his peak success came as a senior golfer in the USA. From his debut year of 1986 until 1993 he was always at least among the top-ten money winners and topped the list in both 1988 and 1989. Senior British Open champion in 1989 and 1993, his senior career saw him rack up 23 titles and more than $9.5 million.

Stewart Cink

Born: May 21, 1973
Huntsville, Al, USA

Voted the country's best collegiate player in 1995, Stewart Cink set the Nationwide Tour alight in his first year as a professional by winning three tournaments on his way to breaking the single-season earnings record; he also finished in the top 20 of the US Open for good measure. His first victory on the PGA Tour came the following year at the Greater Harford Open – a closing 66 saw him emerge a one-stroke winner over Jeff Maggert. This win, and season's earnings of $809,580, saw Cink become the first player to be voted Nationwide Tour Player of the Year and PGA Tour Rookie of the Year in successive seasons. Consistency started to become the watchword for Cink: a steady performer on the US Tour, he added further victories in 2000 (MCI Classic), 2004 (MCI Heritage and the World Cup Championship), and in 2008 (at the Travellers Championship), but was starting to run up a catalogue of near-misses in the majors. Tied for the lead going into the final round of the 2001 US Open, a double-bogey on the final hole saw him miss out on a play-off spot by one stroke. He went on to win the British Open in 2009 in a play-off against Tom Watson.

Howard Clark

Born: August 26, 1954
Leeds, England

Blessed with one of the best swings in British golf, Clark has probably not done his talents full justice, though he came back to form in 1994 and captained the England team in the Dunhill Cup. Before this his game appeared to be in decline, partly perhaps owing to an elbow injury. He had been a consistent performer from 1976 to 1989, with his best years being 1978 and the period from 1984 to 1986. Clark has been very successful in team events, playing in six Ryder Cup teams from 1977

to 1995 and representing England in several World Cups, where he was the individual winner in 1985. He has also made five Dunhill Cup appearances. In addition, he has won 11 times on the European Tour, once winning two tournaments in a row. His most prestigious win was the PGA Championship at Wentworth in 1984. He had to wait six years to add his sixth Ryder Cup appearance to his fifth, but the match at Oak Hill greatly revived his reputation. His singles point at the expense of Peter Jacobsen was crucial to Europe's victory, achieved with the help of a hole-in-one at the short sixth. His final season on tour came in 1999, and he is now an on-course commentator for television.

Darren Clarke

Born: August 14, 1968
Dungannon, Northern Ireland

The number plate on his Ferrari, DC60, bears testament to the fact that when Darren Clarke is on his A-game, he is very good indeed. What does the moniker stand for? In the 1999 European Open, the genial Irishman became the first player in the history of the European Tour to shoot 60 twice (his first low-round epic came at the 1992 European Monte Carlo Open). After a stellar amateur career, Clarke emerged on the world scene by finishing runner-up to Justin Leonard in the 1997 British Open at Troon. The following year he finished second on the European Order of Merit following two wins. In 2000, he became the first European to win a World Golf Championship event, beating Tiger Woods in the final to secure a $1 million pay cheque. Victory in the 2001 European Open at the K Club saw him become the first Irishman to win a tour event on native soil for 19 years and he completed a successful year with a third-place finish at the British Open. In 2003, he became only the second player to win multiple World Championship Golf events with a four-shot victory

DARREN CLARKE Personal tragedy seemed to stop his promisng career in its tracks.

at Akron. His career was on the up. Then, in August 2006, his wife Heather died of cancer and, with his priorities no doubt altered, his game suffered. He made himself available for the Ryder Cup a month later – at the K Club in his native Ireland – and, amid emotional scenes, won all three of his matches. Then he started to slip down the world rankings. Two tournament wins in 2008 hinted at a return to form – the entire golfing world hopes his best days are still ahead of him.

Neil Coles

Born: September 26, 1934
London, England

Coles turned professional at the age of 16. Seven years on, he started to make his mark, and from 1961 began a run of astonishing consistency. From then until 1980 he was never worse than 12th on the money list, was leader twice and second once. He finished in the top six on 12 occasions. But he was not merely a money winner. At a time when the

tournament schedule was limited and based largely in Britain, he racked up 28 wins. Coles is probably the best British player since the war never to have come really close to winning the British Open. However, he did very well on occasions, coming third as early as 1961. A relatively poor last round at Carnoustie in 1975 saw him fall away after having been in strong contention. In 1973, by contrast, he played one of his best rounds, a 66, but had gone out too far behind to have any real chance. He tied for second. Apart from having played in eight Ryder Cups, his proudest achievements are probably his victories in the Matchplay Championship (three times) at Wentworth, the Dunlop Masters and the PGA Championship. He has won 14 times on the Senior Tour (when he won in 2002, he became the oldest ever winner on the European Senior Tour at the age of 67 years, 276 days). He has been chairman of the European Tour board since its inception in the 1980s.

CHARLES COODY His greatest moment came at Augusta in the 1971 edition of the Masters.

Glenna **Collett (Vare)**

Born: June 20, 1903
New Haven, Ct, USA

Glenna Collett was perhaps the greatest American woman amateur ever; her record of six victories in the US Amateur is approached only by JoAnne Carner. Her wins in the US Amateur came in 1922, 1925, 1928, 1929, 1930 and 1935. She was runner-up in 1931 and 1932, and was medallist on four occasions (the leading strokeplay qualifier for the matchplay stages). During her career, which spanned a period of 18 years, she won a total of 49 leading amateur events. These included the French title in 1925 and the Canadian in both 1923 and 1924. She was a keen baseball player in her youth, and this may have helped with her muscle development, for she hit her tee shots a very long way indeed. At the age of 18, she struck one drive which was measured at a little over 300 yards – and all this with grace and precision rather than brute force. During her peak years, her only rival on the world scene was Joyce Wethered, who defeated her on two occasions in the British Amateur championship. The second of these matches came in the final at St Andrews in 1929. Collett was out in 34 and seemed home and dry at 5 up. However, at lunchtime after 18 holes, the lead had been cut to just 2 up and, in the afternoon, the English player pulled ahead to win by 3 and 1.

Charles **Coody**

Born: July 13, 1937
Stamford, Tx, USA

Charles Coody was a consistent money earner rather than a prolific winner, collecting just three victories during a long career on the PGA Tour. One of those victories happened to be a major, however. Over four days at the 1971 Masters, he proved that not only could he live with the game's greatest players, but he could also beat them sometimes, too. His rivals that year were none other Jack Nicklaus and Johnny Miller, and although Coody had to fend off memories of a late collapse at the same tournament two years earlier, he held firm to birdie two of the last four holes on the way to running out a two-shot winner. He was also in with a shout at the US PGA Championship in 1976. Leading the field after 54 holes, a final-round 77 saw him lose out to Jack Nicklaus. Since joining the Senior Tour in 1987, he has racked up five victories to date.

Harry **Cooper**

Born: August 4, 1904
Leatherhead, England

Cooper, whose family moved to America when he was a child, is one of the best PGA Tour players never to have won a major championship, although he came very close. He finished one stroke behind Horton Smith in the 1936 Masters after being in the lead going into the final round, and was second again two years later. His experience of close encounters with the US Open was probably even more disappointing. In 1927, he three-putted the last green while Tommy Armour holed a good one to earn a play-off, which Cooper lost. In 1936, he broke the scoring record for the same event, but the relatively unknown Tony Manero still came in two strokes better. However, Cooper, nicknamed "Light Horse Harry" because of his speed about the golf course, was

an extremely successful tournament player. His total number of victories is not known, but is probably about the 25 mark. His best year was 1937, when he took nine titles and was both leading money winner and holder of the new Vardon Trophy for the lowest stroke average. He is today almost a forgotten man. It's the major championships that earn immortality.

Henry **Cotton**

SEE PAGE 151

Fred **Couples**

Born: October 3, 1959
Seattle, Wa, USA

Fred Couples first began to make a name for himself on the PGA Tour when he took the 1983 Kemper Open, and since then he has had 15 tour wins and six placings among the top-ten money winners. He was leading money winner in 1992, when he won three US events. The most important of these was the Masters, his only major to date, though he has often featured among the contenders. He has also been a very effective player for the US in team competition. In 1995, he and Davis Love III became the first pairing to win the World Cup four times in a row, on the third of these occasions with phenomenal scoring. Couples won the individual International Trophy by five strokes after rounds of 65, 63, 68 and 69. Seemingly a very relaxed golfer, Fred has his problems like anyone else. Putting is one of them, and one that has cost him numerous tournaments. Fred's long game is extremely fluent and effective, perhaps aided by what appear to be very loose shoulder joints. Back problems limited his appearances on the PGA Tour, but he threatened at the US Masters in 2006. In 2010 he made an astonishing transition to the Senior Tour, winning three of his first four tournaments – and finishing second in the other – and challenging at the 2010 Masters before finishing sixth.

HENRY COTTON
Arise, Sir Henry

Henry Cotton lived like a millionaire in the days when professionals were not paid in kind. He was Walter Hagen's most faithful disciple, and, accordingly, played a part in assuring that those who came after him were afforded the respect they deserved.

He never made any attempt to disguise the fact that he worked all hours at the game to earn money. He was once handed a cheque for £52 for finishing runner-up in the French Open and told the organizers: "It is almost an insult to give such a ridiculously small sum of money to some of the world's best golfers. You've got to pay if you want the best."

That was Cotton: he would embarrass anyone who denied him what he felt he was worth and, such were his talents both for the game and repartee, the tactics worked. By 1931 he had built a £10,000 house, kept five servants, and even topped the bill at the Coliseum Theatre.

On the course, he played several rounds that have become part of golf folklore, and none more so than at the 1934 British Open at Sandwich, where he led the field after three rounds by nine shots. That was largely courtesy of an astonishing 65, a score that would remain the championship record for 43 years. Dunlop, his sponsors, were so impressed that they named a ball after it. Indeed, the Dunlop 65 was probably the most famous golf ball to have been manufactured in the 20th century.

Cotton was born in 1907, the son of a prosperous iron founder. Whereas most professionals scrimped and saved during their early years, Cotton went to Alleyn's public school and gained his taste for privilege.

He turned professional at the age of 16, and four years later finished ninth in the British Open played at St Andrews. Cotton was so impressed by the technique of the winner, a certain Bobby Jones, that he decided to go to America "to find out what made them tick".

In all he would win three British Open championships, and among British players who have taken up the game since the First World War, only Nick Faldo can match that. Cotton would surely have won more if the Second World War had not robbed him of some of his best years.

He almost threw away the first of those titles at Sandwich. Holding a nine-stroke lead going into the final round, he closed with an error-strewn 79. Fortunately none of the chasing pack could manage anything better than a 71 and Cotton won by five strokes. The Englishman's victory ended a period of American domination in the tournament, but it had also exposed Cotton's greatest weakness – nerves.

His finest hour came at Carnoustie in 1937, when he secured his second Open title in a field that contained the entire US Ryder Cup team. A best-of-the-day final round of 71 was enough to see him to a two-stroke victory.

Following the six-year break for the Second World War, Cotton's third, final and almost certainly his most convincing triumph came at Muirfield in 1948. He was a five-stroke winner over second-place Fred Daly and confirmed his status as the greatest British player since the Great Triumvirate.

At the end of his career, Cotton became involved in both journalism and golf-course architecture; his designs included Penina in Portugal, while in the print game he became the golf correspondent of the *News of the World*, a position he would hold for more than 30 years.

It is an indication of the respect in which he continues to be held that at Arnold Palmer's Bay Hill club in Florida, a Cotton report on one of Palmer's British Open wins holds pride of place in the men's locker room.

1907	1934	1937
Born on January 26 in Holmes Chapel, England	Wins British Open for the first time – shooting a 65 in the second round.	Second triumph in the British Open

1948	1987
Third and final win at the British Open, played at Muirfield	Knighted for his contributions to golf shortly before his death

Bruce **Crampton**

Born: September 28, 1935
Sydney, Australia

Nicknamed "The Iron Man" because he used to play in nearly every event on the PGA Tour, Crampton has continued along the same path on the Senior Tour. Playing his first full season there in 1986, he won seven events and was leading money winner. Up to the end of 1994, Crampton had collected a total of 19 Senior victories and had won over $3.5 million – more than twice the sum he won on the main tour. Crampton first came to the fore in 1956, when he won the Australian Open at the age of 20. Having joined the PGA Tour in 1957, he was very unsuccessful for a few years, but had his first victory in 1961. More followed fairly regularly until he had totalled 14 by the end of 1975. Although he never won a major, he was twice second in the US PGA, once in the Masters and once in the US Open. In fact, in 1972, he was second in three of the four majors. After his good years his form fell away rapidly and his health gave way. He retired and went into the oil business, before making his triumphant return as a senior.

Ben **Crenshaw**

Born: January 11, 1952
Austin, Tx, USA

Crenshaw was a youthful prodigy whose first success came on his debut as a PGA Tour member. In his early days he looked set to be an all-time great, and although that did not quite materialize, he proved in the 1995 Masters that he still had the game to win a major championship. Some swing analysts have thought that the weakness in his game is an overlong backswing, past the horizontal, which can mean a lack of control. Ben has certainly hit his share of fairly wild wooden club shots. In contrast, his putting is extremely compact. Many regard him as the best putter in the game, especially after his biggest career victories, the 1984 and 1995 Masters. On the PGA Tour, Crenshaw

was extremely consistent. He finished in the top eight on the money list seven times and has 19 career victories. He captained the United States team in the controversial Ryder Cup at Brookline in 1999 and switched to the Senior Tour in 2002.

Ben **Curtis**

Born: May 26, 1977
Colombus, Oh, USA

When Ben Curtis finished tied for 13th place at the Western Open in 2003, he could not have known that his best PGA Tour finish to date would change his life. Why? The Ohio native's first top-25 finish had secured him a spot in the following month's British Open, where he would pull off one of the greatest upsets in the game's history. Rounds of 72, 72, 70 and 69 saw him become the first first-time winner of a major championship since Francis Ouimet won the 1913 US Open and the first person to win the British Open at his first attempt since Tom Watson in 1975. His victory saw him leap from 396th to 35th in the world rankings – the largest single leap since the rankings began in 1986. For the keener observers of the game, though, Curtis's triumph came as no surprise. Back-to-back victories in the Ohio Amateur tournament saw him end 2000 as the world's number one ranked amateur golfer, and three years on he had made a telling mark on the game. Now a regular feature on the PGA tour – upon which he has notched up two victories – he came close to collecting another major championship at the 2008 US PGA at Oakland Hills, when he finished second to Pádraig Harrington.

Fred **Daly**

Born: October 11, 1911
Portrush, Northern Ireland

By the age of 30, Daly was becoming consistently successful on the Irish golf scene, but as tournament play in Britain and Europe was suspended during the war, he lost what might well have been several of his most

productive years. As soon as the war was over, however, Daly began to enjoy his heyday, which lasted until 1952. The biggest victory of his career was the 1947 British Open, over Royal Liverpool's course at Hoylake. He began with rounds of 73 and 70 in testing conditions, then sagged to a 78 on the morning of the final day. In the afternoon, he played a good 72 in reasonable weather and set a target that none of the later starters,

in worsening conditions, could match – he was champion by a stroke. The following year he was second and then third in 1950. In 1952 he was third again, having led after two rounds but then having fallen away fairly badly on the final day. He played in every Ryder Cup match between 1947 and 1953, once winning his singles by 9 and 7, and a further eight important tournaments in the British Isles also came his way.

BEN CRENSHAW The two-time Masters winner was one of the best putters in the business.

LAURA DAVIES
The Crowd Puller

Laura Davies' penchant for giving the ball an almighty clout has earned her a worldwide reputation. She has been exciting galleries for 20 years.

More or less self-taught, she played in the Curtis Cup in 1984 and turned professional in 1985, having borrowed her stake from her mother, Rita. It proved a sound investment and the loan was quickly repaid when Laura won one tournament and the Order of Merit in her rookie season in Europe.

In 1986, Davies gave the first indication that she was not just a big-hitting fish in a small pond when she finished 11th in the US Women's Open and a few months later, when she won the British Women's Open at Birkdale. She finished as Europe's number one for the second time.

Even so, the golfing world was shocked when the 23-year-old Englishwoman won the US Women's Open in 1987, defeating JoAnne Carner and Japanese idol Ayako Okamoto, who was US number one that season, in an 18-hole play-off.

In America, the LPGA changed its constitution so that Davies was granted automatic membership without having to plough through qualifying school, and she was widely expected to take the States by storm.

In 1988 she won twice, finishing 15th on the money list. Davies refused to concentrate solely on the American circuit and also won three times in Europe, and once in Japan. However, the going was tougher in the US.

There were low times – in 1990, she won only once – but, in 1992, she was Europe's number one again and inspired Europe to an unexpected victory over the USA in the Solheim Cup. It was one of the great sporting upsets and Davies, in an incredible display, won all three of her matches.

The win boosted European confidence and self-belief and Davies was one of four Europeans to win on the LPGA Tour in 1993. She also won in England, Thailand and Australia, but surpassed that in 1994 when she became the first player – man or woman – to win on five tours in one calendar year, and realized her dream of being the world number one. She was the leading money winner in the US and won three tournaments, including her second major championship. She won twice in Europe, once in Thailand, once in Japan and once in Australia.

In 1995, Davies won six times worldwide, but had to settle for number two spot in Europe and America behind Annika Sorenstam.

She bounced back in 1996 with the best season of her career (nine wins) and regained the number one spot. She was Europe's number one for the fourth time and was Player of the Year in the US, winning three events – two of them majors.

A streak of 23 wins in three seasons is hard to follow and, in 1997, Davies won a mere three times, once in the US. Typically, there was nothing low key about it: she won the Standard Register Ping in Phoenix for the fourth consecutive year, to set a tour record and put her alongside Gene Sarazen and Walter Hagen as the only players to manage the feat. In 2003, she was invited to play an event on the men's European Tour, but failed in her attempt to become the first ever woman to make the cut in the men's game – it was an experience she vowed never to repeat.

Since then, her victories (five of them) have been confined to the Ladies' European Tour, for which she remains a standard-bearer. In 2009, she became the only woman to play in every Southern Cup (11 of them) since its inception in 1990.

LAURA DAVIES She has been a dominant force in the women's game for the past 20 years.

1963	1985	1987	1992
Born on October 5 in Coventry, England	Turned professional and wins both a tournament and the Order of Merit	Stuns the golfing world by winning the US Women's Open	Inspires Europe to shock win over US in Solheim Cup

1994	1996	1997	2009
Leading money winner in US. Wins tournaments on five different tours worldwide and claims second major, the LPGA Championship	Double major year with wins at LPGA Championship and du Maurier Classic	Wins Standard Register Ping tournament for fourth year in a row	Becomes the only woman in history to play in every Southern Cup match - 11 since 1990.

John Daly

Born: April 28, 1966
Sacramento, Ca, USA

At golf tournaments there is sometimes a buzz of expectation and a rush of spectators – usually indicating that the leaders are approaching. The exception was, till the arrival of Tiger Woods, John Daly. He can still attract a crowd even when well down the field. They enjoy gasping at the distance he can hit the ball. The length comes from natural power, aided by a huge shoulder turn and a backswing that is absurdly long by modern standards. He is also prepared to take risks and let fly from the tee with the driver when others might be thinking about a prudent three-iron. Daly first came to attention with his dramatic appearance in the 1991 US PGA Championship at Crooked Stick, to which he drove "on spec", to find that a late withdrawal had given him a place in the field. His first chance to see the course was during his first round when he shot a 69, two behind the leader. He added rounds of 67, 69, 71 to win by three strokes. Marital or drink problems have dogged his career, though his one 1995 victory was typically spectacular, the British Open, this time beating Costantino Rocca in a four-hole play-off at St Andrews. Then the tournament wins dried up. His ten-year exempt status on the PGA Tour came to an end in 2001, and on the European Tour in 2005. Victory at the 2004 Buick Invitational offered his fans hope, but it proved a rare highlight. In 2008, a series of infringements led to a six-month suspension on the PGA Tour and he now relies on sponsor's exemptions to compete. Interestingly, he is the only eligible two-time major winner never to have played in the Ryder Cup.

Beth Daniel

Born: October 14, 1956
Charleston, SC, USA

Daniel had a short, but outstanding, amateur career, making two Curtis Cup appearances and winning the US Amateur title in 1975 and 1977. She was also a member of the World Cup team. When she began competing on the LPGA Tour in 1979, she was immediately successful. She had her first win and finished tenth on that year's money list. She was soon doing much better and threatening to replace Nancy Lopez as the wonder of the age. In both 1980 and 1981 she topped the money list and increased her tour victories to eight. However, she did not top the list again until 1990, her best year, when she won seven times – a feat rarely achieved in modern times – and her winnings of over $860,000 set a new record. So far she has finished in the top-eight money winners ten times. By the end of the 1994 season she had racked up 33 tour wins. Oddly, only one of these is a major, the 1990 LPGA Championship. By the end of the 2009 season, she stood in eighth place on the career money list on the LPGA Tour.

Laura Davies

SEE PAGE 153

Rodger Davis

Born: May 18, 1951
Sydney, Australia

Many professional golfers like to identify themselves by their clothing. Davis has had two trademarks for long periods in his career: his long socks and plus-twos. He has been a strong contender in the British Open. In Ballesteros's first year at Lytham in 1979, for instance, he held the lead with five holes left to play but, like a few others, fell back over the testing finish. At Muirfield in 1987, he started with a blistering 64, which gave him a three-stroke lead, but his following rounds of 73 and 74 took him out of strong contention. On the final day he never quite looked like winning, but his 69 was eventually good enough to earn him a tie for second with Azinger, leaving Faldo victorious by a single stroke. Davis was a winner in Australia when he first decided to try his luck in Europe in 1977. He made the occasional impact, sometimes fading out of contention after good starts. His first win came in 1981 and he has had half a

JOHN DALY The crowds flock to see the "Wild Thing" thrash the golf ball mighty distances.

dozen more since then, the most important being the PGA Championship in 1986 and the Volvo Masters in 1991. A switch to the Senior Tour in 2001 brought one victory and $2 million.

Jimmy **Demaret**

Born: May 10, 1910
Houston, Tx, USA

One of the greatest players not to have won a US Open, Demaret was the first to win the Masters three times. He did this in 1940, 1947 and 1950, once managing a 30 over the second nine at Augusta, Georgia. Despite his numerous tournament successes, Demaret was noted above all for his flamboyant clothes. Walter Hagen was probably the first golfer to attire himself in, for example, two-tone shoes, a bow-tie and matching slacks and top. Demaret went much further and

RODGER DAVIS A consistent performer, he has twice come close to winning the British Open.

might grace the course topped by a tam-o'shanter, with vivid shirt and trousers, the ensemble completed from his vast collection of shoes. If Demaret was the Ian Poulter of his time, there is no evidence to suggest that he had a lucrative clothing contract. As a golfer, he was very influential in his shape of shot. Before him, most top professionals favoured a draw, because of the greater run on the ball. Demaret decided that the fade was better, because the side-spin imparted on the ball held both the fairways and the greens more effectively.

Bruce **Devlin**

Born: October 10, 1937
Armidale, Australia

Devlin came to the fore in 1959, when he won the Australian Open and decided he was good enough to turn professional. He then played worldwide before settling in the United States. Between 1964 and 1972 Devlin won eight events on the PGA Tour, but continued to make appearances in Europe, most notably in 1966 when he was the leading money winner. For a long time, Devlin was considered to be a likely winner of a major championship. His best performances however were two fourth places in the Masters and two sixths in the US Open. One of the latter came at Pebble Beach, in his mid-40s, when he held a two-stroke lead after two rounds but dropped back to six strokes behind winner Tom Watson.

Leo **Diegel**

Born: April 27, 1899
Detroit, Mi, USA

"They keep trying to give me the championship, but I won't take it," said Leo Diegel after yet another title had been cast to the winds, but it might all have been so different. He contended strongly for the US Open as early as 1920. A win then might well have given him the self-assurance so much needed

by a young player. Though blessed with a great talent, Diegel never quite fulfilled it. Perhaps his main problem was his lack of composure at crisis points in the majors. In the 1933 British Open at St Andrews, for example, he needed only a par four at one of the easiest last holes in golf to tie, but his putting let him down. It often did, despite endless experiments with different putters and a revolutionary method. The latter involved crouching low over the ball, with the club grip almost touching his chin and pointing both elbows outwards. He hoped that this would take his jerky wrists out of the putting stroke. It was much imitated. Despite his failings, Diegel was still a formidable tournament player and is credited with some 30 victories. The most important of these came in the Canadian Open, which he won four times, and the US PGA Championships of 1928 and 1929 - the first of which ended Walter Hagen's great run.

Chris **DiMarco**

Born: August 23, 1968
Huntingdon, NY, USA

Some players rise through the ranks of the game with ease; others have to work their way up the hard way. Chris DiMarco falls into the latter category. His claw-like putting grip may not be the most aesthetically pleasing on the circuit, but it has become one of the most effective and has helped the American become one of the most consistent players on the PGA Tour. It took eight seasons before DiMarco truly established himself on the US circuit in 1999. His first victory came a year later at the Pennsylvania Classic and five further top-ten finishes and 25 made cuts in 33 events saw him amass over $1 million in prize money. A second tour victory followed in 2001 when he won the Buick Challenge in a play-off; the same year he led the Masters through 36 holes before falling back

to finish tenth. By 2002, DiMarco had broken into the top ten in the world rankings and was a regular feature in the United States teams in both the President's Cup and the Ryder Cup. He has come agonizingly close to capturing a major title: losing in two play-offs - the first to Vijay Singh in the 2003 US PGA and the second to Tiger Woods in the 2005 Masters and then, at the 2006 British Open, losing out to Woods yet again. The defeats seemed to halt his progress: winless since 2002, he has started to slide down the world rankings.

Luke **Donald**

Born: December 7, 1977
Hempstead, England

Like fellow countryman Paul Casey, Luke Donald is another player who made a name for himself in the Walker Cup and in American collegiate golf. In 1999, he was voted the top collegiate golfer, an accolade that earned him an invite to the 2000 Memorial Tournament where he finished in a tie for 51st place. After turning professional in 2001, he decided to ply his trade Stateside: his first tour victory came in just his 37th tournament start - at the Southern Farm Bureau Classic - and he became only the 11th rookie in the history of the PGA Tour to earn $1 million in his first season. Victory on the other side of the Atlantic came in 2004. He won the Scandinavian Open by five strokes. The display was enough to earn him a captain's pick for the 2004 Ryder Cup, where he went on to play a significant part in Europe's record victory. He finished third at the 2005 US Masters - his first appearance - and had his best season to date in 2006 when his second PGA Tour title (the Honda Classic) put him into the world's top 10 for the first time. He finished 29th on the money list in 2007, but endured a curtailed 2008 season that ended with wrist surgery. By 2009, he was some way back to his impressive best.

Flory van Donck

Born: June 23, 1912
Tervueren, Belgium

Easily the finest golfer Belgium has so far produced, van Donck was almost a dominant figure in continental Europe and highly effective in Great Britain. The extent of van Donck's dominance in his native land can be seen from his record in the Belgian Professional Championship. Between 1935 and 1968 he won it 16 times. In 1979, at the age of 67, he was still representing his country in the World Cup, an event in which he played regularly from 1954 to 1970 and was individual winner in 1960, when it was at a peak of its prestige. He won five times in the British Isles, and finished in second place in the British Open twice. He had a smooth and rhythmic swing, but was less elegant on the greens, putting with the toe of his club high.

George Duncan

Born: September 16, 1883
Methlick, Scotland

Duncan was still young when he emerged onto the British golf scene, and was in the Scotland team by 1906. However, it was several years later, when he beat both Braid and Taylor in the News of the World Matchplay Championship, that he really became a household name. In 1913, he beat Braid again, in the final. By this time he was just about on a level with the Great Triumvirate and Sandy Herd, and was much in demand for both challenge and exhibition matches. After the war, much was expected of George Duncan and Abe Mitchell, but even they could not prevent the growing American dominance of the British Open. However, Duncan won at Deal in 1920, and an amazing victory it was, too. He began with a couple of 80s, which put him out of contention. His driving had been the main problem, but after playing his second round he picked up a driver in the exhibition tent, had a few swishes with it – and money changed hands.

His game was transformed. On the final day, he had rounds of 71 and 72 and won by a couple of strokes.

Olin Dutra

Born: January 17, 1901
Los Angeles, Ca, USA

Olin Dutra carved out his place in golfing history over the first half of the 1930s. A tall, heavy-set man with a fine touch on the greens, he won two major championships in three years and also served as chairman of the US PGA Tournament Committee in 1935. His first major success came in the 1932 US PGA, which he won in an impressive manner. First he led the 32 qualifiers by posting a 36-hole score of 140; then he demolished anyone who stood in his way in the matchplay stages. Dutra was only extended as far as the 17th green in his semi-final against Ed Dudley; in the first round he handed out a fearful 9&8 hammering to George Smith, before rounding it all off with a 4&3 victory over Frank Walsh. His win at the 1934 US Open was achieved under starkly contrasting circumstances. This time he had to come from behind, making up no fewer than eight strokes on the halfway leader, Bobby Cruikshank, with two final rounds of 71 and 72 at Merion. What made the achievement still more remarkable is that Dutra had not played golf for ten days prior to the tournament owing to illness. There was no rustiness at the death of the game, however, as he overtook Gene Sarazen to win by one stroke.

David Duval

Born: November 9, 1971
Jacksonville, Fla, USA

It may have taken him 86 starts before he recorded his first victory on the PGA Tour – he had finished runner-up seven times – but once David Duval had tasted victory for the first time, in 1997, he could not stop winning. He won the next two events he played in as well

DAVID DUVAL The American has struggled with injuries since capturing the 2001 British Open.

to become the first player since Nick Price in 1993 to win three consecutive tour events. The only surprise was that it had taken the former US Amateur champion so long. Four more wins came the next season, and the next – the highlight coming in the final round of the Bob Hope Chrysler Classic when he became only the third player in the history of the PGA Tour to shoot a 59 – the others: Al Geiberger in 1977 and Chip Beck in 1991. By the end of 1999, he had overtaken Tiger Woods at the top of the world rankings. Duval's 2000 campaign was beset with persistent back problems, but, in 2001, he won his first major championship, the British Open at Royal Lytham – a final-round 67 gave him a three-shot victory over Niclas Fasth. It appeared that this

win would provide a springboard to greater things, but Duval, troubled by back and wrist problems, has not won since, and many observers considered his career to be over. However, magically, he reappeared at the top of the leaderboard at the 2009 US Open, before a bogey on the 71st hole saw him slip back to second place. He failed to earn his PGA Tour card for 2010 and now relies on sponsors' exemptions to compete.

J. Douglas Edgar

Born: September 30, 1884
Newcastle-upon-Tyne, England

Although Tommy Armour said he was "the best golfer I ever saw", and Bobby Jones called him "a magician with a golf club", Edgar is now a largely forgotten figure in the history of golf. The reason he has been forgotten is that he died prematurely – and mysteriously – in Atlanta, Georgia, as a result of a small, but deep, wound in his thigh. He had bled to death. Was it a mugging? Perhaps murder for an unknown reason? Or was he simply the victim of a hit-and-run driver? There were headlines for a short time and then the story became a shadowy part of golf history. The crime was never solved. Edgar became a name to be reckoned with when he won the 1914 French Open by six strokes from Harry Vardon. Then came war, after which he emigrated to America. There, his greatest achievement came quickly when he won the Canadian Open by 16 strokes from Bobby Jones and Jim Barnes, still the greatest margin ever in a national Open against a top-class field. He won the same event again the next year and also reached a US PGA final. He was killed in 1921. A revolutionary feature of Edgar's game was that, like many others, he had a very full shoulder turn but, unusually, a much more restricted hip movement. He always felt that he would play his best when his hands felt "thin".

Lee **Elder**
Born: July 14, 1934
Dallas, Tx, USA

Lee Elder is famous above all as the first black golfer to play in the Masters. There is little or no doubt that those who used to rule at Augusta hoped that no black would compete. When it was a purely invitational event this was relatively easy to achieve – there were in any case few blacks in the US playing to a really high standard. However, once it was decided to introduce a direct qualifying system, in addition to invitations, winners on the PGA Tour were allowed in. Thus, in 1974, when Lee Elder won his first title, the Monsanto Open, beating Peter Oosterhuis in a play-off after a dramatic last round, he qualified to play in the 1975 Masters. There,

ironically, he failed to survive the half-way cut. Elder had three further wins on the main tour and played on the 1979 Ryder Cup team. He was successful during the 1980s on the Senior Tour. Between 1984 and 1988 his worst finish on the money list was 19th, and in his best year, 1985, he was second. During this period he notched up eight victories – in one of them he opened with a 61, a Senior Tour record.

Steve **Elkington**
Born: December 8, 1962
Inverell, Australia

Elkington won the Doug Sanders Junior World Championship in 1981 and immediately attracted college interest in the United States. Success while a student at Houston showed that he was undoubtedly a promising prospect, and by 1987 he had qualified for the PGA Tour, immediately achieving some good results. In 1990, he won the Greater Greensboro Open, and, the following year, the Tournament Players' Championship, after a tough fight with Fuzzy Zoeller. This is an event which ranks just below the four major championships. It earned him nearly $300,000 and a ten-year exemption from having to qualify for the PGA Tour. In 1992, he took the Australian Open, another event just below major championship status. His final stride to that level came in the 1995 US PGA at Riviera, where his closing 64 for 267 equalled the lowest ever aggregate for a major (Greg Norman at Sandwich in 1993). Even this was not decisive. Colin Montgomerie tied with a 25ft birdie putt at the 72nd hole. Elkington beat him at the first play-off hole. He won the Players' Championship for the second time in 1997 – joining Jack Nicklaus and Fred Couples as the only two-time winners of the event – and recorded the last of his ten wins on tour in 1999.

Ernie **Els**
SEE PAGE 158

Chick **Evans**
Born: July 18, 1890
Indianapolis, In, USA

The Western Amateur remains one of the top events on the American circuit. Evans won it eight times, including a sequence of four in a row. However, his main target was the US Amateur. It did not come easily. In 1909, 1910 and 1911 he was defeated at the semi-final stage. The next year he got as far as the final, but was heavily defeated, 7&6, by Jerry Travers, after having been 3 up early on. However, Evans was still good enough to defeat the leading professionals of his time, taking the Western Open in 1910. Then came a

trip abroad and a win in the French Amateur – and also a meeting with James Braid, which led him to switch to the Vardon grip. In 1914, he was nearly US Open champion, finishing just a stroke behind Walter Hagen, but he did it in 1916, and in a grand manner. His 286 total brought him a two-stroke win and set an aggregate record that was to last for 20 years. That year, he also took the US Amateur at last – apart from Jones, he remains the only man to win both titles in the same year. He won again in 1920 and also reached the final in both 1922 and 1927. He still qualified for the US Amateur as late as 1953.

LEE ELDER Will go down in history as the first black player to have played in the Masters.

ERNIE ELS
Easy Does It

With his languid swing, the "Big Easy" has been making waves on both sides of the Atlantic through the early 1990s until today. However, just as he was establishing himself as the leading player of his generation, along came Tiger Woods. How he must have wondered what could have been, as Tiger set about thoroughly re-writing golf's history books.

Els first emerged in his native South Africa in 1992 where he won six events. The following year he displayed his talents to a worldwide golfing audience when he became the first player in the British Open to shoot four rounds in the 60s. It wasn't good enough for victory, though, as he finished tied for sixth. His breakthrough in the major tournaments arrived at the following year's US Open when beat Loren Roberts and Colin Montgomerie in a play-off.

He may have surrendered a three-stroke final-round lead at the following year's US PGA, but found consolation in the World Matchplay Championship later that same year, winning the tournament for the second straight year. He went one better in 1996, completing a hat-trick of wins.

Els put his major aspirations well and truly back on track in 1997. Victory at Congressional Country Club saw him become the first foreign player since Alex Smith (in 1906 and 1910) to win the US Open more than once.

The South African may have won tournaments in both 1998 and 1999, but he will surely ponder what could have been in 2000. The history books will record that Tiger won three of that season's four major tournaments: what most people will forget is that Els finished as runner-up in three consecutive majors – the Masters, the US Open and the British Open.

It must surely have had an effect on him. He went winless on the PGA Tour for the first time the following year and won only once worldwide – the Players' Championship in South Africa – but at least he beat Woods. Teaming up with Retief Goosen in November, the duo won the World Cup in Japan.

It seemed to spur him on to greater things: 2002 was a year to remember for the South African, bringing as it did his third major championship. In all he won six times worldwide, including the British Open at Muirfield, when he survived a difficult four-man play-off with five consecutive pars to get his hands on the famous Claret Jug for the first time.

His good form continued: in 2003 he won the European Order of Merit;

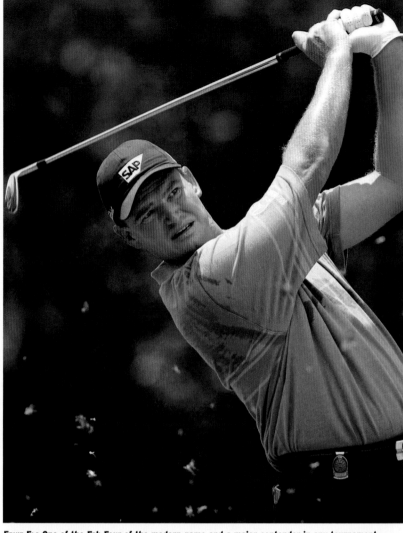

ERNIE ELS One of the Fab Four of the modern game and a major contender in any tournament.

in 2004, he recorded five victories, including a sixth World Matchplay title and finished as Europe's no. 1 for the second consecutive year. But then knee surgery in 2005 halted his progress. His return to form was slow but a first PGA Tour title for three years in 2008, two top-ten finishes in the majors in 2009, and two early-season PGA Tour wins in 2010 prove that when the South African is on his A-game, he is still a match for anyone.

1969	1992	1994	1996
Born on October 17 in Johannesburg, South Africa	Wins six events on South Africa Tour, including the South African Open, the South Africa Masters and the South Africa PGA Championship	Wins the US Open for the first time	Wins the World Matchplay Championship for the third successive year

1997	2000	2002	2007
Wins the US Open for the second time	Finishes as runner-up in three successive majors	Survives a four-man play-off to win the British Open for the first time	Wins his seventh World Matchplay Championship

NICK FALDO
The Modern Hogan

Nick Faldo, despite an already successful career, famously decided in the mid-1980s that he needed to remodel his swing totally, and went on to become the best golfer in the world. Faldo first came into the public eye in 1975, when he won both the British Youths' Open Amateur Championship and the English Amateur. He turned professional the following year and his first tournament win came in 1977. That year saw another boost to his career, when he formed a good partnership with Peter Oosterhuis and also beat Tom Watson – a Watson still with the glow of the Masters and the Turnberry Open Championship about him – in the singles of the Ryder Cup at Royal Lytham and St Anne's.

Determined to be one of the great players of golf's history, and conscious that his swing was not sufficiently reliable under pressure, Faldo astutely chose David Leadbetter as his coach. The swing that emerged after much tutelage took time to work. Faldo won in 1984, but no more successes came his way until the Spanish Open of 1987, the year that saw his arrival as a world figure. Faldo's 68 in the first round of the British Open saw him very well placed, despite the fact that Australian Rodger Davies held the lead with a

64. Few saw him as a real threat, but Faldo's second-round 69 brought him level. His 71 in the next round put him a short head behind leader Paul Azinger, just a stroke behind.

Faldo's final round is already part of golfing legend, for in misty, chilly weather he parred every single hole. In the end, he won because of Paul Azinger's failing. With a three-stroke lead and with nine to play, the American faltered with bogeys on the last two holes. Faldo did not, and his play on the difficult final hole was exemplary – a good drive, an excellent five-iron to the front of the green and two putts.

However, his reputation wasn't yet made in the US. Many thought all those 18 pars could hardly be inspirational golf. Winning the Masters in 1989 changed all that, although he had an apparently disastrous third round when he took 77, which dropped him five strokes behind the leader Ben Crenshaw.

It was very different on the final day. He shot a 65 to tie with Scott Hoch, who then proceeded to assist Faldo to his second major win. On the first play-off hole Hoch missed from about 2ft and a grateful Faldo birdied the next for the title. When it was all

over, it seemed that Faldo had birdied almost everything in the final hours.

Faldo's best year was in 1990, when he came close to equalling Ben Hogan's 1953. First there was another Masters. After rounds of 71 and 72, a 66 then put him in third place, three shots adrift of Raymond Floyd, and a final round of 69 was good enough to force a play-off with the overnight leader. The second hole was again decisive, as Floyd put his second shot into the water and that was that. Only Jack Nicklaus, in 1965-66, had won two straight Masters.

In the US Open that same year, he missed the play-off by one shot. Soon it was time to go to St Andrews, where he played his most devastating golf ever. Four majors in the record books. By now Faldo was a millionaire many times over, and his rise to pre-eminence had done much to win Leadbetter his reputation as the new guru of golf.

Muirfield in 1992 saw some silly betting, but Faldo did seem invincible at 130 for 36 holes. When John Cook overtook him on the final day, he recovered with "the best four holes of my life", including two birdies, to win his fifth major. Another staunch finish, against Curtis Strange in the 1995 Ryder Cup was instrumental in

NICK FALDO The six-time major winner was the most successful British golfer of his generation.

Europe's win. Faldo added a sixth major, his third US Masters in 1996, capitalizing on Greg Norman's collapse on Sunday afternoon, with a best-of-the-day 67.

He won on the PGA Tour the following year at the Nissan Open and partnered David Carter to success in the World Cup in 1998. He made the last of his 11 Ryder Cup appearances in 1997 and holds the record for the most matches played (46) and the most points won (46).

He captained Europe during their Ryder Cup defeat at Valhalla in 2008, and was knighted for services to golf the following year.

1957 Born on July 18, Welwyn Garden City, Hertfordshire	**1987** British Open champion at Muirfield	**1989** First Masters win	**1990** Repeats Masters victory and wins his second British Open title
1992 Wins third British Open Championship	**1996** Overtakes Greg Norman for third Masters title	**1997** Becomes all-time Ryder Cup record points scorer at Valderrama	**2008** Captains Europe to defeat in the Ryder Cup at Valhalla	**2009** Knighted for services to golf

Johnny Farrell

Born: April 1, 1901
White Plains, NY, USA

Farrell is one of the very few players who beat Bobby Jones when this great American was in his peak years. It happened at Olympia Fields in the 1928 US Open. The two tied on 294, and went into a 36-hole play-off, as was then the norm. Farrell, with a 70, was three shots better than Jones after the first round, but Jones came back at him in the afternoon. However, Farrell held on, and a 7ft putt on the very last hole was good enough for a one-stroke victory. That was his only major victory, though he was second in 1929 in both the US PGA and the British Open. He also finished one behind the Jones-Willie Macfarlane play-off in the 1925 US Open. In the period of 1923-24, he made money in every tournament he entered, but an even better spell came early in 1927, when he won seven consecutive tournaments. He had eight wins in all that year, to follow his five the previous season. Farrell played in the first Ryder Cup team in 1927 and again in the next two events. He is widely considered to be one of the greatest putters the world has ever seen.

Max Faulkner

Born: July 29, 1916
Bexhill, England

Faulkner was one of the more eccentric players of modern times. In his search for putting perfection he assembled a vast collection of putters – making most of them himself – said to have reached a total of around 300. He must have experienced many disappointments! Faulkner was constantly experimenting with subtle variations of the other clubs, too, and seems virtually never to have played with a full conventional set. This was because Faulkner had great feel for the shape and flight of a shot and was one of the few players who found it easy to bend the lofted irons either way. His victory in the 1951 British Open at Portrush was achieved with an extremely light putter with a pencil-like shaft and grip. Faulkner went into the event with his long game in a dreadful state. That gradually improved under the influence of all the unlikely putts that were dropping. He began the final round with a six-stroke lead and was scarcely troubled as he ran out the winner by two strokes over Argentine golfer Antonio Cerda. He was the last British golfer to win the championship until Tony Jacklin 18 years later. Faulkner made the Ryder Cup team five times and recorded 16 wins in Britain and Europe.

Jim Ferrier

Born: February 24, 1915
Sydney, Australia

Ferrier came into professional golf having dominated the Australian amateur scene for several years, winning the Australian Amateur title four times in the late 1930s. He also won the Australian Open twice as an amateur, in 1938 and 1939, and at St Andrews in 1936, became the first Australian to reach a final of the British Amateur Championship. He turned professional in 1940 and, deciding that Australian golf was rather a small pond, departed for the US the following year. He made money but no great impact on the PGA Tour until the mid-1940s, and scored his first win in 1944. His only major came in 1947 when he won the US PGA, then a matchplay event, defeating Chick Harbert in the final. Ferrier also finished second in the 1950 Masters to Jimmy Demaret – but he ought to have won. He only needed to score 38 on the final nine holes to take the green jacket, but his game fell apart. However, as consolation that year, he finished second on the money list. Altogether he had 21 wins on the PGA Tour, the last of these coming in 1961.

Dow Finsterwald

Born: September 6, 1929
Athens, Ga, USA

There was not much dash about Finsterwald's play. Although he was an excellent shot-maker, he always had safety in mind. Once he was on the green, he knew that his excellent putting would be the equalizer. As a result, he was one of the most consistent scorers of his era. His lack of adventure meant that he seldom had a bad round, and at one time he held the record for the most tournaments played without missing the halfway cut. He joined the PGA Tour in 1952 and had some very bad years, but things started to go a great deal better from 1956, when he finished second in the money list. The next year he won the Vardon Trophy for the lowest stroke average. He was a good performer in the majors, though he won only one, the 1958 US PGA, the first year the event switched over to strokeplay. He had been second, under the matchplay format, the year before. In 1962, he tied Arnold Palmer and Gary Player for the Masters, but Palmer won the 18-hole play-off easily. Finsterwald won 12 events on the PGA Tour and played in four Ryder Cups between 1957 and 1963. He was later a non-playing captain.

RAYMOND **FLOYD**
The Ultimate Competitor

RAYMOND FLOYD A party animal in his younger days, he matured into a doughty match-player.

Everything that you need to know about Raymond Floyd was present on the day he collected the US Open trophy at Shinnecock Hills in 1986.

It was present in his own golf, as he mastered one of the world's great links courses with a supreme variety of shots. Mostly, though, it was there in the press conference that Payne Stewart gave afterwards by the side of the 18th green.

Stewart and Floyd had been partners on the final day, and it was the former who leapt out of the blocks with a wonderful front nine of 33. He then birdied the 11th, a scary par three. From there on in, however, Stewart could not quite shake the feeling that a pair of malevolent eyes was burning a hole in the back of his head. "I could not escape the Raymond Floyd stare," he admitted.

Floyd had a swing for which, had you seen it on the practice ground, you would have told him to find a good coach. From 70 yards in, however, he was brilliant, and had few equals as far as mind games were concerned.

This was seen to best effect when he was on his knock and in front. Most players regard leading for a long time as the most difficult element of the game. Floyd, meanwhile, was a front-runner par excellence; three of his four major championships were won in this manner.

His skills at front running were seen

to best effect in the 1976 Masters, where he opened with a 65 to top the leaderboard. Would he be nervous? You must be joking. He followed it up with a 66 to lap the field. There would be no respite. He went on to equal Jack Nicklaus' then-record 72-hole score of 271 to win by eight strokes.

What Floyd would have won had he dedicated himself to his sport in his early years one can only imagine. But our Raymond was a party animal. No one could say that he did not make up for it in his later years, indeed at 49 he was still playing Ryder Cup golf, and a valuable role at that.

At the time of the 1991 match in Kiawah Island, Fred Couples was an enormously skilful player whose brain scrambled when confronted by a pressure situation. Floyd asked to be his partner, because he believed that he could bring the best out of him, and on the first day the pair were invincible. Couples went on to play in all five matches, losing only once. It proved the making of him.

Some players have games that are suited to various courses, but only at the US Open did Floyd feel less than comfortable. It is surprising, too, that he never won the British Open, because he was a wonderful

improviser. He came awfully close, though. He finished fourth in 1976 at Royal Birkdale and second, two strokes behind Jack Nicklaus, at St Andrews in 1978, thanks to a second-round 75. But the prize that would have enabled him to become only the fifth player to win all four major championships always eluded him and, given the competitor he was, one suspects that there will be one or two regrets lingering towards the back of his mind about that.

He joined the Senior Tour on his 50th birthday and more success followed. He won three events in just seven starts in his rookie season, the highlight of which came when he won the Senior Tour Championship in Puerto Rico. He also won on the regular PGA Tour that year - at the Doral-Ryder Open - to become the first player to win on both tours in the same year (a feat since matched by Craig Stadler in 1993). Thirteen more victories have followed on the Senior Tour, the last of them coming at the Senior Players' Championship in 2000, the fourth of his senior major championship titles. In a stunning career, Floyd had notched up 66 wins and had amassed more than $20 million in prize money when he retired from competitive golf in April 2010.

1942	1963	1969	1976	1982
Born on September 4 in Fort Bragg, NC, USA	Wins first tournament on PGA Tour, the St Petersburg Open Invitational	Wins first major, the US PGA Championship	Wins the Masters	Wins the US PGA Championship for a second time

1986	1989	1992	1993
Fourth major title comes with victory at the US Open	Captains US Ryder Cup team	Becomes first player to win an event on both the PGA Tour and the Senior Tour in the same season	Makes eighth and final appearance as player in Ryder Cup at the age of 50

Jim Furyk US Open winner in 2003.

Ross **Fisher**

Born: November 22, 1980
Ascot, Berkshire

A product of the famous Wentworth club in Surrey, Ross Fisher joined the European Tour in 2006 and made a flying start to his rookie season, finishing fourth in his first event and ending the year an impressive 66th on the Order of Merit. His first victory came in 2007, when he won the KLM Open by one stroke over local favourite Joost Luiten, and he finished the year 44th on the Order of Merit. He lost out to Phil Mickelson in a playoff at the HSBC Champions tournament in Shanghai at the start of 2008, but, in July, went on to collect his second European Tour title with a seven-stroke victory at the European Open, which included a first round of 63, despite neither playing nor practising on the London Golf Club course. He showed he was of the highest calibre in 2009, reaching the semi-finals of the WGC Matchplay Championship, finishing second at the PGA Championship at his home course, Wentworth, and, most notably, in the majors. The Englishman led all four at one stage, finishing tied for 30th at the Masters, fifth at the US Open, 13th at the British Open – where he held a two-stroke lead in the final round before a quadruple bogey on the fifth ended his chances – and 19th at the US PGA. His place among the game's elite was confirmed by his victory at the 2009 World Matchplay Championship.

Jack **Fleck**

Born: November 8, 1922
Bettendorf, Ia, USA

For an hour after Hogan had completed his four rounds in the 1955 US Open, he sat in the locker-room accepting the congratulations on a record-breaking fifth US Open. He was five strokes better than anyone who had finished, and there was only one player still out on the course with a statistical chance: Jack Fleck, an unknown pro from a municipal course in Davenport, Iowa. He had once finished as high as sixth in a tour event and had also gone around the Olympic course in 87 in a practice round. But he was playing well enough now, and, needing a birdie at the last to tie Hogan, he duly hit a very difficult approach shot to about 8ft and then holed the putt. Words failed him in the Press tent afterwards. As for Hogan, he was in peak form and no one, least of all the inexperienced Fleck, was going to beat him over 18 holes. But he did. Taking a one-stroke lead into the last hole, he took four while Hogan hooked into deep rough and took three to get back to the fairway. This was very easily Fleck's finest hour. He did win a couple of tour events several years later, but little

else, and the Senior Tour came a bit too late for him.

Raymond **Floyd**
SEE PAGE 161

Doug **Ford**

Born: August 6, 1922
West Haven, Ct, USA

Not many men hole a bunker shot to win a major, but Ford did so to take the 1957 Masters. It gave him a 66, and a three-stroke margin over Sam Snead. This was his second major championship, following his success in the 1955 US PGA. Ford's swing was quite short and ugly, and although he attacked with venom, he was by no means a long hitter. However, the short hitter has a better chance of keeping the ball on the fairway and leaving a precise shot to the green. Once there, Ford was right up among the best putters of his day. He came into the game as the son of a club professional and, from the age of 18, had a successful amateur career, mainly in his home area. His first professional victory came in the Houston Invitational and he joined the PGA Tour full-time in 1950. By the end of his main career, he had won 19 events and tied in seven others which he lost in play-offs. His peak years were from 1951 to 1960, when he never finished worse than tenth on the money list and was second twice. Ford was on every US Ryder Cup team between 1955 and 1961.

Fred **Funk**

Born: June 14, 1956
Takoma Park, Md, USA

The former golf coach at the University of Maryland may not have racked up the number of titles of many of his contemporaries, but there can be few more consistent players ever to have played the game. The key to his success? There can be few straighter hitters in the game than Fred Funk: during his 20-year career on the PGA Tour he

has finished in top spot in driving accuracy ten times. A relatively late starter, Funk won the first of his eight tour titles in 1992 (the Houston Open). It is not titles however, but the relentless number of top-ten finishes that mark his career. He was runner-up four times in 2002 and recorded a career-high nine top tens in 2003: his consistency was recognized by Jack Nicklaus, who made him one of his captain's picks for the President's Cup the same year. It was much of the same for 2004, as a first tournament win for six years, coupled with a sixth-place finish in the US Open, saw him qualify for his first Ryder Cup at the age of 48: in doing so he became the oldest player to finish in the top ten in the Ryder Cup points list. A switch to the US Senior Tour in 2006 has been a successful one, with five further victories, including the US Senior Open title in 2009, by six strokes, over Joey Sindelar.

Ed **Furgol**

Born: March 22, 1917
New York, USA

Ed Furgol's story is one of complete triumph over adversity. As a child he broke his arm and it was badly set; as a result it was permanently bent rigid. Consequently, in the golf swing it was of little use to him except to guide the club towards the ball. Furgol compensated for his disability in a number of ways: he built up the left-hand grip on his clubs so that they were the thickness of a tennis racket; by necessity he had a short swing, but he made amends by thrashing hard at the ball. Accordingly he was able to hit the ball very powerfully, and enjoyed a distinguished amateur career. His most successful year as a professional came in 1954 when he won the US Open and was named the US PGA's Player of the Year. His Open triumph came paired with the then-first-year professional Gene Littler. What a contrast they made; on this occasion, the verdict went to the manufactured play of Furgol over the cultured swing of Littler – the margin was just one shot. The following year Furgol demonstrated it was no fluke by taking the World Cup for America in partnership with Chick Harbert, collecting the individual title as well. Having reached the highest level, however, Furgol appeared to grow tired of the lifestyle soon afterwards, retreating to become a club professional. He remained a formidable competitor, though, as he demonstrated at the 1963 Masters, where he finished fifth, trailing the winner, Jack Nicklaus, by just two strokes.

Jim **Furyk**
Born: May 12, 1970
West Chester, Pa, USA

If you ever needed any evidence that a golf swing does not have to be beautiful to be effective, look no further than Jim Furyk. Armed with an out-to-in swing that had been shaped by his father, the West Chester-born player recorded his first victory just a year after joining the tour in the 1995 Las Vegas Invitational – a tournament he has gone on to win on two other occasions. A second win followed in 1996 at the Hawaiian Open, and although the following year remained winless, it marked Furyk's emergence onto the world stage: he finished tied for fifth at the US Open, fourth at the British Open and tied for sixth at the US PGA Championship. The major victory finally arrived at the 2003 US Open at Olympia Fields, where Furyk tied the mark for the tournament's lowest 72-hole score with 272. Victory at the Buick Open later in the season saw him move up to third in the world rankings and he became only the fourth player in tour history to earn more than $5 million in a single season. A wrist

injury curtailed his 2004 season, but he returned with one victory in 2005 and two in 2006 – a year that saw him finish a career-high second on the money list. A pair of wins in 2010 has seen him re-establish himself in the world's top ten.

Sergio **Garcia**
Born: January 9, 1980
Castellon, Spain

The Spaniard has achieved so much to date in the golfing world that you have to remind yourself that he has only just turned 30. That has much to do with the fact that "El Nino" has now graced golfing circles for 16 years. He first came to prominence as a talented amateur golfer making the cut as a "guest" amateur in the Turespana Masters at the tender age of 14, the youngest player ever to do so on the European Tour. Just 19 when he turned professional, he won his first tournament – the Irish Open – in just his sixth start.

He came to global prominence when he pushed Tiger Woods all the way at the 1999 US PGA Championship at Medinah thanks to a blistering first round of 66, and made the first of his five Ryder Cup appearances to date the same year and in the process became the youngest player (19 years, eight months and 15 days) ever to appear in the event.

Major swing changes in 2003 saw him become firmly established inside the world's top ten. He came close at the 2006 British Open (tied for fifth), but still major championship success eluded him. He looked set to break that duck at the 2007 British Open at Carnoustie, leading the tournament through the first three rounds, before a bogey on the 72nd hole placed him in a play-off with Pádraig Harrington – which he lost. He won the prestigious Players Championship in 2008, but it is major championship success that he craves.

Al **Geiberger**
Born: September 1, 1937
Red Bluff, Ca, USA

Geiberger will always be specially remembered for being the first player to break the magic 60 in a PGA Tour event, which he did on June 10, 1977, in the second round of the Danny Thomas-Memphis Classic. He went on to win, one of 11 successes on the main tour between 1962 and 1979. His most important victory came with the 1966 US PGA Championship (which he won by five strokes from compatriot Dudley Wysong), but others of almost equal significance were his wins in the 1975 Tournament of Champions and the Tournament Players' Championship, both of them

events which rank just below major championship status. Geiberger has always been plagued by stomach problems and found it helped him to eat little and often. His chosen snack on the golf course, famously, was the peanut butter sandwich, but even this could not contain the stomach problems and he has had to have several operations. When be became eligible for the Senior Tour at the age of 50, Geiberger immediately became one of the most effective competitors. Apart from being injured in 1994, he has performed consistently, notching up ten wins by the time he stopped competing regularly in 2002. Geiberger was on the US Ryder Cup team in 1967 and 1975.

Sergio Garcia Supremely talented, but a major tournament victory continues to elude him.

Lucas **Glover**

Born: November 12, 1979
Greenville, SC, USA

A member of the 2001 US Walker Cup team, Lucas Glover's rise to the top of the game has been based on length and accuracy off the tee, steadiness on the greens, and impressive consistency. He earned his US Tour card for 2004 with a joint 26th-place finish at the 2003 season-end qualifying tournament (after finishing 17th on the Nationwide Tour money list), and finished 134th on the money list in his first season. Glover's first tournament win came at the 2005 Funai Classic with birdies on the final two holes. He ended the year looking to be one of the game's rising new stars: he finished inside the top 30 on the money list and passed the $2 million mark in prize money for the first time. But between 2006 and 2008 he struggled to take his game to the next level. There were consistently strong performances, with a string of top-ten finishes (but no tournament wins). Glover's long wait for a second Tour victory ended in spectacular style in June 2009, however, when he dug deep to hold off the challenge of Ricky Barnes, David Duval and Phil Mickelson over the closing holes to win the US Open at Bethpage Black.

Bob **Goalby**

Born: March 14, 1931
Belleville, USA

Goalby was involved in perhaps the most famous rules decision of all time. It happened at the end of the 1968 Masters. Roberto de Vicenzo, having dropped a shot at the last, after a great round, glumly signed his card – marked by a fellow competitor. Alas, he had failed to notice that his score on the 17th was wrongly shown as a par, not a birdie. Roberto was not disqualified for his error, as he had merely signed for a higher score than he had actually achieved, but that score had to stand, and instead of de Vicenzo being in a play-off for the Masters, Goalby had won. This was very unfortunate – for both men.

Goalby, after all, had finished with a superb 66 and would have tied de Vicenzo anyway. He had played a great tournament and, as like as not, would have gone on to win the play-off. But what is remembered is that Roberto was the real winner but that someone else got the green jacket. Goalby had joined the PGA Tour in 1957, and in 1958 was named Rookie of the Year. He won 11 tour events in his career and was second in the 1961 US Open and the 1962 US PGA. With a lively temper and a pronounced in-to-out swing, his great problem was a draw which could become an uncontrollable hook. Despite this, he had his very hot streaks and once set a tour record with eight consecutive birdies.

Retief **Goosen**

Born: February 3, 1969
Pietersburg, South Africa

A former South Africa Amateur champion and a product of the Southern Africa Tour, Retief Goosen has become one of the most consistent and successful players on either side of the Atlantic. His first European Tour victory came in 1996 at Slaley Hall: the following year he captured the Peugeot Open of France title, an event that started a love affair with the country as he went on to win twice more in France. His breakthrough year came in 2001. He earned over $1 million in prize money in just ten starts on the PGA Tour and captured his first major title, the US Open. After three-putting the 72nd hole, he defeated Mark Brooks in an 18-hole play-off to become only the eighth player in 50 years to make the US Open his first PGA Tour title. That win was enough to see him to the European Order of Merit title too, the first South African to do so since Dale Hayes in 1975. He repeated the feat the following year. 2004 saw him collect his second US Open title, in the process he became the 21st multiple winner of the event, and he ended the season on a high by capturing the Tour Championship by four strokes to finish

RETIEF GOOSEN By 2005, the South African had catapulted himself to the forefront of world golf.

a career-best sixth on the US money list. Wins on both the European Tour and PGA Tour in 2005 moved him up to fourth in the world rankings, a peak he has not since surpassed. He won once in 2006 (at the South African Open) and once in 2007 (at the Qatar Open) – finishing in a tie for second at the Masters that year. 2008 saw him finish outside the top 20 of the US money list for the second consecutive year, but he returned to the winner's circle in 2009 with victories at the Transition Championship and at the Africa Open.

Wayne **Grady**

Born: July 26, 1957
Brisbane, Australia

Though he didn't win the British Open at Troon in 1989, it was perhaps Grady's finest hour. A 67, following a first-round 68, gave him a one-stroke

lead. After the third round, Grady had retained his narrow lead of one – over Tom Watson. In the final round, Grady did little wrong, but some inspired golf from Greg Norman, who had started the day seven behind, and some very good, if occasionally lucky, play by Mark Calcavecchia, produced a three-way tie – and a four-hole play-off, which was won by the American. For Grady, it was a rare encounter with the possibility of greatness. However, a major championship did come his way the very next year when he won the US PGA. Grady had made his PGA Tour debut in 1984, finishing 217th on the money list, improving to 45th in 1985. The next three years were less kind, but Grady broke through in 1989 when he won the Westchester Classic and was 27th on the money list. The following year he improved to 21st, mainly a result of his US PGA win.

Lucas Glover He hit the headlines with an unexpected victory at the 2009 US Open.

Twice the Australian PGA Champion, Grady also won the 1984 German Open. He is now a television commentator.

David **Graham**
Born: May 23, 1946
Windsor, Australia

With the Australian Tour having limited seasons, Graham, like many of his countrymen, has had to make himself an international golfer. Indeed, he has won all over the world, though his principal efforts have been on the PGA Tour, where he has won eight times, and as a part of the Senior Tour, which he joined in 1996. Putting has always been a very strong feature of his game. Graham has won two major championships. The first of these is the 1979 US PGA. This

was the first success by an Australian in a major since Peter Thomson won the 1965 British Open. He started off four behind the leader in his final round, but got to the turn in 31 and had birdies at the next two holes. With the event in his hands, Graham then showed considerable clumsiness around the green on the last hole, and could only tie. However, he won the play-off against Ben Crenshaw with the aid of some truly remarkable putting. In 1981, he became the first Australian to win the US Open. He did it with a last-round 67, thanks largely to his precision through the green. He took 33 putts – but missed only one fairway and no greens. He enjoyed relative success on the Senior Tour, winning five times

and amassing more than $4 million in prize money before retiring in 2004.

Lou **Graham**
Born: January 7, 1938
Nashville, Tn, USA

Lou Graham's time came in the mid-1970s, and particularly in 1975, when he won the US Open at Medinah. Dropping a shot at the last to fall into a play-off is not usually the portent for glory the next day, but Graham managed it with a level-par round of 71 to beat John Mahaffey by two strokes. Later that year, he teamed up with Johnny Miller to win the World Cup for America in Bangkok. Two years later, Graham mounted a wonderful weekend charge and almost secured a second US Open title. Playing the last 36 holes at Southern Hills in 136 shots – equalling the record for the event – he placed tremendous pressure on Hubert Green, who just managed to stave off the onslaught to claim the title by one shot. Three more titles in the space of just eight weeks came two years later. He eventually joined the Senior Tour, where he enjoyed three productive years, including six top-five finishes in 1989, before a wrist injury curtailed his play.

Hubert **Green**
Born: December 18, 1946
Birmingham, Al, USA

Hubert Green's years at the top were over by the time practice grounds on every professional tour became crowded with gurus pacing up and down. Which is just as well, because can you imagine the impact it would have had on his psyche if every time he looked up he saw a coach looking his way with a frown on his face thinking: "You can't swing a club like that and hope to be successful." But Green was successful, and so probably stands as the ultimate example of the fact that in golf it is not how, but how many. Green was the youngest of four in a family of golfers, and joined the PGA Tour in 1970. His two major championship successes were well spread out. The first was the 1977 US Open and formed part of

his golden summer, where he was also third at the British Open at Turnberry – where Jack Nicklaus and Tom Watson had their unforgettable shoot-out. As for his own major success at Southern Hills, Green managed to hang on to a lead that he held following an opening round of 69. Eight years on, it was Green who was doing the pursuing at Cherry Hills, chasing Lee Trevino as he sought back-to-back US PGA Championships. It was a third-round 75 from the not-so-merry Mex that allowed Green back into it and a last-round 72 was enough to see him to the title. A switch to the Senior Tour after he became eligible has brought him four victories.

Ralph **Guldahl**
Born: November 22, 1912
Dallas, Tx, USA

Guldahl may well be an example of a golfer ruined by writing a golf instruction book. It caused him to think about the way he himself played the game, which was extremely unorthodox. He had very little flow – with either his legs or in foot roll – and compensated for a lack of cock in his right wrist action on the backswing by letting the club move in his grip. Thinking and writing about it may have ruined him, for he suffered a permanent loss of form. Guldahl himself had various other explanations, ranging from a bad back to the fact that he had done it all in competitive golf. The latter was certainly true – if only for a brief spell. He first hit the headlines in 1933 when he came to within a 4ft putt of a tie for the US Open. Guldahl then disappeared for a few years, but came back in 1936 as the second highest money winner. The next spring he experienced his famous loss in the Masters, largely due to a disastrous 5-6 sequence on the 12th and 13th holes, but his time was coming. Two months later, he won the US Open and then had a rare repeat victory the following year. The Masters came his way the next year, partly because of those previously fatal holes. This time he played them 3-3 and that was just about the end of it for Ralph Guldahl.

WALTER HAGEN
"Eddie - hold the flag, will you?"

The above remark came during a round of golf with Edward, Prince of Wales, soon to be, briefly, Edward VIII. It shows how much Hagen felt at ease with everyone, from kings and presidents to ordinary followers of golf.

Hagen had come to the top very quickly. He played the 1912 Canadian Open and finished 11th. Asked at his home club how he had done, Hagen replied, "I lost." This was an early variation on his famous adage that no one remembers who finished second. He lost again in the 1913 US Open, finishing a stroke behind the play-off between Vardon, Ray and Ouimet. The following year, 1914, was better. He began the US Open with a record 68 and held on to win. He won the US Open again in 1919 and was ready to spread his wings further afield and prove himself in the British Open.

Hagen arrived at Deal for the 1920 event. Since, as a professional, he was not allowed to enter the clubhouse, he hired a limousine, had his chauffeur park it in front of the clubhouse and enjoyed the contents of his hamper. It was a typically grand gesture from a man who enjoyed cocking a snook, but Hagen's play did not impress the spectators nearly as much. He came in 53rd of the 77 qualifiers.

He realized that, to compete more effectively on links courses, he must learn the pitch and run. Having done so, he enjoyed a great run in the British Open during the 1920s. After being sixth the following year, he won in 1922, was second the next year and won again in 1924. For his next entries through to 1929 he was third, first and first. With that last victory, he was nearly finished with the British Open.

In the US Open, he was far less successful in the 1920s, not adding to his two titles. The fact that Bobby Jones was always in the field had a great deal to do with this.

But Jones as an amateur was not eligible for the matchplay US PGA, and Hagen proceeded to compile perhaps the greatest run of success of anyone in a major championship. In 1916, he reached the semi-finals and next played in 1921, when he won. His next appearance was in 1923, when he lost to Gene Sarazen in the final. Then came his unparalleled run of four in a row.

The strength of his game was from, say, 100 yards in. He was a short pitcher of excellence, could nip the ball off the sand nervelessly when in a greenside bunker and was the best putter in the business. Hagen's long game was less impressive. Not particularly long off the tee, his swaying swing was perhaps the cause of wildness. However, when surveying a shot from wild country he had the sang-froid to be able to say: "Well, I put it there." And then his recovery shots were as fabled as those of Seve Ballesteros later.

By the end of the 1920s, Hagen had collected 11 major titles and was close to entering his 40s. His tally of majors could well have been higher: he did not have the chance to compete in the Masters, which began in 1934, until his best days lay well behind him. To some extent he may have lost his appetite for centre-stage and by this time his name was easily big enough for him to spend much time on exhibition tours worldwide where he could both enjoy himself and make the money he needed. Hagen had a great capacity for enjoyment and only a brief interest in family life, though he was much addicted to the company of attractive women and kept a little black book to record their phone numbers around the world.

He fulfilled his ambitions. Perhaps he didn't passionately desire the major and tournament titles he amassed over the years. They were the means to an end: enjoying life. As he used to say: "I didn't want to be a millionaire. I just wanted to live like one."

WALTER HAGEN No more colourful figure has ever played the game.

1892	1914	1919	1921	1922	1924	1927
Born on December 21, Rochester, New York	Wins first US Open	Second US Open title	Begins a sequence of five US PGA titles from 1921 to 1927	First victory in the British Open	Second victory in the British Open	Captain of the winning US Ryder Cup team in inaugural match against Britain

1928	1929	1931	1933	1935	1937
Third victory in the British Open	Fourth victory in the British Open and losing Ryder Cup captain	Successful Ryder Cup captain	Ryder Cup captain for the fourth time and second time on the losing side	Third victory as Ryder Cup captain	Ryder Cup captain for sixth time, first victory for away team

Jay Haas

Born: December 2, 1953
St Louis, Mo, USA

A smooth, easy swing is often the key to a long career and few swings come smoother and few careers have been as long as those of Jay Haas. St Louis-born Haas secured the first of his nine tour victories way back in 1978, winning the San Diego Open by three strokes. His last victory was back in 1993, when he claimed the Texas Open, but since then he has hit perhaps the most consistent streak of his career: a streak that has been rewarded by captain's picks for both the President's Cup (in both 1994 and 2003) and the Ryder Cup (in 2004). In 1996, Haas tied the record for the most consecutive rounds of par or under at the Masters – with nine – and Augusta, in 1999, was the scene of his best performance in a major championship to date when he finished third. In 2003, Haas earned over $2 million in prize money for the first time: he also finished fifth in the US PGA Championship. Equally consistent form in 2004 saw Hal Sutton select him as a captain's pick for the Ryder Cup: it was a surprise choice for many, but Haas was one of the few Americans who could hold his head up high after his side's crushing defeat at the hands of the Europeans.

Todd Hamilton

Born: October 18, 1965
Galesburg, Il, USA

The word "journeyman" is often seen as a derogatory term, but Todd Hamilton has had to travel to make a living out of the game. After making just one cut in four tournaments on the Nationwide Tour, the American crossed the Pacific to ply his trade in Asia and the move brought years of success. In 11 years on the Japan Golf Tour, Hamilton recorded 14 tournament victories before finally gaining his card for the PGA Tour in 2003: it was an event that triggered a fairytale year in 2004. Hamilton won his first event, the Honda Classic, by birdieing the final two holes of the tournament. Then came his first major championship with victory at the British Open at Royal Troon. After bogeying the 72nd hole, the American beat Ernie Els in the four-hole play-off to become the second consecutive rookie to win the tournament and the eighth American to lift the Claret Jug in the last ten years. In what had been the greatest and the most surprising story of the year in golf, Hamilton took the Rookie of the Year honours at the tender age of 38. But the fairytale has not continued. Hamilton has not ended a year inside the top 100 on the US Money List since.

Chick Harbert

Born: February 20, 1915
Dayton, Oh, USA

With his ability to hit the ball vast distances, and a sure touch on the greens, it was not surprising that Chick Harbert proved particularly adept at matchplay. Accordingly, his finest performances in the majors were reserved for the US PGA Championship, in which he was the runner-up once and the victor in 1954 at Keller Country Club. Two years earlier, Harbert had lost in the final to Jim Turnesa, a hard defeat to bear since the match went all the way to the home green. Now he enjoyed his moment in the sun, beating Walter Burkemo by the margin of 4&3 in the final, having seen off Tommy Bolt a round earlier – this time by the slenderest of margins (1 up). Harbert had shown early promise when he won the Michigan Open in 1937 while still an amateur. He would win it on two more occasions when he joined the professional ranks, together with five other titles. In tandem with Ed Furgol, he also helped America lift the 1955 World Cup.

Pádraig Harrington

Born: August 31, 1971
Dublin, Ireland

Given his recent staggering success, it seems strange to think there was a time when Pádraig Harrington was considered one of the nearly men of golf. A string of nine runner-up spots was finally broken when he won the Brazil Sao Paolo Open in 2000. It all seemed a long way away from the man who burst onto the professional scene in 1996 by making the cut in his first nine tournaments, recording five top tens and finishing in 11th place in the Order of Merit in his first full year. He followed his impressive debut season with fifth place at the British Open, and partnered Paul McGinley to take Ireland to World Cup success at Kiawah Island. Then came the drought. Following the success in Sao Paolo he won again later in the year. Victory at the season-ending Volvo Masters in 2001 saw him break into the world's top ten for the first time. Victories in each of the following three seasons have cemented his reputation as one of the most dangerous golfers on the circuit. He switched mainly to the PGA tour in 2005, won twice and pocketed $2.6 million in prize money. In 2006, he won the European Order of Merit for the first time, but in 2007, he overcame a double-bogey on the 72nd hole at the British Open in Carnoustie to beat Sergio Garcia in a play-off and become the first Irishman to win the Open for 60 years. The following year, he became the first European to win back-to-back British Open titles since James Braid in 1905-06 with victory at Royal Birkdale. The year got even better when he won the US PGA at Oakland Hills.

Pádraig Harrington The Irishman won three out of six majors between 2006 and 2007.

Sandra **Haynie**

Born: June 4, 1943
Fort Worth, Tx, USA

Haynie is one of the great figures of the LPGA Tour. In the period from 1963 to 1975, her worst placing on the money list was ninth, and she had at least one victory every year. Usually, however, she was a multiple winner, with 1974 being her most successful year. Then she won six times, including the LPGA Championship and the US Women's Open, two of the four majors she has won in a long career. Haynie was troubled by arthritis from the age of 33, and soon after her great years she became only an occasional competitor, playing just 17 tournaments in the space of the four years from 1977 to 1980. Yet 1982 saw her in peak form once more. She had two victories and finished second on the money list, one of the five times she has been in this position (while never being number one). Once Haynie was into her 40s, she became a receding force, and has not competed since playing a full season in 1989 without any real success. Sandra Haynie was inducted into the Hall of Fame in 1977, and, in 1970, won the Player of the Year award.

Sandy **Herd**

Born: April 22, 1868
St Andrews, Scotland

Always just a notch below the standards set by the Great Triumvirate of Vardon, Taylor, and Braid, Sandy Herd outlasted them all. His long professional career began in 1892 at Huddersfield Golf Club. The same year, he won three tournaments and made a good run at the British Open, being held for the first time at Muirfield, finishing tied for second place behind Harold Hilton. Herd was second again in 1895, this time at St Andrews, and looked likely to win at Muirfield the following year when he started with a 72 – five strokes better than anyone and 11 better than the eventual winner, Harry Vardon – before his form collapsed. His finest hour came at Hoylake in 1902, when he won the British Open by a stroke from Vardon and Braid. He was the first champion to use the "modern" rubber core ball instead of the guttie. After Herd's win, the guttie was finished. It was to be many years before Herd was. He was second in the 1920 British Open, having been in the lead with a round to go, and played for the final time in the event in 1939, 54 years after his first appearance. In 1926, he upstaged even the Great Triumvirate with what is probably the greatest feat ever performed by an "old" golfer. At the age of 58, he took the News of the World Matchplay Championship, then ranked second only to the British Open.

Dave **Hill**

Born: May 20, 1937
Jackson, Ms, USA

Like a Hogan or a Nelson, Dave Hill has always delighted in trying to achieve perfection in his lonely vigils. "You paint pictures out there," he said, "and each good shot is a deft stroke." During the 1960s, Hill earned an outstanding reputation as a ball striker and also because he tended to be more outspoken than the various authorities liked. He was particularly rude about the Hazeltine National course, the site of the 1970 US Open, in spite of the fact that he eventually finished second. "All the course needs," he declared, "is 80 acres of corn and four cows." This, and similar comments, brought him a $150 fine. Hill joined the PGA Tour in 1959, and from 1960 to 1975 was in the top-30 money winners 11 times. He achieved his best placing of second in 1969, his peak season, which included three wins. Altogether Hill won 13 times on the main tour and also made three Ryder Cup appearances. Eventually, he tired of tournament golf, particularly because he felt that success depended too much on putting. When he became eligible, however, he returned on the Senior Tour in 1987 and went on to record six wins.

Harold **Hilton**

Born: January 12, 1869
West Kirkby, England

Hilton is generally ranked alongside his fellow Royal Liverpool club member John Hall as one of the two greatest British amateur golfers. He may only have taken four Amateur Championship titles to Ball's eight, but he won two British Opens to Ball's single victory. He remains the only British amateur to have taken the Open twice and, perhaps surprisingly, the only British amateur to have taken the American title, when he succeeded at Apawamis in 1911. Hilton's first British Open victory came in 1892 at Muirfield. He had not intended to play and gave himself time only for a day's practice. His start wasn't promising, but his final rounds of 72 and 74 were truly outstanding for the time. Five years later, on his home course of Hoylake, he did it again, beating James Braid by a stroke. Oddly, he found winning the British Amateur Championship more of a problem, partly because his great rival, Freddie Tait, used to get the better of him. However, he won in 1900 and 1901 and then, during a revival shortly before the First World War, came two more victories.

HAROLD HILTON The only British amateur to have won twice at the British Open.

BEN HOGAN
Long Game, Grand Slam

Ben Hogan had a long game the accuracy of which has probably never been matched. The man's shots always seemed to home in on the flag. It then became almost a matter of the luck of the bounce if they stuck a little too short or skidded through a little too far. But, as legend has it, they were always on line.

In his peak years, Hogan was almost as accurate with the driver, but he was never a supreme putter. His method was perhaps too mechanical, so that he always lacked real delicacy of touch. But, like his nearest modern counterpart, Nick Faldo, he could reliably stuff the ball into the hole from 6ft and under.

At the outset, there were many years of failure, but Hogan was persistent. He first played on the PGA Tour in 1931 and, from time to time, for several years afterwards. There was little if any sponsorship in those far-off years. Hogan would do odd jobs, save up the dollars and then play for as long as the money lasted. He won virtually no prize money. In 1937, he did win some money and, the following year, his first event, a fourball. He was already 34 years old.

But 1940 saw the beginning of the Hogan legend. He won the North and South event over Pinehurst 2 and was on his way.

Then came the war, with Hogan becoming a dominant player, playing 39 events in 1941 and being only once out of the top five. The reasons for this astonishing improvement were that he had become a good short-range putter and had trained himself on the practice ground to shorten the length of his backswing, which had been absurdly beyond the horizontal. As a result, his long game immediately became more consistent.

He emerged as a supreme talent after the war, with 21 wins in the first two seasons, which included the 1946 US PGA Championship. He was by no means satisfied. Hogan was aiming for a level of consistency that would lead to greatness. Over the winter of 1947-48 he worked on changing his low drawing hook into a slice. Although he succeeded, he lost much of his length, but the ball finished on the fairway, Hogan's main aim. That slice quite quickly became a slight fade. The length was little altered and the shape of shot was consistent. You rule out the trouble along the left and then have the whole of the fairway to aim at. Hogan won his first US Open.

But Fate had a trick up its sleeve.

Early in 1949, Hogan was very severely injured in a road accident. Many thought he would never play again and he was indeed out of the game for nearly a year. When he returned, walking was agony and he had to restrict himself to just a few events. The majors became his aim, though he had to exclude the US PGA – then a 36-hole matchplay event – because he knew his legs wouldn't take him around that many holes in a day.

Having missed the 1949 US Open, Hogan took the title on three of his next four entries. His winning last-round 67 at the spectacularly difficult Oakland Hills course in 1951 was, he thought, the best round he ever played. His last US Open win came in 1953, his greatest year, when he also took his second Masters and won the British Open on his only entry to complete the modern grand slam.

It was thought at the time that Hogan would go on winning the majors as long as he wanted to. As Hogan himself said, desire was what counted. But he was wrong. Hogan kept both desire and will, but his putting stroke went. He developed what is variously called "the twitch", "the jerks" or "the yips". In one US Open, when still in contention on the final green, he was

BEN HOGAN He spent hours honing his swing and was rewarded with nine major championships.

noticed apparently trying out a variety of putting methods on the edge of the green. A friend later commented on this. Hogan explained that he hadn't been trying to find a stroke that would hole a putt, but one that would make missing look respectable.

After 1953, Hogan went into a slow decline, but remained a force to be reckoned with until towards the end of the 1960s.

1912	1938	1946	1947	1948
Born on August 13, Dublin, Texas	First tournament win, Hershey Fourball	The US PGA became his first major title	Victorious Ryder Cup captain	Wins his first US Open title and second US PGA in a double-major year

1949	1950	1951	1953	1967
Involved in serious car accident, but recovers enough to be non-playing Ryder Cup captain at Ganton, Yorkshire	Second US Open title	Wins both the Masters and the US Open	Wins the Masters, the US Open and the British Open (on his only entry)	Non-playing Ryder Cup captain as US wins in his home state of Texas

JULI INKSTER She compiled a prolific amateur record before going on to win six majors.

Ben **Hogan**
SEE PAGE 169

Tommy **Horton**
Born: June 16, 1941
St Helens, England

Horton's early career was boosted by a man called Ernest Butten, who had a passionate desire to see a British player win the British Open. The last to do so had been Max Faulkner at Portrush in 1951. The scheme was that Butten would put some money into grooming three players with the potential to become superstars. Faulkner would teach them how to swing the club, putt and have the mental toughness to be winners. As it turned out, none of them came really close to winning the tournament, but Brian Barnes and Tommy Horton did become very considerable players. Horton was twice joint leading British player in the British Open - in 1976 and 1977. His finest hour was probably his victory in the 1978 Dunlop Masters, then very much a top tournament. Quite a small man, Horton was somewhat underpowered and often found himself having to hit long irons into greens when Brian Barnes, for example, might have needed just a firm wedge. So Tommy Horton became one of the best long-iron players in European golf. He had

eight tournament wins in Europe, was second on the money list in 1967, had three victories overseas and was in the 1975 and 1977 Ryder Cup teams. He was PGA captain in 1978. He has enjoyed a highly successful career on the European Senior Tour winning 23 events - he shot a tour-record 62 at the 1997 Scottish Senior Open - and stood at the top of the all-time money winners' list until 2007.

Jock **Hutchison**
Born: June 6, 1884
St Andrews, Scotland

Hutchison was one of many Scots who emigrated to America to find fame and fortune and played a leading role in developing the game there. He began to make his mark around 1910, and was fifth in the US Open the following year. His best finishes in the event were two second places, in 1916 and 1920, and he was third on two other occasions. In 1916, he came close to winning his first major, the US PGA, but was beaten in the matchplay final by the Cornishman Jim Barnes. However, all was well in 1920 when he defeated another English export, J. Douglas Edgar, in the final of the same event. His greatest success came on home ground, in the 1921 British Open at St Andrews. After the four rounds, he was tied with the English amateur

Roger Wethered, but easily won the 36-hole play-off. There was some controversy afterwards. Hutchison's clubs were heavily scored, and it was felt that it was this factor that enabled him to stop the ball so quickly on hard and fast greens. Such designs were later banned. Hutchison won an estimated eight events of significance on the fledgling PGA Tour.

Trevor **Immelman**
Born: December 16, 1979
Cape Town, South Africa

Trevor Immelman enjoyed a successful amateur career - winning the US Amateur public links championship in 1998 and making the cut at the 1999 Masters - before turning professional later that year. In 2000, he created a stir by winning the South African Players Championship and became a full member of the European Tour in 2001. He endured three second-place finishes in 2002 before discovering the winning formula at the 2003 South Africa Open. Later in the year, playing alongside Rory Sabbatini, he helped South Africa win the World Cup. In 2004, Immelman became the first player since Gary Player (1976-77) to make a successful South Africa Open title defence and collected a second win of the season at the Deutsche Bank Open. A fifth-place finish at the 2005 Masters prompted Player to make him his captain's pick for the Presidents Cup, and he rewarded him by going unbeaten in four matches. Taking advantage of a two-year PGA Tour exemption for Presidents Cup players, Immelman moved to America and claimed his maiden US title at the 2007 Western Open and moved into the world rankings' top 15 for the first time. In December 2007, medical problems led to the removal of a golfball-sized benign tumour from his diaphragm, but Immelman bounced back magnificently in 2008, capturing his first major title with a win at the Masters. He not only held off Tiger Woods by three strokes but also became the first player since

Raymond Floyd in 1976 to lead after all four rounds.

Juli **Inkster**
Born: June 24, 1960
Los Altos, Ca, USA

Inkster had a glittering amateur career. Between 1980 and 1982 she became one of only three women - the others being Glenna Collett and Virginia van Wie - to have won the US Women's Amateur title three years in a row. In her last amateur season, heading the US team, she won both her Curtis Cup matches by 7&6 and later went on to take the individual prize in the Women's World Amateur Team Championship by a comfortable four strokes. She was, without doubt, the world's best woman amateur. After turning professional, she quickly captured her first LPGA title. In 1984, she was named Rookie of the Year and won two majors, the Nabisco Dinah Shore and the du Maurier Classic. The demands of motherhood appeared to have taken their toll, but a third major, the Dinah Nabisco Shore, came her way in 1989. Ten years later, in a wonderful return to form, she romped home with both the US Open (by five shots) and the McDonald's LPGA Championship (by four shots) to become only the fourth woman - along with Mickey Wright, Louise Suggs and Patricia Bradley - to have won all four of the designated majors. She successfully defended her McDonald's LPGA Championship in 2000 and increased her major tally to seven in 2002 by winning the US Women's Open for a second time. By 2010, she had 38 professional wins to her name.

Hale **Irwin**
Born: June 3, 1945
Joplin, Mo, USA

In the 1990 US Open at Medinah, Irwin played one of the most dramatic shots in the history of golf. He holed a putt of about 60ft on the last green to tie with Mike Donald. They finished level after a further round and Irwin then holed a birdie putt on the first sudden-death hole to win. At 45, he had become the oldest winner of the US Open. Irwin has two more US Opens on his record. His first came over the very difficult Winged Foot course in 1974, where seven-over par was good enough for a two-stroke victory. This win demonstrated one of Irwin's great strengths. He is by no means an outstanding putter or a genius at close range, but he does find most of the fairways and greens, so tough courses bring out the best in him. His second US Open win came in 1979 and included the shot of the year in his third round, a two-iron to a couple of feet or so. He won 20 titles and $5.9 million in 27 years on the US PGA Tour. Those statistics have been blitzed by his performances on the Senior Tour since he became eligible in 1995. By the end of the 2009 season, he had amassed 45 victories (including 5 senior major championships) and won more than $25.2 million in prize money – he has won more than $8 million more than his nearest rival on the all-time seniors' money-winners list.

Tony **Jacklin**
Born: July 7, 1944
Scunthorpe, England

Not many players lead a major after every round, but Jacklin did so at the US Open at Hazeltine in 1970. He cruised home to win by seven strokes, becoming the first Englishman to win the US Open since Ted Ray in 1920. Jacklin had won the British Open in 1969, and for a month or so was one of the select few to hold both of the national championships. He was a British national hero and seemed on the verge of becoming an all-time great, but thereafter the big prizes eluded him. Lee Trevino had much to do with this, holing some outrageous, and very telling, shots at Muirfield in 1972, when the pair were locked in combat for the Claret Jug. Playing the penultimate hole, Jacklin had victory in his grasp as Trevino struggled, but he three-putted for a six. Later that same season, he played brilliantly against Trevino in the World Matchplay Championship – but again it was the American who came out on top. Though Jacklin was to play other excellent tournaments, he was never in contention again for a major championship. He was a brilliantly successful Ryder Cup captain during the 1980s and did much to revitalize Europe's fortunes in the event.

Peter **Jacobsen**
Born: March 4, 1954
Portland, Or, USA

This player is in high demand for US golf clinics and company days. The main reason is that he is a jovial fellow who enjoys communicating. He also provides good copy for Press tent interviews. Overall, his career has been impeded by medical problems, but he suddenly found top form at the age of 41, winning $1 million in 1995. Jacobsen likes to play internationally and it is appropriate that his first win came in the 1979 West Australian Open. The following year he won his first event on the PGA Tour, the Buick Open. The next 14 seasons brought a meagre three wins (but $3.5 million) before his back-to-back 1995 victories raised him to his highest ranking yet, seventh. He won again in 2003, his final year before switching to the Senior Tour. He won once in his debut season and what a tournament to win – the US Senior Open. Jacobsen first broke through in 1980 in the Buick Open at Warwick Hills, MI. In 1984, he won twice and finished tenth on the US money list. That remained his highest position till 1995. The strongest feature of his game is consistency through the green. He hits the fairways more than most and then goes on to find the greens. He is also thought to be the best there is at imitating the swings and mannerisms of other players.

Don **January**
Born: November 20, 1929
Plainview, Tx, USA

January has been an important figure in US golf since he joined the tour in 1956. He had his first victory that year and continued to win occasional tournaments until his victory in the Tournament of Champions in 1976. In this phase of his career he was always a consistent money winner and finished in the top-60 money winners 20 times. This was despite the fact that he was not a hard worker in terms of tournament entries. He left the tour in favour of course design in 1972, returning when that activity slumped to achieve ninth place in 1976. He won ten times on the main tour, including the US PGA in 1967, and subsequently gained 22 Senior titles.

Lee **Janzen**
Born: August 28, 1964
Austin, Tx, USA

Lee Janzen is an accomplished if unspectacular golfer who seems to relish the pressure moments. Accordingly, two of his eight victories on the PGA Tour have come in major championships, and he also showed his mettle in the 1997 Ryder Cup, birdieing the final two holes of his singles match against José-Maria Olazabal to come back from one behind with two to play to win. Janzen's first win in the US Open in 1993 followed four successive rounds in the 60s that enabled him to tie Jack Nicklaus' 72-hole record for the event. On that occasion it was Payne Stewart whom he defeated to the finishing line. Oddly enough it was the same player who again duelled with him for the title five years later, at the Olympic Club in San Francisco, as Janzen joined the select group of players who have won America's national Open on more than one occasion. However, he has not recorded a PGA Tour victory since.

TREVOR IMMELMAN The South African led after all four rounds to win the 2008 US Masters.

Miguel Angel **Jimenez**

Born: January 5, 1964
Malaga, Spain

Nicknamed "The Mechanic" for his love of fast cars, the cigar-smoking, Rioja-loving Spaniard finally secured his European Tour card in 1988. His first victory on tour came four years later, at the Belgian Open in 1992, and he ended the season in 14th place on the Order of Merit. A second victory came at the Dutch Open in 1994 and he ended the season in fifth place on the money list. Any disappointment at missing out on a spot for the 1997 Ryder Cup was alleviated when he played a vital role as vice-captain to Seve Ballesteros during Europe's memorable victory at Valderrama. He bounced back the following year to take the Lancôme Trophy by chipping in for a birdie two at the final hole and made his mark on the international stage in 1999. Two tour victories were consolidated when he took the runners'-up spot at the WCG-American Express tournament when he lost in a play-off to Tiger Woods. A slump in form in 2002 saw him slide to 66th in the money list, but he returned to the winner's circle in 2003 and continued that form into 2004, when he was Europe's most prolific winner – taking four tournaments. He was consistent for the next few seasons, but in recent years has gone on to collect the most prestigious titles of his career – the PGA Championship at Wentworth in 2008 and the Dubai Desert Classic in 2010.

Zach **Johnson**

Born: February 24, 1976
Iowa City, IA

A promising, but by no means a standout, collegiate player, Zach Johnson is a prime example of how far sweat and graft can take a player. After turning professional in 1998, he spent two years on the Prairie Tour, before joining the Nationwide Tour where, in 2003, two victories saw him finish top of the money list

ZACH JOHNSON Held off a charging pack to win the 2007 US Masters.

– earning a then-record $432,882– to claim his PGA Tour card. He got off to an impressive start making 24 out of 30 cuts, collecting his first victory (in only his 13th start) at the Bellsouth Classic and ending the season as only the second player in Tour history to surpass $2 million in earnings in his rookie season. His progress continued with five top-ten finishes in 2005 and a debut Ryder Cup appearance at the K Club in 2006 (where he went 1-2-1 in a losing cause). He made worldwide headlines, when he made three birdies in a four-hole stretch to win the 2007 Masters by two shots from Tiger Woods, Retief Goosen and Rory Sabbatini at a cold, windswept Augusta National. Victory at the AT&T Classic later in the year saw him end up seventh on the money list. Johnson's progress continued in 2008 with his fourth Tour victory, at the Texas Open, and in 2009, when he recorded eight top-ten finishes and two victories (at the Mercedes-Benz Championship and the Sony Open in Hawaii) to surpass $4 million in single-season earnings for the first time.

Bobby **Jones**

SEE PAGE 173

Steve **Jones**

Born: December 27, 1958
Artesia, NM, USA

The career of this son of Artesia (population 10,610) is a tribute to persistence. He was prospering on the PGA Tour, notably with three wins in 1989, till a dirt-bike accident late in 1991 damaged his left ring finger. Jones got back on tour in 1994, his long game relying on the reverse overlap grip normally used in putting. A year on he was back to six-figure earnings and, in 1996, inspired by Ben Hogan's "focus on each shot" exhortation, became both the US Open champion and the Comeback Player of the Year. Jones began 1997 with an 11-stroke win at Phoenix, his home town: his 72-hole total of 258 was the third lowest in PGA Tour history. He won again in 1998 at the Quad City Classic. He has suffered from injuries since then and missed all of the 2004 season following surgery on his elbow in 2003. Shoulder and elbow surgery in 2008 and 2009 have blighted his switch to the Senior Tour.

BOBBY JONES
The Emperor Who Had Had Enough

Bobby Jones achieved a success rate that was, and remains, beyond compare. In his whole relatively brief career he played only 52 tournaments, either amateur or professional, and won 23 of them.

By around the age of 20, Jones was already nearly the golfing phenomenon of the age and there could have been few who doubted that he would become the greatest golfer ever. In that decade up to 1930 he provided the proof.

It all took off in 1923 when he won his first major, the US Open. He achieved the victory despite completing his final round bogey, bogey, double-bogey. Was there a flaw in Jones' armour in that he tended to let up when in a commanding position? He was clearly better when under the whip.

That came in the play-off against Bobby Cruickshank. At the last he had to risk all to win, needing to hit a long iron from a sandy lie over water to the green – or play short of the hazard for safety, with the likelihood of having to play another 18 holes. Jones went for the bold shot and played it to perfection.

With the knowledge that he had it in him to win a major, Jones was on his way. In the US Amateur, for instance, from 1924 to 1930, he won five of his seven entries and was runner-up once.

In the US Open, Jones's four victories still give him a share of the record. In the other years between 1922 and 1930 he finished 11th – a dismal failure in Jones's terms – was second twice and lost two play-offs.

His record in the British Open was the most remarkable of all. He first appeared in 1921 at the age of 19. After two rounds he was four behind the leaders, but then had a disastrous 46 to the turn at St Andrews, double-bogeyed the next two holes – and tore up his card. He did not appear again in a British Open until 1926. As it was a Walker Cup year, his travelling expenses were paid and the US team then went on to compete in the British Amateur.

Miffed at not winning, and wanting to show the British public what he was made of, Jones decided to stay on for the Open at Royal Lytham and St Anne's. He won, in the end as a result of a cracking mid-iron to the heart of the 71st green from a sandy lie in the rough.

Though he couldn't really afford the trip, Jones felt as though he had to return for the St Andrews Open the following year. He won comfortably this time with a record score and no theatrics were necessary.

His final British Open appearance was at Hoylake in 1930. He won again, despite once dropping eight shots in the space of three holes and, in his final round, once taking five more to get down when being just short of a par five in two. it seemed 1930 was the miracle year, with Jones winning the Amateur and Open Championships of both Britain and America. He had had a hunch that this might just be possible, and in the winter had taken the unusual step – especially for those days – of trying to keep fit.

Shortly after the completion of the never-to-be-repeated Grand Slam at Merion in 1930, Jones decided to retire. Alexander the Great always felt that his empire could be even bigger. Jones, however, felt that there were no more fields left to conquer.

Instead, he designed some of the best iron clubheads ever, and was instrumental in the design of the Masters Tournament and of the Augusta course. With his amateur status gone, he also made a lot of money from his golf fame.

BOBBY JONES For many, he was the greatest player ever to have played the game.

1902	1923	1924	1925	1926
Born on March 7 in Atlanta, Georgia	First US Open win	First US Amateur win	Wins US Amateur for the second time	Wins both the US Open and the British Open

1927	1928	1929	1930	1934
Wins his second British Open and his third US Amateur	Fourth US Amateur	Third US Open	Wins the Grand Slam – the US Open, the British Open, the British Amateur and the US Amateur	Plays in his invitational tournament at the course he designed at Augusta, which quickly becomes known as the Masters

CATHERINE LACOSTE Many consider her to be the best golfer that France has ever produced.

Anthony **Kim**
Born: June 19, 1985
Los Angeles, CA, USA

A three-time All-American (2004–06) and a member of the 2005 US Walker Cup team, Anthony Kim turned professional in 2006 and finished in a tie for second on his Tour debut at the Texas Open. He earned his full Tour card at the 2007 qualifying school and, as the youngest rookie on Tour, enjoyed a successful debut season, recording four top-tens. He broke into the world's elite in 2008, making 19 of 22 cuts, with eight top-ten finishes, and wins at the Wachovia Championship (to become the youngest winner on Tour since Sergio Garcia in 2002) and the AT&T National. Kim capped a superb breakthrough year by playing a pivotal role in the United States' Ryder Cup win over Europe, where he defeated Ryder Cup veteran Garcia 5 and 4 in a highly charged opening Sunday singles match. In November 2008, he made the final of the prestigious World Matchplay Championship, only to lose 4 and 3 to England's Ross Fisher. At the 2009 Masters he broke the record for the most birdies in a single round, shooting 11 during his second round. In 2010, he won the Houston Open to become only the fifth player in 30 years to have won three times on the US PGA Tour before the age of 25. He displayed his enormous talent at that year's US Masters, posting rounds of 68, 70, 73 and 65 to finish in third place, his best performance in a major championship to date.

Mi Hyun **Kim**
Born: January 13, 1977
Inchon, South Korea

Mi Hyun Kim is one of a number of Koreans who have broken into the ranks of the LPGA in recent years – collectively they have been dubbed the "Seoul Sisters". Turning professional in 1996, she won 15 times on the Korean LPGA Tour before she had reached 22 years of age and shared a fierce rivalry with compatriot Se Ri Pak. Whereas Pak was offered a lucrative sponsorship deal to go to the States, Mi Hyun Kim had to earn her LPGA Tour card the hard way. Although she earned her card at the first attempt, she spent her first year on tour driving between events with her parents in a van and staying in cheap hotels to save money. Two tournament wins and Rookie of the Year honours soon changed that. Sponsors stepped forward and her life in the States changed. Further tournament wins have followed (eight of them on the PGA Tour) and by the end of 2009 she had amassed more than $8 million in career earnings. An exceptionally long hitter, despite her 5ft 1in frame, her best performance at a major championship is second at the 2001 British Women's Open.

Betsy **King**
Born: August 13, 1955
Reading, Pa, USA

Betsy King first attracted notice at the 1976 US Women's Open, when she finished in eighth place. However, after joining the LPGA Tour in 1977, she found it all a very slow learning process, and her first successful season only came in 1983. That year she finished 14th on the money list, but she was on her way. From 1984 until 1995 her worst placing was ninth, and she has finished in the top three seven times. She was leading money winner in 1984, 1989 and 1993. Since her first success in Japan in 1981 the victories have piled up. Her first LPGA success came in 1984. Two others followed that same year, after which she did not have a winless year until 1994. In 1989, she set a new target (broken the next year) for a season's money winnings with over $650,000. She had won six times, including the US Women's Open. This was one of her five major titles to date, the others being the Dinah Shore in 1987 and 1990, the LPGA in 1992, and the rare feat of a second Women's Open in 1990. In 1995, she became the first LPGA player in history to pass the $5 million mark in career earnings. She captured her 31st tour title in 2001 when she won the LPGA Classic.

Tom **Kite**
Born: December 9, 1949
Austin, Tx, USA

Tom appears a rather anonymous player, partly because his face is normally shielded by a very large pair of spectacles and hooded by a sponsor's eye shade. He is perhaps more famed for blowing major championships than he is for winning them, but he is still a good enough player to have amassed more than $10 million in career earnings. Kite has achieved this by his consistency rather than by winning tournaments. After joining the PGA Tour in 1972, he had only three tournament victories to his credit ten years later. His strike

BERNHARD LANGER The two-time Masters champion's story will always be associated with a putter.

rate, however, has greatly increased since then. He is not a long hitter but a master with the wedge, often carrying three. His peak year was 1989, when he set what was then the PGA Tour money-winning record at just under $1.4 million. However, having long been described as the best player never to have won a major championship, he was probably far more pleased by his victory in the 1992 US Open at Pebble Beach. He was captain of the unsuccessful 1997 American Ryder Cup team at Valderrama in Spain and joined the Senior Tour in 2000, where he has racked up ten tournament wins to date, including one senior major.

Catherine **Lacoste**
Born: June 27, 1945
Paris, France

For a while Lacoste was arguably the best woman player in the world. She also has a strong claim to be ranked as the greatest French player, of either sex, of all time. She had a lot to live up to, coming from a very sporting family. Her father René had been a great tennis player; her mother became the first overseas player to win the British Ladies Golf Championship. Catherine's finest achievement was her victory in the 1967 US Women's Open, when she was just a few days past her 22nd birthday. She was the youngest player to win this event, the first and only amateur, and only the second overseas player. An even better year for her came in 1969, when she became only the third player to win both the British and US Amateur titles in the same year. Catherine would undoubtedly have become a highly effective player on the LPGA Tour. Instead, she married a Spaniard and competed relatively little afterwards. She did, however, add two Spanish national titles to her record following four earlier victories in the French Open Amateur championship.

Bernhard **Langer**
Born: August 27, 1957
Anhausen, Germany

No man has conquered a putting twitch as successfully as Germany's greatest ever golfer, Langer, who managed to find an all-round level of consistency matched by few of his peers. Even by his teens, Langer was renowned as someone who was a great approach putter but who was very ineffective from short range. Then he found a putter that worked, for a year or two, and later resorted to the left-hand-below-right grip. When this failed him too, he had to discover another method to eliminate a convulsive twitch in his left wrist. He found an extremely effective, but very weird, method of putting, one of the oddest yet seen. He placed his left hand well down the grip with the shaft well up the inside of the left forearm. The right hand then clamped the shaft to the forearm. It worked and took him to the greatest victories of his career: wins at the 1985 and 1993 US Masters – at Augusta of all places, a supreme test of a player's putting skills. A winless year in 1996 (his first since 1979) was followed in 1997 by four wins and three Ryder Cup points in four games. However, the lasting memory from the event was when the German missed a putt from 5ft to hand the cup to the Americans. He returned to the winner's circle again in 2001 – with victories at the TNT Open and the German Masters and qualified for the 2002 Ryder Cup – where he went undefeated. He won again in 2003, his 61st career victory, at the Volvo Masters, and proved an inspirational choice as captain of Europe's 2004 Ryder Cup team, leading them to a record victory. A switch to the Senior Tour in 2007 has been highly successful, bringing him ten tournament wins and over $5 million in prize money.

Tom **Lehman**
Born: March 7, 1959
Austin, Mn, USA

Lehman was 37 when, in 1996, he became the first US professional to win the British Open at Lytham, a month after tieing second in the US Open. In 1991, he was still seeking a way out of the mini-tours. Big Tom's career blossomed with his first PGA Tour win – the Memorial – in 1994. In 1995, despite colon surgery, he won again. His bravura finale to 1996 earned him the Tour Championship by six strokes at Tulsa, made him US PGA Player of the Year, the leading money winner and moved him up to second in the world rankings (he led briefly in 1997) behind Greg Norman, and confirmed his claim to the Vardon Trophy for the best scoring average. He recorded his fifth PGA Tour title when he triumphed in a play-off to take the Phoenix Open. He captained the US to defeat at the 2006 Ryder Cup at the K Club in Ireland, and in 2009, switched to the Senior Tour, winning his first event.

Cecil **Leitch**
Born: April 13, 1891
Silloth, England

Charlotte Cecilia Pitcairn Leitch was perhaps the first woman to give the golf ball an uninhibited thump. Her style was based on a broad stance and she used a palm grip with the right hand. For a few years, she was probably the best in the world – until the arrival of Joyce Wethered. Cecil won the British Ladies' Championship in 1914, 1920, 1921 and 1926.

Tony Lema

Born: February 25, 1934
Oakland, Ca, USA

Lema is remembered chiefly for two events in his career, one a triumph, the other perhaps the most remarkable defeat in the history of matchplay. In 1964, when the British Open still attracted only a few of the top US players, Lema decided to enter at St Andrews. Even so, he took it casually. He hardly knew the course, and mainly just tried to hit it where the caddie told him. Nevertheless, on his first appearance in the British Open, and with no previous experience of golf on linksland, he won by five strokes from Jack Nicklaus. If this was remarkable, his defeat by Gary Player the following year in the World Matchplay Championship at Wentworth was astonishing. Lema completed the first 18 holes 6 up and then won the first hole in the afternoon. Alas for Lema, Player then became inspired, drew level

on the last hole and won the first hole of the play-off. From 1957 until his death in a plane crash in 1966, Lema won 16 events worldwide.

Justin Leonard

Born: June 15, 1972
Dallas, TX, USA

The year after Justin Leonard was born, Craig Stadler won the US Amateur title. Like Jerry Pate who won in 1974 and Mark O'Meara (1979), Stadler later won a major championship. In 1997, Tiger Woods and Leonard increased the tally of major victories by former US Amateur champions over the past 25 years to five (and Phil Mickelson made it six when he won the 2004 Masters). José-Maria Olazabal is the only British Amateur champion to have won a major title in that time. So US college boys tolerate the giddy heights well. A graduate in business studies from the University of Texas, Leonard overtook Jesper Parnevik and Darren Clarke at

Troon, impressing the galleries with his calm course management and his modest demeanour as he became the youngest British Open champion since Seve Ballesteros. He cemented his reputation as one of the world's leading players by overcoming a five-shot deficit to win the Players' Championship the following year. In 1999, it was his 45ft putt on the 17th hole at Brookline that sparked the celebrations that caused so much controversy at the Ryder Cup. A couple of lean seasons followed, but the Texan returned to the top ten in the money list in 2002. He led the US PGA Championship after 54 holes the following year before a final-round 77 saw him fall back to fourth place. He claimed his eighth tour title in 2004 when he won the Honda Classic, and then won twice more in 2005. Consistent performances in 2007 and 2008 saw him qualify for the US Ryder Cup team at Valhalla, where he collected two-and-a-half points out of four as the home team romped to victory.

Thomas Levet

Born: September 5, 1968
Paris, France

After struggling on the European Tour for the better part of the mid-1990s, Thomas Levet received an invite from the French Federation to play in the Cannes Open and won to become the first Frenchman to win on home soil since Jean Garaialde took the French Open in 1969. His next victory came at the British Masters in 2001, when Levet became the first Frenchman to win on British soil since Arnaud Massy took the British Open in 1907. He almost equalled Massy's feat the following year at Muirfield. He made his way through the initial four-man play-off along with Ernie Els before losing out to the South African at the first extra hole. However, his performance in

the British Open, coupled with an 18th-place finish in the US Open, saw him gain exempt status for the PGA Tour. The 2004 season saw him post his third tour success, when a final-round 63 saw him come from seven strokes behind to grab a one-shot win ahead of New Zealand's Michael Campbell at the Scottish Open. Levet then played a winning part in Europe's victorious 2004 Ryder Cup campaign against the US.

Bruce Lietzke

Born: July 18, 1951
Kansas City, Mo, USA

If Lietzke's ambitions had matched his undoubted talents he might have been a superstar. However, perhaps his limited golf workload suits his temperament. It may also have given him a longer career. He likes to spend as much time with his wife and two children as he can, to support the Dallas Cowboys and do some "serious fishing". Lietzke's first very good year came in 1977, winning his first two tournaments and finishing fifth on the money list. He won 13 times on the PGA Tour, most recently in 1994, and seems to win as much money as he needs – more than $6 million in all. A switch to the Senior Tour brought instant success. He won twice in his rookie season, and has since added five more titles to his collection and a further $6 million in prize money to his already significant pot.

Lawson Little

Born: June 23, 1910
Newport, RI, USA

This long-hitting New Englander came to the fore in 1933, reaching the semi-finals of the US Amateur and earning a Walker Cup place which took him to Britain the following year. The British opposition was completely overwhelmed in both of his matches, and Little moved on from St Andrews to Prestwick for the

BRUCE LIETZKE With a little more ambition, who knows what he might have gone on to achieve...

NANCY LOPEZ Her five successive wins in 1978 brought the crowds flocking to see her.

British Amateur Championship. Having progressed smoothly to the final, he beat a strongly supported local man by a landslide 14 and 13, after arguably the best stretch of golf ever produced by an amateur. He then went home and won the US Amateur, beating his opponent by 8&7. How do you follow that? Well, 1935 was nearly as good for Little. First he took the British Amateur Championship again, after a close fight with an English doctor, and then proceeded to win the US title again – the only time both championships have been won by the same man in two successive years. With four major championships under his belt, Little turned professional, but failed to become the dominant force he was expected to be. He did, however, win the 1940 US Open, beating Gene Sarazen in the play-off.

Gene **Littler**
Born: July 21, 1930
San Diego, Ca, USA
"Here's a kid with a perfect swing like Sam Snead's ... only better." This comment came from Gene Sarazen when Littler was a young man. The player also earned the nickname "Gene the Machine", because he made the golf swing look so effortless and the results were so predictably perfect. With his near-perfect swing, really excellent putting and precision short-iron play, it is surprising that Littler did not become a superstar. Lack of a driving passion to be the best might have been the reason. He sometimes seemed content to make a good start to the season and then to take things relatively easily. He first emerged in 1953, by winning the US Amateur, and his profile became more distinct the very next

year when he won a PGA Tour event as an amateur – a very rare feat indeed. On turning professional, he continued to be successful, winning four events in his first full season, 1955. His best year came in 1959, when he won five times. In 1961, he took the US Open and later lost play-offs for the 1970 Masters and the 1977 US PGA. He won 29 times on the PGA Tour, eight times on the Senior Tour, and also made seven appearances in the Ryder Cup.

Bobby **Locke**
SEE PAGE 178

Nancy **Lopez**
Born: January 6, 1957
Torrance, Ca, USA
Lopez once seemed destined to be regarded as the greatest woman player ever, but it didn't quite happen. Why? One reason could be her liking for family life. Another is faulty technique – her backswing finishes in a very shut position at the top. Most of the time, however, she has it all adjusted by the time she gets the clubhead into the strike zone. She is also an outstanding putter. It was in 1978 that she set the LPGA Tour on fire, recording five straight wins. Of course, it could not go on forever, but she won nine times that year and the publicity ensured that the LPGA has never looked back. She was also highly successful the following year with eight wins, but then lost her absolute dominance. She remained a formidable competitor, having won 48 events and headed the US money list three times. Alison Nicholas administered a painful defeat in 1997 as Lopez looked certain to win her first US Women's Open. She retired from tournament play in 2002 and attempted a comeback in 2007 and 2008, entering six events but failing to make the cut in any of them.

Davis **Love III**
Born: April 13, 1964
Charlotte, NC, USA
Love was overtaken in the long driving stakes at first marginally by John Daly, then to the tune of 15 yards or so by Tiger Woods. In a similar manner to Woods, Love hits in a far more controlled fashion, and despite the fact that he is now past his 40th year, he is still one of the major contenders for any tournament he enters. He joined the PGA Tour in 1986 and clinched his first tournament win, in the Heritage Classic the following year. He emerged as a major figure in world golf in 1992, taking the Heritage Classic for the third time as well as the Greater Greensboro Open and the Players' Championship and, in 1993, the Tournament of Champions, another of the high-prestige events just below "major" ranking. Playing with Fred Couples he has won four World Cups, and he has also represented the United States in the Walker, Dunhill and Ryder Cups. Love's outstanding driving – and long-iron play – has been crucial to his success on the PGA Tour, but when it comes to majors, putting errors at the death have cost him dear. He put that behind him in the 1997 US PGA Championship at Winged Foot as he held off a strong challenge by Justin Leonard to win by five shots. Five more tour wins have followed, most notably when he captured the Tour Championship in 2003 – a final-round (and a tournament-record) 64 saw him run out a comfortable six-stroke winner. Age may have restricted his big-hitting prowess, but he recorded further wins in 2006 (at the Chrysler Classic) and 2008 (the Network Classic). By 2010, he had amassed a huge $29.3 million in prize money to stand fifth on the all-career money list. He has made six Ryder Cup appearances, the last in 2004.

BOBBY LOCKE
Master of the Greens

One of the most fascinating things about sport is to wonder how players who dominated their own era would have fared if placed among another generation. Clearly players like Jack Nicklaus and Ben Hogan would have succeeded, whatever the time frame. But what about Arnold Palmer? In particular, what about Bobby Locke?

One can only think that he would have had to change his style completely to have stood a chance. For in these days, of dauntingly narrow fairways and snooker-table greens, how could Locke have hoped to compete with a hook that was so pronounced that he often aimed right of the target as much as 45 degrees before winging the ball back towards the flag.

No player could hope to stop the ball with such a shape of shot to a flag cut on the right of the green behind a bunker. Having said that, Locke was so good on the greens he would probably have played to 20ft and holed more than his share of putts.

Locke won his first tournament, the Transvaal Open, in 1934 and thereafter made the South African Open practically his own.

He turned professional in 1938 at the age of 20 and quickly made his presence felt in Britain. The war

intervened, however, and when it ended he went to America. He was not popular. He was slow and deliberate and talked little. Still worse, he was a winner. In two-and-a-half seasons he played in 59 tournaments, winning 13 of them.

When Locke decided to stay in Britain the year after winning the British Open in 1949, it was alleged that he had broken various contracts to play in America and was barred from the PGA Tour.

Locke contented himself with playing in Europe and enjoyed many successes, most notably in the British Open. For a decade, he and Peter Thomson dominated the championship.

His first British Open success came at Sandwich in 1949, but he had to work hard for it, beating Harry Bradshaw by 12 strokes in a 36-hole play-off after the pair had both recorded. He successfully defended his title the following year at Troon with a two-stroke victory over Roberto de Vicenzo.

Two years later, at Royal Lytham and St Anne's, he outlasted Peter Thomson for a one-stroke win after Fred Daly had fallen away badly with a

BOBBY LOCKE The South African was perhaps the best putter the game has ever seen.

76. Ben Hogan, during his year of years, dominated proceedings in 1953 and Locke could only sit back and watch as Peter Thomson racked up a hat-trick of victories between 1954 and 1956 – the South African finished second to the Australian during the first of those wins, at Royal Birkdale. Locke returned to centre stage in 1957, though, to record his fourth and final Open victory, this time at the home of golf, St Andrews, and no doubt to his immense satisfaction, beating his nemesis Peter Thomson by three strokes.

His reputation as a loner did not stand four-square with his great

passion, which was playing the ukulele. He even played it once on stage at a Southport nightclub.

In February 1960, Locke was on his way to visit his wife when his car was struck by a train on a level crossing. He was in a coma for several days and virtually lost the sight in one eye. But for that accident, he would have gone on at least to match Peter Thomson's record of five British Open championships. The career of the man who became the first player to dominate golf on three separate continents – Africa, Europe and America – was effectively over.

1917	1934	1938	1949
Born on November 20 in Germiston, South Africa	Wins first tournament, the Transvaal Open	Turns professional at the age of 20	Wins the British Open for the first time

	1950	1952	1957	1960
	Successfully defends his British Open crown	Wins the Claret Jug for the third time	Fourth success at the British Open	Involved in a car accident that leaves him in a coma for several days

Sandy Lyle

Born: February 9, 1958
Shrewsbury, England

The first of Lyle's two supreme achievements came at Sandwich in 1985, when he won the British Open, helped somewhat by Bernhard Langer and David Graham falling away. Even on the final day Lyle made no dramatic move until he posted successive birdies on the 14th and 15th, to move into the joint lead. Disaster loomed at the 18th, when a little pitch shot from rough at the edge of the green almost came back to his feet. However, he got his bogey five and that was good enough. Lyle's greatest year came in 1988. Having won the Phoenix Open and the Greater Greensboro Open, he enjoyed his finest hour at the Masters. He began with a 71 in high winds and then moved two strokes ahead of the field with a 67. A third-round 72 was good enough to keep that advantage. On the final day, he began to pull well away from the field, but faltered on the second nine. At the last he put his tee shot into a fairway bunker along the left, but nipped a seven-iron off the sand past the flag, and his ball drifted back to about three yards. The putt went down and he was champion – the first British player to achieve the feat. Later the same year, he won the Dunhill Masters and the World Matchplay. He won only three more times on the European Tour and switched to the Senior Tour in 2008. In 2009, he made a strong showing at the Masters – finishing in a tie for 20th – but it seems that his glory days are now some way behind him.

Johnny McDermott

Born: April 12, 1891
Philadelphia, Pa, USA

In 1911, McDermott became the first native-born American to win the US Open. He had already come very close to victory the previous year, aged 19, losing in a play-off to Alex Smith. He found himself in a play-off once again in 1911, this time opposed to George Simpson and Mike Brady, both formidable players who were destined never to win their national championship. With his victory, McDermott became the youngest player, then or now, to win a major championship. The following year he won again with scores of 74, 75, 74, 71, making him still one of the select few to have achieved consecutive victories. In 1913, he proved in a US tournament that he could beat the best of the British. Harry Vardon and Ted Ray, who were until then all-conquering on a tour of the United States consisting mainly of exhibition matches, were left miles behind. Much encouraged, McDermott crossed the Atlantic to see if he could win the British Open, and came in fifth. It seemed as though a long and brilliant career lay ahead of him, but instead he had a mental breakdown in 1915 and that was that.

Rory McIlroy

Born: April 5, 1989
Hollywood, Northern Ireland

After enjoying a glittering amateur career – playing in the Junior Ryder Cup in 2004, shooting a course-record 61 at Portrush in 2005, becoming the world's no.1 ranked amateur player a year later, and firing an opening round 68 at the 2007 British Open (the only bogey-free round of the day) – Rory McIlroy turned professional in September 2007. His professional career got off to a blistering start, making the cut in his first event, finishing third in his second (the Alfred Dunhill Links Championship) and fourth at the Madrid Open a week later. In just three events, he had earned enough money to secure a place in the top 115 of the money list and, therefore, secure his card for the following year – the youngest, and quickest, player in European Tour history to do so. By the end of 2008, which included an agonizing play-off loss at the European Masters, he was the youngest player in the world's top 50. He broke his tournament duck with a wire-to-wire victory at the Dubai Desert Classic at the start of 2009 (aged 19 years and 273 days, the seventh youngest winner in European Tour history) to climbed to 16th in the world rankings. He finished tied for third at the 2009 US PGA but lost out to Lee Westwood in the race to become the year's no.1 European golfer. The man from Hollywood has the game to get his hands on the sport's biggest prizes.

John Mahaffey

Born: May 9, 1948
Kerrville, Tx, USA

The classic progression to winning a major championship is to be in contention first before going on to victory, and John Mahaffey followed this trail without any diversions. His first near-miss came in 1975, when he lost a play-off to Lou Graham for the US Open at Medinah; a year later he was again in contention in the same event, but this time he could only stand and admire as Jerry Pate conjured up his miracle birdie to win at Atlanta. When Mahaffey's moment did arrive, however, Pate was among those who had a front-row seat. The occasion was the 1978 US PGA Championship at Oakmont, a fearsome course well set up for Mahaffey's straight hitting and solid putting. When the final round began, though, it was Tom Watson who was well in control – indeed he was fully seven shots ahead of Mahaffey. A 66 from the challenger completely changed matters and Watson's 73 meant a sudden-death play-off, with Pate also involved after a last-round 68. Mahaffey birdied the second extra hole to claim the title. There might have been more majors but for a battle with a series of injuries and an even more difficult battle at the start of the 1980s with alcohol. He won both of those battles, and then returned to win a number of prestigious tournaments, including the 1986 Players' Championship. He has also won once on the Senior Tour.

RORY McILROY The young Irishman is one of the hottest properties in modern golf.

Meg Mallon

Born: April 14, 1963
Natcik, Ms, USA

Not many professional golfers would agree to let a golf journalist with little experience of golf caddy for them in a tournament, but Meg Mallon did – and won. What is more, it was the first victory of her career and led to a season that she has yet to match, including as it did two major championships. The journalist in question, Sonja Steptoe, chose Mallon because of her equable temperament and they both had plenty to smile about at the end of the 1991 Oldsmobile Classic as Mallon ran out a one-shot winner. By the end of the season, Mallon (without Steptoe) had also won the LPGA Championship, the US Women's Open and the Daikyo World Championship to end the season in second place on the money list. A former Michigan Amateur champion, Mallon elevated herself from steadily improving fifth-year professional to potential superstar in the space of just three weeks in June and July: that's when she won the two majors, beating Pat Bradley and Ayako Okamoto in the LPGA and closing with a 67 in the last round of the Open at Colonial to edge out Bradley again. She has played in the Solheim Cup ten times since 1992 and, in 2002, with Michele Redman as partner, posted a record for the most ever birdies by a fourball team (ten). She has now passed the $6-million mark in career earnings, collecting her fourth major, the US Women's Open for the second time, in 2004.

Lloyd Mangrum

Born: August 1, 1914
Trenton, NJ, USA

With his centre parting, thin moustache and an ever-present cigarette between his lips, Mangrum had a bit of the air of a Mississippi river boat gambler. He was indeed a hard man; hard enough to win two Purple Hearts while under the command of General Patton during the 1944 Battle of the Bulge. Apparently undeterred by his wounds, he went off to recuperate at St Andrews and won a GI tournament there before returning to the United States for the 1946 golf season. He had already made his mark there, and had in fact caused a sensation in 1940 by setting what was then an Augusta record with a first-round score of 64 in that year's Masters. In the end, he finished second to Jimmy Demaret. In 1946, he won his only major championship, a marathon US Open. He tied with Byron Nelson and Vic Ghezzi, and in the 18-hole play-off all three had 72s. So out they went again for another 18 holes. This time, Mangrum's 72 was enough for a one-stroke victory. This was the beginning of his great years, when he twice won the Vardon Trophy, topped the money list and was always up there near the top. Tournament wins piled up and he is credited with 34 on the PGA Tour.

Graham Marsh

Born: January 14, 1944
Kalgoorlie, Australia

This Australian is a truly international golfer who has won all over the world, from Switzerland to Malaya. He never made a prolonged assault on the PGA Tour, though he did win the important Heritage Classic in 1977. Elsewhere, he has won at least 56 significant events worldwide, including 24 in Japan. Marsh qualified by age for the Senior Tour in 1994 and showed that he maintained his very consistent game by being only once out of the top 25 in 22 events. His best performance was to finish in second place in the US Senior Open. He notched up his first Senior Tour win the following year and has since gone on to claim five more victories – including the US Senior Open in 1997. He has also racked up more than $8 million in prize money during his time on the tour. The gap in Marsh's record is that he failed to win a major championship, though he has won both the European Open and the World Matchplay. Marsh is always meticulous in his preparations before playing a shot, particularly making sure that all the right parts are in precise alignment with the target. He then strikes neatly and with enough power and always seems to finish well balanced. He also controls his emotions and avoids histrionics, which is more than ever could have been said about his brother Rodney, the famous Australian cricketer.

Shaun Micheel

Born: January 5, 1969
Orlando, Fl, USA

Between 1993 and 2001, Shaun Micheel had been in and out of the tour and a regular visitor to qualifying school – his best season during that time came in 2000, when he posted three top tens and four top 20s to finish just outside the top 100 in the money list. It was hardly the form of a future major winner. After returning to Q-school in 2001, he fared better in 2002, when he posted two further top tens: one of those was a third-place finish at the B. C. Open. Then came 2004: he secured his first PGA Tour win in his 164th start and shocked the golf world as he became the first player since John Daly in 1991 to make the US PGA Championship his first tour win. Holding a slender one-stroke lead over Chad Campbell going into the final hole, he fired a seven-iron to within inches of the flag to secure a famous victory and, perhaps more importantly, exempt status on the tour until 2008. He finished in the top 100 of the money list for the second time in his career the following year, but then started to slump. He returned to prominence at the 2006 US PGA, finishing runner-up to Tiger Woods, but has not made the cut in a major since 2007.

Phil Mickelson

Born: June 16, 1970
San Diego, Ca, USA

The big left-hander has been winning for most of his career. The real surprise is that it took him so long to record a major championship among those 38 PGA Tour victories,

MEG MALLON The genial American has posted four major victories.

PHIL MICKELSON The big left-hander laid a few ghosts to rest when he won the 2004 Masters.

but that moment finally came in 2004 when he recorded his seventh top-ten finish at Augusta – this time, though, he was the player at the top of the pile. He had to work hard for the green jacket, though – his five-under back nine of 31, including an 18ft birdie putt on the 18th, saw him squeeze past Ernie Els by just one stroke. It did not matter. It was the major that Mickelson had come so close to winning in his previous 46 attempts. The Californian had a stellar amateur career: he is one of only three players to win the US Amateur (the only left-hander to do so) and the NCAA Championship in the same year – the other two being Jack Nicklaus and Tiger Woods – and, in 1991, he won the Northern Telecom Open on the PGA Tour, the last amateur player to win a professional event. Success on the PGA Tour came immediately as he recorded two wins in his first year, 1993. In 1994, he made the first of his seven appearances in the Ryder Cup at Oak Hill. He won eight

times between 1996 and 1998, and although 1999 was winless, it was the closest he had come to winning a major: he lost out by one stroke to Payne Stewart in a thrilling finale to the US Open at Pinehurst. The wins kept coming. He finished third in the Masters and runner-up in the US Open. He finished third again at Augusta in 2003 before victory finally came the following year. A couple of near-misses followed – second at the 2004 US Open; third at that year's British Open – but a final-round 72 was enough to take him to the 2005 US PGA by one stroke. Mickelson was by now fast mounting a challenge to Tiger Woods's dominance of the game. A second Masters title followed in 2006, before he endured yet another runner-up finish at the US Open (his fifth would follow in 2009). In 2010 however, he emphatically confirmed his status as one of the game's all-time great players when he bagged his third Masters title.

Cary **Middlecoff**

Born: January 6, 1921
Halls, Tn, USA

Middlecoff was one of the players who helped to turn golf into the slow game it is today. He took a long time to align himself to the ball, and Bobby Jones was moved to remark that it was not a visually attractive process. A serious analyst of the golf swing, Middlecoff was among the first to grasp how important the set-up can be. Another of his theories concerned getting the clubhead in the right position at the top of the backswing, where he would bring it to a careful halt before initiating the downswing. Such was his slowness, by the standards of the times, that in the play-off for the 1957 US Open his opponent, Dick Mayer, took out a camping stool on which to perch himself while Middlecoff took his time. If this was a psychological ploy it may have worked. Middlecoff went around in 79; Mayer won rather comfortably with his 72. Even so, Middlecoff's overall record was far superior. He won the US Open twice, in 1949 and 1956, and the Masters in 1955. He was also the leading PGA Tour player during the 1950s with a total of 37 victories, which puts him well up the all-time list. The end of his career came, like so many greats, because of a twitch on the short putts.

Johnny **Miller**

Born: April 29, 1947
San Francisco, Ca, USA

For a short span of time, Miller played golf as well as it has ever been played. He was undeniably the best golfer in the world in 1974, when he headed the PGA Tour money list, but his peak years lasted only from 1973, when he won the US Open, to his victory in the 1976 British Open at Royal Birkdale. At Oakmont Country Club in the US Open, Miller was six strokes behind the leaders when the final round began, but a start of four birdies immediately brought him into contention. There were more birdies

to come and Miller finished with a 63, still the lowest score ever recorded in major championship golf. His putting had by no means been phenomenal. It was the supreme quality of his iron play that counted the most. In 1974, he had no fewer than eight victories on the PGA Tour, followed the next year by four more and a close encounter with the Masters. His 1976 British Open triumph marked the end of his great run. He lost form dramatically, but did make a comeback during the early 1980s. Remarkably he won again early in 1994, having made no money in the previous year, then began spending most of his time commentating for American television.

Abe **Mitchell**

Born: January 19, 1887
East Grinstead, England

The Great Triumvirate of James Braid, J H Taylor and Harry Vardon certainly set standards that no British trio have achieved since. By the end of the First World War, however, the Victorian greats were all well past their prime, and the question of their successors arose. The two more obvious candidates were George Duncan and Abe Mitchell, although the latter had not established himself to the same extent. Duncan was to win a British Open; Mitchell did not. Perhaps he never quite recovered from his disappointment at Deal in 1920, when he was 13 strokes ahead of the eventual winner, Duncan, after two rounds and then three-putted the first three greens, had a seven on his card and finished in 84. However, Mitchell was still the top British golfer through the 1920s, and had a formidable record in matchplay, winning the PGA Matchplay championship three times. He was highly feared in the Ryder Cup, where, either in singles or with partners, he had such winning scores as 8 and 7, and 9 and 8 to his credit and, overall, took seven points out of a possible ten.

Larry Mize

Born: September 23, 1958
Augusta, Ga, USA

Mize had his finest hour in the 1987 Masters, where his birdie at the final hole produced a tie with Seve Ballesteros and Greg Norman. A play-off began in which death was indeed sudden – Seve departing in despair after just one hole. On the next Norman played a good safe shot, away from the water on the left, to the right side of the green. If he could get down in two, he looked sure to be the champion, for Mize was well off the green further right. However, from 140ft away he played a good running pitch that seemed just a touch too strong – but down it went and that was that. It was a fluke, of course, but a highly popular one in the town of Mize's birth. The rest of his career has been less spectacular, though he has been a good journeyman since he joined the PGA Tour in 1980. His first win came in 1983, and he has since added three more tour wins before moving to the Senior Tour in 2008. His other great achievement was his fine win in the 1993 Johnnie Walker World Championship in Jamaica – a victory that was worth over $1.2 million.

Shigeki Maruyama

Born: September 12, 1969
Chiba, Japan

Japan has been blessed with some great golfers, Jumbo Ozaki and Isao Aoki to name but two, but none of them have performed particularly well outside of their own country. For a short while, the exception to this appeared to be Shigeki Maruyama. After recording seven victories on the Japan Golf Tour, the diminutive Japanese player first came to the attention of a wider golfing public when he recorded a 100 per cent record in the 1998 President's Cup.

He secured his card for the PGA Tour the following year and, in 2000, passed the $1-million mark in his first year on tour – the first Japanese player to do so. In 2001, he captured his first title – the Greater Milwaukee Open – to become the first Japanese player to win an event on American mainland soil. Two more tour victories followed and, in 2003, Maruyama became the first player in history to pass $1 million in earnings in each of his first four seasons on tour. He finished 32nd on the Money List in 2005, but started to slip down the rankings in 2006 (79th) and barely squeezed into the top 125 in 2007. He lost his card after a disastrous season in 2008 and now plays mainly in Japan.

Colin Montgomerie

Born: June 23, 1963
Glasgow, Scotland

There's that saying that you drive for show and putt for dough. However, if you can't hit the ball quite long and fairly consistently straight from the tee, you will putt in vain. Montgomerie's game is strong in both of these departments. He is a long hitter who can usually be confident that his fade will "take". This means that he can rule out trouble along the left, aim more or less at it, and leave himself the whole width of the fairway to play with. Thereafter, he is one of the best putters in the world. One achievement that has so far eluded Montgomerie is a win in a major championship, but he has performed very well in the US Open. In 1992, he finished third to Tom Kite at Pebble Beach. He was closer still two years later, tied for second behind Ernie Els, and, in 1997, he finished second on his own by a stroke – to Els again. His best chance, however, came in 2006 at Winged Foot when he stood in the middle of the fairway on the 72nd hole holding a one-shot lead, only to finish with a double-bogey to lose out to Geoff Ogilvy by one stroke. Steve Elkington was his nemesis in a sudden death play-off in the 1995 US PGA. On the European Tour he,

SHIGEKI MARUYAMA **The Japanese player has played impressive golf on the PGA Tour.**

unbelievably, headed the money list from 1993 to 1999. The incredible run of success came to an end in 2000 when he was toppled from the top of the tree by Lee Westwood. He maintained his 15-year sequence of winning at least one worldwide event a year since 1992 by winning the Singapore Masters in 2004. His best performances in recent times, though, have been reserved for the Ryder Cup. He has been a pillar of strength for the European team in eight performances and remarkably remains unbeaten in singles matches. On 28 January 2009, it was announced that Montgomerie would captain the European team at the 2010 Ryder Cup at Celtic Manor in South Wales.

Gil Morgan

Born: September 25, 1946
Wewaka, Ok, USA

Most American golfers have been to university and some emerge with prefixes to their names. One example is Cary Middlecoff, who qualified as a dentist but found that golf paid even better and paid no further attention to teeth. In 972, Morgan graduated with his doctorate from the Southern College of Optometry and fixed his eyes firmly on the PGA Tour, for which he first qualified to play in 1973. His first big year came in 1977, when he won his first tournament, but 1978 was better still. Winning twice and finishing second on the PGA Tour money list, he seemed to have established himself as a name player. That did not quite happen, but he continued to perform well: by the end of 1996 he had exceeded $5 million in money winnings, had won seven times on the PGA Tour, and played in two Ryder Cup teams in 1979 and 1983. His greatest triumphs and disasters, however, came in one particular event, the 1992 US Open. Here he became the first golfer to reach ten-under par, and even improved that by another two – only to subside dramatically to tie for 13th place. He has enjoyed huge success on the Senior Tour, racking up an impressive 25 victories and standing in second position on the all-time money-winners list on that tour with $19.6 million.

Tom **Morris Sr**

Born: June 16, 1821
St Andrews, Scotland

Winner of the first truly British Open Championship in 1861 (the first the previous year was not open to amateurs), Old Tom Morris went on to further victories in 1862, 1864 and 1867. He began playing over the Old Course at St Andrews when he was about six, and became apprenticed to Allan Robertson to make both clubs and feathery balls. The pair then became a formidable partnership in foursomes challenge matches for large sums of money. They fell out, however, when Robertson spotted Old Tom playing with a gutta percha ball at a time when these were rapidly replacing the feathery from 1848 onwards. Robertson felt that they would kill his trade. Morris set up his own workshop but, in 1851, moved

Colin Montgomerie In recent years, the Scot has reserved his best golf for the Ryder Cup.

away to become professional and keeper of the green at the new Prestwick Golf Club. Returning later to his home town to take over a similar role, he became a revered and much-loved figure in golf. He did the original designs for many courses in the British Isles.

Tom **Morris Jr**

Born: April 20, 1851
St Andrews, Scotland

"Young Tommie", as he was usually called, was a brief comet on the golf scene, dying at the age of 24, just a few months after his wife in 1875.

However, if only for a few years, he was the dominant player of his time. Indeed, like several players in succeeding generations, he changed the whole notion of how well the game could be played. A long hitter, he was also excellent in his recovery shots from bad lies in the rough, and his iron shots to greens were revolutionary. Where earlier players had tended to use short-shafted lofted woods, he used a rut iron. This was a small-headed club, originally intended to enable players to, literally, escape from ruts. Young Tommie used it to gain far greater

backspin in his short approaches. He won the British Open for the first time in 1868, in succession to his father, at the age of 17, and retained it the next two years. Then a problem arose. The original trophy was a Morocco leather belt, presented with the proviso that anyone who won it three titles in a row got to keep it. With no trophy to hand, no championship was held in 1871. The following year, Tommie won the replacement, a claret cup. He remains the only man to have won four British Open Championships in a row.

Kel **Nagle**

Born: December 21, 1920
Sydney, Australia

Nagle was one of the late developers in golf. Although he first won a tournament in his late 20s, he then almost totally disappeared from view for several years. When he became a factor once more in tournament golf, his game had been transformed. Formerly a long but wild hitter and a relatively poor putter, he was now shortish, but he was particularly steady from the tee and a very sound putter indeed. However, he continued to be a primarily Australasia-based golfer. As he approached the age of 40 he had won the Open Championships of both Australia and New Zealand, while elsewhere his record was unimpressive. Then came the British Open at St Andrews in 1960. The new hero was Arnold Palmer, making his first appearance in the tournament, but although he played well he trailed Nagle by five strokes after two rounds. Nagle had gone round in 69 and 67, but was still given little chance. The climax came in the final round. Palmer holed out for a birdie on the last while Nagle faced a par putt on the treacherous 17th of some 7ft. He got it and went on to par the last for a one-stroke victory. After this his confidence blossomed, and some 25 titles followed.

BYRON NELSON
The Man Who Could Not Stop Winning

No golfer before or since has amassed a winning streak quite like that of Byron Nelson in 1945. All right, it is fair to point out that the fields were not as strong as they might have been because many of the best American professionals were still in military service. Even so, 11 tournaments in a row deservedly earn Nelson a place among the giants who have played the game.

Backing up this judgement are some of the statistics amassed during the streak. Nine of the victories came in strokeplay tournaments, and Nelson played them in 113-under par for a barely credible stroke average of 67.92 shots per round.

Nelson was born in the same year and brought up in the same postal district as Ben Hogan, and for years both toiled to make a living. It was Nelson who struck gold first: indeed, it would be 1946 before Hogan won his first major (Nelson had won five by 1945) and by that time the haemophilia that had exempted Nelson from war duties was preventing him from being in peak condition on the course. He retired from full-time golf to his Texas ranch shortly after, paid for by the war bonds that he received for his victories the previous year, cash being in short supply at the time. He was only 34 years old.

The first of his major victories came at the Masters in 1937, the first year that the Augusta members began wearing their symbolic green jackets. Nelson strode onto the first tee complete with a set of clubs featuring the new steel shafts that had just been invented – he was the first player to use the pioneering technology, and to what effect. He proceeded to give such a masterful demonstration that it ensured there was no going back. He hit every green in regulation, with the exception of the four par-fives which he reached in two, and signed for a 66 – a new course record. A bad third-round 75, however, appeared to have cost him the tournament: it gave Ralph Guldahl a four-stroke lead going into the final round. Nelson prevailed, though, with a final-round 70 as Guldahl faded away with a 76.

Nelson's next major success came at the US Open in 1939 – an event that will be remembered more as the tournament that Sam Snead threw away than the one that Nelson won. Sat in the clubhouse on 284, Nelson could only sit back and watch as Snead stood on the 17th tee requiring bogey-par to win. He bogeyed the 17th and was rattled ... a disastrous eight followed. Nelson entered a three-man play-off and emerged victorious after a 36-hole tussle with the ever-unfortunate Craig Wood – Denny Shute had fallen by the wayside after 18 holes.

Nelson proved Snead's nemesis in the US PGA Championship in 1940, winning the final 1 up. He then claimed his fourth major, and his second Masters title, when he beat his rival Ben Hogan in a play-off in 1942.

Then came 1945, the year golf became locked in a full Nelson. In all, he won 18 of the 30 tournaments he entered (including a second US PGA title). In strokeplay events, his average lead over those who finished second measured out at 6.3 strokes.

There is a tendency to dismiss Nelson as a lightweight when compared with the overwhelming achievements of his peers at the time, Hogan and Sam Snead. Certainly he cannot match them for longevity, but he made his contribution all the same to an American triumvirate who dominated golf in the period.

One player who appreciated the contribution that Nelson had made to the game was Tom Watson, and the pair were lifelong friends. It was Nelson who became an important force behind Watson's development, who guided him during his early years as a professional and told him not to fret, that the victories would come.

Since 1968, the Byron Nelson Classic has been a staple fixture on the PGA Tour, and Nelson actively promoted it every year. It says something about his standing in the game that while the courses it is now played upon are hardly from the top drawer, the field always is. He died in 2006, aged 94.

BYRON NELSON In 1945, the Texan won 18 of the 30 tournaments he entered.

1912	1937	1939	1940
Born on February 4 in Fort Worth, Tx, USA	Wins the Masters by two strokes using steel-shafted clubs	Wins the US Open as Sam Snead collapses over the final two holes	Wins the US PGA Championship beating Snead 1 up in the final

1942	1945	1968
Wins the Masters for a second time	Wins 11 successive tournaments and the US PGA Championship for the second time. Retires from the game at the end of the season	The Byron Nelson Classic is played for the first time

Tsuneyuki Nakajima

Born: October 20, 1954
Gunma, Japan

It may well be Tommy Nakajima's sad fate to be remembered chiefly for two disasters which befell him in one year – 1978. Qualifying to play in the Masters, he managed to run up a score of 13 on the 13th hole at Augusta, where most players are thinking about eagles, or birdies at the very least. Three months later, at St Andrews in the British Open, he earned a cruel kind of immortality. The famous Road Hole bunker, hard by the 17th green on the Old Course at St Andrews, has almost, but not quite, been renamed "The Sands of Nakajima" following his toils there while in close contention for the championship. Nakajima was, and is, a superb sand player, but the shot was exceptionally demanding, with the flag close by and a narrow thread of green beyond and then the road. Trying for a delicate shot which would just clear the steep face of the bunker and gently settle on the green, poor Nakajima took four attempts to succeed, and eventually a nine went down on his card. In Japan, however, he has been prodigiously successful, with four Opens, three PGAs and three Matchplays to his credit, and has won more than 50 events.

Byron Nelson

SEE PAGE 184

Larry Nelson

Born: September 10, 1947
Fort Payne, Al, USA

In terms of money winnings, Larry was only outstanding between 1979 and 1981, particularly in 1979 when he was second on the US money list. However, he has occasionally played superbly in the major championships when, after none too good a year, he has had moments of inspiration. The greatest of these came in 1983, when he won the US Open at Oakmont. He had been having a poor season and was seven strokes off the lead after two

JACK NEWTON The Australian twice came close to major success before injuries sustained in an horrific accident ended his career.

rounds. However, a 65 then brought him right back into contention and in the final round play was suspended because of thunderstorms: at that point there were only two players left in it – Watson and Nelson. They restarted on the 16th, a 226-yard par three. Nelson found the green and then holed out from about 20 yards. It proved the decisive shot of the championship. Nelson also went on to win the US PGA on two occasions, 1981 and 1987. He has since forged a successful career on the Senior Tour, collecting 19 victories and pocketing over $13.6 million in prize money.

Jack Newton

Born: January 30, 1950
Sydney, Australia

Newton's finest hours came in two major championships. In 1980, he came second to Seve Ballesteros in the Masters. Five years earlier, he had come tantalizingly close to glory in the British Open at Carnoustie. He

began with rounds of 69 and 71, and a 65 then brought him up to within a single stroke of the leader, Bobby Cole. In the final round he looked to be doing even better. With the leading pack faltering, only Newton was playing consistently. Then, two strokes ahead on the leaderboard with four holes to play, he began to make his own errors. After dropping a shot at the difficult 17th, he needed to birdie the last to win – and couldn't quite do it. He had, however, tied with the then little known Tom Watson. In the 18-hole play-off the next day, the pair were level after 17 holes. However, Newton then bunkered his shot to the green on the 18th and didn't get his recovery close – a par for Watson was enough to secure him the first of five British Open titles. Newton won in America, Australasia, Africa and Europe, but his career ended abruptly when he walked into an airplane propeller in the dark and was very seriously injured.

Bobby Nichols

Born: April 14, 1936
Louisville, Ky, USA

Bobby Nichols had two golden years. In 1962, he won two tournaments, finished third behind Jack Nicklaus and Arnold Palmer in the US Open and sixth in the US PGA Championship. In 1964, he again showed that he kept the right company when once more he, Palmer and Nicklaus occupied the top three positions in a major. This time, and certainly something to tell the grandchildren about, Nichols' name was at the top of the US PGA Championship leaderboard three shots ahead of Nicklaus and Palmer. And all in the Golden Bear's lair, to boot – Colombus Country Club, Colombus, Ohio. It was a fairytale for Nichols, who had been paralysed for 13 days and kept in hospital for three months as a youngster following a car accident. He went on to record 11 PGA Tour wins over the dozen years between 1962 and 1974.

JACK NICKLAUS
The Course Manager Who Changed

Nicklaus knew he was the best there was and, many would say, played too cautiously. If he had a weakness, it was arrogance. He didn't want to let the others in as a result of playing bold shots which could have gone wrong. Safety was almost always his watchword.

That is, until the final round, when he no longer had anything to lose. Then, for his last-round tee shots, he would leave the long irons in the bag. At Muirfield in 1966, he manoeuvred his way round, mostly playing irons from the tee for placement. He won. Several years later, at the same course, he arrived as both Masters and US Open champion. To achieve the modern grand slam (Masters, US Open, British Open and US PGA in the same year) was a serious possibility.

Nicklaus, with a round to play, lay six strokes behind the leader, Lee Trevino. Now he would have to go for everything. For a while, it all came off. About two holes behind, Trevino and Jacklin heard the roars come back to them as the Nicklaus birdies mounted. He was out in 32 and then birdied the next two holes. Suddenly he was in the lead, but there were no more birdies and one dropped shot meant, in the end, that Nicklaus finished a

shot behind Trevino's winning total.

There were many of these magnificent last-round charges in both major championships and tournament play, but it makes one wonder how much greater his record might have been if he had attacked from the very first shot in the first round.

Like Jones about 40 years before, Nicklaus (with two US Amateurs under his belt and a near-miss in the 1960 US Open) was quickly recognized as a rising star. He truly became one with a win in his first professional season – in the 1962 US Open, which included the added drama of beating the great Arnold Palmer in an 18-hole play-off.

Nicklaus soon became the new wonder and easily the dominant golfer on the world scene. In 1963, his stature was confirmed when he added both the Masters and the US PGA to his record.

When he won the 1965 Masters, breaking the Hogan scoring record by three strokes, winning by a record nine strokes and including a single round of 64, Bobby Jones was moved to remark that his performance was "the greatest in golf history".

Without a doubt Nicklaus had become the greatest golfer in the world, and his dominance lasted from

the early 1960s until, you could say, 1977, when Tom Watson managed – just – to beat Nicklaus in both the Masters and the British Open.

Even so, Nicklaus was not to be out of the reckoning for a good many years to come. In 1980, he came back from his worst year to take both the US Open and the US PGA. In 1982, he came agonizingly close to adding a record-breaking fifth US Open to his record at Pebble Beach,

only to be foiled by Watson's little pitch from greenside rough on the 71st which astonishingly went into the hole. He had one more major in him, however, surging up the field over the last nine holes with one of his greatest charges to win the 1986 Masters. Surely he couldn't do it again? Aged 58 and not walking too freely in his 40th Masters, he gave the leaders a fright in 1998, finishing joint sixth at five-under par.

JACK NICKLAUS His tally of 18 majors and two US Amateurs may never be beaten.

1940	1961	1962	1963	1965	1966	1967	1970	1971	1972
Born on January 21 in Columbus, Ohio	US Amateur champion for second time	Wins first US Open, defeating Arnold Palmer in play-off at Oakmont	Adds both the Masters and US PGA to his major collection	Second Masters victory	Completes grand slam of all four majors when he follows a third Masters victory with his first British Open	Second victory in US Open	British Open champion for the second time	Second US PGA title	Another two-major year with victories in the Masters and US Open

1973	1975	1978	1980	1983	1986	1987	1996
Wins his third US PGA title	His fourth two-major season, as in 1963, taking the Masters and US PGA	Becomes British Open champion for the third time when he wins at St Andrews	His fifth two-major year: a fourth US Open win and fifth US PGA title	Winning Ryder Cup captain	Aged 46, wins his record sixth Masters	Losing Ryder Cup captain, as US goes down 13-15 on the course he built	Won 100th tournament with a closing-round 65, and made the cut in all four majors

GREG NORMAN
The Story of What Could Have Been

GREG NORMAN A two-time British Open winner ... but there should have been more majors.

What to make of Greg Norman has become one of golf's classic debates. Is he the Great White Shark or the Great White Flag? Was he supremely unlucky or simply foolish?

There is certainly a fatal flaw in the Australian's game: the only possible explanation for all the endless failures to win a major championship in America when in contention to win. Put simply, Norman is vulnerable when placed under pressure.

The positives should not be overlooked, however, and those centre around a sublime talent and the pleasure that he has given to galleries and television audiences alike during his years at the top.

Norman is responsible for some of the greatest rounds of golf ever played. Three in particular stand out. The first came in the 1986 British Open at Turnberry, when he conquered atrocious conditions and an awesomely difficult course to shoot 63.

Seven years later, again at the British Open, this time played at Sandwich, Norman came close to such perfection again when he shot 64 in the final round to hold off the challenge of many of the most redoubtable competitors of the time.

He did it again at Augusta in 1996, when he equalled the course record with a 63. It gave him a two-shot lead – which was extended to six shots by the time he stood on the first tee going into the final round. What followed will go down as one of the greatest collapses in golf history.

Up against Nick Faldo, any doubts that may have been lingering in the back of the Australian's mind would not have been eased when he bogeyed the first hole. Norman's lead was down to two by the turn; by the 11th they were all square. The galleries watched in paralysed silence as Norman found the water on the 12th and again on the 16th – two double-bogeys. A birdie on the final hole gave Faldo a five-stroke win – the swing over the final round had been 11 strokes.

His detractors would say that this epitomizes Norman: brilliant one minute but hopeless when it really matters. The line of failures has certainly been spectacular, with countless pushed shots on the 18th at Augusta costing him the chance of victory. He has been unlucky too, though. Bob Tway holed a bunker shot to beat him for the 1986 US PGA Championship; nine months later, Larry Mize holed a freak chip to steal a green jacket from his back.

Norman's other weakness is also his drawing card. Like Arnold Palmer before him, he would often go for the daring play rather than the sensible one. Unlike Palmer, though, he has enjoyed a remarkably long career at the highest level. Even after missing almost all of 1998 with a shoulder injury, Norman still rebounded with a win in his first tournament back.

Like many a man when he reaches 40, Norman looked around and found other interests. These days he is more involved in his many business ventures than in playing the game and his successes have helped fund a lifestyle that used to be the preserve of Hollywood movie stars, not golfers.

In 2008, having not appeared in a major tournament for three years, he sensationally led the field at the British Open after 54 holes before eventualy finishing third.

So what to make of Norman? A great life and a great golfer – just. Despite his talent, he may be remembered for what may have been rather than what he actually achieved.

1955
Born on February 10 in Mount Isa, Queensland, Australia

1976
Wins his first tournament in Australia – the Westlakes Classic

1977
Collects first title on the European Tour – the Martini International

1980
Claims the first of his three World Matchplay titles

1984
Wins for the first time on the PGA Tour

1986
Shoots a 63 on the way to winning the British Open at Turnberry

1993
A final-round 64 is enough to secure second British Open title

1996
Becomes first player to break $10-million mark in earnings on PGA Tour

2001
Inducted into golf's Hall of Fame

GEOFF OGILVY A solid performer who found his A-game at the 2006 US Open.

Norman **von Nida**

Born: 1914
Strathfield, Australia

Australian golf was a very small world when von Nida arrived on the scene. During the 1930s he had to content himself mainly by winning state titles and money games with wealthy amateurs. Having tried the Far East Tour, then in its infancy, and finished as runner-up in the 1939 Australian Open, he decided to try his luck in the United States. However, the outbreak of the Second World War put a stop to that project. It was in 1946 that he really emerged as an international golfer. He turned

up in Britain with total reserves of £17, but immediately began winning money. The following year he dominated the tournament scene, taking four of the first six events. By the end of the season, he had won or tied for first place seven times and was leading money winner with over £3,000. That year he had also shared the lead in the British Open after three rounds, but faded on the final afternoon. He was never to repeat the success of 1947, but remained a force to be reckoned with for a few more years. He won the Australian PGA four times and the Australian Open three times.

Greg **Norman**

SEE PAGE 187

Andy **North**

Born: March 9, 1950
Thorp, USA

Of the 21 golfers to have won more than one US Open, North is perhaps the least distinguished. Oddly, he has won only one other tournament on the PGA Tour, the 1977 Westchester Classic, and has never finished higher than 14th on the money list. Plagued by injuries, he competed rarely on the PGA Tour, and was able to do so only because of his exemption as a former US Open champion. His first US Open came at Cherry Hills, Denver, in 1978, where he had a four-stroke lead with five holes to play, but rather staggered home. Needing a bogey five at the last to win, he only just did it. Short of the green in two, he then played his short pitch into a bunker, but came out fairly close and was relieved to hole the putt. After a series of poor years he re-emerged to win the 1985 US Open by a stroke. That was a surprising year, for the runners-up were hardly great names – T. C. Chen, Dave Barr and Denis Watson. North then disappeared again but, as Walter Hagen said: "Anyone can win one US Open, but it takes a great player to win two." He has since won once on the Senior Tour.

Christy **O'Connor Sr**

Born: December 21, 1924
Galway, Ireland

Many Irish players are unorthodox, and O'Connor, nicknamed "Wristy Christy", was no exception. Nevertheless, he was not only one of the greatest Irish golfers ever, but was also at the top of British golf for many years. He came very close to winning the British Open in 1958, when his start of 67, 68 was the best since Henry Cotton's 67, 65 back in 1934. He faltered a little, thereafter, but came to the last hole at Lytham needing a par to tie. On this difficult hole, he did not quite manage

it, and it was Peter Thomson who went on to win, beating Dave Thomas in the play-off. O'Connor was third, a position he repeated in 1961 and, in 1965, he was second. It is tempting to speculate on what he might have achieved had his putting stroke been more solid and far less wristy. He played in every Ryder Cup match from 1955 to 1973 and also represented Ireland 15 times in the World Cup, partnering Harry Bradshaw in the winning team in Mexico City in 1958. More important for him was probably the fact that he won 24 European tournaments and dominated domestic golf in Ireland.

Geoff **Ogilvy**

Born: June 11 1977
Adelaide, Australia

In 2004, six years into his professional career, the casual observer could have been forgiven for thinking that Geoff Ogilvy was yet another of a growing number of Australian golfers earning a comfortable living on the PGA Tour without ever threatening to challenge for the game's major honours. But those within the golfing world knew his mixture of long, straight driving coupled with excellence around the green, was a cocktail for future success, and it all started to come together for him in 2005. In his 108th start, at the Tucson Classic, he beat Kevin Na and Mark Calcavecchia in a sudden-death playoff to collect his first PGA Tour title; later in the year he recorded back-to-back top-ten finishes at the British Open (T5) and the USPGA (T6). Ogilvy won twice in 2006 – beating Davis Love III 4 and 3 in the the WGC Matchplay Championship final and profiting from late collapses by Colin Montgomerie and Phil Mickelson to win the US Open, at Winged Foot – and earned $4 million in a season for the first time. He continued his love for WGC events by making it to the final of the Matchplay Championship again in 2007, only to lose out to Henrik Stenson, but made amends by winning the strokeplay event at Doral in 2008. Now firmly established in among the

Jumbo Ozaki Who knows what he might have achieved had he been prepared to travel.

world's top-20 golfers, Ogilvy won twice on Tour for the second time in 2009 and has become a contender to win every tournament he enters.

José-Maria **Olazabal**
Born: February 5, 1966
Fuenterrabia, Spain

That the career of so talented a player as Olazabal should suddenly be terminated by such a banal-sounding affliction as sore feet became a dreadful probability soon after his 29th birthday in 1995. He resisted doggedly, limping in April in defence of his Masters title at Augusta to 14th place, the highest placing by a European that year. He was only able to enter eight European events in 1995. From ninth in the world he slid to 225th, brought low by what was at first diagnosed as incurable rheumatoid arthritis. Salvation came by way of a meeting with Dr Hans-Wilhelm Muller-Wohlfahrt, known as "Dr Feelgood" to other athletes he had helped. The German detected a spinal hernia, and specified a rugged programme of exercise and physiotherapy. Five months of this brought Olazabal – who had been forced to give up his 1995 Ryder Cup place – to Dubai in February 1997, after two years of doubt and despair. The limp, though not all of the pain, was gone and the

talent was as sharp as ever, proved by a 65 in the third round, and 12th place overall. His comeback gained a "Golfer of the Month" award for Olazabal, who surprised even himself by winning his third event back on tour – the Turespana Open in Gran Canaria – and inside a month he finished joint 12th in the 1997 Masters. Aggressive with his irons and armed with a short game and putting stroke comparable to that of Seve Ballesteros, Olazabal has a Ryder Cup record of 14 wins to eight losses in five appearances on top of 28 victories in both Europe and America. He rounded off his comeback in emphatic style in 1999, as he held off the charge of Greg Norman and Davis Love III to collect his second major triumph, and his second victory at Augusta, by two strokes. He has won three times since, in Europe and America. His last victory came at the Mallorca Classic in 2005.

Mark **O'Meara**
Born: January 13, 1957
Goldsboro, NC, USA

In his own words Mark O'Meara was a "nice golfer". Nice career, nice lifestyle – and so what, if he was one step down from the best players of his generation? Then came a friendship with a young player named

Tiger Woods. Soon they became inseparable, and for the first time in his life O'Meara saw the game in a completely different light. Put simply, by 1998, O'Meara found himself infected by new goals, new ideals and, welded to a fine swing and a golden putting touch, he set about achieving the Indian summer to end them all. Birdies on the final two holes to win the Masters? No problem. A four-hole play-off for the British Open? No sweat: his opponent, Brian Watts, never stood a chance. He came close to winning a third major that summer as well as he challenged for the US PGA, but two in a year was more than enough. Just for good measure he rounded off the year by winning the World Matchplay Championship at Wentworth. He moved to the Senior Tour in 2007, but despite a series of top-ten finishes, is still to record a win.

Francis **Ouimet**
Born: May 8, 1893
Brookline, Ma, USA

Ouimet became a national hero overnight when he beat the great Harry Vardon and recent British Open champion Ted Ray in an 18-hole play-off for the 1913 US Open close by his home town. Oddly, it seems his victory the next year in the US Amateur Championship gave him more pleasure. Perhaps that was because his performances had earlier been poor. In his four previous entries, he had failed to qualify three times and had once been knocked out in the second round. Much later, in 1931, he was to win this title again, but that was after Bobby Jones was safely retired. Despite his working-class background, Ouimet never considered turning professional. Nevertheless, he did lose his amateur status for a few years when the USGA decided that he was profiting from his golfing fame by opening a sports shop in Boston. There was an ironic sequel in 1951, when the R&A decided to choose their first American captain. The obvious choice was perhaps the greatest golfer

of all time, Bobby Jones, who had not broken the rules of playing golf as an amateur, but who had certainly made a great deal of money after his retirement. Yet it was Ouimet who was invited, and he performed his tasks with both grace and diplomatic skill.

Masashi **Ozaki**
Born: January 24, 1947
Tokushima, Japan

There are plenty of reasons why Japanese players have made so little impact outside their native land. Chief among them is their reluctance to travel, be it through homesickness, diet or the fact that the best players can earn untold wealth without ever using their passports. The leading example of this is Jumbo Ozaki, who has achieved superstar status in Japan and earned more money than he could ever spend if he lived to be a thousand years old. Furthermore, he has clocked up more than 65 victories. But outside Japan? He did little to justify his place through the 1990s as one of the top ten players in the world rankings. Yet with a little more ambition there is every chance that he could have become the first player from his country to win a major championship. He has proved this time and again in the Japanese tournaments that regularly attract the best players from around the globe: when the world comes to Jumbo, he has invariably beaten the world. Ozaki's penchant for colourful silk shirts and outrageous golf bags makes him instantly recognizable. What a shame that he has never exploited his talents to the hilt, and now, into his 60s, he clearly has no desire to do so. Invited to take part in the International President's Cup team for the historic first match outside America, at Royal Melbourne in 1998, Ozaki said thanks, but no thanks. He is the leading member of a trinity of brothers who have all made impacts in Japan, all becoming multi-millionaires through their golfing exploits. It is quite a collective achievement.

ARNOLD PALMER
Battling Arnie Thrills His Army

It was Arnold Palmer's style of play that was largely responsible for his unique charisma. In his prime, he always made the game seem like a battle against the golf course. Both spectators at an event and television viewers at home loved to see him play and even today, when he is into his 70s, many would rather see him open a soft drink can than others hole a full bunker shot.

Top players have mostly hit the ball very hard, but that has often been disguised by a rhythmic swing with the real acceleration only coming in the strike area, followed by a finish that is poised and sometimes elegant. Not so with Arnold. The take-away is quite fast, and after impact the club is flung towards the sky.

It may not look pretty, indeed it looks forceful – but it worked. Palmer is one of the best drivers of a golf ball the game has seen. The method worked equally well for long and medium irons, usually full shots. However, Palmer was never up with the best when he had to play a finessed wedge or a gentle eight-iron.

At his best, the same applied to his game around and on the greens. The aim wasn't to get the shot stone dead, but to hole it. This was especially true of his putting. Many players concentrate on trying to achieve perfect pace, so that the ball drops gently into the hole. Not Palmer in the great years. He gave it a firm rap. If he missed, there was no problem with the return from 4ft or so.

With the wear of the years, Palmer became less confident. Arguably his long game actually improved, but his putting, in particular, was increasingly cautious. Instead of aiming to bang it into the hole, he began to want to be sure of getting down in two. He also partly abandoned his policy of always going for the flag – and never mind the penalties for failure – in favour of more percentage shots.

A second important element of his appeal is his expressive face. Spectators always felt they could feel what Arnie was going through. Joy, amusement, anger, disappointment, amazement, ecstasy and even de-pression – all were on view.

Although Palmer had won two Masters by April 1960, his legend really began when he won the US Open in June 1960. He went into the final round six strokes behind the leader, but thought that a 65 might still swing things his way. Out in 30, he parred his way home while his two closest rivals, the aging Ben Hogan and a young Jack Nicklaus, faltered.

He instantly gained the reputation of being the man who could mount a last-round charge to victory, and it remained with him throughout his main career, even though it was by no means entirely true. Palmer was probably better at seizing an early lead and then keeping his nerve right through to the finish.

In Britain, he transformed the British Open almost overnight from a slightly parochial affair which interested few Americans (in 1960 the dominant force in world golf) into a major event on the world scene. He came second in that centenary Open and then won the championship the next two years, producing his greatest major championship performance in the Troon Open of 1962. Player entries from the United States gradually grew from that period onwards, and a great debt is owed to Palmer for the fact that the British Open field is more representative of world talent than any of the other three majors.

The appeal of Arnold Palmer continues, even though it is over 40 years since he last won a major. Indeed, it was there for all to see when a tearful Arnold bade farewell to the Augusta galleries in his final appearance at the Masters in 2004 – he received a standing ovation throughout the 36 holes he played.

ARNOLD PALMER Until Tiger Woods's arrival, no man did more to enhance the game's popularity.

1929
Born on September 10 in Latrobe, Pennsylvania

1954
US Amateur champion, after which he turns professional

1955
First professional win, the Canadian Open

1958
Wins his first major, the Masters

1960
Two majors in the year, the Masters and the US Open

1961
Wins British Open

1962
Two more majors, a third Masters and second British Open

1963
Becomes the last Ryder Cup captain to play in the event, leading the US to a 23-9 victory

1964
Wins his fourth, and last, Masters

1975
Ryder Cup captain for the second time, this time in his home state

Alf Padgham

Born: July 2, 1906
Caterham, England

There are many ways of putting and, for a while at least, Padgham found an unusual answer to his putting problems. Instead of keeping his eye over the ball, he lined up with it very much further away from his body. Padgham decided on this method because it helped him to imitate his excellent chipping stroke. The extended arm action worked for him, and for a while he carried all before him. Of course, Padgham didn't do it all on putting alone. He had one of the best swings in the British game. Vardon thought it perfect and his contemporary Dai Rees considered it the equal of Sam Snead's. In the few tournaments of his time, Padgham set a record, between 1935 and 1936, of winning four consecutive tournaments. He was also very effective in matchplay, taking the News of the World event twice and reaching the final on another occasion. He won his only British Open in 1936, after breaking into a pro's shop – at Hoylake. Arriving early in the morning to begin the day's final 36 holes, he found it shut and resorted to smashing the window in order to collect his clubs.

Se Ri Pak

Born: September 28, 1977
Taejon, South Korea

Such was the impact that Se Ri Pak made in her debut season on the LPGA Tour, she was dubbed women's golf's answer to Tiger Woods. And what a year it was. 1998 saw the Korean take two major championships in her rookie season. First came the LPGA Championship, when she led the tournament from start to finish. Her homeland went mad. More was to follow two months later in July. Pak beat Jenny Chuasiriporn on the second extra hole of a play-off, following the designated 18 holes. On the 18th hole of regulation play, Se Ri had removed her shoes and socks and stood in the water hazard in an attempt to keep her dreams afloat. Korea exploded. When she returned at the end of the season, such were the demands being placed on her that she collapsed and had to spend a few days in hospital. She had come a long way from the days when her father used to force her to camp in a graveyard at night to "develop her bravery". She cites her father as her major influence, and although such training techniques may be a little extreme, Se Ri has developed an unflappable temperament on the golf course. Three more majors have followed – the British Open in 2001 and the LPGA Championship in 2003 and 2006, although she hasn't won on the LPGA Tour since 2007.

Arnold Palmer

SEE PAGE 190

Ji Eun (Grace) Park

Born: March 6, 1979
Seoul, South Korea

Grace Park is another of a contingent of South Korean players to take the women's golf world by storm. Saying that, she took a very different path to her compatriots Se Ri Pak and Mi Hyan Kim. The daughter of wealthy restaurant owners in Seoul, Park first took up golf at the age of ten. Before that she had been a national junior champion at speedskating, but she took to golf in such a way that, recognizing her talent, her parents sent her to live with relatives in Hawaii, where she received specialist golf tuition. It paid dividends. In 1998, she won all of the amateur major championships, the first player to do so since 1938. The following year, she played ten events on the Futures Tour, winning five of them, finishing on top of the money list and earning her card for the main tour. She got off to a bad start, but a win finally came four months into the year. She settled down in 2001, winning her second title and won again in 2002. She started to show her true potential in 2003, posting an astounding 19 top-ten finishes on the way to third place in the money list. In 2004, she finished second to Annika Sorenstam, and collected her first major, the Nabisco Championship. Back and neck injuries sidelined her through 2005 and 2006 and she struggled on her return. In April 2009, she underwent further surgery on her hip.

Willie Park Sr

Born: 1834
Musselburgh, Scotland

Willie Park Sr has the distinction of being the first winner of the British Open, in 1860. He went on to win three more times – in 1863, 1866 and 1875. For a good many years, the principal players of their time were Park and Tom Morris Sr, both of whom were eventually eclipsed by the genius of Tom Morris Jr. Park first came to notice in the mid-1850s when he challenged all and sundry to play for £100 a side, very large stakes indeed for the time. Most tended to avoid confrontation with him because he was a very long driver of the ball and also an excellent putter – a difficult combination of talents to beat. Perhaps it came from his upbringing as a golfer when he used just one club for both of these parts of the game. Besides this, he would sometimes challenge club golfers, offering to play them standing on one leg and using just one hand. Legend has it that even like this, he lost just once.

Se Ri Pak She set the women's game alight when she arrived on the LPGA Tour in 1998.

Willie **Park Jr**

Born: February 4, 1864
Musselburgh, Scotland

Although golf professionals had previously been makers of clubs and balls as much as expert players, William Park Jr can be called the first businessman golfer. His success as a British Open winner in 1887 and 1889 (the third member of the family to win, after his father and uncle Mungo) gave him the prestige to branch out into other fields, almost certainly to the detriment of his golf. He also went into club-making, but was soon tending to employ other craftsmen rather than doing the work himself as had been the case with his predecessors. Park had shops in both London and New York, but this business gradually faded as the mass manufacture of golf clubs began to develop. He then made himself the first great golf architect and worked intensively in design and construction in Britain, continental Europe and North America. The Sunningdale Old course is his masterpiece.

Jesper **Parnevik**

Born: March 7, 1965
Stockholm, Sweden

The volcanic-dust eating Swede with the inverted peak of a baseball cap cuts a peculiar figure on the fairways, but perhaps that's what you should expect from the son of his country's most famous comedian. His performances on the golf course have been anything but a joke, however. Parnevik took his first win on the European Tour at the 1993 Scottish Open and challenged for the British Open at Turnberry the following year. Going to the 72nd hole with a one-stroke lead, a bogey left him with a clubhouse total of 11-under par. He could only sit back and watch as Nick Price finished eagle-birdie to lift the Claret Jug. The following year, Jesper claimed the Scandinavian Masters to become the first Swede to win a European Tour event on home soil. He finished second best at the British Open for the second time in his career in 1997 before a switch Stateside in 1998. Five wins in the next four seasons on the PGA Tour propelled him up the world rankings before a hip injury restricted his appearances and saw a slump in form. He recorded five top-ten finishes in 2004 to signal a return to form, before the hip injury returned to curtail his tournament play. Parnevik has represented Europe in three Ryder Cups to date and has been on the winning side on two occasions.

Jerry **Pate**

Born: September 16, 1953
Macon, Ga, USA

Golf is a more stressful game, physically, than many might think. Professionals often practise for hours on end, with the clubhead frequently crunching into the turf, and the results are a variety of injuries, mainly to wrists, elbows and shoulders, while the lower back suffers from the twisting motion of the golf swing. Pate seemed set to become one of the modern greats, but shoulder problems killed him off after a brilliant early career. In 1974, he won the US Amateur and also tied for the individual prize in the World Amateur Team Championship. Off he went to the PGA Tour qualifying school and was medallist in 1975. What more can you do than win the US Open the very next year in your first season as a professional? That is what Jerry Pate did, also hitting what many would say was the shot of the season. This was a five-iron from the rough, over water, and to a tight pin position. Pate got his ball to about 2ft and was the US Open champion. That year, and until 1982, Pate was a big money winner, and at the age of 27 became the youngest player to achieve career winnings of $1 million. Then came injury.

Corey **Pavin**

Born: November 16, 1959
Oxnard, Ca, USA

After an excellent amateur career, Corey Pavin turned professional in 1982 but he had to wait until 1984 for his first title on the PGA Tour. He went on to win 14 more titles. The highlight of his career came when he won the 1995 US Open at treacherous Shinnecock Hills. His final score of level par 280 is a testament to how solidly he played. Until his US Open victory, Pavin had been recognized as the best golfer never to win a major. He had come close at Royal St George's in the 1993 British Open when, after tying Nick Faldo for the lead after three rounds, his final-round 70 was overshadowed by Greg Norman's blistering 64 and Pavin finished fourth. That year he won the World Matchplay Championship. His success has been achieved despite not having a powerful drive, but it is accurate, and he is one of the best putters and sand players in the business. His lack of power also means that he is inventive in his shot-making. Where others will be thinking of cracking a mid-iron directly at the flag, Pavin may shape a wood onto the green, perfectly illustrated by the magical second shot he played to 4ft in the final round to ensure his US Open victory. In 2006, to the surprise of everyone, he rolled back the years to win the US Bank Championship – setting a Pan Tour record in the first round for the fewest strokes ever taken over nine holes when he completed the back nine in 26 shots. In 2008, he was named as US Captain for the 2010 Ryder Cup.

Calvin **Peete**

Born: July 18, 1943
Detroit, Mi, USA

Peete had an unusual introduction to golf. One of 19 children, he did not take up the game until the age of 23, and even then was hampered by a broken left elbow, which means he cannot straighten that arm. At his peak, Peete had superb balance through the strike area which helps to account for his legendary accuracy from the tee. He topped the PGA Tour averages for finding the fairway. Perhaps more importantly, he was also among the most consistent at hitting greens in regulation. Alas, for some time his putting did not equal his other abilities, but he broke through in 1979 to win his first tournament. Peete's top years came between 1982 and 1985, when he won nine events on the PGA Tour and finished in the top-four money winners three times. After 1986, though, his success rate dropped rapidly, partly as a result of shoulder and lower back problems. His last two victories came in the Tournament of Champions and the USF&G Classic in 1986, bringing his total of tour victories to 12.

Dottie (Mochrie) Pepper

Born: August 17, 1965
Saratoga Springs, NY, USA

Pepper joined the LPGA Tour in 1988 and was an immediate success. Her first three years on tour were very respectable, for she totalled about $500,000 in money winnings. Then her career really began to take off. In 1991, she won no tournament but was extremely consistent, rising to third on the money list. Since then her status remained much the same as she continued to be in the top five up to the end of 1996. Her best year came in 1992, when she had four wins, the most important of which was the Dinah Shore, her first major championship, a tournament she would win again in 1999. Pepper was well known for what some people consider to be over-aggressive demonstrations during the Solheim Cup, in which she has competed on five occasions. She retired in 2004 due to injury, and now works as a television commentator.

Kenny Perry

Born: August 10, 1960
Elizabethtown, KY, USA

Kenny Perry seems to get better with age. In 2003, his 13th season as a professional, he recorded three tournament victories, the first multiple win season of his career, ten top-ten finishes (three of them coming in the major championships) and amassed nearly $4.5 million in prize money. The first of those wins came with a six-stroke victory at the Bank of America Colonial; a week later he took the Memorial Tournament. In doing so he became (at 42) the oldest player to record back-to-back wins on the PGA Tour since Hale Irwin won the US Open and the Buick Classic back-to-back in 1990 at the age of 45. His 2003 form cemented his place in the US 2004 Ryder Cup team (where he lost both of his matches). His good form continued into 2005 with two victories, at the Bay Hill Invitational

and the Bank of America Colonial, the latter by seven strokes. Knee surgery sidelined him the following year and it took him until 2008 to return to winning ways. But what a return: he won three more times and made a second appearance in the Ryder Cup. He won twice in 2009 and should have added the Masters title to his collection – only to falter on the 72nd hole and lose to Angel Cabrera in a play-off. A lucrative switch to the Senior Tour beckons.

Henry Picard

Born: November 28, 1907
Plymouth, Ma, USA

Picard was essentially a 1930s golfer and well up among the most successful of that era. He might, for instance, have won the first Augusta National Invitational (later to become known as the Masters), in 1936, and came close the following year when a 67, 68 start put him four ahead of the eventual winner, Gene Sarazen. He put that right three years later, in 1938, by producing four very consistent rounds of 71, 72, 72, 70 to win by two strokes from Harry Cooper and Ralph Guldahl. Picard won the US PGA Championship in 1939, beating Byron Nelson 1 up in the final. Picard first became a tournament winner in 1934 and remained extremely successful until around the beginning of the Second World War when ill health virtually halted his career. By that time he had won 27 tournaments and had been leading money winner – with a little over $10,000!

Gary Player

SEE PAGE 194

Ian Poulter

Born: January 10, 1976
Hitchin, England

Although perhaps best known for his colourful dress sense and hairstyle, the young Englishman has made his mark on the European Tour for the way he plays the game, and has

Ian Poulter The colourful Englishman is starting to challenge for the game's major honours.

proved himself influential. Playing on the Challenge Tour in 1999, he looked set for a top-15 finish and a tour card that such a position warrants, before tripping over his golf bag leaving the Luxemburg Open and damaging the ligaments and tendons in his ankle. The lay-off meant a trip to qualifying school, but he did enough to earn playing privileges on the European Tour for the 2000 season. He marked his debut season with a win at the Italian Open (a feat he would go on to repeat in 2002) and followed that up with victory at the Morocco Open in 2001. Two more victories followed in 2003 and he made sure that he had won at least once in each of his four seasons on the European

Tour when he defeated Sergio Garcia in a play-off at the season-ending 2004 Volvo Masters in Spain. He made his debut in the Ryder Cup the same year, and played his part in Europe's crushing victory by winning his singles match on the final day. He was winless in 2005, but took the Madrid Open title in 2006 and ended the year ninth in the European Order of Merit. In 2008, he recorded his best finish in a major when a final round 69 propelled him to the runner-up spot at the British Open – his performance helped to make him Captain's Pick for the 2008 Ryder Cup. In 2010 he collected his biggest prize to date when he won the WGC Matchplay title.

GARY PLAYER
The Great Practiser

Gary Player could hole a chip or bunker shot or play a ball dead by the hole side. No fluke was involved. The results were achieved only with remorseless practice. For both these shots Player has a method which may be unique. The stroke is a downward stab.

GARY PLAYER The diminutive South African possessed a sensational short game.

His short game has remained Player's greatest strength over a career which has lasted over 50 years, more than 25 of those seeing him contend for, and win, major championships. Yet when he first arrived in Britain in the mid-1950s, he was advised by professionals of the time to give up the game as a livelihood, go back to South Africa and just play for fun. Opinion was that Gary had a hooker's grip, that his swing was too flat and that he lacked both rhythm and feel for the game. Perhaps the effectiveness of that stab on the short shots went unnoticed. You could say he was the first great golfer to expect to get down in two once he was near the green.

Another first for Player was the emphasis he put on physical fitness and diet. Before his time, most golfers considered that just playing the game was enough to keep you trim. The same was largely true of eating and drinking. Moderation was good enough.

Because Player is a small man, one of the main aims of his fitness regime was to increase his length from the tee. Compared to a Nicklaus, hitting a wedge for his second shot on a long par four, he found himself using a medium iron. Player once said he had gained about 25 yards from his healthy foods and strenuous exercise. Though those yards were undoubtedly important, far more significant was his will to win. As someone else said: "Gary just likes beating people."

He began doing that in the mid-1950s and, by 1958, had become one of the rare overseas golfers to win in the US. But his breakthrough on the world scene came in 1959 when he won the British Open at Muirfield. Successes in the Masters and the US PGA followed in the early 1960s, and his victory in the 1965 US Open made him one of the happy band of players to complete the slam of all four majors. Even more, with Nicklaus and Palmer, he was a founder member of what came to be known as the Big Three. The advertising and sponsorship money poured in.

In his native South Africa, with the decline of Bobby Locke, Player was by far the dominant golfer. But he had to be an international golfer, and over the years has probably clocked up more air mileage than anyone else. The United States was his main arena, but he also made annual appearances in Britain and played in Australia often enough to take their Open seven times. In Britain he won the World Matchplay Championship five times. His 1959 Open success at Muirfield was perhaps a little lucky. At Carnoustie in 1968, however, he had to battle head-to-head with Jack Nicklaus. Six years later, at Royal Lytham and St Anne's, he gave one of his finest performances which involved much use of his one-iron in the strong wind.

Perhaps his finest hour, however, came at Augusta in 1978, when Player was becoming a figure of the past. Entering the final round of the Masters, he was seven behind leader Hubert Green. His outward nine of 34 was good, but it seemed unlikely to affect the outcome of the tournament. His inward nine changed all that. With six birdies, he was home in 30. Player's remarkable 64 – one of the greatest final rounds in the history of major championship golf – gave him victory when Hubert Green missed a short putt on the last green.

Perhaps that was Gary Player's last hurrah, but he still competes enthusiastically on the Senior Tour and has notched up an impressive 19 victories to date – the last of which came in 1998.

1935	1958	1959	1961	1962
Born on November 1 in Johannesburg, South Africa	Earns his first PGA Tour win	Wins his first major, the British Open	Collects the Masters	Wins his third major, the US PGA

1965	1968	1972	1974	1978
Takes the US Open to become only the fourth player to win all four majors	Wins his second British Open	Wins his sixth major, the US PGA	Wins two majors in the year, the Masters and British Open	Wins his ninth major, the Masters at the age of 42

Nick Price

Born: January 28, 1957
Durban, South Africa

In 1994, Price won six times and soared to the top of the World rankings. Perhaps most importantly, he won two major championships back to back, the British Open and the US PGA. With his five wins in the United States it is hardly surprising that he finished the season as leading money winner with just under $1.5 million. Though Price won the World Series of Golf as long ago as 1983 and has been a name player since 1982, he did not become a really major figure on the world stage until very much later. His performance in the 1982 British Open at Troon did cause a stir, however, and for years he probably lived with the memory of the major he should have won – but for lost strokes over the closing holes. Price lost another British Open, at Lytham in 1988, but this time as a result of inspired play from Seve Ballesteros. Two wins in 1997 were clouded by an illness to his caddie, Squeak Medlen, who subsequently died from leukaemia. He won his 16th tour title, and his 15th of the decade (only Tiger Woods, also with 15, won as many times in the 1990s) when he won the St Jude Classic. A 17th tour title arrived in 2002 when he won the Mastercard Colonial. Incredibly, Price finished in the top 50 on the money list in the United States for 19 consecutive seasons. In all, he has claimed 45 victories worldwide. He switched to the Senior Tour in 2009, where he won once.

Judy Rankin

Born: February 18, 1945
St Louis, Mo, USA

Judy Rankin was a very early developer, winning the Missouri state title at the age of 14 and going on to finish as low amateur in the US Women's Open the following year. By the age of 17 she was playing on the LPGA Tour, though with very modest success – $701 in her first season.

NICK PRICE The South African bagged three major titles in two years between 1992 and 1994.

However, she made good progress and was ninth on the money list by 1965. In 1968, her stroke average came down substantially and she also had her first victory. She was on her way, and over the next ten years the victories piled up. In both 1976 and 1977, when she had six and five wins respectively, she was leading money winner on the LPGA Tour. From 1969 to 1979, her worst placing was 15th, and she was ninth or better nine times. By the end of 1979 she had notched up 26 tournament wins in the US, but that was more or less it. Rankin had a very strong left-hand grip, which tends to put stress on both the left wrist and can lead to an increased twisting movement of the lower spine. Her victorious Solheim Cup captaincy in 1996 assuaged the back pains that ended her playing career.

Betsy Rawls

Born: May 4, 1928
Spartanburg, SC, USA

Rawls did not begin playing golf until her late teens, but was soon winning the Texas state title and the more important Trans-National and Broadmoor Invitational. While still an amateur, she finished second in the US Women's Open. From 1951, she played as a professional and her first win came in the US Women's Open, the most important of women's titles, which she won again in 1953, 1957 and 1960. She also won the Western and the LPGA Championship twice each. Her total of 55 LPGA victories ranks her behind only Kathy Whitworth, Mickey Wright and Patty Berg. As a money winner, she was in her prime from the mid-1950s (for which records are incomplete) until 1970. She was leading money winner in 1959 when she won a truly remarkable ten times, and never finished worse than 16th in a 14-year period. Yet in those years women's golf did not attract high prize money. The most she won in a season was about $26,000. Rawls went on to become tournament director of the LPGA Tour during a period of rapid growth in the last half of the 1970s.

Ted Ray

Born: March 28, 1877
Jersey, Channel Islands

European success is now a common occurrence in the Masters, but not in the US Open. Only three British players, for instance, have managed to add this title to a win in the British Open: Harry Vardon (when, to be frank, it didn't matter very much), Ted Ray in 1920, when Americans were on the verge of dominance of world golf, and Tony Jacklin in 1970. Ray first really announced himself on the British golf scene by reaching the 1903 final of the News of the World Matchplay Championship and losing to James Braid, then at the height of his powers. Ray began to contend for the British Open, but had to cope with the stiffest competition from Vardon, Taylor and Braid. He finally broke through in 1912 at Muirfield, beating Vardon into second place by a comfortable four strokes. Ray was a dramatic player to watch because of his prodigious power. Even Bobby Jones was in awe of him while watching him on a US exhibition tour. The power showed to good effect when Ray took his US Open title. On one par-four hole, he managed a long carry of some 280 yards over a ravine and birdied the hole in all four rounds. He excelled at thrashing the ball out of bad lies, but also had a delicate touch on the greens.

Dai Rees

Born: March 31, 1913
Barry, Wales

Rees's greatest achievement came at Lindrick in the 1957 Ryder Cup. He was in the only winning pairing on the Great Britain and Ireland side, of which he was captain, and on the second day trounced his opponent, 1954 US Open champion Ed Furgol, by 7 and 6. Equally notable was his failure to win a British Open, well though he played. Either he or Abe Mitchell must be the best British player not to win. Rees first began to make some impact in the event towards the end of the 1930s, but became a really significant factor after the Second World War. He might well have won in 1946, when he had the lowest round of the championship, a 67, and went into the final round tied with the eventual winner, Sam Snead. Alas, he then had a disastrous start and could only partially recover. He finished fourth. In 1950 and 1953, he outscored the eventual champions for two rounds, but they lasted better. In 1954, he needed a par on the last to tie, but his ball skipped through the green. Rees thought it had hit a small stone. His last chance came at the age of 48, when he was one behind. In compensation, he was a most consistent tournament winner with 28 victories to his credit.

Chi-Chi Rodriguez

Born: October 13, 1935
Rio Piedras, Puerto Rico

Rodriguez is an even more talkative player than Lee Trevino, and, in his younger days on the PGA Tour, was known to many as "the clown prince of the tour". Others, who disliked his chatter and on-course antics, called him "the four-stroke penalty". They felt that was about the number of strokes he cost them with his distracting behaviour. Such august figures as Arnold Palmer and Jack Nicklaus told him to moderate it, and he did so, while still remaining exuberant. Rodriguez had a successful career on the PGA Tour between the beginning of the 1960s and the early 1980s. His first win came in 1963, his last in 1979, and he totalled eight in all. However, he prospered far more as a Senior since 1985. In 1986, he won three times and the next year took seven events, including the PGA Seniors. That year he also managed the feat of birdies on eight holes in a row, a record, which helped him to his record fourth straight win in a single season. He continued to take a title every year until the end of 1993. Rodriguez was a member of the US Ryder Cup team in 1973 and played for Puerto Rico in 12 World Cup teams.

Bill Rogers

Born: September 10, 1951
Waco, Tx, USA

Rogers worked his way gradually to the top and then subsided rapidly. As an amateur, he made the 1973 Walker Cup team. He then turned professional and first made a real impact by winning the 1977 Pacific Masters. The following year he took the Bob Hope Desert Classic, the first of his eventual five victories on the PGA Tour. In Britain, Rogers attracted much attention when he won the 1979 World Matchplay Championship at Wentworth. By this time, the strengths of his game were becoming apparent. Not long off the tee, he was very accurate and his scoring average was always good. His excellent putting involved an action with relatively stiff arms, the stroke coming from the shoulders. In 1981, he reached his peak. He won three times on the PGA Tour and was named Player of the Year. More importantly, he took the British Open at Royal St George's, going into the last round with a five-stroke lead. That year he had five wins in six entries, worldwide. He only won once on the PGA Tour after that, in 1983. "Then I had a very positive attitude," he said recently. "It was never the same after that."

Eduardo Romero

Born: July 12, 1954
Cordoba, Argentina

Before Angel Cabrera came along to eclipse his considerable achievements, Eduardo Romero was the best player to have come out of Argentina. After turning professional at the relatively advanced age of 28, Romero first won his own country's PGA back in 1983, and has repeated that success twice. The Argentine Open, however, eluded him until 1989, but he has also won the Chile Open twice. Golf in South America, however, is on a somewhat small scale and players have to make their names and earn their fortunes abroad. Romero plays mainly in Europe, with excursions to the US and elsewhere. He began his European career in 1984 and started to make real progress in 1988 when he reached the top 50. Since then he has done a great deal better, his first big season coming in 1989 when he moved up to 13th on the money list and also won the Lancôme Trophy, which has a select field. He won the Open di Firenze in 1990, and had two successes in 1991 – the Spanish Open and the French Open. These meant that he was comfortably in the top-20 money winners in the years 1989–91. In 1994, he took the Italian Open and the European Masters, a tournament he won for the second time in 2000. When he won the 2002 Scottish Open, just before his 48th birthday, he became the third oldest winner on the European Tour – behind Des Smyth and Neil Coles. He switched to the Senior Tour in 2004 and has recorded five wins, including two senior major championships.

CHI-CHI RODRIGUEZ The fairways have never seen a more vocal competitor.

Bob Rosberg

Born: October 21, 1926
San Francisco, Ca, USA

Bob Rosberg played on the PGA Tour for almost 20 years and won seven titles, including the US PGA Championship in 1959. It was the year in which he proved the old adage that a man who can putt is a match for anyone. After finishing runner-up in the US Open at Winged Foot to another great putter, Billy Casper, Rosberg collected his sole major at Minneapolis by virtue of a storming finish. Trailing Jerry Barber by nine at the halfway stage and by six shots going into the final round, he putted his rivals into place money with a 66 to win the tournament by one shot.

Paul Runyan

Born: July 12, 1908
Hot Springs, Ark, USA

Paul Runyan was a case in point for those who said that size isn't everything. Diminutive in stature and short off the tee, there weren't many people who gave him a chance to beat Sam Snead in the final of the 1938 US PGA Championship. The bookmakers made Snead 10-1 to win; some odds in a two-horse race. The one person who thought that he could win was Runyan himself. Despite being outdriven by 70 yards off the tee, he plugged the gap in skill by exhibiting his remarkable skills from 80 yards in. He was nicknamed "Little Poison" because of his talents on and around the greens and gradually it seeped into Snead's system. Never the most patient of golfers, he could not cope and Goliath was eventually toppled by the staggering margin of 8 and 7. Matchplay was the perfect format for Runyan and it is not a surprise to learn that his other major success also came at the US PGA Championship when he defeated Craig Wood at the 38th hole. But Runyan could play the strokeplay game, too: all told he won 20 PGA Tour events. His career lasted longer than most because it was built around an imperious short game, the skills of which did not diminish until well beyond middle age. Indeed, Runyan enjoyed great success as a senior, winning both the US and the World senior titles.

Doug Sanders

Born: July 24, 1933
Cedartown, Ga, USA

Doug Sanders won 19 times on the PGA Tour between 1956 and 1972, and had five wins in 1961, but his fame rests on one never-to-be forgotten shot. Unfortunately for him it was a missed putt, which cost him the 1970 British Open. By then past his prime, Sanders had had to prequalify, but he was a master of improvised shots and St Andrews was his ideal arena. He came to the last two holes needing a couple of pars to win the championship. It was not easy, because the 17th is just about the most difficult hole in world golf. With the aid of an exquisite bunker shot, Sanders got his par four. The Open then seemed to be his, for the last hole at St Andrews is as easy a finishing hole as you can find. Sanders hit a good enough drive, slightly thinned his approach so that he ended up to the back of the green, putted up to 4ft or less and then contemplated that putt for the championship. You have to make up your mind. Sanders did, but then noticed a mark along the line. He paused to remove it and then did not go through the usual routine – and missed. He then lost the 18-hole play-off with Jack Nicklaus by a stroke. Never mind, he is still better remembered for that missed putt than many are for a dramatic winning shot. If you ask Doug today if it preys on his mind he is likely to reply, "No, sometimes I don't think about it for five minutes."

Gene Sarazen

SEE PAGE 198

DOUG SANDERS He will always be remembered for the missed putt that cost him the 1970 British Open.

Adam Scott

Born: July 16, 1980
Adelaide, Australia

Adam Scott claimed both the Australian and New Zealand Amateur titles before earning his card for the European Tour. He finished 13th in the Order of Merit in his first full year, 2001, and claimed his first professional title at the Alfred Dunhill PGA Championship. A second title came the following year, the Qatar Masters. He earned an invite to play in the Masters and finished up joint-ninth. In 2003, he claimed his first PGA Tour win in just his 34th start, at the Deutsche Bank Championship. A fourth success on the European Tour, the Scandinavian Masters, followed later in the year. Scott's most significant victory to date came at the 2004 Players' Championship, considered by many to be the "fifth" major. With a two-stroke lead over Padraig Harrington going into the 72nd hole, he hooked his approach shot into the water. An up-and-down recovery shot gave him a pay cheque of $1.44 million. Victory at the 2005 Nissan Open saw him break into the world's top ten for the first time. In 2006 he captained the prestigious Tour Championship and finished a career-high third on the PGA Tour money list. Major championship success beckoned, but then his form fell away and he slipped out of the world's top 50.

GENE SARAZEN
The Shortest Champion

Gene Sarazen had a career that fell into two distinct and highly successful phases – the second culminating in the achievement of the first professional grand slam. First came a change of name. Born of Italian stock, he decided that Eugene Saraceni didn't sound right for a 17-year-old who wanted to be a professional golfer. So he went into his career as Gene Sarazen.

By the time the 1922 US Open came around, even though he had won a tournament, he was very little known – not surprising at 20 years and four months of age. At the end of that week in Illinois, he had become a national figure on the golf scene. Sarazen closed with a 68 to win.

In the same year, he also won the US PGA and beat Walter Hagen in a challenge match for the "World Championship". He beat Hagen again the following year, this time in the final of the US PGA.

Suddenly, Sarazen seemed to be the dominant player. However, Hagen was far from finished and Jones was emerging as the golfer who could beat them all. Sarazen also began to experience technical problems. His swing was compact and powerful (especially so for a man of only 5ft 3in, the shortest of major champions),

but his grip was laughable by modern teaching standards. With the left hand, he could see four knuckles and explained that there were advantages: the left wrist didn't break down when almost side on to the line of fire.

There was an even weirder feature of his grip: his left thumb played no part but flapped in the air. Sarazen also, like Jack Nicklaus, used the relatively rare interlocking grip, where the little finger of the left hand is fitted between the index and middle finger of the right.

The fast reactions of extreme youth, it could be argued, could cope with these unorthodoxies but, after the first flush of success, Sarazen did not maintain his pace. He could win tournaments from time to time, but the majors were beyond his grasp.

Then he entered his second phase. By the late 1920s and early 1930s he was winning good tournament money and was featuring often in the majors.

He was a potentially great player once again – and then also had a revolutionary idea. During this time even players of true excellence had trouble with bunker shots. Today most would prefer to have a good lie in a greenside bunker rather than a good

grassy lie from the same distance. The lofted clubs of the day were not effective. Because they bit into the sand, the only way to use them was either to flick the ball off the surface or explode it out.

Sarazen decided that what was needed was a clubhead that would glide through the sand, slicing underneath the ball, instead of digging in. So he took a club with a broad sole and added lead solder to raise the height of the rear. After much experimenting and test driving he had cracked the problem. Future players would be able to aim at getting near the flag from a greenside bunker instead of just being content to get their ball out of the hazard.

Sarazen himself was on his way to more major championships and had a glorious 1932, first winning the British Open at Prince's, Sandwich, in 1932 by five strokes and then, a fortnight after, the US Open.

A year later, he took the US PGA for the third time, but his most mystical achievement came in the second – and his first – Masters. With no apparent chance of catching Craig Wood, he suddenly holed a four-wood second shot at the par-five 15th, in front of just a handful of spectators.

GENE SARAZEN The ultimate proof of the old adage that size is not everything.

Sarazen had drawn level and went on to win the play-off the next day.

In 1940, he lost a play-off for the US Open and continued to play on the PGA Tour. Much later, he still had a couple of spectacular shots left. On day one of the 1973 British Open at Troon, at the tender age of 71, he holed in one with a five-iron shot on the Postage Stamp hole (the 8th). The next day he missed the green and was bunkered. No great problem: he holed his shot from the sand.

1902	1922	1923	1932
Born on February 27 in Harrison, New York	Aged just 20 wins two majors, the US Open and US PGA	Retains his US PGA Championship	After a nine-year gap, wins British Open and US Open

	1933	1935	
	Wins his third US PGA	Wins the second (his first) Masters, thanks to a double-eagle at the 15th	

Patty **Sheehan**

Born: October 27, 1956
Middlebury, USA

As an amateur, Sheehan won a string of state titles and climaxed her career with a win in the 1980 AIAW National Championship. She played in the Curtis Cup that same year and won all her matches. Turning professional later on that year, it was not long before she made an impression, her first win coming the following year in the Mazda Japan Classic. In the US she first won in 1982 and had two other victories that same year. She was already a star and has remained so. She crossed the $5-million mark in earnings in 1996 and captured her 35th career victory at the Nabisco Dinah Shore to earn her sixth major championship (seven, if you include her victory at the British Women's Open in 1992 which was not then classified as a major but is now). In addition to that 1996 win, she has also won the LPGA three times (in 1983, 1984 and 1993) and the US Women's Open twice (in 1992 and 1994). She captained the United States team to victory in the 2002 Solheim Cup at Interlachen Country Club in Minnesota in 2002.

Denny **Shute**

Born: October 25, 1904
Cleveland, Oh, USA

There was little money on the fledgling PGA Tour of the 1930s, so Shute had to devote much of his time to his club professional's job. Even so, his achievements were very considerable, notably his victory in the 1933 British Open at St Andrews. The course was playing very short, which does not mean easily, because the greens were not holding and that placed a premium on the precise judgment of the pitch and run. Shute had the odd result of four rounds of 73, which gave him a total one lower than Syd Easterbrook and in a tie with Craig Wood. He went on to win the play-off. Easterbrook had already featured in Shute's year at Southport

JAY SIGEL Having amassed an incomparable amateur record, he turned professional at the age of 50 to join the Senior Tour and made a fortune.

and Ainsdale in the Ryder Cup. There, at the climax of the match, Shute had three-putted the last green to lose to Easterbrook, and the United States went down. Revenge was very likely sweet. In the previous Ryder Cup matches in the United States, Shute had been a great deal more successful. He and Walter Hagen won their foursomes by 10 and 9, and Shute his singles by 8 and 6. Shute won two major championships in his own country, the 1936 and 1937 US PGAs, a feat emulated by Tiger Woods in 1999-2000. He was elected to the PGA Hall of Fame in 1957.

Jay **Sigel**

Born: November 13, 1943
Narberth, Pa, USA

In 17 lucrative years on the US Senior Tour, Jay Sigel has won more than $9.4 million, but what makes this level of performance all the more astonishing is that he did not turn professional until his 50th birthday. In other words, he never tested himself against the best competition through all his prime years. Instead, Sigel sold

insurance policies and concentrated on compiling the finest amateur record of the modern era. No one comes close to his achievements. He won the US Amateur on two successive occasions and also the 1979 British Amateur; he won three US mid-Amateur Championships and also played in seven American teams that contested the World Amateur Team Championship. He will be best remembered for his feats in the Walker Cup. He played in the competition seven times and amassed more points than any other player. He signed off in 1993 by winning both of his matches on the second day in a crushing American victory. Then, on turning 50, he joined the ranks of the Senior Tour where he has compiled eight victories and all that money.

Scott **Simpson**

Born: September 17, 1955
San Diego, Ca, USA

After a successful amateur career, which included Walker Cup status, Simpson twice failed to qualify for the PGA Tour before eventually making it

in 1979. He always made reasonable money but tended to disappear from the public view for long periods. His greatest season came in 1987, when he finished fourth on the US money list but, much more importantly, won the US Open after a very close confrontation with Tom Watson. All this took place at the difficult Olympic Club. Since then, Simpson seems to have become a US Open specialist, though he has not won again. He tied for sixth place in 1988 and 1989, and for first place in 1991, before losing in a play-off to Payne Stewart. Simpson is regarded by some as a journeyman professional, but he is much more accurate from the tee than many, which can give him an advantage when players are confronted by the tight drive zones and dense rough that are normally part of a US Open set-up. Besides his US Open, he won seven events on the PGA Tour, the last in 1998 when he won the Buick Invitational, and four important events overseas. A switch to the Senior Tour in 2005 has yielded one victory.

VIJAY SINGH
Practice Makes Perfect

VIJAY SINGH Nobody hits more practice balls on the range than the likeable Fijian.

It speaks volumes for Vijay Singh's determination and application that, at the end of the 2004 season, the number-one-ranked golfer in the world did not hail from one of golf's traditional powerhouses but from tropical Fiji. When it comes to practice, nobody works harder.

Singh is a truly international golfer. With the exception of 1996, he won at least one tournament worldwide between 1988 and 2008.

He learned his trade from his father in his native Fiji. He was then forced to travel to earn his stripes and collected his first tournament victory in 1984 at the Malaysian PGA Championship.

Singh then switched to the more lucrative European Tour and recorded his first victory in 1988 at the Swedish PGA Championship. He won at least one tournament on the European Tour over the next four years before earning his card for the PGA Tour. He was an instant success, gaining Rookie of the Year honours in his first year, and recording his first victory.

Back and neck problems may have restricted his appearances Stateside during 1994, but he still won twice on the European Tour and followed that with a double-win season on the PGA Tour in 1995.

He put his winless 1996 year behind him in 1997 by earning $1 million for the first time and rounded off a memorable season by winning the prestigious World Matchplay title at Wentworth.

He collected his first major title in 1998: the US PGA Championship at Sahalee with a one-stroke victory over Steve Stricker.

A second major followed in 2000, with a surprise victory at the Masters. If the next two seasons were years of consolidation, then any work fine-tuning his game paid dividends as Singh ended the 2003 season on top of the money list for the first time with four victories under his belt and $7,573,907 in his pocket.

If 2003 had been a year to remember, however, Singh's 2004 season will go down in the history books as one of the finest ever played. During the course of a stellar year, the Fijian became one of only six players in history to win nine tournaments in a season.

The highlight came at Whistling Straits when the Fijian collected his third major title and his second US PGA Championship. Singh came through a three-man play-off (beating Justin Leonard and Chris DiMarco after registering the only birdie) after shooting a final-round 76 – the highest final-round score by the winner of a major since Reg Whitcombe shot a closing 78 at Royal St George's to win the 1938 British Open.

At the end of the season, Singh had pocketed a single-season record $10,905,166 in prize money and had ended Tiger Woods's reign as the world's number one player. He confirmed his status in 2005 with four victories and 18 top-ten finishes, four of them in the majors.

2006 may have not been as prolific (with just a solitary victory to his name), but the Fijian impressively finished inside the top ten of the money list for the ninth straight season. He captured two tour titles in 2007 and three in 2008, but has remained winless since then.

1963	1984	1988	1993
Born on February 22 in Lautoka, Fiji	Wins first tournament, the Malaysian PGA Championship	Wins first title on European Tour	Rookie of the Year on PGA Tour following win at Buick Classic

1998	2000	2003	2004
Wins his first major, the US PGA Championship	Wins the Masters for second major title	Ends the year on top of the US money list	Wins US PGA for the second time and ends year as world's number-one-ranked golfer

Jeff Sluman

Born: September 11, 1957
Rochester, NY, USA

Jeff Sluman has earned some $21.4 million during the course of his 30-year professional career, which is a tribute to both his tenacity and his determination. Somewhat surprisingly, he has just six PGA Tour victories to his name, with the pick being the 1988 US PGA Championship. Sluman trailed Paul Azinger by three shots going into the final round, but reversed that with a wonderful closing 65. His doggedness has served him particularly well in the major championship arena, and he can count himself slightly unfortunate not to have won the 1992 US Open at Pebble Beach. This was the Open where the wind rose in intensity throughout the final day and Colin Montgomerie, who finished two hours before the leaders went off, was congratulated by Jack Nicklaus when he came off the course because he thought the Scot's level-par total would be good enough. But Sluman beat it, with a last-round 71. Unfortunately for him, so did Tom Kite, finally flying high in a major. And so it added up to yet another second place for Sluman. Another notable runner's-up spot was the 1988 Players' Championship, when he lost a play-off to Sandy Lyle. The other time he looked destined for major championship glory was at Augusta in 1992, where he led after an opening round of 65, before stepping back and having to settle for fourth. At 5ft 7in, Sluman was never going to be a golfing heavyweight, but he has made a name for himself by always being there or thereabouts. A switch to the Senior Tour in 2007 has brought him three wins.

Alex Smith

Born: January 28, 1874
Carnoustie, Scotland

Alex Smith was one of four brothers from Carnoustie who made their way to America in the early years of the 20th century to help with the development of the game on the other side of the Atlantic. He won the US Open on two occasions; in the first, in 1906, brother Willie finished in the runner's-up spot, while another brother, George, tied for 18th. Four years later, it was almost a family affair once more, when Alex was joined by brother Macdonald and Johnny McDermott in a three-way play-off. Alex shot a 71 and won by four shots from McDermott, with Macdonald, who had only just emigrated to join his brothers, a further two strokes behind.

Horton Smith

Born: May 22, 1908
Springfield, Ma, USA

Being the first to win an event gives you a better chance of entering the history books – if only because yours is the first name on the trophy. Horton Smith won the first Augusta National Invitational in 1934, the tournament which was soon to become known as the Masters. The event aroused great interest, mainly because Bobby Jones, who had retired from all competitive golf four years before, was making a re-appearance in "his" tournament. But Jones never repeated his previous form in any of the Masters he played. Smith won this first event by a stroke from the ever-unfortunate Craig Wood. He repeated that success a couple of years later, this time by one from Harry Cooper. Those two Masters were his only majors, but he was third twice in the US Open and once in the British Open. He played on three Ryder Cup teams and won some 30 tournaments.

Macdonald Smith

Born: March 18, 1890
Carnoustie, Scotland

Bing Crosby, himself a low handicap golfer, watched most of the greats over nearly half a century and considered that Smith had the best-looking swing of the lot. However, although he won over 30 times in the United States, Smith is often rated the best player not to have won a major. But how close he came. As early as 1910, for example, when only 20, he tied for the US Open and lost the play-off. He was never to come quite as close to a major again. By far the most famous failure came at Prestwick in 1925, after he took an almost impregnable five-stroke lead into the final round. The Scots turned out in their thousands to see their man from Carnoustie win. Crowd control was very poor on a course that presents difficulties in this respect. Smith sometimes had to wait too long to play his shots and occasionally, it is said, had to fire blind over spectators. As it turned out, a 76 would have been good enough but, alas, he took 82.

JEFF SLUMAN Now on the Senior Tour, Sluman has been a tenacious and determined competitor throughout his 30 year-professional career.

SAM SNEAD
Slammin' Sam

SAM SNEAD He was a prolific winner, but success in the US Open always eluded him.

Sam Snead won more events on the PGA Tour than any other golfer. He is also the only player to win tournaments in six different decades, and was the first golfer to shoot 59 in competition. He also made 34 career holes-in-one, and is reckoned to have shot below his age on more than a thousand occasions. Even at 62, he was still good enough to finish third in the US PGA Championship.

What do all these things tell us? That Samuel Jackson Snead was probably the most talented golfer who ever lived. He certainly had the most graceful swing. But he was not without his flaws, and most of them were from the neck upwards.

In all Snead won seven major championships but never the US Open: he played in it on no fewer than 26 occasions, but never came closer than his excruciating loss in 1939, when he made a triple-bogey eight on the 71st hole at Spring Hill in Philadelphia to blow a two-shot lead.

Snead was the youngest son of five and grew up in the backwaters of

Virginia. Legend has it that he carved his first club from a branch that had broken off while he was climbing down from a tree. The truth is not quite so lyrical; he did carve out clubs from the limbs of swamp maple.

His swing was all his own work, inspired by the sight of his brother Homer flashing huge drives across the farms near his homestead. Soon Sam graduated to a set of cast-off clubs and then a caddying job, which later led to an assistant's post at the Greenbrier. It was while there that he was invited to make up a four with Lawson Little, the former British and US Amateur champion, and two past US Open winners, John Goodman and Billy Burke: Snead shot 61.

It was so good that the members immediately carried out a whip-round to raise some funds to allow him to try his hand at the professional circuit. He went to California with $300 in his pocket and with the intention of finding, as he called it, "a real job when the money ran out". It never did. He won $600 the first week and then, in his third start, the $1,200 prize in the Oakland Open. Snead won four further times that year and finished as runner-up in the US Open.

"Slammin' Sam" became his moniker, and he was quickly a popular figure with the spectators, who had not had anyone to idolize since the retirement of Bobby Jones.

His one appearance in the British Open came at St Andrews in 1946. It is said that as he came towards the Old Course, he pronounced: "Why the hell have they built a golf course on this cow pasture?" Snead remained unimpressed to the end, railing against the austere accommodation and the food that was prevalent in a country still picking itself up following a long war. It did not stop him winning, however: his final-day rounds of 74 and 75 giving him a four-stroke victory.

In 1949, Snead won the Masters and the US PGA in his home state of Virginia, but perhaps his best year came in 1950 when he won no

fewer than 11 tournaments. It was not without its disappointments, however. Ben Hogan returned following his car accident, won the US Open, and was declared golfer of the year. To say that hurt Snead would be an understatement. He never played a full PGA Tour schedule again.

He was one of the founder members of the Senior Tour, and naturally cleaned up on it for years. He was still turning up at the odd tournament well into retirement and was one of the honorary starters at the Masters until shortly before his death in 2002.

In terms of career longevity, no one will surely ever come close to Snead. His achievements stand comparison with virtually every golfer who ever lived, but one question will always be asked: what would have happened had he had the cool temperament to match his smooth swing?

1912	1942	1946	1949	1950
Born on May 27 in Ashwood, Va, USA	Wins US PGA for the first time beating Jim Turnesa in the final	Wins the British Open at St Andrews on his only visit to the tournament	Double major year with wins at both the Masters and the US PGA	Claims 11 tour titles during the course of the year

	1951		1952		1954
	Wins the US PGA for the third time, beating Walter Burkemo 7 and 6 in the final		Wins the Masters for the second time with a victory margin of four strokes		Wins the Masters for the third and final time, beating Ben Hogan by one stroke in an 18-hole play-off

ANNIKA SORENSTAM
In a League of Her Own

A graduate of the University of Arizona, where she was College Player of the Year and NCAA Champion in 1991, Sorenstam turned professional in 1992 and finished second on her first outing on the European Tour – the Ford Classic at Woburn. She finished her rookie season third in the Order of Merit. She turned her attentions Stateside in 1994, finished the season 39th on the money list and won Rookie of the Year honours. She notched up her first tournament victory when she won the Australian Open at Royal Adelaide.

That win provided a trigger for what was to follow in 1995. She started the season with a victory in the OVB Damen Open in Austria – her first success in Europe – won two weeks later, at the lucrative Hennessy Cup, and again two weeks later, this time beating Meg Mallon by one stroke at the US Women's Open. By season's end she stood on top of the money lists on both sides of the Atlantic – the first player ever to achieve the feat.

She slipped to third on the US money list in 1996, despite winning the US Women's Open for the second successive year, but bounced back in 1997 by winning six events.

Sorenstam was number one again in 1998, winning four tournaments, topping the money list and becoming the first player to win the Vare Trophy with a scoring average under 70.00 – it was 69.99. The arrival of Karrie Webb seemed to knock Sorenstam off her stride. A three-win season in 1999 was followed by a four-win season in 2000, but it was the Australian who stood on the top of the US money list, not the Swede. It was a rivalry that sparked new life into her and Sorenstam redoubled her efforts during the off-season.

The hard work paid dividends. During the course of the 2001 season she set or tied 30 LPGA Tour records, collected her first major title since 1986 – the Nabisco Championship – and regained the number-one spot.

If 2001 had been good, 2002 was even better. She won 13 of 26 events entered and in the process broke or tied 20 LPGA Tour records. Among those victories came her fourth major – when she successfully defended the Nabisco Championship.

It was a tough year to follow, and although she only won six tournaments on the LPGA Tour, two of them were majors – the LPGA Championship and the British Women's Open, to complete the career grand slam. Later in the year, she accepted an invitation to play in an event on the PGA Tour – becoming the first woman in 58 years to compete against the men. She missed the cut by four shots with rounds of 71 and 74, although surprisingly it was her short game that really let her down.

The roll continued into 2004. She won half of the 20 tournaments she entered around the world – including her seventh major, the LPGA Championship. Among the ten titles she collected in 2005 were two more majors – the Nabisco Championship and the LPGA Championship. She added the US Women's Open, her tenth major, to her tally in 2006.

A neck injury sidelined her in 2007 and despite returning to winning ways in 2008 – capturing her 72nd LPGA Tour title at the Michelob Open – she announced her retirement in May of that year.

ANNIKA SORENSTAM Her dedication has seen her become the dominant golfer of her generation.

1970
Born on October 9 in Stockholm, Sweden

1992
Turns professional and finished third on the European money list

1995
Tops both European and US money lists. Wins the US Women's Open

1996
Wins the US Women's Open for the second time

2001
First women to shoot 59 in a tournament. Collects third major with win in the Nabisco Championship

2002
Wins 13 tournaments worldwide and successfully defends Nabisco Championship

2003
Completes career grand slam with wins at LPGA Championship and British Women's Open

2004
Collects seventh major championship with victory at LPGA Championship

2005
Wins Nabisco Championship and LPGA Championship

2006
Wins US Women's Open – the tenth and final major of her career

Mike Souchak

Born: May 10, 1927
Berwick, Pa, USA

How is this for nine holes of golf – 2, 4, 4, 3, 3, 3, 3, 3, 2? That was how Souchak played the second nine at Brackenridge Park during the 1955 Texas Open, for a total of 27. If he hadn't gone out in a relatively "poor" 33 he would have broken the magical 60. However, he was inspired that week, and rounds of 60, 68, 64, 65 gave him an aggregate of 257 which stood as a record low in tournament play until 1981, when Peter Tupling beat it over a 6,000-yard course. On the PGA Tour, only Al Geiberger, Chip Beck and David Duval have bettered that first-round 60. However, it should be said that Souchak's score was achieved on a fairly easy course, while Tupling's involved putting on sand greens, which are easier than grass. Souchak played on the 1959 and 1961 Ryder Cup teams and won 16 times on the PGA Tour.

Craig Stadler

Born: June 2, 1953
San Diego, Ca, USA

Nicknamed "The Walrus" on account of his profuse moustache and a 210-pound outline, Stadler is one of the most recognizable figures in world golf. He recorded his first two victories as a professional in 1980 and shot up the money list from 55th to eighth, a position he repeated in 1981. The following year he finished as leading money winner, with close on $500,000. More importantly, he also won four times in the United States. The most significant of his victories undoubtedly came at the Masters, though that was a trying experience for him. After 11 holes of the final round he held a five-stroke lead, but then dropped shots on the 12th, 14th and 16th. He came up the last hole needing a par for victory, but three-putted to tie with Dan Pohl. However, he parred the first play-off hole, Pohl bogeyed, and that was good enough. Stadler has played in two Ryder Cups and won 13 times on the PGA Tour – the last of his victories came in the 2003 BC Open, the year he became eligible for the Senior Tour. And what a transition he made, winning two tournaments, including two senior major championships. Stadler was famously disqualified in a 1987 event for kneeling on a towel to play a shot from under a tree for "building a stance". In 1995, he was permitted to cut down the (by now) diseased tree.

Jan Stephenson

Born: December 22, 1951
Sydney, Australia

Like Laura Baugh, Jan Stephenson has sometimes received more attention for her sex appeal than for her golf. She has turned down offers to pose for both Playboy and Penthouse, but has appeared topless in a French magazine. "I'm not ashamed of my body," she said, "and I'll flaunt it if I want to." In her teens, Stephenson was phenomenally successful in Australia, winning a host of girls' and junior titles and then, after turning professional in 1973, dominating what there was of an Australian Tour. Her future obviously lay in the United States and she began to play the LPGA Tour in 1974, winning good money and being named Rookie of the Year. Her first win came in 1976, since when she has taken 16 titles on the LPGA Tour plus two Australian Opens, the 1981 World Ladies, the French Open and a Japanese event. Her peak years in the United States were between 1976 and 1988, when she only finished out of the top 20 once. She has won three major titles and did so in consecutive years: the 1981 Peter Jackson Classic, the 1982 LPGA Championship and the 1983 US Women's Open.

Payne Stewart

Born: January 30, 1957
Springfield, Ma, USA

Before he was tragically killed in 1999 when the plane he was travelling in en route to the Tour Championship crashed in South Dakota, Payne Stewart stood out for many years by virtue of the bright colours of the clothing he wore under a contract to advertise American gridiron football clubs. When that contract expired, he changed to a line of designer wear made on his own account. He certainly attracted a great deal of attention, though it is not quite the gear to be wearing if you have to back into a gorse bush to play a shot.

Stewart often found himself in gorse bushes, not because of bad play, but because he was one of the few Americans who are fond of playing outside the United States. His first professional wins came in India and Indonesia during 1981, and another followed in Australia the following year. He won in the United States in both 1982 and 1983, but thereafter found it easier to win large amounts of money than tournaments. In 1993, for instance, he set a PGA Tour season record for money winnings – nearly $1 million – without scoring a victory. His first major victory came in 1989 in the US PGA. Two years later came the US Open after an 18-hole play-off with Scott Simpson, a formidable championship player, at Hazeltine National. A second US Open title followed in spectacular fashion at Pinehurst in 1999 when he edged out Phil Mickelson in a thrilling finale just months before his untimely death.

Dave Stockton

Born: November 2, 1941
San Bernardino, Ca, USA

Stockton is one of those players whose greatest achievements have been in over-50s golf. In a long career on the PGA Tour, which effectively lasted from 1964 to 1980, he won 11 times. This may seem a modest total, but it did include two major wins, both in the US PGA Championship. In the 1970 event, Arnold Palmer was one of the players he forced into second place; in 1976, Ray Floyd and Don January were the two who came in second after Stockton holed a putt to win from several yards. Putting was, and is, the main strength of his game. He had a severe back injury in his early teens, and since then has never been able to hit the ball full out. He himself has claimed that he merely guides the clubhead through the ball – but he still manages to drive it 250 yards or so. Stockton twice played on the US Ryder Cup team – in 1971 and 1977 – but will be best remembered for his captaincy

PAYNE STEWART The charismatic American had won three majors before his untimely death.

of the winning team in 1991, when Bernhard Langer's famous missed putt at Kiawah Island allowed Hale Irwin and the United States off the hook. Stockton was rewarded by his team tossing him into the Atlantic. He has been a prolific winner on the Senior Tour, claiming 14 wins, topping the money list in both 1993 and 1994 and earning $10 million in prize money.

Frank **Stranahan**

Born: August 5, 1922
Toledo, Oh, USA

Stranahan, an amateur, was one of the first golfers to introduce the idea that extreme physical fitness might be important for golf. Earlier it had been thought that no excessive consumption of food, alcohol and nicotine was all you had to aim at. Stranahan caused a sensation when, shortly after the Second World War, he arrived at a famous British hotel with his weight-lifting kit. Whether or not it did his golf much good is open to question, for in golf the ability to accelerate a light clubhead counts for a great deal more than the muscles required to shift inert weights. In Britain, if not in America, the methods earned him the nickname "Muscles". His ideas of fitness apart, Frank was one of the great amateurs of the immediate post-war years. He won a host of US regional titles, though he never did better than reach the final of the US Amateur, when he lost on the 39th. In Britain he was much more formidable, winning the British Amateur comfortably in both 1948 and 1950 and reaching the 1952 final. He was a very frequent competitor in the British Open and tied for second place in 1947 and 1953, when he was the world's best amateur.

Curtis **Strange**

Born: January 30, 1955
Norfolk, Va, USA

In 1988 and 1989, Strange became the first man since Ben Hogan to win consecutive US Opens. 1988

Karen Stupples Hit the big time in 2004 with her British Open victory at Sunningdale.

also saw him become the first player to pass $1 million in a year's PGA Tour earnings, as well as achieving the rare feat of winning four times. If Strange's proudest achievements are his US Open victories, which are in the record books for ever, there is another that certainly won't be in the future. That is his 62 over the Old Course at St Andrews in the 1987 Dunhill Cup. This achievement is slightly devalued because the event is played as stroke matchplay, and over the closing holes, Strange would have been under little real pressure. Strange has had an up-and-down career, and since 1990 has not really featured as a major player. His first outstanding year came in 1980, when he emerged as a significant force and finished third on the US money list. He then subsided a little before being top money winner in 1985, 1987 and 1988. Altogether

he has won 17 events on the PGA Tour, and nearly $7 million. In his early professional days he earned the reputation of being far better at winning money than tournaments, but later became known as an "iron man" when in contention, a reputation belied by his costly slip against Nick Faldo in the 1995 Ryder Cup. He captained the United States Ryder Cup team at The Belfry in 2002 and made his debut on the Senior Tour in 2004.

Karen **Stupples**

Born: June 24, 1973
Dover, England

For six years, Karen Stupples, a former Curtis Cup player with England and a former collegiate player with Florida State University, cut a somewhat innocuous figure on the LPGA Tour. Then came 2004: her first tour title came in record-breaking fashion at the start of

the year when she shot a final-round 63 to take the Welch's/Fry's Championship at Tucson. Her finishing total of 258 (a mammoth 22-under par) was the lowest 72-hole score in the history of the LPGA Tour. It became a year of final rounds for Stupples. She started her final round of the British Women's Open one stroke off the pace and went eagle, albatross on her first two holes. The albatross came when she holed a five-iron from 202 yards on the 475-yard second. Her finishing total of 269 (19-under) equalled the low 72-hole in majors (set by Dottie Pepper at the 1999 Nabisco Dinah Shore) and Stupples had become the first Englishwoman to win the British Women's Open since Penny Grice-Whittaker thirteen years before, in 1991. She has not won on tour since, but has performed consistently enough to pass the $1 million mark in career earnings.

J H TAYLOR He shot to prominence by winning the British Open in 1894.

Louise **Suggs**
Born: September 7, 1923
Atlanta, Ga, USA

Louise Suggs ranks as one of the greatest of women players. As an amateur, she won numerous state and regional titles and capped that part of her career in some style. She won the US Women's title in 1947 and followed up by capturing the British version of the event in 1948 and playing in the Curtis Cup. She then turned professional and was a founder member of the LPGA. As a professional, she had a great record in what were then ranked as major championships. She won the 1957 LPGA Championship, the US Women's Open in 1949 and 1952, the Titleholders in 1954, 1956 and 1959 and the Western Open in 1949 and 1953. The most remarkable of these was her first US Open victory, which she won by a record 14 strokes from Babe Zaharias. In these early years of the LPGA tournaments there were really only usually three players in contention – herself, Patty Berg and Zaharias. Louise fought very well. In her best years she was always among the top money winners and won consistently. Her last success came in 1962. It was her 50th.

Hal **Sutton**
Born: April 28, 1958
Shreveport, La, USA

Sutton was a player who seemed destined to become one of the stars of the modern game. He had made a big impression as an amateur, making the Walker Cup team, winning several regional events and taking the 1980 US Amateur. At Pinehurst, he was the individual winner in the World Amateur team championship, winning by nine strokes while his 276 total set a record for the event at 12-under par. In 1981, he was leading amateur in the British Open and again played in the Walker Cup team. Following a very good first professional season, crowned by victory in the last event, the Disney Open, 1983 was even better. He led the US PGA from start to finish, beating Jack Nicklaus by a stroke. He also won the Players' Championship. These and other results made him leading money winner for the year and saw him elected PGA Player of the Year. A no-win 1984 was followed by two titles in 1985 and 1986. Then came an eight-year drought, when Sutton "won only money". His career brightened in 1995 at the BC Open with a startling final round of 61, the best by a tournament winner in 20 years, since Johnny Miller at Tucson in 1975. It was like a return to the old days in 1998 – his best season since 1983 – when he won the Texas Open and then went on to win the Tour Championship at East Lake, beating Vijay Singh at the first hole of the play-off. His return to form continued into 1999, when he won the Canadian Open by three strokes, and into 2000: first he went head-to-head with Tiger Woods at the Players' Championship – and emerged the one-stroke winner – and then he took the Greater Greensboro Classic. His victory in the 2001 Houston Open saw him pass the $1-million mark for the fourth consecutive season and secured him a place in the 2002 US Ryder Cup team. He was their captain in 2004 and could only look on in despair as his team subsided to a record defeat. He became eligible for the Senior Tour in 2008.

J H **Taylor**
Born: March 19, 1871
Northam, England

Forever immortalized as part of the Great Triumvirate that dominated golf at the start of the 20th century, J H Taylor was the first of the three – James Braid and Harry Vardon were the others – to come to prominence, winning the British Open in 1894 and then successfully defending his title the following year. He also won it three times after the turn of the century, and would finish as runner-up on no fewer than six occasions. Taylor grew up close to the links at Westward Ho! and worked there as a youngster. By the time he left his teenage years behind, he had blossomed into a fine player and, after a short period at Winchester, moved to Royal Mid-Surrey where he was the resident professional for 47 years until his retirement in 1946. His victory in the 1894 British Open came in only his second appearance in the event, and led to him becoming the most famous professional in England. This Open, at Sandwich, was the first to be staged outside Scotland and Taylor won by five strokes to end the domination of the championship by the Scots. Like Braid, Taylor was instrumental in the founding of the Professional Golfers' Association; so much so that Bernard Darwin, in applauding his contribution, wrote that he had "turned a feckless company into a self-respecting and respected body of men". In addition to his qualities as a golfer, Taylor had a rare charm, which was recognized when he was made an honorary member of the Royal and Ancient Golf Club in 1947.

Peter **Thomson**
SEE PAGE 207

David **Toms**
Born: January 4, 1967
Monroe, La, USA

Toms first came to the attention of the wider golfing public at his first visit to the Masters in 1998. He shot a final-round 64 (one shot off the course record and one shot off the record round for any of the major championships) to finish in a tie for sixth place. His back-nine 29 tied the tournament record, as did his six consecutive birdies between the 12th and the 17th. That performance seemed to spur him onto greater things. He won twice on tour the following year and once more in 2000. Then came 2001 and a dramatic victory at the US PGA Championship. Holding a one-stroke lead over Phil Mickelson going into the final hole, he chose to lay up short of the water hazard after finding his ball in a poor lie 213 yards from the flag. He wedged to 12ft and then sank the par put for the title after watching Mickelson's birdie attempt stop short of the hole. The following year he was the pick of the US players in their losing Ryder Cup effort at The Belfry. Three more wins between 2003 and 2004 saw him become one of only five players under the age of 40 to reach the ten-win mark on tour. The others: Tiger Woods (40), Phil Mickelson (23); Ernie Els (13) and David Duval (13). He captured the prestigious WGC Matchplay title in 2005 and won again in 2006, but has yet to recapture the form that brought him a major championship.

PETER THOMSON
Master of the Links

PETER THOMSON His best moments came at the British Open – he was a five-time winner.

Peter Thomson will be remembered for more than just his exploits on the course. Indeed, one might have to go back to Bobby Locke to find another player with such a diverse spread of interests.

Thomson played the game in cerebral fashion. He was no fan of Arnold Palmer's smash-and-find-it tactics, believing instead in the simple virtues of finding the fairways, locating the greens and, above all, preparing thoroughly and remaining cool at all times.

His record shows such a level of success in Britain and Ireland in the 1950s as to lead to the conclusion that the decade could be summed up as "the Thomson era". But what about America? Why no joy there when confronted with players of the quality of Hogan and Snead? It has led some to conclude that Thomson was one step down from the very highest calibre of player. For a start, he was not completely unsuccessful in America. From 1953 to 1959 he amassed no fewer than 42 top-ten finishes, and this despite leaving every July to return to Australia.

It is true, however, that his style of play was particularly suited to links golf, where a player has to think his way round to make a score. While many a great player would rage at an unfair lie, Thomson would always remain serene, retaining his un-shakable self-belief.

Given such qualities, it comes as no surprise that Thomson reserved his best performances for the British Open. And how. In 1952 and 1953 he finished as runner-up: first finishing one stroke behind Bobby Locke at Royal Lytham and St Anne's, and then to Ben Hogan – when the American rounded off an incredible three-major season with victory at Carnoustie.

Thereafter, however, Thomson could call the British Open his own – he would win the tournament four times in the next five years and become one of only three golfers in the 20th century to win the tournament five times when he triumphed at Royal Birkdale in 1965 (the other two being Harry Vardon and Tom Watson). True, with the exception of the final win, his opposition was not perhaps as strong as it might have been, but the fact that between 1952 and 1958 no British player ever finished above him in the tournament is some measure of his brilliance during that time.

His first triumph came at Birkdale in 1954, when he turned the tables on Bobby Locke, this time lifting the Claret Jug for the first time after a one-stroke victory. He won again the following year, this time at St Andrews, and became the first player to complete a hat-trick of titles since Bob Ferguson (winner in 1880-82) when he won by three strokes at Royal Liverpool. He came through a play-off with Dave Thomas to take the title for a fourth time in 1958, but his fifth and final triumph, at Birkdale, was probably his best – he overcame a field that contained the greatest names of the day, including Nicklaus and Palmer.

The one time that he did commit himself completely to America, Thomson proved practically unbeatable. This was in 1985, and the Senior Tour. He shelved his other interests and devoted himself to playing there, winning ten times. But at the end of it he was bored.

Now he travels the world in his various capacities in the game, most notably as one of the great architects around today. Not for Thomson some of the modern obsessions with water, water everywhere: "A great golf course can be judged by the number of balls that a reasonable player needs to finish it," he said. "If it is a one-ball course, with all the usual features in place, then it must be a great course. If you need a dozen balls to play it, like some of the courses where fairways are surrounded by man-made lakes, then it is rubbish."

Thomson was perfectly suited to golf. He was not a loner, but he enjoyed his own company and would often whistle Beethoven's "Appassionata" while making his way around the course. No golfer proved more the words of the old saying: "If you can keep your head while all around are losing theirs..."

1929	1954	1955	1956
Born on August 23 in Melbourne, Australia	Wins the first of his British Open titles at Birkdale	Successfully defends British Open title	Claims a hat-trick of British Open titles with a three-stroke win at Royal Liverpool

1958	1965	1985
Wins the British Open for a fourth time	Captures his fifth and final British Open at the scene of his first triumph, Birkdale	Plays on the Senior Tour and wins ten times

Sam Torrance

Born: August 24, 1953
Largs, Scotland

Torrance's long and largely successful career is a testament to his long hitting and rhythm as much as anything. For a time, a twitching putter looked likely to bring his career to a premature end. Then he decided to experiment with a long putter. An avid snooker player, he practised with it on his table and the balls started to go in without that fatal tremor. On his day, he is now as good a performer as any on the greens. He first played on the European Tour in 1971 and made moderate progress until 1976, when he won twice and was third on the money list. His highest ranking was second, in 1984, and again, by a whisker, in 1995, to fellow Scot Colin Montgomerie. His best period came between 1981 and 1985, and he continues to be a very strong performer, though not at his best in major championships. He has won 20 times on the European Tour and his career money winnings surpass £4 million. He will always be remembered for holing the putt on the 18th green at The Belfry in the 1985 Ryder Cup that ended a 28-year drought for the Europeans. It was fitting that Torrance was awarded the captaincy of the team for the 2002 event, again at The Belfry. He now plays on the Senior Tours on both sides of the Atlantic with considerable success, capturing 11 titles to date, and also works as a television commentator.

Jerry Travers

Born: May 19, 1887
New York, NY, USA

There was a time when players carried far fewer clubs than they do today – one British Open champion carried just seven! Travers was rather a different case, however. He was seldom happy with woods, and may have been the first golfer of high ability to prefer an iron off the tee. But if Travers suffered the severe problem of being erratic with his woods, he usually made up for it with his brilliance on and around the greens. He was one of the first to concentrate on this, while others thought more of excellence through the green. His putting was particularly outstanding. Travers worked on various methods to see what worked best for him. He settled on an upright stance, keeping the body still throughout the stroke and making the head of the putter follow along the line - all conventional ideas today. What made Travers unusual in his day was his emphasis on an upright stance: many used to crouch low over the ball, with legs splayed wide. Travers won four US Amateurs – more than anyone except Bobby Jones. He won the US Open in 1915 - and never played in it again!

Lee Trevino

SEE PAGE 209

Bob Tway

Born: May 4, 1959
Oklahoma City, Ok, USA

In 1986 Tway hit one of the most famous shots in modern golf. It came on the final hole of the US PGA Championship at Inverness. After the opening two rounds, Tway lay no fewer than nine strokes behind Greg Norman, but a third-round 64 reduced the gap to four. In the final round, Tway pulled level, and then came the drama of the final hole. Norman hit a good approach which spun back into the semi-rough around the green. Tway bunkered his approach and was left with a very difficult shot to make his par. A touch too strong, and his ball would run off the green; if he came up short, he would be left with a nasty downhill putt. He played a perfect shot, the ball pitching about 20ft short of the hole – and running in. Norman then needed to hole his chip to tie and, not surprisingly, failed. This was Tway's fourth victory of the season in his seventh year on the PGA Tour.

BOB TWAY He won the 1986 US PGA in spectacular style when he holed out from a bunker.

He finished second on the money list, with some $650,000, and was named PGA Player of the Year. Since then he has had four more victories on the tour, the last of them, in 2003, coming eight years, four months and 21 days after his previous win, at the 1995 MCI Classic – a span of 233 events.

Harry Vardon

SEE PAGE 210

Ken Venturi

Born: May 15, 1931
San Francisco, Ca, USA

Venturi will never forget the Congressional and the 1964 US Open. He had suffered a disastrous slump in form and had qualified to play in the championship for the first time in four years. Earlier his career had been as promising as anyone's. While still an amateur in 1956 he had come very close to winning the Masters after opening with rounds of 66 and 69, followed by a 75 in poor weather. Alas, in the final round he took 80, but had still been in the lead with two holes to play. Another Masters disaster followed in 1960. With two holes left, he had a one-stroke lead over Arnold Palmer. But the great man was unkind enough to birdie the last two holes and that was that. Even so, at this stage Venturi had the consolation of ten wins on the PGA Tour, including four in 1958. Thereafter his consistency went, and he also suffered problems with his hands. In 1964, his game began to come back and he made a sound start to that US Open, followed by a 66 on the final morning. In extreme heat, he had to be accompanied by a doctor on the final afternoon, but managed to make it through to victory. That was the happy end to Venturi's story, for his game soon faded because of poor health.

LEE TREVINO
Unorthodox Can Work

Lee Trevino is an odd-looking golfer indeed, but at his peak around the early 1970s this effervescent Mexican-American could beat the best. Trevino's method centres on having a hooker's grip with his left hand

and then doing a variety of things to ensure that he plays with a slice. It seems Trevino was never willing to change his grip and so he had to produce counter-measures to avoid a right-to-left shape of shot.

For a start, he takes up the classic slicer's stance, very open to his target line. The club is then taken away on an outside path, but eventually is inside to out in the impact area. To stop that clubhead being shut at impact, Trevino drives strongly with his legs and also pulls the club through with his left side and arm. Ben Hogan once remarked that he liked watching Trevino because he worked his hands so beautifully through the ball.

Even though his swing proved effective, no one praised it as he took centre stage. It was described as being that of a weekend hacker.

In his 20s, Trevino served in the US armed forces overseas and returned to work in local golf. He did not attempt to qualify for the PGA Tour. However, he did play in the 1966 US Open. His 54th position made no headlines, but it was a respectable performance when he had previously

LEE TREVINO Of the major tournaments, only the Masters failed to come his way.

done little more than win the Texas State Open, which was not a tour event. The following year, he gave it another go and came in fifth. Again no headlines, but it gave Trevino the feeling of certainty that he could compete with the best.

He proved it at Oak Hill in 1968 when he destroyed Bert Yancey in head-to head play over the final round to win by four, the first man to break 70 in all four rounds of a US Open. Some thought this was a fluke win, that Trevino had happened to hit peak form for one week, and that this was his first and also his last tournament win. In fact he was about to embark on a great career.

In retrospect, his peak years ran from his US Open victory to around the mid-1970s, though he remained a player to be reckoned with for long after that, with his last major victory coming with the US PGA as late as 1984. Again, at Shoal Creek, all his rounds were below 70.

Partly through his consistency, Trevino always won very large amounts of money on the PGA Tour and never had a bad year. For a time it seemed as though he would be a likely rival to Jack Nicklaus for world supremacy. After being leading money-winner on

the PGA Tour in 1970, he went on to have an even better year in 1971. In the space of five weeks he took the US Open, the Canadian Open and the British Open. And in the US Open he had beaten Jack Nicklaus in a play-off. In 1972, he beat Jack Nicklaus again – and Tony Jacklin – for the British Open. But Nicklaus continued on his winning ways while Trevino's peak years were already over. No threat to Nicklaus for supremacy in world golf, he continued to pile up tournament victories instead.

Trevino is unusual in his relationship with spectators. Most players look as if they are having rather a bad day at the office. Sometimes they seem anguished, distressed, pained or just plain bored. Trevino is always full of chat. He does quiet down when in contention, but not completely.

For a time during the 1980s he seemed to be losing interest in tournament golf. In the sunset of a great career he was perhaps thinking more of TV, company days and the like. But the Senior Tour came as a gift when he reached 50. In a 15-year career on the Senior Tour he has won 29 times and earned $13.3 million to stand at 31st in the all-time money-winners' list.

1939	1967	1968	1971
Born on December 1 in Dallas, Texas	Wins his first tournament, the Hawaiian Open	Wins US Open	Wins his second US Open and follows it with British Open

1972	1974	1984	1985
Successfully defends British Open	Wins his fifth major, the US PGA	Wins his second US PGA eight years after being struck by lightning at Western Open	Losing Ryder Cup captain at the Belfry

HARRY VARDON
The Father of Modern Golf

Harry Vardon was golf's first supreme stylist, his swing a study in effortless grace. No one has ever managed to equal his haul of six British Open championships that straddled either side of the 20th century. He also won the US Open in 1900.

It was Vardon who popularized the overlapping grip, although it is a common misconception to think he invented it; the concept belonged to the famous Scottish amateur player Johnny Laidlay – and perhaps others.

In addition to that, his name is immortalized through the award of two prestigious trophies on either side of the Atlantic that both carry his moniker. The Harry Vardon Trophy goes to the player with the leading stroke average on the PGA Tour and the winner of the Order of Merit on the European Tour.

Vardon was introduced to the game in Jersey, where he worked as a caddie. When his brother Tom went to England and made some money at the game, Harry soon followed.

His first job was at a nine-hole course in Ripon in Yorkshire, but it was as the professional at Ganton that he first made his name. When he arrived, in 1896, J H Taylor was the great name of the day, but the members were so confident that their man could defeat the then British Open champion that they raised the money to stage an exhibition match. Vardon won 8 and 6.

The confidence that victory gave him was obvious a month later at Muirfield when he succeeded Taylor as British Open champion, beating him by three strokes in a 36-hole play-off after the pair had tied after 72 holes. Together with James Braid, this pair would dominate the British Open for an era, and they became known as the Great Triumvirate.

Vardon was the best golfer of the three. He had a revolutionary swing

HARRY VARDON No man has won the British Open more times than this man from Jersey.

Compared to the conventional "St Andrews swing", which involved a wide stance and a flat path back and through, producing a lower ball flight, Vardon's swing path was very much higher and, naturally, the resulting downswing was very much steeper. This resulted in a high ball flight and led to Vardon's consistency at holding the ball on both the fairways and the greens – it also placed him at a distinct advantage when the ground was hard. It soon became apparent that nobody could equal Vardon when it came to playing wooden club shots to the flag, and both his driving and ball striking became legendary: indeed, his ball striking was so pure that he saw no need to take a divot. From 1896 to 1903 he was absolutely at the peak of his powers, and with four British Open titles under his belt already, anything seemed possible.

But just as the future dawned with exciting possibilities, Vardon was struck down by tuberculosis, from which he never really recovered, although there were two more British Open victories. The first of those came in 1911, when he beat Arnaud Massy in a play-off. Vardon's last hurrah came at Prestwick in 1914 – the last British Open before the First World War –

when, fittingly perhaps, he beat J H Taylor by three strokes.

There was also one memorable showing in the US Open in 1913 that would mark the awakening of interest in golf in America. Over the closing holes, Vardon was disputing the title with Ted Ray, before a little-known American amateur from the host club of Brookline called Francis Ouimet tied both of them with the back nine of his life. The next day it was Ouimet who won the play-off. A country erupted.

Vardon's play through the greens in that championship was as good as ever, but he suffered some pathetic putting lapses. They would get worse, too, and he would become one of the first sufferers of that dreadful affliction now known as the yips.

In his book, *This Game of Golf*, Henry Cotton recalled "the unbelievable jerking of the clubhead in an effort to make contact with the ball from 2ft or less from the hole".

Amazingly, for such a thoroughly accomplished striker of the ball, it was not until well into his retirement years that Vardon managed his first hole-in-one. He died in 1937, and is buried close to the South Hertfordshire club where he was the professional for many years.

1870	1896	1898	1899
Born on May 9 in Jersey, Channel Islands	Wins the British Open for the first time beating J H Taylor in a play-off	Wins the second of his British Open titles	Successfully defends his British Open title

1900	1903	1911	1914
Wins the US Open	Raises the Claret Jug for the fourth time	Wins the British Open beating Arnaud Massy in a play-off	Wins sixth and final British Open title at Prestwick

Scott **Verplank**

Born: July 9, 1964
Dallas, Tx, USA

For a player who has had to contend with both injury and illness throughout his career, the diminutive Texan has achieved great things on the golf course. He first came to the attention of the golfing world when he won the Western Open as an amateur in 1985 – becoming the first amateur for 29 years to win an event on the PGA Tour (the last to do so was Doug Sanders at the 1956 Canadian Open). His second tour title came at the 1988 Buick Open. Then came the injuries which limited his appearances for the next four years. Regaining his card via qualifying school in 1993, he rebounded to finish 18th on the money list and won the individual honours at the World Cup the same year. He returned to the winner's circle for the first time since 1988 with victory at the Reno-Tahoe Open and followed that up by ending the 2001 season in the top ten in the money list for the first time in his career: his reward was being selected as one of the two captain's picks for the Ryder Cup team. In 2004, he finished in the top 30 in the money list for the fourth straight season. In 2006, he became the first American golfer to get a hole-in-one during a Ryder Cup match.

Roberto **de Vicenzo**

Born: April 14, 1923
Buenos Aires, Argentina

De Vicenzo is still best known for an error in checking his scorecard on the last day of the 1968 Masters, which also happened to be his birthday. He played the round of his life, a 65, but he failed to notice that his playing partner had marked him down for a par four on the penultimate hole, which Roberto had birdied. He was a little distracted by his bogey five on the last hole of all. He thought he had lost the event by his errors there, but it was the calligraphy on the 17th that cost him the chance of a play-off. "What a stupid I am," he said. He was less stupid at Hoylake the previous year in the British Open. A third-round 67 gave him a two-stroke lead over Gary Player and a three-stroke advantage over the defending champion, Jack Nicklaus. He held on to win, his round climaxed by three superb tee shots. At 44 years and 93 days he was the oldest British Open champion of modern times. De Vicenzo won over 30 national titles around the world. His overall total of wins is not known, but at well over 200, he may well be the most prolific winner of all time. Roberto, a very easy-going character, has likely not kept count.

Lanny **Wadkins**

Born: December 5, 1949
Richmond, Va, USA

Wadkins plays brilliantly when the inspiration flows. Almost as quick a player as there is, he goes for the flag rather than for safe parts of the green. Sometimes everything comes off; sometimes it doesn't. Perhaps this accounts for his fluctuating results in money winnings on the PGA Tour since his career began in 1971. His iron shots at the flag are probably the strongest part of his game, while his putting has been more variable. When his game is on song, Wadkins seizes his chances and he wants to win rather than just finish well up the field and pocket a respectable cheque. As a result, he has been a frequent winner on the PGA Tour and totalled an impressive 21 victories: he has also won almost $6 million. Wadkins has played on seven Ryder Cup teams, but his one turn as captain in 1995 turned sour in that while one of his personal selections, Fred Couples, did well, the other, Curtis Strange, lost all three matches as Europe regained the trophy. He now competes regularly on the Senior Tour and commentates on US television.

Art **Wall**

Born: November 25, 1923
Honesdale, Pa, USA

Art Wall may not be considered among the very élite of his profession but he has, by most considerations, enjoyed a remarkable life. He won the Masters with one of the great finishes that even that tournament has seen and then, over the course of a long career, was still winning events on the regular tour at the age of 51. He also managed a few holes-in-one – 45 at the last count and believed to be a world record. Wall's big year came in 1959 when he won four times on the PGA Tour, including an unforgettable Masters triumph. There appeared little hope for him as he came to the 13th hole on the final day, the last leg of Amen Corner. All his prayers were answered from there on in, however, as he played the sequence in no less than five-under par to win by a stroke from Cary Middlecoff, with Arnold Palmer a further stroke behind. Wall turned professional in 1949, and once he had notched his first victory, in 1953, he managed a regular stream of victories until 1966. Given that he was 42 years old at that point, it seemed that time had caught up with him, but there was still to be one more victory no fewer than nine years later in the Greater Milwaukee Open. Wall played in three Ryder Cup matches, the pick of them coming in 1961 at Royal Lytham, when he claimed three points out of three, including a singles victory over Henry Weetam.

Tom **Watson**

SEE PAGE 212

Karrie **Webb**

Born: December 21, 1974
Ayr, Queensland, Australia

Karrie Webb certainly hit the ground running when she made it onto the LPGA Tour. That she got there at all was in doubt; she was forced to play the qualifying tournament with a broken wrist, but she still finished second to earn her card. Her rookie year was nothing short of sensational. She captured four tournaments on the way to breaking the million-dollar barrier in earnings in her first season. Only Nancy Lopez, with nine wins, has done better. The following year she collected the Vare Trophy for the lowest scoring average on tour; her 70.00 was the lowest in the 45-year history of the trophy. She had to wait until 1999 before collecting her first major, the duMaurier Classic, and got her second the following year, the Nabisco, by the stunning margin of ten strokes. The following year saw her win both the US Women's Open and the LPGA Championship as she became the youngest player in the history of the game to complete the career grand slam (at 26 years, 6 months and 3 days). She successfully defended the US Open the following year and claimed a third British Women's Open in 2003. The young guns may have pushed her out of the limelight in recent years, but her game has still been good enough to win the 2006 Nabisco Championship, her seventh major, along with a 36th LPGA Tour win in 2009.

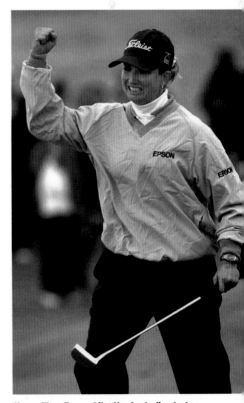

KARRIE WEBB For a while, the Australian had no equal on the LPGA Tour.

TOM WATSON
Fresh-faced Kid From Kansas City

Tom Watson made his majestic mark on the game with five British Open victories in only nine entries, and wrested away from Jack Nicklaus the crown of the world's leading golfer.

Early in his career (he turned professional in 1971) Watson earned the reputation of being a "choker", a man who was found wanting when the pressure was on. That was first turned around when he won the 1974 Western Open, shortly after having "choked" in the US Open, blowing the one-stroke lead he held going into the final round with a disastrous 79.

It was the British Open that began to establish him as a force to be reckoned with. In 1975, he arrived unheralded at Carnoustie, having finished poorly in both the Masters and the US Open, and without even the time to play a full practice round. Eyes were on others as Watson went quietly about his business. He was hardly noticed by the television cameras until he holed a long birdie putt on the final hole to set a target which no one could better. However, one matched it, Jack Newton, but Watson narrowly won the 18-hole play-off the following day.

This success sparked winning ways, and he soon became the dominant player on the PGA Tour, being five times leading money-winner in the period from 1977 to 1984. It seemed as though this might be the man who would dethrone Jack Nicklaus as world number one. Psychologically, that came in the 1977 British Open at Turnberry, when, playing the last two rounds head to head, Watson became champion when some great play brought a one-stroke margin over Nicklaus.

Watson was now the man to beat in this event. His next success was even more emphatic. He swept into a comfortable lead at Muirfield after a 64 in the third round and cruised home by four strokes.

Troon in 1982 saw tougher going for Watson. There were others, such as Nick Price and Bobby Clampett, who "ought" to have won. As he said: "I didn't win it. It was given to me." Even so, it was Watson who shot a firm last round while others wavered.

It was a different story at Royal Birkdale the following year. Several players subdued the course, which was not playing at its most difficult. In the final round, Watson lost his narrow lead and didn't regain it until he birdied the 16th. He came to the last, a long par four, needing a par to win. The way he achieved it was classic. First he banged a long drive down the middle and he followed up with a superb long iron to the heart of the green. That was that.

With five British Opens to his credit in only nine entries, Harry Vardon's record six victories were nearly in his grasp and he was ready to make that mark at St Andrews in 1984. However, a loose long iron to the 71st hole (the 17th) finally killed his chances.

Like Tony Jacklin after his 1972 Open disaster, Tom Watson has not been quite the same man since. He is still a threat in majors, and his first US win in nine years, at the 1996 Memorial Tournament, was hugely popular.

His long game remains imperious but his short game – especially his putting – is not what it was. At his peak, Watson used to give the hole a chance, with a firm rap. If he went a few feet past he was confident he could hole the return. In more recent years he has been far more tentative. There are still good days, though, such as in 1998 when he won the Mastercard Colonial, his last win on the PGA Tour; in 1999, when he won the Bank One Championship, his first Senior title in just his second start on

TOM WATSON He was the man who knocked Jack Nicklaus from the top of the golfing tree.

the tour; and, most magically of all, at the 2009 British Open at Tunnberry. Aged 60, he threatened to write the greatest story in the game's history, leading the tournament through 71 holes only to falter at the last and, emotionally spent, lose to Stewart Cink in a play-off.

1949
Born on September 4 in Kansas City, Missouri

1974
First US Tour win, the Western Open

1975
Wins his first major, the British Open

1977
Wins two majors, the Masters and the British Open

1980
Collects his third British Open

1981
Wins his second Masters title

1982
Has another two-major year, the US Open and the British Open

1983
Joins Peter Thomson as a five-time British Open champion

1993
Successful Ryder Cup captain, as the US win at The Belfry

Lee Westwood

Born: April 24, 1973
Worksop, England

By the end of the 2000 season, Lee Westwood had the golfing world at his feet. Six victories throughout the year saw him end Colin Montgomerie's seven-year tenure at the top of the European Order of Merit. What's more, an early-season victory at the Dimension Data Pro-Am meant that he had won a tournament on every continent – a claim that cannot be made by too many golfers. Two things then coincided to knock Westwood out of his stride. The birth of his son and a break from the game coupled with some restructuring work on his swing saw him fall away to 75th on the Order of Merit in 200, but he showed a glimpse of his former self in the Ryder Cup that year. Westwood ended three years of drought with victory at the BMW International Open in 2003 and followed that up with another win at the Dunhill Links Championship a month later. But then came another drought. To his great credit, he battled away and returned to the winner's circle twice in 2007 and moved back into the top 50. By the end of 2008, he was back in the world's top 20, and confirmed his return amongst the game's elite in 2009: he finished third in that year's US Open, British Open and US PGA and won the inaugural Race to Dubai. He suffered another near-miss at the 2010 Masters, finishing second.

Mike Weir

Born: May 12, 1970
Sarnia, Ontario, Canada

At the age of 13, Mike Weir wrote to Jack Nicklaus asking him whether, in his opinion, he should switch to being a right-handed player. Nicklaus' response was to stick to his natural swing and the Canadian can be glad that he took Big Jack's advice. Weir broke onto the PGA Tour in 1998 after five successful years on the Canadian Tour. His first tour victory came on native soil the following year, at the Air Canada Championship: his victory made him the first Canadian to win a tour event on home soil since 1954. In 2000, Weir became the first Canadian to represent the International Team in the President's Cup and went unbeaten throughout the competition. His breakthrough season came in 2003, a year which included three tour wins, including his first major title – the Masters. He recorded just the fourth bogey-free final round by a winner in the 67-year history of the tournament (and the first since Doug Ford in 1957). A bogey at the first extra play-off hole was enough to see off Len Mattiace and saw him become the first left-hander to win a major since Bob Charles took the 1963 British Open. He started 2004 with victory at the Nissan Open, and finished in the top ten in two majors that year, but has recorded only one win on the PGA Tour since 2009.

Tom Weiskopf

Born: November 9, 1942
Massillon, Oh, USA

Nicknamed "Terrible Tom" by the Press, Weiskopf was sometimes his own worst enemy. A perfectionist, gifted with a magnificent swing, he didn't feel it was "proper golf" to miss greens and scramble pars by means of a chip and single putt. His play in the 1969 Masters was characteristic. He missed only four greens in the tournament, but still managed to finish second, having three-putted 13 times. More dramatic was his play in the 1980 Masters. This time he came to the par-three 12th having played competent golf. This shot to the green must be exact for distance: just a touch short and you are in Rae's Creek; a little long and it's difficult to salvage a par. Tom emerged with a 13. His great period was quite short. Towards the end of 1972 he won the World Matchplay Championship. The following year he won four PGA Tour events and the British Open at Troon in generally unpleasant weather.

Joyce Wethered

SEE PAGE 214

Kathy Whitworth

Born: September 27, 1939
Monahans, Tx, USA

Whitworth played on the LPGA Tour from 1959 until 1991, and was consistently successful between 1962 and 1985. Her money-winning achievements were truly remarkable. She was leading money winner eight times and on another ten occasions finished no worse than ninth. She racked up a total of 88 victories, beating Mickey Wright's record of 82. She was captain of the United States Solheim Cup team in both the inaugural event in 1990 and again in 1992.

Craig Wood

Born: November 11, 1901
Lake Placid, NY, USA

Craig Wood earned a reputation as a man who always just missed out on major championships. Easily the most famous one was the second Masters in 1935. Wood was in the clubhouse and no one on the course had a chance of catching him, unless you counted Gene Sarazen, who had to birdie three of the last four holes to tie. No one has done that in a major before or since. Playing that perilous second shot over water at the 15th, Sarazen let fly with a four-wood – and holed out for an albatross. Not surprisingly, Wood lost the 36-hole play-off by a wide margin – five strokes – the next day. By this time he had also lost the first Masters by a stroke to Horton Smith and had a close encounter in the 1933 US Open. That same year he tied Denny Shute for the British Open and, of course, lost the play-off. The US PGA in 1934 wasn't any kinder to him: he lost the final on the 38th hole, his massive driving overcome by short-game expert Paul Runyan. Wood later lost the 1939 US Open to Byron Nelson, again in a play-off. Double consolation came in 1941, with the Masters plus the US Open, from which

Tom Weiskopf He won the 1973 British Open, but there should have been more majors.

he was persuaded not to withdraw with back trouble.

Ian Woosnam

Born: March 2, 1958
Oswestry, England

Only 5ft 4½in tall, Woosnam is probably the longest-hitting short man ever. A superb striker of the ball, he hits a right-to-left shape of shot, his one pronounced weakness being with the putter. However, even on the greens he is often very good indeed – no one can have his kind of tournament-winning record without a very considerable putting talent. Woosnam has not performed as well in the major championships as his abilities would suggest. His single major came in the 1991 Masters, though he went close to a US Open win. His most consistent performances came on the European Tour, where he notched up 33 victories. In 1987, he and David Llewellyn won the World Cup for Wales. Woosnam appeared in the Ryder Cup on eight occasions and captained them to success in 2006. In 2001, he became the first player to win the World Matchplay event in three different decades when he beat Padraig Harrington in an epic final.

JOYCE WETHERED
The Greatest Woman Golfer

One of the best-known remarks ever made about any woman golfer was that of Bobby Jones about Joyce Wethered. Jones said of Wethered that she had the best swing of any golfer, male or female, he had ever seen, adding: "I have never played with anyone, man or woman, amateur or professional, who made me feel so outclassed."

Outclassed! Bobby Jones! The man who, in 1930, became the only man ever to win the grand slam, the Open and Amateur championships of the USA and the United Kingdom. And yet it was that same year that he played a match against Wethered at St Andrews, with both hitting from the very back of the back tees, and with Wethered, by then retired from championship golf, going round in 75. It was after that match that Jones gave that considered opinion, which has gone into golf folklore.

Nor was the great man alone in his opinion. Gene Sarazen, looking back at the age of 95 in 1997, said emphatically: "Joyce Wethered was the greatest woman golfer who ever lived." That two Americans could ignore the claim to that title of players like Mickey Wright and Babe Zaharias perhaps tells you all you need to know about the excellence of the English player.

Wethered was playing her best golf in the 1920s, winning the English championship five times in a row starting in 1920, and also winning the British championship on four occasions. Such was her pre-eminence that Sir Henry Cotton said of her: "In my time, no golfer has stood out so far ahead of his or her contemporaries."

That was a judgement endorsed, even in those chauvinistic times, by a general recognition that had the Walker Cup team been open to players of both sexes, then Wethered would not only have been an automatic choice, she would probably have played no lower than four down the order.

Part of the secret of her success was her intense concentration. Her first English championship was won at Sheringham, that lovely, cliff-top, north Norfolk golf course which is sandwiched between the sea and a railway line running the length of the coast.

Nowadays only holiday specials use the line, but then it was in regular use and golfers commonly had to wait until a train had passed in order to play. This was particularly so at the 17th, where the green is only a few yards from the line and where, in one of her matches in the championship, Wethered faced a crucial putt.

She studied it, went briskly to it and holed it – despite the fact that at that precise moment a train was thundering past, all smoke and sparks. Afterwards Wethered was asked if she had considered waiting for the train to pass before attempting the putt and replied famously: "What train?"

She won 33 successive matches in the English championship, largely thanks to her ability to shut out extraneous matters, and always looked in complete charge of both her situation and herself. The latter, though, was not always the case. She once said: "I was very nervous and used to shake tremendously... But I was quite alright the moment the match was over."

Or she was usually. It was after her epic victory over Cecil Leitch in the British at Troon in 1925 that Wethered decided to retire. The reason? She wrote: "A yard putt to win faced me on the 37th hole, a thing that I had always prayed not to have. It went in, and I went and sat down on a hillock by the beach ... I was dead tired. My legs had left me. Usually when you won the elation would carry you on, but not that time."

The retirement lasted until St Andrews in 1929, when she was lured back for the British championship by the fact of the venue. "There is a magic about St Andrews," she said, "and I couldn't resist it."

It was there that she won her fourth title, beating Glenna Collett (later Mrs Vare) in one of the classic matches of all time. Bernard Darwin, golf correspondent of *The Times*, summed it up thus: "It was a great match, greatly played. As to Miss Wethered, if she prefers once more to retire into private golf, she can do so with the knowledge that she has given as complete proof of surpassing greatness as any game player of either sex that lived."

JOYCE WETHERED She had no equal in the women's game and even pushed Bobby Jones.

1901	1920	1922	1924
Born on November 17	First of five successive wins in the English Amateur	Wins the first of her British Amateur titles	Second triumph in the British Amateur

1925	1929
Successfully defends Amateur title, but decides to retire from the game	Comes out of retirement to win fourth British Amateur title, at St Andrews

TIGER WOODS
Record-breaker

Woods's explosive arrival on the scene created an unprecedented interest in the game: television ratings soared, galleries swelled and money flowed into the game like never before. The young American had managed to do what no player had achieved before him – make golf cool.

Woods won the US Junior Amateur Championship from 1991 to 1993 when no one before or since had won more than one. In 1994, he became the youngest winner of US Amateur, aged 18, a title he successfully defended the following year. He went one better in 1996, completing the hat-trick and recording two wins on the PGA Tour.

If America had taken note of Tiger Woods in 1996, then the whole world stood up and admired the following year. At the 1997 Masters, his first major tournament as a professional, he shot rounds of 70, 66, 65 and 69 – a 72-hole record for the tournament – and romped to victory by 12 strokes.

He may have failed to live up to the hype the following year – he won only once – but Woods came back strongly in 1999 with eight tournament victories, including his second major: the US PGA Championship at Medinah. He finished the season by winning four consecutive tournaments – the first player since Ben Hogan in 1953 to manage to do so.

If 1999 was impressive, then 2000 was spectacular. For the record, Tiger Woods set or tied 27 PGA Tour records during one of the finest seasons of golf ever played. During the course of the year, he won three consecutive majors, completed the career grand slam, totalled nine PGA Tour victories and became the youngest player in PGA Tour history to have won 20 times. Here's a simple measure of how far ahead of his rivals he was: during the course of the year he was 53 under par in the majors – the next best mark was Ernie Els's still-impressive 18-under.

The record breaking started at the US Open played at Pebble Beach. Woods's total of 12-under 272 tied the 72-hole record for the competition and broke the low-score record in relation to par. This almost pales into insignificance when you consider the winning margin – a record 15 strokes, breaking the 13 set by Tom Morris Sr at the 1864 British Open. More records tumbled at the British Open at St Andrews: Woods cantered to an eight-stroke victory, set a new low mark in relation to par in both the British Open and

TIGER WOODS Can the American go on to surpass Jack Nicklaus's haul of 18 majors?

a major championship (19-under) and became the youngest member of the quintet of players to have completed the career grand slam. He then beat Bob May in a play-off to become the first player since Denny Shute in 1936-37 to defend a US PGA title successfully. When he won the Masters the following April, he became the first player in history to hold all four major championships at the same time: it was the Tiger slam.

Tiger had much to live up to: he won the US Open in 2002, but no more majors followed and his critics started to talk of a drought: he was even overtaken by Vijay Singh at the top of the world rankings.

But he was back to his intimidating best by the beginning of 2005 and capped his comeback by defeating Chris DiMarco at the first play-off hole to win his fourth Masters and his

ninth major. For the record, his victory at Augusta also saw him reclaim the world number-one spot.

He took a nine-week break from the game in May 2006 following the death of his father, and celebrated an emotional and dominant victory at that year's British Open at Hoylake; four weeks later he won the US PGA – his 12th major. He defended his US PGA title the following year and added a 14th major when he battled and overcame a serious knee injury to win the 2008 US Open at Torrey Pines. Knee surgery led to 18 months out of the game.

Woods won four times in 2009, narrowly lost out to YE Yang at the US PGA and then took a break from the game following a series of lurid revelations about his private life that left his image damaged. He returned amid great fanfare at the 2010

1975	1991	1994		1997	1999	2000
Born on December 30 in Cypress, Ca, USA	Wins the first of three successive US Junior Amateur titles	Becomes youngest ever US Amateur champion		Wins the Masters – his first major as a professional	Wins the US PGA Championship	Wins three consecutive majors – the US and British Opens and the US PGA

2001	2002	2005		2006	2008
Wins the Masters to become only player in history to hold all four majors concurrently	Collects eighth major when he wins the US Open	Picks up his fourth green jacket and his ninth major when he beats Chris DiMarco in a play-off at Augusta		Wins British Open and US PGA Championship	Collects 14th major with victory at the US Open

Ian Woosnam The Welshman will captain the European side in the 2006 Ryder Cup.

Lew Worsham

Born: October 5, 1917
Alta Vista, Va, USA

There are just a few shots which enter golfing legend. Worsham was involved in two of them, even if one was actually Sam Snead's rather than his. In 1947, the great Sam Snead holed a sizable putt to tie Worsham over 72 holes. In the 18-hole play-off, the pair were level as they played the 18th. Both then had quite short putts to lose or win – or carry on. Snead saw he was further from the hole and settled down to putt. Worsham, as he was quite entitled to do, questioned the distances and asked for measurements to be made. They were; Snead was right; he putted first – and missed. Worsham then holed out to be US Open champion. They say that no one remembers who finished second, and this is almost invariably true, but Snead's miss is far more a part of golfing legend than Worsham's US Open victory. In 1953, Worsham produced an authentic great shot of his own. He was playing in the Tam o'Shanter World Championship, and approached the 18th needing to get down in two from about 100 yards to tie Chandler Harper. He holed his approach.

Mickey Wright

SEE PAGE 217

Yang Yong-Eun

Born: January 15, 1972
Jeju-do, South Korea

The fourth of eight children of a vegetable farmer on a small island south of South Korea, YE Yang first picked up a golf club at the age of 19. He learned the game by copying the swings of customers at the driving range where he worked part-time picking up golf balls, and by studying instructional videos. Yang coupled his natural aptitude for the game with sheer hard work, practising on the range early in the mornings and late at night, before his progress was halted at the age of 21 by two years of military service. He turned professional in 1996 and although he was named the Korean Tour's Rookie of the Year in 1997, he had to wait until 2002 before registering his first victory - at the SBS Championship on the Korean Tour. More titles on the Korean, Japan and Asian Tours followed, but it wasn't until 2006, and victory at the European Tour-sanctioned HSBC Champion's tournament in Shanghai (by two strokes over Tiger Woods) that his career stated to gather pace. His first forays on the PGA Tour were difficult – he had to come through Qualifying School in both 2007 and 2008 – but, in 2009, he made history. In March, Yang recorded his first PGA Tour victory, at the Honda Classic; five months later, he became the first Asian-born player to win a major championship, overhauling Tiger Woods down the stretch to claim the US PGA Championship at Hazeltine.

Babe Zaharias

Born: June 26, 1914
Port Arthur, Tx, USA

The Babe was not the greatest woman golfer of all time, but she was possibly the greatest athlete. Just before the 1932 Olympics she entered eight events in the US National Championships and won six of them – and all this in well under three hours. At the Los Angeles Olympics she won the 80 metres hurdles, setting a new world record, and the javelin, and was second in the high jump. When she took to golf a couple of years later, the Babe was soon hitting the ball a very long way. It took her many years to master the game though, and for some of that time she was something of a freak show in exhibitions. Her peak began around 1946, when she won 16 consecutive amateur tournaments. This sequence included the US Women's Open, and she went on to take the British equivalent in 1947. Turning professional, she won about a third of all the events she entered, including the US Women's Open in 1948, 1950 and 1954 and was also leading money winner for four years consecutively. She died of cancer at the age of 41.

Fuzzy Zoeller

Born: November 11, 1951
New Albany, In, USA

Fuzzy Zoeller is one of the few pros who looks to be enjoying their day on the golf course. Despite career-long back problems, he always has a jaunty stride. He must also spend less time over the ball than any other figure in world golf. He takes his stance quickly, glances towards his target and swings. On the PGA Tour, Zoeller was a consistent performer from the mid-1970s, but seemed to be fading towards the end of the 1980s. However, he came back strongly in 1993 and 1994, in the latter year contending for the British Open. He had two major victories, both after play-offs. The first of these came in the 1979 Masters, the first time Zoeller had qualified to play. After a slow start, Fuzzy won on the second hole of a play-off with Ed Sneed and Tom Watson. His play-off win in the 1984 US Open was very different, with Zoeller cruising round in 67 to Greg Norman's 75. He has won twice on the Senior Tour – one of those victories came at the 2002 Senior US PGA Championship.

Babe Zaharias A gold-medal winner in the 1930 Olympic Games and a major winner in golf, she was one of the finest athletes ever to have lived.

MICKEY WRIGHT
The Perfect Swing

It is the measure of the true greatness of Mickey Wright that there was hardly a professional – man or woman – who did not look up to her. Many agree that she possessed the most technically proficient swing that the women's game has ever seen, and 82 career wins (including four US Women's Opens) testify to the fact that she had a temperament to match. It is estimated that she won over a quarter of the tournaments she entered.

Of those 82 victories, 44 came between 1961 and 1964, her invincible period when she averaged 11 wins per season. It was a time when she achieved an impregnable mix: she knew she going to win, her opponents knew she was going to win, and she knew that her opponents knew that she was going to win.

Not that she would ever have let on. Miss Wright was, even during her days of public performances, essentially a shy person – a golfer who, after the round was played, would retire rapidly to her hotel. Her idea of a good night out was dinner with some friends, when the talk would preferably be about something other than golf.

That would be difficult, though, if there were others golfers around, for she did so many remarkable things on the golf course that they all wanted to know the secret. There wasn't one, of course, except that, just like Severiano Ballesteros, she had an instinctive understanding of what to do in impossible situations. The difference between her and the Spaniard was that she got on with the job in hand with a minimum of fuss and a complete absence of the dramatics that always accompanied a Ballesteros special.

One of the reasons that Wright is not perhaps as well-known as she certainly should be is that the height of her career, in the early 1960s, clashed directly with the time that Arnold Palmer and Jack Nicklaus were breathing fire at each other and dominating the golf coverage. It was the time, too, of fledgling television coverage, and the cameras concentrated almost exclusively on the men.

This was a pity, because Wright was more than just a good golf swing. She was both attractive and intelligent, and had an aura about her that instinctively appealed. What was it about her, though, that made her special? The leading American golf writer, Herb Warren Wind, felt that her technique was much as a man would play.

In *The Story of American Golf*, Wind says: "She struck the ball with the same decisive hand action that the best men players use, she fused her hitting action smoothly with the rest of her swing, which was like Hogan's in that all the dysfunctional moves had been pared away, and like Jones' in that its cohesive timing disguised the effort that went into it."

Perhaps the most instructive part of that commentary is the players that Wind used as comparisons, although Wright herself thought of her swing slightly differently. Once, when it was pointed out to her that people had said she had the perfect golf swing, Wright replied: "There's no such thing... You don't score well just by swinging it nicely and hitting it well, but that was always extremely important to me. A good golf swing has always been much more important to me than scoring well."

She went on: "My strength was my good swing which allowed me to be a fine long-iron player. I was able to hit the ball high, carry it a long way. Jackie Burke Jr [a Ryder Cup player and captain] watched me hit

MICKEY WRIGHT If it were not for Palmer and Nicklaus, she would have had a higher profile.

a few balls back in the '50s. He said: 'I'll give you one tip. You hit the ball high. Learn to hit it higher. Don't ever forget that.' I thought that was one of the keys that helped make me a good player. You cannot hit the golf ball high with a bad golf swing."

Nor, of course, with a swing like Wright's do you hit many bad shots, and during her career she held just about every record available on the women's tour. Once, in 1964, she remarked on this to Leonard Wirtz, then the LPGA tournament director, who called her attention to the fact that there was one she didn't hold: the lowest score for 18 holes.

The very next tournament she went out and shot 62, a score that would not be beaten for 34 years, in an altogether different era.

1935	1958	1959	1960	1961
Born on February 14 in San Diego, Ca, USA	Wins the US Women's Open and the LPGA Championship	Collects second US Women's Open	Wins her second LPGA Championship	Triumphs in US Women's Open, the LPGA Championship and the Titleholders' Championship

	1962	1963	1964	1966
	Wins the Titleholders' Championship and the Western Open	Wins the LPGA Championship for the third time and the Western Open	Wins fourth and final US Women's Open	Wins the Western Open for the third time

PART FOUR:
THE FAMOUS COURSES

An integral part of golf's unique charm is that the game is played in such imposing settings. The golfing landscape encompasses Florida swamplands, Arizona desert, Persian Gulf oases, English country estate parklands and the bare dunescapes of so many links courses around Britain. The most famous links course of all may be the Old Course at St Andrews, pictured below, where the R&A clubhouse stands behind the 18th green.

KEY

CC	Curtis Cup
RC	Ryder Cup
TC	Tour Championship
USAM	US Amateur Championship
USO	US Open
USPGA	US PGA Championship
USWAM	US Women's Amateur
USWO	US Women's Open
WATC	World Amateur Team Championship
WC	World Cup
WKC	Walker Cup
MAST	Masters

BALTUSROL

USO	1903, 1915, 1936, 1954, 1967, 1980, 1993
USAM	1904, 1926, 1946
USWO	1961, 1985
USWAM	1901, 1911
USPGA	2005

MERION

USO	1934, 1950, 1971, 1981
USAM	1916, 1924, 1930, 1966, 1989, 2005
USWAM	1904, 1909, 1926, 1949
CC	1954
WATC	1960
WKC	2009

OAKMONT

USO	1927, 1935, 1953, 1962, 1973, 1983, 1994, 2007
USAM	1919, 1925, 1938, 1969
USWO	1992

PEBBLE BEACH

USO	1972, 1982, 1992, 2000, 2010
USPGA	1977
USAM	1947, 1961, 1999

THE UNITED STATES

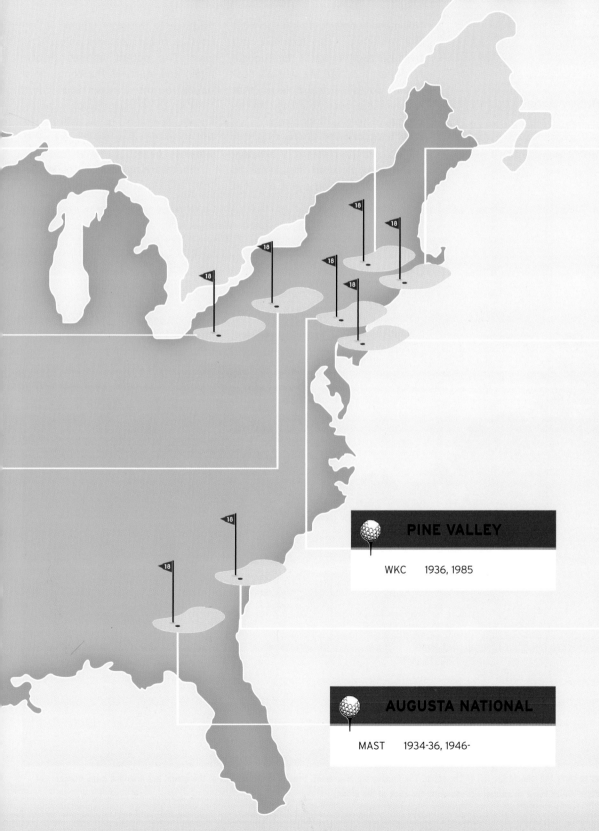

BROOKLINE

USO	1913, 1963, 1988
USAM	1910, 1922, 1934, 1957, 1982
RC	1999

WINGED FOOT

USO	1929, 1959, 1974, 1984, 2006
USAM	1940, 1999
USWO	1957, 1972
WKC	1949

PINE VALLEY

WKC	1936, 1985

PINEHURST

USO	1999, 2005
USPGA	1936
RC	1951
USAM	1962
USWAM	1989, 2008
TC	1991, 1992

AUGUSTA NATIONAL

MAST	1934-36, 1946-

AUGUSTA NATIONAL

Augusta, Georgia, USA

Opened: 1933
Designers: Alister Mackenzie, Bobby Jones
Yardage: 6,925
Par: 72
Major event: Masters 1934-42, 1946-

Not many people could tell you what the first nine holes look like, but from the tenth onwards the Augusta National is by far the world's best known course. Every hole on that last nine has become etched on the retinas of keen golf followers.

It hardly needs saying that this is because the Masters is the only major championship that keeps to the same venue every year, and that

Augusta is the only course which hosts a major championship every year. The potent images return again and again as the contenders battle for the Masters title - not least on the crucial stretch of holes known as Amen Corner. Will he go for a perilous flag set close to the water at the left of the 11th?

What will happen when the leader tries to judge the swirl of the wind

A view down to the 16th green at Augusta. The tee shot has to carry the lake on the left to the green. The Sunday pin placement, usually at the far left of the green, has provided many moments of magic over the years - none more so than in 2005, when Tiger Woods holed an outrageous chip from the back of the green.

The 13th hole at Augusta is perhaps the most famous, and certainly one of the most challenging, par fives in world golf.

above the tops of the trees on the short 12th? And then at the 13th, quite a short par five, he must surely go for the green with an eagle a possibility and a birdie almost certain if he carries the creek which fronts it... Yet many have found that creek and then been unable to get enough bite on their fourth shot.

Perhaps the most effective golf shot of all time was played at Augusta in 1935, in only the second year of what was then the Augusta Annual Invitational Tournament. With four holes to play, Gene Sarazen needed three birdies to tie Craig Wood, home and dry in the clubhouse. At the par-five 15th, Sarazen hit a good drive and then let rip with

his four-wood. His ball hit the bank beyond the water hazard and ran on and on, and into the hole for a double-eagle. With that one shot he had caught Wood.

Only a handful of spectators saw the shot, but among them was Robert Tyre Jones Jr, who had taken a stroll from the clubhouse to see how his old opponents, Gene Sarazen and his playing partner Walter Hagen, were finishing off their rounds – and how the course was playing. As well as being arguably the greatest golfer of all time, Bobby Jones was also highly influential in the creation of one of the world's great courses. But he was a modest man. Incontestably

the greatest player of the 1920s, he didn't think that this qualified him in the least to design a golf course. That was a job for a specialist. However, when Jones was first taken to see the Augusta property by an investment banker, Clifford Roberts (who would become the mainstay of the Masters organization until his death in the late 1970s), he immediately grasped the potential, and together they called in the British course architect Alister Mackenzie, whose work at Cypress Point in California had impressed Jones so much, when he had played there in 1929.

Opinions differ as to how much Augusta owes to Jones, Mackenzie,

course superintendents and later architects who were called in to undertake revisions. What is beyond dispute, however, is that Mackenzie produced the original design in consultation with Jones. In particular, Jones hit hundreds of shots to help show how a hole would play for players of high quality. Between them, they came up with a course where a club player might play to his handicap. The fairways are broad, the rough is almost non-existent, and the greens are not too fearsome – until they are cut to Masters pace, that is. It's this last factor, together with often-fiendish pin placements, which make Augusta a terror in Masters week.

BALTUSROL

Baltusrol, Springfield, New Jersey, USA

Opened: 1895
Designer: Albert W. Tillinghast
Yardage: 7,022
Par: 70
Major events: US Open 1903, 1915, 1936, 1954, 1967, 1980, 1993
US Amateur 1904, 1926, 1946
US Women's Open 1961, 1985
US Women's Amateur 1901, 1911
US PGA Championship 2005

Baltusrol's history had a somewhat macabre beginning. The club derives its name from Mr Baltus Roll, a wealthy farmer of Dutch extraction, who, in 1831, was murdered in front of his wife by two thieves who believed he had a fortune hidden in his house.

The Baltusrol property eventually came into the hands of Louis Keller, a gentleman farmer and socialite, who decided to build his own course in the early 1890s. His first professional was Willie Anderson, the Scot who won four US Opens between 1901 and 1905, one of those over that original course at Baltusrol. Today there are two courses, the Upper and Lower, neither of which bears any resemblance to their predecessor. Albert Tillinghast was brought in to handle the design around 1922, at a time when golf was experiencing another boom.

While the Upper occupies the high ground, it is the Lower that has been the venue for a host of major

Baltusrol is unusual in that it is one of the few courses to finish with two par fives. What is even stranger is that they are the only two par fives on the course.

Baltusrol has played host to the US Open on seven occasions. The most recent, in 1993, saw Lee Janzen shoot an equal-record-low score of 272 – it matched the mark set by Jack Nicklaus in 1980, also over the New Jersey course.

A hole that has a genuine photogenic appeal, it is also a hole of no in-betweens: you either find the green – which with its two levels provides the tournament committee with many options for pin placement – or your ball comes to rest in a watery grave. The water hazard that surrounds the green is unique: rather than there being a gentle slope from green to water, as is the case with most, the two are separated by a stone wall. The hole is also a triumph for the architect, Robert Trent Jones. Baltusrol's committee members questioned the fairness of his decision to lengthen the tee. In response, he pulled out a four-iron from his bag and hit the ball to within 6ft of the flag: "Gentlemen, I think the hole is eminently fair," he said. Thus the argument was settled.

championships, including seven US Opens. Far from picturesque, it makes up for it in the challenge that it presents to golfers of all standards. It is long, varied and something of an architectural anomaly in that it has only two par fives and they are the 17th and 18th, thereby providing a sting in the tail. The 17th measures a monstrous 630 yards, which is a three-shot hole even for the longest of hitters. Just a few have covered the distance in two lusty blows. In the last US Open held at the course, in 1993, many were expecting John Daly to provide the fireworks, and he didn't disappoint, but the Scot Sandy Lyle

was the first to reach the putting surface in two and he did it first with aplomb.

Long before you reach the 17th there are other mountains to conquer, starting with the dog-leg par-four third at a cool 466 yards. Around the landing area, the fairway turns left and slopes downhill towards a creek that cuts across just in front of the green. The green is big but undulating and one of the most difficult to putt on because of its subtle rolls.

The short fourth can measure between 150 and 200 yards depending on the placement of the tee, and requires just a solid iron shot

across a lake to a green that slopes left-to-right and back-to-front.

The straight sixth and the dog-leg 11th, both well over 400 yards and requiring two solid blows, can easily see shots surrendered, as can the 401-yard 13th, where the drive must carry the ditch which runs parallel to the fairway after crossing it. After the ultra-long 17th, the 542-yard 18th is played from an elevated tee down into the fairway then over a creek up to an elevated green protected by four bunkers at the front, left and right.

Baltusrol's US Opens have produced some famous winners as well as some daring deeds. In 1954,

Ed Furgol, hooked his drive on the final hole, then played his second through the trees onto a fairway of the Upper course before playing back to the 18th green to win. In 1967 and 1980, Jack Nicklaus emerged victorious. On the first occasion he carded a closing 65 to beat Arnold Palmer by four strokes. In 1980, he opened with a record-equalling 63, matched by Tom Weiskopf, then went on to win his fourth US Open with a record aggregate of 272. This was matched by Lee Janzen at Baltusrol in the 1993 Open – as the American shot four rounds in the 60s to win his first major tournament.

BROOKLINE

Brookline, Massachusetts, USA

Opened: 1893
Designer: Willie and Alex Campbell,
William Flynn
Yardage: 7,033
Par: 71
Major events: US Open 1913, 1963, 1988
US Amateur 1910, 1922, 1934,
1957, 1982
Ryder Cup 1999

Country clubs abound in the United States: it seems as though every town, every village even, has one. When it comes to golf, however, The Country Club in the upper-class Boston suburb of Brookline stands alone: it is a club that is intertwined with so much of the history of the game in the United States.

Brookline was one of the five founding member clubs of the United States Golf Association in 1894 and, in 1913, hosted the US Open: it was an event that would change the face of the game in the United States. Francis Ouimet's shock victory, beating two of the game's most established stars – Harry Vardon and Ted Ray – in a play-off, kick-started the game's popularity on that side of the Atlantic – at last the Americans believed that they could produce a star to take on and beat the best in the game. Golf in the United States has never looked back.

All of which seemed a long way off back in the 1890s, when three of the club's members approached the committee with a request to build six golf holes. They were allowed to do so, as long as the cost of the holes' construction did not exceed $50.

That price limit did much to shape the character of Brookline. The holes march through banks of trees and outcrops of rock: there wasn't the money to engage in the earth-shifting exercises of today. But the greens were small, and the rough long. It may look easy upon first glance, and in fairness there are tougher tests of a golfer's armoury around the world, but the course, and especially the greens, presents a tough challenge. That was shown when the US Open came back to the club in 1963, on the 50th anniversary of Ouimet's win: Julius Boros' winning score was the highest the tournament had seen for 18 years.

Anyone hoping to make a good score around Brookline needs to make inroads into the first eight holes: the first five holes are all par fours and all of them require a certain degree of bravery off the tee. If bravery was asked for on the first eight holes, then it is a prerequisite on the ninth – a hole that is rather aptly called The Himalayas. When you stand on the tee, you are confronted by a rocky outcrop that you either have to avoid or drive over. The test increases from the ninth hole onwards, a quartet of par fours where if you emerge with regulation figures you have truly earned your stripes.

The character of the championship

At first sight, Brookline may not seem to present the greatest of challenges, but with its tree-lined fairways and difficult-to-read greens, the course poses quite a threat. It has also played host to some of the most memorable moments in the history of golf in the United States.

If it were not for this hole golf would not be the sport it is today in America: three US Opens and one Ryder Cup have been decided here. In 1913, Francis Ouimet made a decisive birdie here to force his way into a play-off and then holed out for a birdie here the following day and went on to record his dramatic victory. When the US Open returned to the course in 1963, Tony Lema carded a bogey to fall out of a tie for the lead, Arnold Palmer followed suit to fall out of contention and Jacky Cupit, who needed only a par-bogey finish to win took six. The winner, Julius Baros, needed only one putt for a birdie. Then, in 1988, leader Nick Faldo overshot the green, took a five that effectively put him into a play-off with Curtis Strange: the following day the American won. And then came Justin Leonard's "miracle" putt to secure the half point that won the Ryder Cup for the home side in 1999.

course changes on ten: indeed, three holes from one of Brookline's three courses are used here (from the Primrose course) and the fairways become tighter and the greens more severe. And it is both on and around the greens where the player's game is truly tested.

As Ben Crenshaw said: "It [the course] tests your approaching ability from all angles, with all sorts of looks. The greens have beautiful, natural undulations, which are very difficult to pick up sometimes. They are anything but straightforward. This is a course that requires a lot of knowing."

The last comment is one of the reasons why Brookline was chosen by the Americans as the venue for the 1999 Ryder Cup. At the end of the second day it seemed as though the plan had backfired. On the last day, however, home knowledge prevailed and the home side produced the greatest comeback in the history of the competition. Brookline has been kind to American golf.

MERION

The original Merion course, in the 1890s, was squeezed into 100 acres, formerly used for cricket, on the outskirts of Philadelphia. When the rubber-cored ball made it obsolete, the club had to look further afield.

Soon a plot of 127 acres of old farmland together with a stone quarry was bought and the club assigned a group of young members to handle the designing. Among them was Hugh Wilson, an insurance salesman and first-class golfer. Before any work was carried out, however, Wilson spent seven months travelling around Britain, learning the fundamentals of constructing outstanding golf holes. On his return, he set to work with the assistance of Richard Francis to build the new course at Ardmore, opened in 1912. He continued to refine the course for another dozen years, but unfortunately, it was the only complete layout to bear his name, as he died prematurely in 1925 at the age of 46.

Merion is noted above all for its greens. They come in all shapes and sizes, beautifully shaped, cleverly contoured, sometimes on two levels, sometimes shelved into a shoulder of a hill, sometimes sloping away to the back. But each is protected by a bunker, a creek or heavy rough.

A curiosity of the course is that, instead of flags, Wilson decided to mark the holes with a wicker basket atop the flagsticks. He is believed to have got the idea from Scotland, where it used to be the practice to place lobster pots as markers.

Another feature of Merion is the infinite variety of its holes. There are long par fours and short par fours, two par fives, one of 600 yards, the fourth, while the short holes measure between 129 yards and 224 yards. There are right-hand dog-legs and left-hand dog-legs, while the final three holes provide what many feel is the toughest finish of any of America's US Open courses.

The 16th is the celebrated Quarry Hole of 430 yards, where the approach must carry the old quarry workings to a plateau green. The 17th is a 224-yard par three from an elevated tee back across the quarry to a green encircled by bunkers. The 458-yard 18th requires a blind drive across the quarry once again, then a medium- or long iron, often from a downhill

FEATURE HOLE: 11th – 370 yards, par four

Some holes are etched into the minds of the golfing public as much as for the achievements that took place on them as for their architectural splendour. One such hole is the 11th at Merion, for it was here that Bobby Jones completed his grand slam in 1930 – a feat that will never again be repeated as long as people play the game. Described by former USGA executive director and PGA Tour Commissioner Joe Day as "the classic pitching hole", it is a short par four that demands precision rather than force. Few will take a driver off the tee, looking instead to position the blind shot on the flat piece of land before the brook in front of the green – known by some as the "Babbling Brook" and others as the "Baffling Brook". From there it is a wedge to the green that is guarded at the front by a bunker.

lie, to a green flanked right and left by bunkers. Golfers who manage par figures over that trio can count themselves good players.

One of Merion's first claims to fame was in 1930 when it was the scene of the final act of Bobby Jones's grand slam. On its famous 11th, Jones, who was eight up on Gene Homans in the final of the US Amateur, drove safely, hit the green with his second and two-putted for par and a half to win 8&7, adding his national title to the British

Amateur won at St Andrews, the British Open at Hoylake, and the US Open at Interlachen.

Merion has staged many of America's national championships. Its first US Open came in 1934

when Olin Dutra won by a single stroke from Gene Sarazen, who fell away with a final round of 76. The 1950 event saw Ben Hogan, hardly recovered from his horrific road accident a year earlier, tie with Lloyd Mangrum and George Fazio, then win the 18-hole play-off by four strokes. In 1971, Jack Nicklaus finished tied with Lee Trevino, but it was the latter who prevailed in the play-off, 68 to 71. Merion's most recent US Open, in 1981, went to Australian David Graham with a final round of 67 which was little short of perfection – he missed one fairway, but still got a birdie, and hit every green in regulation.

Merion, squeezed into a tiny pocket of land, has played host to some memorable US Opens. Although not long, it is characterized by the variety and the difficulty of its greens. It is also unique: holes are not marked with flags, but with wicker baskets on the flagsticks.

OAKMONT

Oakmont, Pennsylvania, USA

Opened: 1904
Designer: Henry C. Fownes
Yardage: 6,921
Par: 71
Major events: US Open 1927, 1935, 1953, 1962, 1973, 1983, 1994, 2007
US Amateur 1919, 1925, 1938, 1969
US Women's Open 1992

Oakmont, on the outskirts of Pittsburgh, is arguably the most penal layout in America, with hard, slick greens, bunkers everywhere, narrow fairways with thick rough, and a length of almost 7,000 yards.

It begrudges low scores and these are almost impossible when it comes to major championships.

The club has also been renowned for doing its own thing, especially when it comes to staging US Opens.

The 1953 and 1962 championships were marked by heated disputes between the USGA and the club over how the bunkers should be raked. This was because the rakes used at Oakmont were oversized and left wide furrows into which the ball would drop. It led to a famous remark by Jimmy Demaret, who said: "You could have combed North Africa with that rake, and Rommel wouldn't have got past Casablanca."

In 1983 there was another disagreement with the USGA – about the length of the rough. In the event, the players were greeted by thick, dense grass, some nine inches high in places, and could only hack the ball back on to the fairway. The dispute lasted two days of the championship before the mowers were summoned.

Oakmont is not the most beautiful course in the world. It was built on a stretch of flatlands at the foothills of the Alleghenies by a steel magnate, Henry C. Fownes, in 1903. In those days, the course was split by a railway line which curved through a gorge. In 1952, the Pennsylvania Turnpike was constructed, but as it followed the path of the railway, the damage to the course was minimal.

Fownes certainly knew how to get things done. Work began in September 1903 with 150 workers and 25 teams of horses, and 12 holes were finished within six weeks; the other six holes in the spring. The whole layout opened that autumn with a "bogey" of 80, eight par fives, a par six, and a total of 220 bunkers. A year later it boasted no fewer than 350. Bunkers were something of a fixation with Fownes and the eighth underlines this. The hole is a par three of 244 yards, but contains the Sahara bunker, which is 75 yards long and 35 yards wide and required 11 lorry-loads of sand to fill it.

While the bunkers may dominate the course, it is the greens which visitors remember most. They have taken an awful toll on the top names over the years. In Oakmont's first US Open, in 1927, Tommy Armour, the Silver Scot, won with 301, 13-over par; then, in 1935, Sam Parks, a Pittsburgh man who knew the course like the back of his hand, won with 299, the only player to break 300.

After the Second World War, it was agreed to make Oakmont less intimidating. Some fairways were widened in the driving area and the number of bunkers was reduced to fewer than 200. In 1953, Ben Hogan came to Oakmont as Masters champion and spreadeagled the field with an opening 67. He won by six from Sam Snead and his awesome shotmaking was illustrated by the fact that he covered the final four holes in 13 strokes – against a par of 15.

In 1962, Jack Nicklaus won the first of his four US Opens at

Oakmont, characterized by its hard, fast greens and the enormity of its seemingly infinite bunkers, has fallen foul of the USGA over how these giant sandtraps should be raked on more than one occasion when it has played host to the US Open.

The most famous of Oakmont's bunkers is the "Church Pews" positioned between the third and fourth fairways.

FEATURE HOLE: 3rd – 426 yards, par four

Oakmont is a course renowned for its brutality: hazards abound that punish the errant shot. There is one hazard on the course that catches the eye more than any other, however. Positioned between the third and the fourth fairways lies a bunker that is, quite literally, the size of a football field. Lying within this large, sandy waste are eight mounds of earth, lying in strips and rising 3ft from the sand. These mounds have given the bunker its name: "the Church Pews". According to Tom Watson: "That is why they call it the Church Pews: you pray that you can get the hell out of that thing." The bunker is particularly threatening on the third: with that hazard on the left, and a trio of bunkers guarding the fairway on the right, accuracy is placed at a premium from the tee. The second shot plays uphill to a green that slopes away from the player.

Oakmont, beating Arnold Palmer in a play-off; then Johnny Miller took the title at Oakmont in 1973 with a closing 63 which was no doubt helped by very wet greens. After Larry Nelson's win at Oakmont in 1983, the 1994 event promised a possible British victory when Colin Montgomerie tied with Ernie Els and Loren Roberts. But, in the three-way play-off, Els clinched his first major success after he and Roberts had tied again with 74s, four ahead of the fast-fading Scot. It handed the South African his first major title.

PEBBLE BEACH

Pebble Beach, Monterey Peninsula, California, USA

Opened: 1919
Designer: Jack Neville
Yardage: 6,799
Par: 72
Major events: US Open 1972, 1982, 1992, 2000
US PGA Championship 1977
US Amateur 1947, 1961, 1999

There is perhaps no finer place on earth to play golf than over the links course at Pebble Beach - particularly the stretch of holes that run along the coastline of the Pacific Ocean.

Most great golf courses have been designed by acknowledged great architects. But there are exceptions, the most famous being the Old Course at St Andrews, where local golfers evolved a route through the linksland over the years. Pebble Beach was also an amateur creation, but came from the creativity of one man, Jack Neville. He was an amateur golfer of great local distinction, winner of the California Amateur on five occasions and a choice for the 1923 US Walker Cup team. The property developer Sam Morse thought he was the man to design him a golf course. It was a decision which

Trying to pick a feature hole at Pebble Beach is like trying to choose between a bottle of Chateauneuf du Pape and a Barolo - an almost impossible task. For guidance, perhaps it is best to take the advice of the man who won two national titles here, Jack Nacklaus, who describes the approach to the eighth as "the greatest second shot in golf". After hitting a perfect drive, the player still has some 170 yards left to the green: and they are quite some 170 yards - the player has to hit the ball over a deep oceanic chasm and must hit the centre of the green - a green that Alister Mackenzie spiced up by moving closer to the ocean and sloping towards the sea. The challenge of the shot is the only thing that will take your breath away more than the scenery that confronts you.

worked out very well.

In later years, Neville said: "The golf course was there all the time. All I did was find the holes." And what holes they are.

Though nearby Cypress Point has been described as the Sistine Chapel of golf, and also as "the dream of an artist who had been drinking gin and sobering up on absinthe", the Pacific holes at Pebble Beach are no less dramatic.

The drama begins at the fourth, which is a short par four, usually playing at about 325 yards but with the cliffs threatening any approach shot that drifts right. The fifth, like so many par fives, is not particularly difficult and, if the golf is not going well, there is at least the reward of a splendid view along to the tenth green. The seventh is apparently an easy par three at 120 yards, but the green is set at an angle to the line of play.

Then comes the eighth - one of the toughest par fours in world golf. The next two holes are well over 400 yards, play into the prevailing wind and call for tee shots close to the cliff edge to ease the shots to the greens.

The 17th, particularly at the close of a championship, is a very demanding par three, close on 220 yards, with a green set across the line of play and tightly bunkered. It was here, in the final round of the 1983 US Open, that one of the truly momentous shots in golf history was struck. Tom Watson had just dropped a shot at the 16th to be only level with Jack Nicklaus. Here his tee shot missed the green, leaving him a little pitch shot from the rough which seemed doomed to race past the hole. But Watson thought positively. He tried to hole it, and did so. He was back in the lead and needed only to par the final hole to win. In fact, he birdied it, to win his first and only US Open, and to deprive Jack Nicklaus of his fifth.

That spectacular last hole presents a classic tee shot situation. The bold line is along the cliff edge, having carried an inlet. To the right is less dangerous, but a pine can then block the second shot. This is one of very few par fives that have been seldom reached in two. Although Jack Nicklaus, playing in his final US Open at Pebble Beach in 2000, gave his fans one last hurrah by reaching it in two … it may not have settled many championships, but those who win have been brave. Or simply brilliant: as was the case when Tiger Woods obliterated the rest of the field in the last US Open to be played there, in 2000.

PINE VALLEY

Pine Valley, Clementon, New Jersey, USA

Opened: 1919
Designer: George Crump
Yardage: 6,765
Par: 70
Major events: Walker Cup 1936, 1985

A beautiful monster is how Pine Valley has been described. Laid out on a huge 184-acre bunker, with forests of pine, larch and oak trees, a generous amount of water and thick, dense undergrowth, it is the most terrifying course in golf. There are no continuous fairways, just islands of green amid the never-ending sandy wasteland, plus tees and greens which can be regarded as refuges to which the golfer inevitably struggles out of the mire.

Pine Valley is the work of Philadelphia hotelier George Crump, the leader of a band of golfers from the Philadelphia Country Club who made occasional trips to play at Atlantic City. One day on their journey by train, Crump spotted a piece of land which he felt would be ideal for golf and, on investigation, found virgin forest, swamps and impenetrable bush, but all on a sandy soil.

After spending some days at the site, Crump persuaded 18 of his friends to contribute $1,000 each, and the land, reported to be the highest ground in southern New Jersey, was bought in 1912. The course took seven years to build,

There are few sterner tests in golf than that to be found at Pine Valley. Due to its layout, though, it has never staged a major tournament.

From the moment you step onto the tee at the tenth hole at Pine Valley, one bunker looms large - the infamous D A.

and Crump took to living in a small bungalow on the site, directing the felling of trees, the building of dams to form lakes, the layout of holes and the positioning of greens.

However, in January 1918, Crump suddenly died with only 14 holes completed. He had spent $250,000 of his own money, but there was enough left in his estate to complete the remaining four holes. Hugh Wilson, the creator of Merion, and his brother Allen were called in to direct the remaining work.

The end product drew plaudits from course designers and leading players alike, but there have been thousands of ordinary golfers who have been shattered by Pine Valley's penal qualities and have left the course wishing they had never bothered.

It is not so much the problems that lie in wait in the apparently endless sand, as the pressure that builds up in the mind through having to hit from one green oasis to the next, with little room for error, and the increasing sense of desperation with each disaster.

The story goes that club members have a standing bet that first-timers at Pine Valley never break 80. One who did was Arnold Palmer, who went there in 1954 as US Amateur champion. As he was about to get married, he took all the bets he could find, knowing that if he had lost he couldn't afford to pay them. In the event he shot 68 and left with a sizeable wedding present.

Then there was the late Woody Platt, a good amateur, who knew

Pine Valley well and started with a birdie three at the first, where the drive is over the inevitable sandy wasteland, followed by a dog-leg right to a green that steeply drops away. The second is just 367 yards, but again the tee shot must carry 180 yards of sand, then a second to an elevated green surrounded by even more sandy wastes, Platt left nothing to chance and holed a seven-iron for an eagle.

On the short third, there is nothing between the tee and green but 185 yards of sand. Platt went for it and holed-in-one. The fourth measures 461 yards with a blind tee shot over more sand to an island fairway which turns right. Even more sand must be carried to the green, and Platt hit a driver, a four-wood and

then holed from 30ft for a birdie to be six-under par. As the fourth returns to the clubhouse, he retired to contemplate the next 14 holes, especially the 226-yard fifth across a lake. He fortified himself with a drink and never came back out.

Despite its fame and reputation, Pine Valley has never staged, nor sought to stage, a major championship, its layout being unsuitable for large crowds. Perhaps it is just as well, as it could damage many a reputation.

PINEHURST

Pinehurst, North Carolina, USA

Opened: 1895
Designer: Donald Ross
Yardage: 7,020
Par: 72
Major events: US Open 1999, 2005
US PGA Championship 1936
Ryder Cup 1951
Tour Championship 1991, 1992
US Amateur 1962, 2008
US Women's Amateur 1989

Paradise can be a somewhat overused word when linked to golf courses, but in the case of Pinehurst it fits the bill perfectly. There are more than 35 courses in a 30-mile radius, and the club has seven of its own, designed by the likes of Ross, Fazio, Trent Jones and Maples. Little wonder that the great Bobby Jones dubbed Pinehurst the "St Andrews of United States golf".

Like so many top courses around the world, Pinehurst is situated among sandhills, thus affording magnificent terrain and, as the name implies, acres of towering pines that form majestic avenues for every hole.

Pinehurst was the brainchild of a Boston soda fountain magnate, James W. Tufts, whose idea was to set up a resort in the south where New Englanders could avoid the harsh winters in their home state. He eventually found what was then a desolate area of North Carolina. There was a natural progression to golf in the latter part of the 19th century, and a club was formed in 1895.

In 1900, Harry Vardon is reported to have played the original 18 holes and, later that year, a Scot, Donald Ross, who had been professional and greenkeeper at his local club, Royal Dornoch, was appointed as club professional.

Within a year of arriving in North Carolina, Ross started to build a second course. Opened in 1907, Pinehurst No. 2 has become the signature layout and has staged a number of top championships. Ross also re-designed the original course, then went on to build No. 3 (1910) and No. 4 (1919) during a 48-year stay at the resort. More recently, Ellis Maples was the creator of a fifth course (1961), Tom Fazio added a sixth (1979), and the seventh was completed in 1986 by Rees Jones. But that isn't the end of the story. An eighth course, The Centennial, designed by Tom Fazio was opened in 1996 to add yet another jewel to Pinehurst's glistening crown.

But it is Pinehurst No. 2 that evokes such delight and nostalgia. Ross called it "the fairest test of championship golf I have ever designed". The great Sam Snead said he rated it as his "number one course" because it constantly challenges the player. "You have to be alert and sharp for 18 consecutive holes; otherwise it will jump up and bite you. I guess that's why the experts rate No. 2 as one of the ten greatest courses in the world." It has staged a number of major events over the years, from the US Open, the US PGA and the Tour Championship to the US Amateur, Women's Amateur and the Ryder Cup in 1951.

It is a course where you have to drive the ball well, hit your long irons well and, most of all, have a razor-sharp short game. The greens are small by modern standards because they fall off around the edges, allowing balls to run off into dips and swales.

Getting on to No. 2 is not easy, but it becomes a lot easier if you stay at the luxurious Pinehurst Resort Hotel, known as the Queen of the South, as tee times are

Every major championship in the United States has paid at least one visit to Pinehurst over the years – a true testament to the course's quality.

reserved for guests. Access to the other courses is much easier, while staying at the New England-style village is an exercise in quiet and pristine living. Here you can enjoy wandering the sandy path from the resort to the village's quaint shops and boutiques, stocking everything from sportswear to antiques, fine wines and every gift imaginable for the golfer.

In every way, Pinehurst is, indeed, a golfer's paradise.

Every aspect of a golfer's armoury is tested on the North Carolina course – you have to drive long and straight, hit solid irons and putt well if you want to succeed here.

WINGED FOOT

Winged Foot, Mamaroneck, New York, USA

Opened: 1923
Designer: Albert W. Tillinghast
Yardage: 6,980
Par: 70
Major events: US Open 1929, 1959, 1974, 1984, 2006
US PGA Championship 1997
US Amateur 1940, 1999
Walker Cup 1949
US Women's Open 1957, 1972

When Albert Tillinghast was commissioned to design a new layout in Westchester County, not far from New York City, he was tersely instructed: "Give us a man-sized course." The message was delivered by the gentlemen of the New York Athletic Club, from whose emblem the golf club takes its name, and the end result was the best golf course in Westchester County.

To create his masterpiece, Tillinghast had to move 7,200 tons of rock and cut down almost 8,000 trees. In fact, he created two courses, but it is the longer and more treacherous West course which has played host to four US Opens.

The key to Winged Foot is its 12 gruelling par fours, ten of which measure 400 yards or more. These require long, straight driving, then a controlled second shot, often with a long iron, to greens that are fiercely contoured and guarded by deep bunkers.

Tillinghast's thinking was that "a controlled shot to a closely guarded green is the surest test of any man's golf". By the standards of some of America's top courses, Winged Foot's total of 60 bunkers is on the conservative side, until you consider that every green has at least two deep ones.

There are not many bunkers on the Winged Foot course, but every green is protected by at least two of them: the course's designer, Albert Tillinghast, considered the shot to the green to be the sternest examination of a golfer's talent.

The club has not only produced a lot of low handicap players with excellent bunker skills, it has also had more than its fair share of national champions. At one time in the early 1940s it had both the US Open and Amateur champions in Craig Wood and Dick Chapman. Claude Harmon, who became pro six years later, won the US Masters in 1948; his assistants included Jack Burke and Dave Marr, both major winners, while Dick Mayer, the US Open champion

Greg Norman dug deep and produced some remarkable recovery shots in the 1984 US Open played at Winged Foot, but eventually lost out in a play-off to Fuzzy Zoeller.

in 1957, was a Winged Foot member before turning professional.

Winged Foot comprises two nine-hole loops, extending like two parallel arms. There are two 400-yard-plus holes to start, followed by the 216-yard third to a green flanked by two bunkers that run the length of the putting surface. Another long par four heralds the first of two par fives, the dog-leg fifth of 515 yards that is again heavily trapped near the green. After a shortish par

four and a moderate par three, the front nine finishes with two more long par fours completing an outward 3,446 yards. The back nine starts with a par three and finishes testingly with five successive par fours, all over 420 yards.

Bearing that in mind, it isn't surprising that of the four US Opens held there, only one has seen a winning score under the par of 280 for four rounds. Bobby Jones won the first US Open there in 1929.

He tied with Al Espinosa on 294, then won the 36-hole play-off by a stunning 23-stroke margin.

The championship didn't return for 30 years but, in 1959, Billy Casper took the title with 282, single-putting 31 greens in the process. In 1974, Hale Irwin won with 287, beating the unusually named Forrest Fezler by two strokes; then, in 1984, came the memorable tie between Fuzzy Zoeller and Greg Norman. The Australian produced some amazing recovery

shots over the final four holes, including holing a 30ft par putt on the last, to finish on 276, four-under par. Zoeller, waiting down the 18th fairway, thought the putt was for birdie and waved a white towel in surrender. Moments later, he holed out for the same score. In the following day's 18-hole play-off, Zoeller won comfortably by eight shots.

That championship proved that Tillinghast had indeed produced a man-sized course.

KEY

BAM	British Amateur
BO	British Open
BWAM	British Women's Amateur
CC	Curtis Cup
RC	Ryder Cup
WBO	Women's British Open
WC	World Cup
WKC	Walker Cup
WMP	World Matchplay

ROYAL COUNTY DOWN

BAM	1970, 1999
BWAM	1899, 1907, 1920, 1927, 1935, 1950, 1963, 2006
CC	1968
WKC	2007

BALLYBUNION

No Major Events

TURNBERRY

BO	1986, 1994, 1997, 2004, 2009
BAM	1961, 1984, 2008
WBO	2002
WKC	1963
BWAM	1912, 1921, 1937

GREAT BRITAIN AND IRELAND

CARNOUSTIE

BO	1931, 1937, 1953, 1968, 1975, 1999, 2007
BAM	1947, 1966, 1971, 1992
BWAM	1961, 1973

ST ANDREWS

BO	1873, 1876, 1879, 1882, 1885, 1888, 1891, 1895, 1900, 1905, 1910, 1921, 1927, 1933, 1939, 1946, 1955, 1957, 1960, 1964, 1970, 1978, 1984, 1990, 1995, 2000, 2005, 2010
BAM	1886, 1889, 1891, 1895, 1901, 1907, 1913, 1924, 1930, 1936, 1950, 1958, 1963, 1976, 1981, 2004
WKC	1923, 1926, 1934, 1938, 1947, 1955, 1971, 1975
WBO	2007
CC	2008

MUIRFIELD

BO	1892, 1896, 1901, 1906, 1912, 1929, 1935, 1948, 1959, 1966, 1972, 1980, 1987, 1992, 2002
BAM	1897, 1903, 1909, 1920, 1926, 1932, 1954, 1974, 1990
RC	1973
WKC	1959, 1979
CC	1952, 1984

HOYLAKE, ROYAL LIVERPOOL

BO	1897, 1902, 1907, 1913, 1924, 1930, 1936, 1947, 1956, 1967, 2006
BAM	1885, 1887, 1890, 1894, 1898, 1902, 1906, 1910, 1921, 1927, 1933, 1939, 1953, 1962, 1975, 1995, 2000
WKC	1983
CC	1992

WENTWORTH

RC	1953
CC	1932 (East Course)
WC	1956
WBO	1980
WMP	1964-2007

ROYAL ST GEORGES

BO	1894, 1899, 1904, 1911, 1922, 1928, 1934, 1938, 1949, 1981, 1985, 1993, 2003
BAM	1892, 1896, 1900, 1904, 1908, 1914, 1929, 1937, 1948, 1959, 1972, 2006
BWAM	1922, 1964
WKC	1930, 1967
CC	1988

SUNNINGDALE

WKC	1987
BWAM	1956
WBO	1997, 2001, 2008

BALLYBUNION

Ballybunion, County Kerry, Ireland

Opened: 1896
Designer: Anon
Yardage: 6,503
Par: 71
Major events: None

Tom Watson, one of the greatest exponents of links golf of all time, proclaimed that all golf architects should play the Ballybunion course before practising their trade.

FEATURE HOLE: 11th – 454 yards, par five

No less a judge than Tom Watson has declared that all golf architects should live and play at Ballybunion before practising their art. Praise indeed. If one had the chance to select any 18 holes from any course in the world to create the perfect course, then you would have to find room somewhere among that number for the 11th at Ballybunion: put simply, it is one of the toughest holes in world golf. With dunes running along the left side of the fairway, and the sea beneath the cliff upon which this hole runs along the right-hand side, any hopes of achieving par or better on this hole disappear with every stroke that is not caught absolutely flush. The hole, just like the course, is totally in tune with its surroundings.

This course is unlikely to hold major events because, like Dornoch, it is so remote, but with the new Cashen course as well, you have here perhaps the best 36 holes of links golf in the world. The Old, by itself, ranks very high on everyone's list.

If the first hole is a comfortable enough start with a drive to a wide fairway, and downhill at that, the second is more testing by far. You have to miss bunkers from the tee but also have to be long to have much chance of making it up to the green. The third is 220 yards, but plays downhill to a severely undulating green. At the sixth, after two relatively easy par fives, you head for the Atlantic Ocean. It is not a long par four – 364 yards – but the wind can play havoc. At the next two holes you play directly from the

cliff edge and have a glorious view along the Atlantic shore. You play away from the shore at the eighth and normally have a following wind. This is no great help, as the hole is a short par three and the green will be more difficult to hold because of the reduced backspin.

Apparently, on one visit, Tom Watson played the hole four times and didn't once succeed in keeping his ball on the green. At the ninth, the drive is between sandhills but

One of the most spectacular holes in world golf, the eleventh at Ballybunion is also one of the most testing.

can be helped onwards by a couple of steps in the fairway. There is a central bunker short of the green and a steep rise to the putting surface.

This has already been outstanding golf, but many believe most of the real Ballybunion comes on the second nine. The tenth heads back towards the ocean, bending leftwards through a valley, and at the 11th tee it is worth stopping to take in the view.

Then a downhill shot confronts the player – but not an easy one. There is the beach on one side and sandhills on the other. Even a good shot can get into difficulties on the severely undulating fairway. If all has gone well with the tee shot, the second must be well aimed between the sandhills which protect the green.

The 12th, a par three of 192 yards, usually plays into the wind and,

because the green is in the sandhills and is quite steeply sloping at the front, needs a full carry on the shot. The 13th, 484 yards, is not in the least a long par five, but it is a hole that demands caution.

For those going for the green in two there is a stream perhaps 80 yards short. Then come two par-three holes, of which the second presents an extremely testing shot to

a well-protected, two-tiered green.

The 17th has the most spectacular tee shot on the course, high up with dunes on either side. You are also heading straight for the United States of America. There is a sharp dog-leg left.

If the last hole is a bit of a disappointment, you can at least be sure of a warm welcome in the clubhouse.

CARNOUSTIE

Carnoustie, Angus, Scotland

Opened: 1842
Designer: Allan Robertson
Yardage: 7,272
Par: 72
Major events: British Open 1931, 1937, 1953, 1968, 1975, 1999, 2007
Amateur Championship 1947, 1966, 1971, 1992
British Women's Amateur 1961, 1973

When the Royal and Ancient Golf Club announced that the 1999 British Open Championship would be held at Carnoustie, a huge sigh of relief could be heard from the whole world of golf. The return of the world's most prestigious championship to these great links was long overdue. Also rejoicing will be the ghosts of all those past champions who have sampled the links, as well as the many sons of Carnoustie who, in years long past, went out to spread the golfing gospel around the world.

Carnoustie's spell in golf's back-waters had nothing to do with the quality of the course; more with what is required off it. The lack of a suitably large hotel in the town was given as the main reason, difficulty of access as another. The growth in popularity of the British Open made these important considerations, but a lengthy, concerted effort by the good folk of Angus and golf fans in general, plus a new hotel scheme, saw the world's top golfers back where they belonged in 1999.

Carnoustie's history seems to have begun in 1842, when a large tract of land was bought from the Earl of Dalhousie and a ten-hole links was laid out by Allan Robertson. This was extended to 18 holes in 1867 by Tom Morris; Willie Park Jr made further alterations, but it was James Braid who remodelled the links in 1926 to produce what we recognize as today's supreme test.

Carnoustie has neither the deep-seated traditions of St Andrews or Muirfield, nor the breathtaking beauty of Royal County Down or Turnberry. But what it does is throw down the gauntlet to players, and a glance at its British Open roll of honour proves that only a real champion successfully takes it up. Tommy Armour, Henry Cotton, Ben Hogan, Gary Player and Tom Watson are as good a quintet as you could find and each one etched his style into Carnoustie's folklore.

Armour, one of many Scots who left for America, triumphed in 1931 at the expense of Macdonald Smith. Cotton's win in 1937, the second of his three British Opens, was gained against the victorious American Ryder Cup team. Hogan's victory in 1953 on his only appearance at the British Open was, many feel, the greatest seen at Carnoustie. Each of his four rounds was lower than the one before, and he finished with a round of 68. Player completed his second British Open success there in 1968 when the course measured 7,252 yards, the longest in Open history. The 1975 contest brought a young Tom Watson to the attention of golf fans as he beat Jack Newton of Australia in an 18-hole play-off. And, in 1999, Paul Lawrie benefited from Jean Van de Velde's final-hole meltdown to claim the Claret Jug after triumphing in the play-off.

Carnoustie is basically a flat course, but don't let that fool you. It is rugged and can be brutal if you stray from its fairways. It also has some famous features which set it apart from its rivals. It has only three short holes, all far from easy, and three par fives, one of which, the 14th, is named "Spectacles" after the twin bunkers that stand guard in the face of the ridge that

The roll of honour of British Open champions at Carnoustie bears testament to the fact that courses do not come much tougher. Golfing purists breathed a collective sigh of relief when the British Open returned there in 1999.

FEATURE HOLE: 17th - 433 yards, par four

The finish at Carnoustie has often been described as the most punishing sequence of holes in the game: just ask Jean Van de Velde, whose capitulation on the final hole cost him the 1999 British Open. The toughest is the 17th, however, which is characterized by the sweeping flow of the Barry Burn that flows along and through the fairway. Indeed, the hole is called the "Island", because that is exactly what the burn creates in the fairway. A fine drive will carry the burn twice before coming to rest on the island section of the fairway: none too simple a task when the wind is lashing off the North Sea. The ideal line off the tee is to the right-hand side: anything too far left will end up in the water. You are then left with a mid-iron to a green protected front left by three bunkers.

runs across the fairway less than 100 yards from the green.

Yet it is the finishing stretch that poses the greatest threat. It begins with the long 14th, then comes the 461-yard 15th, whose green is set into an attractive bowl, followed by the 250-yard 16th, a tough par three that has a well-guarded plateau green.

The Barry Burn crosses the 17th fairway three times, putting a premium on precise shot-making; and if you negotiate this par four safely, you have to do it all again on the return trip, with the burn lying in wait ahead of the tee and the green on this 486-yard home hole. A finish to be feared.

HOYLAKE

Hoylake, Merseyside, England

Opened: 1869
Designer: Anon
Yardage: 6,780
Par: 72
Major events: British Open 1897, 1902, 1907, 1913, 1924, 1930, 1936, 1947, 1956, 1967
British Amateur 1885, 1887, 1890, 1894, 1898, 1902, 1906, 1910, 1921, 1927, 1933, 1939, 1953, 1962, 1975, 1995, 2000, 2006
Walker Cup 1983
Curtis Cup 1992

Hoylake is considered to be one of the toughest tests in British golf, and can be stretched to around 7,000 yards. This is largely why the British Open has been held here ten times. In 1897, it was only the second English course to be used (after Royal St George's, Sandwich) – the tournament was won by the great English amateur Harold Hilton, who beat James Braid by a single stroke. Here, in 1902, Sandy Herd became the first champion to use a wound ball and, in 1924, Walter Hagen took the second of his four British Open titles. In a final round of unusually high scoring, the American shot a 77 to Ernest Whitcombe's 78 – it included a putt of 8ft on the last – to win by one stroke. A reporter asked Hagen afterwards: "Did you know that you needed that putt to win?" Hagen's typical reply: "Sure, but then no one ever beat me in a play-off..."

However, easily the most momentous British Open came in 1930, when Bobby Jones secured his third championship win in just four entries and completed the English swing of his eventual grand slam of all four British and US Amateur and Open titles. The last British Open was played here in 1967, when Roberto de Vicenzo memorably outplayed Jack Nicklaus and Gary Player over the last two rounds.

It is very unlikely that Hoylake will ever host a British Open again, for the simple reason that there isn't enough room for today's Open crowds, particularly on the closing holes. However, the course is still used for top amateur events

Hoylake has hosted some memorable British Open championships, but its size means that it is unlikely to hold another.

On first appearance, Hoylake may look like a piece of flat land and little more. That initial perception will change the moment you reach the stretch of holes through the sand dunes: at that point, the course is as tough a test of links golf as you can find in the United Kingdom.

– the Curtis Cup, Walker Cup and the British Amateur. It also hosts European Tour events.

The course is extremely variable in appearance. On arrival, the impression is of a flat expanse with some undulating ground in the far distance by the Dee Estuary. That bit looks the most dramatic, but in fact many players find that the flatter holes are the most testing, while the stretch from the eighth to

the 11th has the most visual appeal.

The first is one of the flat holes, but it is a frightener. You have to try to keep your tee shot as close as you dare to the practice ground along the right – but that is out of bounds. You are not in much trouble going left until you play the second shot. Then you have to contend with firing directly towards the out of bounds. The seventh also used to cause much fear. There was

a turf bank just to the left of the green and out of bounds lay beyond the putting surface. That penalty has now been removed. Judgement of distance and quality of strike, however, are just as vital as they ever were. As the course occupies a small area, out of bounds is an almost constant threat.

The course is beautifully maintained, the greens are sometimes the best in Britain, and

the clubhouse is full of interest, including what amounts to a museum of golf in the entrance hall.

Hoylake has seen quite a few firsts. In 1885, the club had the idea of staging a big amateur tournament, which was won by Allan Macfie. A generation later, this was recognized as the first British Amateur Championship. In 1921, the first golf international of any kind between British and American men was played over the course, and it was a forewarning of the imminent American dominance that the British were trounced. In 1925, the English Amateur was inaugurated at Hoylake and, quite appropriately, was won by a Royal Liverpool member, T F Ellison.

MUIRFIELD

Muirfield, Gullane, East Lothian, Scotland

Opened:	1891
Designers:	Old Tom Morris, Harry Colt
Yardage:	6,941
Par:	72
Major events:	British Open 1892, 1896, 1901, 1906, 1912, 1929, 1935, 1948, 1959, 1966, 1972, 1980, 1987, 1992, 2002
	British Amateur 1897, 1903, 1909, 1920, 1926, 1932, 1954, 1974, 1990
	Ryder Cup 1973
	Walker Cup 1959, 1979
	Curtis Cup 1952, 1984

It is often said that Muirfield was designed by Old Tom Morris, and he did indeed lay out the first course. However, his original design was by no means ideal, and little more than the site of one green seems to have survived. The Muirfield of today is largely the work of Harry Colt during the mid-1920s. It was Colt, for instance, not Morris, who produced the two loops of nine holes, each ending at the clubhouse. Since Colt's time, the course seems to have changed little, which is not surprising, for Colt was an architect of genius, whereas Morris certainly was not.

Some say that all courses ought to begin with a hole that causes worry; others that there should be a comfortable start and that the really testing stuff should come at the end. The first hole at Muirfield is one that all the competitors in a British Open are very glad to leave with a par four written on their card. It is long and has threatening bunkers, but overall the most difficult holes are the par threes, each offering a tight target to a raised green, with the fall-away often being to deep bunkers, where it can be necessary to play out sideways or even backwards.

Little of Old Tom Morris's original layout of the Muirfield course survives today; the great golf architect Harry Colt is the man who was responsible for producing one of the toughest British Open championship venues.

One of the best holes is the ninth, a par five. It is reachable for modern professionals in two, but there are dangers. Out of bounds lurks along the left, which seemed to have destroyed John Cook's chances in the 1992 British Open when he produced a snap hook over the wall, but he then played superbly – only to throw it all away on the last two holes of the championship. On this hole, Tom Simpson, the noted architect, placed a bunker more or less in

One of the characteristics of links courses is that – with the exception of St Andrews, perhaps – they have finishing holes which test the ability of the golfer to the absolute limit. This is true of the 18th at Muirfield, which is one of the great finishing holes in golf. It is a hole that demands a long, straight drive and a well-struck mid-iron to set up an orthodox par. It provided the arena in which the world's golf audience finally saw Nick Faldo's career take off. In the 1987 British Open, he struck a five-iron that never left the flag to secure victory. For the Englishman, it was confirmation that all the swing changes he had made over the years worked: if he could find the 18th green at Muirfield, with all the attendant pressure, then he had a game that could succeed anywhere.

When the wind raged off the Firth of Forth in the 2002 British Open at Muirfield, it blew away the title aspirations of some of the biggest names in the game.

the middle of the fairway short of the green. It is now known as "Simpson's Folly", but greatly affects the character of the shot into the green.

Muirfield is one of the most popular links courses for British Open competitors. The movement of the ground is gentle, which generally means that there are very few blind shots. In a Press tent interview at the 1992 British Open, Jack Nicklaus described the course as "just a flat field". Seriously, however, he had

liked it well enough to name his most prized design in the United States "Muirfield Village", though this may partly have been due to his wish to commemorate his first British Open win here in 1966.

The course was extremely testing that year, with the rough allowed to grow so long that Doug Sanders remarked that he didn't mind about the championship but that he would like to have had the hay concession. Nicklaus won largely by keeping his ball out of the rough and choosing to

play irons off the tees – it also helped that at the time he was perhaps the best long-iron player in the world.

Another memorable British Open came in 1972, when Nicklaus played a thunderous last round, coming from behind, while the main battle was fought out between Tony Jacklin and Lee Trevino.

As late as the 71st hole, Jacklin appeared to have the title in his grasp before he pitched a little weakly and three-putted. In the space of a very few minutes the

title was Trevino's after he chipped in on the same hole.

The course is the property of the Honourable Company of Edinburgh Golfers. Founded in 1744, they initially played their golf at Leith Links, and later at Musselburgh, before they moved to what is certainly their final home at Muirfield. Their clubhouse contains some fine paintings, a silver club and a copy of Thomas Mathison's *The Goff*, the first publication in the world that was devoted solely to golf.

ROYAL COUNTY DOWN

Newcastle, County Down, Northern Ireland

Opened: 1889
Designer: Tom Morris
Yards: 6,968
Par: 72
Major events: British Amateur 1970, 1999
British Women's Amateur 1899, 1907,
1920, 1927, 1935, 1950, 1963, 2006
Curtis Cup 1968
Walker Cup 2007

In comparison to today's staggering construction fees, the cost of the course at Royal County Down was very reasonable. Back in 1889, the club's provisional committee convened in the hall of Mr Lawrence's Dining Rooms, and agreed to invite Tom Morris over from St Andrews to lay out a course "at an expense not to exceed £4".

There were already nine holes in existence, which Old Tom played, and he left recommendations for an 18-hole layout which was soon completed. The "outlandish outlay" probably represented his fee, but if such a magnificent piece of land became available today, many of the modern designers would arguably settle for a modest pay day.

Those who have had the good fortune to play this gem some 30 miles south of Belfast will have been enchanted by the sheer beauty of the place, never mind the splendour of the links themselves with their abundance of gorse. This is where, as it says in the song, the Mountains of Mourne sweep down to the sea and, dominated by Slieve Donard, the highest peak in the range, they form a perfect backdrop, plunging some 3,000ft sheer, almost to the edge of Dundrum Bay. Surrounded by such beauty, it is easy to be distracted – a grave mistake given County Down's tough reputation.

In those early days, the club used the nearby railway station facilities but, by 1897, it had opened its first clubhouse. A year later, the club was affluent enough to put up a 100-guinea prize for a professional tournament between Harry Vardon, J H Taylor, Ben Sayers, Andrew Kirkaldy, Sandy Herd, and Willie Fernie, which culminated in Vardon beating Taylor by 12&11 in the final.

The course witnessed several changes in its first century. In 1904, the then professional, Seymour Dunn, suggested some changes; Vardon did the same in 1908, the year the club was granted its Royal Charter; but its current magnificence can be traced back to Harry Colt, who made the last significant changes in 1926.

Unlike many links courses which go out and back, County Down has two nine-hole loops of different character, courtesy of

FEATURE HOLE: 9th – 486 yards, par four

With views perhaps unrivalled on any course in the British Isles, Tom Watson described the outward half of this traditional links course as "as fine a nine holes of golf as I have ever played". The sequence of nine finishes with a 486-yard par four: one of the most photographed holes in the world. Starting with a blind tee shot – in the style of many of the traditional links courses (and to their detriment moan the critics) – the player aims to hug the large sand dune on the left: accuracy is a must, as any errant shot will be ensnared by the gorse-covered dune. This leaves the best line into the green that is protected by two well-placed bunkers some 50 yards short of the putting surface. The green itself, with its mounds and hollows, is one of the most difficult on the course.

George Combe, a founder member and captain of the club in 1895-96, who spent many years as chairman of the greens committee. Its other great virtue is that each hole is separate, occupying its own valley between the sandhills, with rarely a view of the next or the adjacent hole.

The front nine, or sea nine, is uncompromising. The premium is on long, straight shot-making which means that those who

With its narrow fairways, Royal County Down places a premium on accuracy from the tee ... he who brings his best driving game will prevail over this tough course.

With the Mourne Mountains hovering in the background and the Irish Sea present for most of the round, Royal County Down is a heavenly place to play golf.

can handle a driver will be at a distinct advantage. Those who stray from the often narrow fairways find themselves tangling with the dunes, wild roses and heavy bunkering.

On the landward or back nine, the problems are heavy rough in the form of seaside grass, heather and gorse, while many of the greens are small, with subtle slopes and hollows that highlight the merest blemish in a putting stroke.

There are those who criticize Royal County Down because the golfer is required to play a number of blind shots, but that is a minor irritant when there is so much to admire. Best of all is the view from the ninth tee, with the Mourne Mountains towering above the rooftops of Newcastle.

Big events have tended to bypass the club. It has staged two British Amateur Championships, in 1970 when Michael Bonallack won his fifth title, and his third on the trot, romping home 8&7 against American Bill Hyndman after being one down at lunch, and again in 1999, when Graeme Storm took the title. The women have been more frequent visitors, the British Women's Amateur having been held here seven times between 1899 and 1963.

ROYAL ST GEORGE'S

Sandwich, Kent, England

Opened: 1887
Designer: Dr W. Laidlaw Purves
Yardage: 6,857
Par: 70
Major events: British Open 1894, 1899, 1904, 1911, 1922,
1928, 1934, 1938, 1949, 1981, 1985,
1993, 2003
Amateur Championship 1892, 1896, 1900,
1904, 1908, 1914, 1929, 1937, 1948,
1959, 1972, 2006
British Women's Amateur 1922, 1964
Walker Cup 1930, 1967
Curtis Cup 1988

Royal St George's, on the shores of Pegwell Bay, is a great links course with an illustrious history. In 1894, it staged the first British Open to be played outside Scotland, which produced the first English winner in J H Taylor who was a five-stroke winner over Douglas Rolland. It also produced the first foreign winner of the British Amateur Championship, Walter Travis from Australia, who won at Royal St George's in 1904, and the first American winner of the British Open, Walter Hagen, in 1922. Another significant first was when Tony Jacklin holed-in-one at the short 16th during a final-round 64 on his way to winning the 1967 Dunlop Masters. It was the first time that such a feat had been captured on television.

Royal St George's was founded in 1887, when Dr Laidlaw Purves and some 50 friends formed a syndicate called the Sandwich Golf Association, obtained a lease on the links and turned them over to the club. The story goes that Purves spotted the land from a church tower in Sandwich after a long search for such a site.

Purves is credited with the original layout, but Royal St George's has seen some remodelling over the years, first by Alister Mackenzie, and more recently by Frank Pennink. It has long had a reputation as a driver's course, but it also provides some of the most

Royal St George's hosted the first British Open championship to be staged outside Scotland – it has stood the test of time ever since.

The great British golf writer Bernard Darwin described the links at Sandwich as "nearly my idea of heaven".

testing second shots found anywhere, starting with the opening two holes, both par fours.

The third is the first short hole of 214 yards, before the course progresses among the expanse of dunes along fairways that rise and fall continually to heavily guarded greens. At the fourth, a par four of 470 yards, you drive over a cavernous bunker, while the green at the 422-yard fifth is reached between two hills.

The first par five comes at the seventh, which has a slight dog-leg, while the eighth, another par four, has a belt of mounds and rough dividing the fairway from the green. After the ninth and tenth – two more par fours played in opposite directions – the 11th is another short hole of 216 yards before the dog-leg 12th around a sandy ridge heralds a loop of three holes skirting the neighbouring Prince's course.

At the 13th you have to manoeuvre between a maze of bunkers, while

the par-five 14th requires straight driving to avoid the out of bounds before crossing the famous Suez Canal midway down the fairway. After another testing par four at 15 comes the short 16th which, depending on the wind, can play anything from a two- to an eight-iron to a green encircled with traps.

The closing holes, two more par fours, again call for accurate driving and sound second shots. At 18, the front of the green is guarded by bunkers right and left which are to be avoided, but so is Duncan's Hollow, named after George Duncan, the British pro who failed to get down in two from there to catch Walter Hagen in the 1922 British Open, an area of thick grass below a steep bank that is a magnet for many shots.

The 1949 British Open, won by Bobby Locke, from an unlucky Harry Bradshaw, who chose – some say

unnecessarily – to play his ball out of a broken bottle, was the last Open at Royal St George's for 32 years. Despite its pedigree as a course, it was felt to be unsuitable to stage the ever-expanding event, but thanks to the building of a bypass around the old

town and other improvements, its long exile ended in 1981. In 1985, Sandy Lyle became the first British winner since Jacklin in 1969. As the only British Open venue south of Lancashire, and with its close proximity to London, it is unlikely to be left out on a limb again.

FEATURE HOLE: 14th – 551 yards, par five

The great British golf writer Bruce Darwin once wrote that Sandwich was "nearly my idea of heaven as to be attained on any earthly links". On a British Open course that has stood the test of time, rarely do the fairways fail to roll or rise at Sandwich: it is one of the truest, and toughest, links experiences on the planet. And the experience does not come much tougher than at the par-five 14th:

the hole provides the player with one of the hardest tee shots in golf – you have to be long, but you also have to be accurate. The ball has to carry over 200 yards of sand dunes, but beware, out of bounds runs all along the right-hand side of the fairway. A bunker lies in the centre of the fairway at 250 yards and a stream (named after the famous Suez Canal) bisects the fairway at 300 yards. Any thoughts of going for the green in two will be tempered by the bunkers that fall 60 yards from the green.

ST ANDREWS

St Andrews, Fife, Scotland

Opened:	Unknown
Designer:	Anon
Yardage:	7,090
Par:	72
Major events:	**British Open** 1873, 1876, 1879, 1882, 1885, 1888, 1891, 1895, 1900, 1905, 1910, 1921, 1927, 1933, 1939, 1946, 1955, 1957, 1960, 1964, 1970, 1978, 1984, 1990, 1995, 2000, 2005, 2010
	British Amateur 1886, 1889, 1891, 1895, 1901, 1907, 1913, 1924, 1930, 1936, 1950, 1958, 1963, 1976, 1981, 2004
	Walker Cup 1923, 1926, 1934, 1938, 1947, 1955, 1971, 1975
	Women's British Open 2007
	Curtis Cup 2008

This is one of the world's oldest and most revered golf courses and is deservedly known as "the home of golf". It is a favourite course of many top professionals and amateurs, perhaps because it is by no means fearsome in still air, but always demands good strategy and shot-making, though some of the first ten holes are easy in the extreme.

The first exciting hole is the fifth, where you need to be a little left because of a cluster of bunkers along the right. There is a steep upslope, set with more bunkers; on hard ground, with a following wind, Craig Wood drove into one of them during the 1933 British Open. The distance is about 430 yards! Even so, most professionals see this as a clear birdie chance.

The sixth is a typical links hole. When you stand on the tee, you may wonder what has happened to the golf course. Most players simply aim

at the marker post, but even if all goes well that far, the second shot is difficult. There is a rise before the green, and the putting surface then slopes away from the player. The seventh is the only dog-leg on the course, and even then only a slight one. It is best to be right rather than left, because Shell bunker is on line for an approach from the left, and the green slopes from left to right.

Golf has been played on the links of St Andrews for centuries – it is rightly considered as the home of golf.

FEATURE HOLE: 17th - 461 yards, par four

The 17th hole ends a trio of finishing holes at St Andrews that, were it not for the disappointing 18th, would be considered among the finest closing holes in world golf. What the 18th may lack, however, is more than made up for by what the 17th possesses. A left-to-right dog-leg, the player must hit the tee shot over a row of dark green sheds: the further to the right the better, but such a shot also requires the longer carry (180 yards at its shortest point). The second shot is the most famous, and arguably the most difficult, shot in golf. To go for the flag is to invoke danger: in the form of the Road Hole bunker – a hazard that has reduced even the most accomplished of players to a weekend hacker. The sensible play is to find the front of the green and two-putt for a par from there. To escape the 17th having not lost a shot is an achievement indeed.

Standing on the 18th tee, you are presented with one of the most famous views in golf. The only disappointment is the hole itself.

The real tests at St Andrews come on the route back to the clubhouse. The 11th, for instance, is one of the best par threes in world golf, feared because of the deep Hill bunker to the left of the green and Strath to the front on the right. The 13th has been ranked one of the great par fours, enhanced by the skyline of St Andrews. The second shot is played over a heathery bank to a flag which seems to be perched on the top.

Another great hole is the 14th, where the tee shot has out of bounds to the right and bunkers known as "The Beardies" to the left. If you succeed and get your shot down the middle, the large Hell bunker lies directly in your path to the green. For long hitters this 567-yard hole is a birdie opportunity, but few manage to get the ball close to the hole, and to be just short leaves a difficult putt or chip.

By this time, many will begin to worry about the 17th "Road Hole", a devilish par four of 461 yards. The tee shot needs to be nearly out of bounds along the right, because from the left it is extremely difficult to hit and hold the narrow, angled green, behind which are the road and a boundary wall, both potential card-shredders. Hardly any British Open competitors get past this challenge with four pars. In 1885, David Ayton took an 11 to lose by two strokes!

This is not true of the last, one of the weakest finishing holes in all of championship golf – though Doug Sanders memorably lost the 1970 British Open there by taking five!

Seve Ballesteros, 1984 champion here, expressed "great sadness" at the news that five holes were to be lengthened before the British Open in 2000. The Old Course, he said, is "a national monument". True enough, but it has been lengthened several times before and the changes in 2000 brought bunkers at five holes back into play that had ceased to worry leading players armed with modern high-tech equipment.

SUNNINGDALE

Sunningdale, Surrey, England

Opened: 1901
Designer: Willie Park
Yardage: 6,703
Par: 70
Major events: Walker Cup 1987
Women's British Open 1997, 2001, 2008
Women's British Amateur 1956

Sunningdale, like its neighbour Wentworth, is a gorgeous course on the Surrey sand belt. Originally three farms surrounded by heather, gorse and pine trees, the land was owned by St John's College, Cambridge, who, around the turn of the 20th century, were persuaded by their agent T A Roberts to turn their land over to golf and residential development. A committee was formed and Willie Park, twice British Open champion, was commissioned to design the Old course at a fee of £3,800.

Much of the site at that time was open country with few trees. The familiar wooded outlook we know today followed a general redesign by Harry Colt, who was Sunningdale secretary for 17 years before transferring his skills to full-time course architecture.

As a result each hole is self-contained, while nature's work over the years has been instrumental in seeing Sunningdale develop into one of the great inland courses.

Colt also found time to design a second 18 holes, the New course of 6,202 yards, par 68, which opened in 1922. The two courses, both tough layouts, complement each other and together make Sunningdale a delight to play.

Oddly enough, the Old course starts with two par fives, but the first, at 494 yards and slightly downhill, can be reached in two shots during a dry summer, while the second, just ten yards shorter, is another good birdie chance with accurate shotmaking. The third, a short par four, also presents the chance of picking up a shot, but the fourth, the first short hole, requires a solid shot up to a well-protected green. The next short hole, the eighth, which follows three par fours, is somewhat similar, while the 267-yard ninth is eminently drivable.

The tenth tee, at the highest part of the course, provides stunning views over the countryside. On this par five you drive down into a broad valley with bunkers to the right and left, leaving a long second shot to a receptive green. The 11th is another short par four with a drive over sand hills, and providing you avoid the trees and ditch on the right, only a short pitch is required to find the green.

The 12th is another testing par four, and after two teasing par threes and the final par five come three par fours that provide a daunting finish. The 18th is a superb finishing hole. Here, a long uphill drive is required avoiding large bunkers right and left, then a long second shot towards the big oak tree that is the club's symbol and stands between the clubhouse and green.

On the tournament side, Sunningdale has long staged its early-season Foursomes event for both amateurs and professionals, women being admitted in recent years, while it has also been a venue for the Ladies British Amateur, the Golf Illustrated Gold Vase and, in 1987, the Walker Cup. In more recent times,

Because of its length, or rather its lack of it, Sunningdale no longer hosts a European Tour event.

it has played host to the Women's British Open on two occasions.

One of the greatest feats in Sunningdale's history was the famous round of 66 produced by Bobby Jones in a qualifying round for the British Open in 1926. It has often been described as the perfect round, because he covered each nine in 33 strokes, and he had 33 shots and 33 putts. Jones's score was also made up entirely of threes and fours, and he hit every green, except one, in regulation and was bunkered only once. He followed it with a 68, then claimed that he had peaked too early. He hadn't, of course, and he proved it by moving on to Royal Lytham and winning the title by two strokes.

Sunningdale has long had a Royal connection. The Prince of Wales, later Edward VIII, and the Duke of York, later King George VI, were both captains, while over the years the club has become a mecca for the great and famous.

It may not be the longest of courses, but to succeed around the Old course at Sunningdale, players need to bring their A-game.

FEATURE HOLE:
11th – 228 yards, par four

It is a crying shame that, for some, Sunningdale is considered to be too short a course to host any of the great modern championships: for it is Britain's best inland course by some margin. What it may lack in length, however, is more than made up for by what it possesses in trickery. No more can this be true than on the par-four 11th. Standing on the tee of a hole that measures just 228 yards raises the blood pressure in most golfers: the temptation is too great – an eagle chance is in the offing. But temptation is rarely rewarded: just as the hole is short, so it is tricky and the rewards will come to the more restrained. The tee shot is blind: which adds to the problem. The approach, usually to a pin that is tucked away somewhere on the raised table part of the green, has to be precise. On this hole, patience and restraint are rewarded.

TURNBERRY

Turnberry, Ayrshire, Scotland

Opened: 1903
Designer: Willie Fernie
Yardage: 6,950
Par: 70
Major events: British Open 1977, 1986, 1994, 2004, 2009
Amateur Championship 1961, 1984, 2008
Walker Cup 1963
Women's British Open 2002
Women's British Amateur 1912, 1921, 1937

Turnberry is one of Scotland's major golf centres. It has two fine courses – the Ailsa and the Arran – a modern clubhouse incorporating every facility, and an impressive hotel set high on a hill overlooking the complete layout, with the Firth of Clyde and the granite dome of Ailsa Craig beyond.

The original links course was the work of former British Open champion Willie Fernie, while Turnberry, like several other resorts in the early 20th century, owed its development mainly to the coming of the railways. The line being pushed south down the Ayrshire coast required the building of a top-class hotel, and both were opened in 1906. Soon Turnberry became a Mecca for the rich, and a second links course,

the Arran, came to be opened in 1912.

However, the First World War put paid to golf. The area was used as a training ground for Royal Flying Corps pilots, while the hotel became the officers' mess. Much the same occurred in the Second World War, with Turnberry becoming a base for RAF Coastal Command with much of the courses disappearing under concrete runways, hangars and other buildings.

In 1946, the then owners, British Transport Hotels, set about using the compensation from the War Office to restore the courses to their former glory. Philip Mackenzie Ross was brought in to redesign the layout, and the Ailsa course, most of which had to be returfed, reopened in 1951. It occupies undulating terrain, threading its way among the sand dunes along the seashore in a general north-south direction. However, the first six holes of the back nine are more east-west, which means the golfer, having got used to the wind direction, has to readjust.

Like all links courses, Turnberry's character changes with the prevailing conditions, which can vary between the docile and the stormy. It is said locally: "If you can see Ailsa Craig it's going to rain. If you can't see it, it's raining." Depending on the direction of the onshore wind, some greens can enjoy a sheltered aspect, while others can be buffeted as if in a wind tunnel.

Apart from its majestic hotel, Turnberry's best-known feature is the lighthouse. This stands adjacent to the par-four ninth hole, where the tee is built on a rocky outcrop of the cliff, requiring a drive across an inlet to the safety of the fairway beyond. The other signature hole is the 16th, another par four which presents few problems until you consider your second shot to a green perched on a

Turnberry, with its two courses, has become a Mecca for golf tourists, many of whom are housed in the majestic hotel seen in the background.

The lighthouse, which stands next to the ninth hole, is one of the most recognized landmarks in world golf.

knoll, below which bubble the waters of the Wee Burn. The number of shots which have found a watery grave here and the number of ruined cards are legion – for even hitting the putting surface is no guarantee of safety.

The Arran course lies inland from the Ailsa on more gently rolling terrain, but can be equally challenging, especially in the wind.

Despite Turnberry's long-established qualities, big-time golf only arrived with the British Amateur Championship in 1961 and then the Walker Cup in 1963, when the home side crashed to a

12-8 defeat after leading 6-3 after day one.

But Turnberry's finest hour came in 1977 with the first of its four British Opens. The links were at their most benign, the sun shone for all four days, and the low scoring reflected this, right up to the classic final-day shoot-out between Tom Watson and Jack Nicklaus. Watson won by a stroke on 268, the lowest 72-hole aggregate in the event's history.

Conditions were almost the reverse in 1986, when Greg Norman defied wind and rain to secure his first British Open; then, in 1994, it was

FEATURE HOLE:
9th – 454 yard, par four

The majesty of golf can come when the player is faced with the challenge of a truly daunting hole; it can also arrive when playing against a picture-postcard backdrop. When the two are combined, the player is in golfing heaven: and that is exactly where he finds himself as he stands on the tee at the long par-four ninth at Turnberry. This is

the Ailsa Course's signature hole, positioned at the far end of the course set above a craggy inlet with the famous lighthouse tucked away to the left. From the back markers, the tee shot has to carry some 200 yards over wasteland. The player is then faced with a long iron shot to the green. The hole is called "Bruce's Castle", named after the remains of the castle of Robert the Bruce, King of Scotland from 1306 to 1329, which can be seen from the ninth green.

Nick Price's turn to gain his first Open after several near misses. The 2004 event saw another first-time winner:

unheralded American Todd Hamilton edged out Ernie Els in a play-off to lift the Claret Jug.

WENTWORTH

Virginia Water, Surrey, England

Opened: 1924
Designer: Harry Colt
Yardage: 6,945
Par: 72
Major events: Ryder Cup 1953
Curtis Cup 1932 (East course)
World Cup 1956
Women's British Open 1980
World Matchplay 1964-2007

In the days after the First World War, developer Walter George Tarrant, who realized the potential for such facilities and who had gained considerable success in producing quality housing around a golf course at St George's Hill in Surrey, was looking for a similar site to repeat the exercise.

He found exactly what he was looking for at Wentworth and eventually secured 1,750 acres of prime countryside, just 21 miles southwest of London. While Tarrant set about developing the property, complete with swimming pool, tennis courts and a ballroom, his friend Harry Colt laid out two courses.

Colt was delighted with the land at his disposal. The Surrey sandbelt, with its heather, soaring pine trees, silver birch and, in more recent times, huge banks of rhododendrons, lends itself ideally to golf courses. His handiwork has attracted worldwide acclaim, while everyone who plays Wentworth knows he faces quite a test. The East course, at 6,176 yards, par 68, is demanding in its own way. However, it is the West course, completed

FEATURE HOLE: 18th - 531 yards, par five

Given that the course plays host to one of the most famous matchplay competitions in world golf, it only seems right that it should provide scope for excitement all the way to the finish: and how. The closing holes of the West course are as inspired as they are unusual: two par fives, both of them dog-legs, one, the 17th moving from right to left, and the other, the 18th, moving from left to right. Both of the holes provide an opportunity for a birdie, but the most exciting, and arguably the easier of the holes is the 18th. The player is looking to fade the ball around the dog-leg from the tee: if he does not get enough left-to-right movement on the ball then it will end up in a fairway bunker and any chance of a birdie has all but gone. The second shot is the clincher: a long iron to the large green to set up that eagle chance. Anything less almost amounts to disappointment.

two years later and better known now as the Burma Road, which is the more familiar, as more of the top professional events are played on it.

The West, which has always demanded accurate driving, features highly among the tour professionals' choice of top venues. Few of the holes can be seen from any other, while the conditions are seldom less than first class, even in the darkest days of an English winter.

The back nine is regarded as the tougher half, and this is confirmed by the yardage and the par, 37 against the outward half of 35. The homeward run begins with a testing par three and a comfortable par four, after which the long 12th gives a chance of a birdie, if not an eagle for the leading players. But it is easy to give those shots back at the 441-yard 13th, where the line is down the right in order to open up the green to the approach. The uphill

The West course at Wentworth has become one of the flagship venues of the European Tour – both the PGA and the World Matchplay championships are played there every year.

The closing hole at Wentworth has provided great drama over the years: a left-to-right dog-leg, players are disappointed if they finish with anything less than a birdie.

par-three 14th plays every inch of its 179 yards to a two-tiered green, while the 466-yard 15th, with its diagonal ditch, requires strategy as well as a straight, long drive.

The par-four 16th provides a lull before the storm which starts with the dog-leg 17th, one of the great par fives of British golf. The 571 yards is downhill from the tee for about 300 yards and the best line is to hug the trees down the left if you don't want your ball to spill off the sloping fairway into the right rough.

Then the hole turns left uphill before descending to a generous green, but beware the private gardens down the left which are out of bounds. The pros hope to pick up a shot here, as they do at the 18th, another par five, but this time a dog-leg right.

Although a comparatively young course, Wentworth has played its part in golfing history. It was here in 1926 that an informal match was played between the professionals of Great Britain and those of America, which the British won comfortably. This was

to prove the forerunner of the Ryder Cup which began a year later.

In 1953, Wentworth played host to the Ryder Cup, with the United States scraping home by a single point, then three years later the Canada Cup, now the World Cup. The occasion provided Ben Hogan with his one and only appearance in England. He and Sam Snead carried off the trophy by a massive 14 strokes, both players shooting final rounds of 68. The World Matchplay Championship had been played

at Wentworth every year since its inception in 1964 until 2007, and the Volvo PGA Championship has been resident at Wentworth since 1984.

In 1978, Wentworth acquired another 150 acres of land, so it was decided to build a third 18-hole course, the South. The design of John Jacobs, with Gary Player and Wentworth professional Bernard Gallacher, it opened in July 1990 and was renamed the Edinburgh, in honour of the Duke, who performed the opening ceremony.

KEY

DDC   Dubai Desert Classic
AO   Australian Open
AM   Australian Masters
AWO   Australian Women's Open
PC   Presidents Cup
WAMTC   Women's Amateur Team Championship
WC   World Cup

VALDERRAMA, SPAIN

RC   1997

EMIRATES, DUBAI

DDC   1989-

THE REST OF THE WORLD

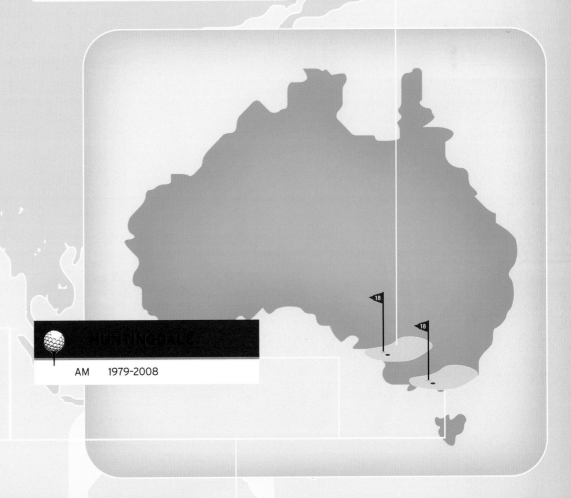

ROYAL ADELAIDE

AO	1910, 1923, 1926, 1929, 1932, 1935, 1938, 1962, 1998

COMMONWEALTH

AO	1967
AWO	1989, 1990

KINGSTON HEATH

AO	1948, 1957, 1970, 1989, 1995, 2000
AM	2009
AWO	2008

HUNTINGDALE

AM	1979-2008

VICTORIA AUSTRALIA

AO	1961, 1981, 2002

ROYAL MELBOURNE

AO	1905, 1907, 1909, 1912, 1913, 1921, 1924, 1927, 1933, 1939, 1953, 1963, 1984, 1985, 1987, 1991
PC	1998
WAMTC	1968
WC	1988

COMMONWEALTH

Commonwealth, Melbourne, Australia

Opened: 1921
Designers: Sam Bennett, Charles Lane,
Sloan Morpeth
Yardage: 6,977
Par: 73
Major events: Australian Open 1967
Australian Women's Open 1989, 1990

If there was ever a case of a club looking after its own interests, then the Commonwealth Golf Club, situated on the Sandbelt near Melbourne, is most definitely a case in point. It is one of the few clubs to have avoided the temptation of luring a high-profile, highly-paid course architect to tinker with its layout: be that as it may, the course, to this day, remains a triumph of the best principles of course architecture.

The club was formed in 1920 when members of the Waverly Golf Club purchased the site near to Melbourne's Metropolitan Club in the South Oakleigh suburb of the city. The first 12 holes were laid out by Sam Bennett, the club's professional, and the course opened for business in March 1921.

Much of the course's legacy can be attributed to Charles Lane. Carrying on in the traditions of doing things

To give the course protection against the big-hitting enabled by modern technology, thousands of trees were planted alongside Commonwealth's fairways in the 1990s.

Classic bunkering is a feature of the Commonwealth course and, although all of the work was all done "in-house", it is still one of the finest examples of triumphant golf architecture in world golf.

FEATURE HOLE:
16th – 398 yards, par four

If you were forced to pick a hole that best summed up the philosophy and challenge of the Commonwealth course, then you would not have to look much further than the 398-yard par-four 16th. This is the ultimate hole in course management: a hole that rewards bravery and skill off the tee. The hole shapes left around a fairway lake and the green is devilishly quick, protected by a fearsome right-side bunker. The message from the tee is clear: the rewards will be there for the player who can hit a long drive as close to the lake as possible – he who dares, and, of course, who manages to pull the shot off, will be rewarded with a relatively simple approach to the green. He who falters, will bring the deep, deep bunker into play.

"in-house", the club's captain (from 1923 to 1933) toured the world to take a closer look at golf architecture and brought his ideas back to the Commonwealth: he shaped much of the course himself, creating a further six holes (by 1926), deepening the bunkers and layering the greens. The club's history records that he could often be seen standing in a bunker, stripped to the waist, digging.

The results of these two men's efforts were anything but amateur and the course that they created conforms to the strictest ideals of golf architecture and strategic design. Commonwealth is not a long course in modern terms, but it requires course management of the highest order if you are to make a good score.

Nothing confirms that more than the name of the winner of the 1967 Australian Open, the only year that the competition was played over the course. Peter Thomson, the five-time winner of the British Open and a player renowned for his meticulous approach to a round of golf, ran out a seven-stroke winner over Colin Johnston.

It is a course made for the likes of Thomson. Position off the tee is at a premium. With deep and beautifully situated bunkers protecting the greens, the golfer is asked to make clear choices throughout his round.

The highlights of the Common-wealth are its par fours. There is the much-revered 16th (see feature hole box-out), a 398-yard par four. Then the 408-yard 11th: the hole is made or lost off the tee where the drive is played around a corner protected by bunkers before hitting an approach to a raised green protected by the deepest of bunkers.

The final two holes complete a much-celebrated closing stretch. The 17th is a relatively short, 336-yard par four protected by a devilishly difficult green. Then comes the 18th, at 442 yards a test of the player's long-iron game and a hole that is protected by some classic bunkering.

The only amendments to the original layout were made in the 1960s, as the course prepared to stage the Australian Open. Extra land was purchased and the tenth and 11th holes were redesigned – all of the work was overseen by the club secretary of the time, Sloan Morpeth.

Time and modern technology have threatened the course in recent years. The first casualty of the new big-hitting generation was the first hole, which was lengthened and made into a dog-leg. Further attempts to toughen the course up came in the 1990s, when thousands of new trees were planted – the result today is that the trees that line the fairways of the course are considered to be among the finest in Australia.

Despite attempts to modernize Commonwealth, the course remains a triumph for the best that traditional golf architecture has to offer.

EMIRATES

Emirates Golf Club, Dubai, United Arab Emirates

Opened: 1988
Designer: Karl Litton
Yardage: 7,102
Par: 72
Major event: Dubai Desert Classic, annually

If you take the road leading north out of Dubai, with the Persian Gulf away to the right, the last thing you would expect to find is a golf course. Each year development increases – more office blocks, more hotels, more traffic – but soon it is the desert, stretching endlessly to the west, that dominates.

Yet, within some 20 minutes of the city's limits, appears the oasis that is the Emirates Golf Club, home of the Dubai Desert Classic which for many marks the serious beginning of the European Tour season. It has been played there each year since 1989 (except for 1991) and has produced some outstanding champ-ions: Severiano Ballesteros, Ernie Els, Fred Couples, Colin Montgomerie and Mark O'Meara among them.

The first feature to catch the eye is the clubhouse, three inter-linked concrete, marble and glass buildings in the style of Bedouin "tents", though it is the golf course that catches the imagination. It is one of the very best on the whole European Tour circuit and one of the wonders of modern technology, which has also proved a magnet for birds of passage and native species. Before course construction began, a mere ten species of bird life were to be found there. Recently 230 have been seen, including some never observed before in the Emirates, such as the Oriental Pratincole. In a climate of negligible rainfall in arid land, this golf oasis has been made possible by pumping in 750,000 gallons of desalinated sea water every day.

So effective is the design that to stand in the middle of the course, set in a fenced rectangle to keep drifting sand at bay, one has no conception of the desert so close at hand.

There is a gentle movement to the land, the fairways are green and lush, the putting surfaces firm and true. It is also a fine test of golf. No wonder the players enthuse, enjoying in late February/early March the sort of temperature hoped for in British high summer. The two loops of nine holes both end beneath the impressive clubhouse, the green of the ninth and 18th shared in the shape of a banana with a lake at their fronts. The ninth is a par four of 463 yards, the 18th a par five of 547 yards. Both demand good shots to the green, the 18th more so since, come the final day, a birdie may be needed, which means the gamble of a long second to carry the water.

No one did it better than Montgomerie in 1996. A stroke ahead of Miguel Angel Jimenez, the Scot knew he would probably need a four to win the title. He faced a shot with a carry of 220 yards, took his driver "off the deck", made it and won the title. It was nominated as the shot of the year.

A year later, Ian Woosnam, in contrast, played a shot which, though the date was only 2 March, became a strong candidate for selection as the worst shot of the year in 1997. All he needed at the 18th was a par five to win. Justifiably, he therefore played the hole as a five, laying up with his second. He then mis-hit a

The Emirates course plays host to the Dubai Desert Classic every year on the European Tour, an event which attracts the leading golfers from around the globe and which, for many, heralds the start of the golfing year in Europe.

straightforward pitch 75 yards into the water, went into a play-off and, together with Greg Norman, lost it to a little-known Australian left-hander, Richard Green.

There is water, too, at two short holes, the fourth and seventh, as well as at the fifth, but there is more to the course than that. There are more splendid holes, notably the eighth, a par four of 434 yards played from a high tee to a rising fairway curving gently left to right. Played invariably into the wind, the second shot, with the flag fluttering against the skyline, is as demanding as any.

So, too, is the golf course itself, but like many another, it needs a good wind for it to be at its best. Whatever the weather in 1997, it seems doubtful if anyone could possibly have enjoyed the Emirates more than José-Maria Olazabal.

His glittering career looked for more than a year to have been ended by foot problems. New treatments brought him back to golfing life to the extent of a 65 in the third round, a £10,605 cheque for his nine-under par total of 279, and joint 12th place.

FEATURE HOLE:
9th – 463 yards, par four

Given that 750,000 gallons of water are desalinated daily and pumped over the course via 19 miles of piping and 750 sprinklers, it only seems right that water should play such a huge part in the best hole on the course – the 463-yard ninth. The water, which forms the largest of the four lakes on the course, is a serious threat from the elevated tee: the aim is as close to the water as you dare, away from the bunkers and trees that protect the right-hand side of the fairway. The approach to the green – shared with the other formidable hole on the course, the 18th – is one of the most testing on the course. The player has to judge the distance precisely: any ball that is short invariably falls back into a watery grave. It is a hole where bravery is rewarded: but a hole where the player has to play to the very best of his ability.

A marvel of modern technology, this glittering oasis surrounded by the Arabian desert, features four man-made lakes.

HUNTINGDALE

Huntingdale, Melbourne, Australia

Opened: 1941
Designer: Charles H. Alison
Yardage: 6,879
Par: 73
Major events: Australian Masters 1979-2009
Australian Women's Open 2008

There are not many courses in the world that become synonymous with the tournaments that are played over them year on year. Augusta National is one, the home of the Masters; Huntingdale is another, as it is a course which, since 1979, has been the home of the Australian version of the event.

It wasn't always the case. The club itself is much older: its affiliations go back to 1896, when the Surrey Hills Golf Club was established, but the birth of Huntingdale itself can be traced to a chance remark made in 1938, when one of the members of the club revealed that some land was available in the Sandbelt area of Melbourne. The land, that up until then had been used by the Melbourne Hunt Club, was duly purchased and the task of designing the course was given to Charles H Allison, an English course architect. Allison drew up a layout for the course based on the topography of the land and handed the papers to Sam Beriman, who oversaw the course's construction. Huntingdale, as the course was named, opened for business in 1941.

It was not until 38 years later, however, that Huntingdale became a stand-out course in the minds of golf followers around the world, and that it did, was due to the fact that it became the home of the Australian Masters: an event which apes its

American counterpart in many ways – from the giving of a jacket to the winner (of the Australian gold variety) to the high quality of the players who take part. A look at the winners list reveals some of the sport's great names: Bernhard Langer (1985), Mark O'Meara (1986) and Colin Montgomerie (1991). Tiger Woods played in 1997, but this was one Masters tournament that he did not win that year. The tournament has perhaps become synonymous with one player above all else: Greg Norman. Australia's favourite son has picked up the gold jacket on six occasions (1981, 1983, 1984, 1987, 1989, 1990).

The course itself, the youngest of the courses on the famous Sandbelt stretch, is characterized by narrow fairways and hard, fast and fairly flat greens: at least in the early years of the tournament. That all changed in 1999, when the course underwent something of a facelift on the back of a record-breaking winning score in the 1998 Masters event (Brad Hughes's 24-under total of 268 smashed the previous low mark by an incredible five shots). As a result, the character of the course, and in particular the greens, changed.

For the worse according to some of the professionals, who complained that the remodelled greens, with their newly added humps and hollows, had lost much of

their originality and now resembled those that could be found on any number of US-style layouts.

The course was toughened up considerably, however. A case in point is the 14th – the longest par five in Australian golf at 607 yards. A number of slopes were introduced onto the fairway after the second set of bunkers that encourage the ball to run off into a pond that protects the front left of the green. A bolder approach is now required from the player who wants to reach the green in two: he has to thread the ball through the narrow gap that exists between the pair of greenside bunkers.

FEATURE HOLE: 18th - 448 yards, par four

Perhaps it comes as no surprise that the final hole of a golf course is often seen as its most important: almost certainly because so many of the tournaments played over the courses are decided on the final hole. This is particularly true of the 18th at Huntingdale, another of the holes that was toughened up after the 1998 Australian Masters. The 448-yard par four was protected by the introduction of an array of bunkers in front of the green. The second shot now has to carry some 220 yards to find the green. In 1999, Craig Spence fired a six-iron long and high over the island bunker in front of the green to within 3ft of the flag to win the Masters by a stroke from Greg Norman.

Another major change involved the creation of a lake in the triangle of land between the 15th, 16th and 17th holes. The 15th itself was a brand new par three that

incorporated an island-style green sitting like an inverted saucer on the lake's edge. If you miss the green on the left, your ball finds a watery grave; miss on the right and there is an army of bunkers ready to welcome your ball.

Although an element of the character of the course has been lost by these changes, the course still graces television screens every year and, perhaps most importantly, provides a stern test of a golfer's skill.

The home of the Australian Masters golf tournament each year, Huntingdale is characterized by its long and narrow fairways and by the speed of its greens.

KINGSTON HEATH

Kingston Heath, Melbourne, Australia

Opened: 1925
Designers: Dan Soutar, Alister Mackenzie
Yardage: 6,947
Par: 72
Major events: Australian Open 1948, 1957, 1970, 1989, 1995, 2000

When Dutton Green, a committee member of Elsternwick Golf Club who was fascinated by the design of British golf courses, was looking to buy land in Melbourne's Sandbelt area for a new course in the early 1920s, he decided to seek the advice of two of the leading players in the game: Harry Vardon and J H Taylor. The advice he got from the former was to buy a piece of land that would be of sufficient length "to stand the test of time".

The search led the committee to Cheltenham, 25km from the centre of Melbourne, and a piece of undulating land with sandy soil – a perfect site for a golf course that would become Kingston Heath.

The committee employed the services of Sydney professional Dan Soutar, who walked around the land twice without saying a word.

Finally he stopped and stated that this is where he would make a start: he was standing on a piece of ground that, he stated, was "an ideal, ready-made, par three".

And so the plans for the course, now described by many as the second-best in Australia (behind Royal Melbourne), started from this point – the 142-yard tenth. Incredibly, seven other holes surround this tiny par three. The construction of the course was entrusted to Mick Morcom, a greenkeeper who had been loaned to the new club from Royal Melbourne. When it was opened for play in 1925, the 6,312-yard course (as it was then) was the longest in Australia: ironic for a course that, in modern times, is criticized for its length, or rather for its lack of it.

On a visit to the course in 1926, even the great Alister Mackenzie could find little wrong with the layout of Kingston Heath – although the Scot left his mark on the course with some classic bunkering.

FEATURE HOLE: 15th – 155 yards, par three

When Alister Mackenzie made an assessment of the course during his visit in 1926 he made only one suggestion to alter it: he thought that the short par-four 15th that existed at the time was "a real blotch on the course". He therefore recommended that it be turned into a par three, with the green placed on top of the dune. The club's committee took his advice, and one of the best par threes in world golf was created. The 155-yard par-three 15th is an uphill shot to a green protected by deep bunkers on both sides: the choice is simple – you have to aim for the middle of the green, regardless of the pin position.

When it opened, Kingston Heath was the longest course in Australia. In recent times, it too has had to be toughened up to protect it against golf's new big-hitting generation of players.

The length is not the only thing that the critics mumble about: they will sight the blind approach on the 17th, the blind drives on both the eighth and the 16th, the fact that all three of the par fives run in a north-south direction, the fact that there are no long par threes and the regularity of the low-flying planes which make their way to and from the nearby Moorabbin Airport.

What the critics fail to notice, however, is how well laid out the course is. Kingston Heath covers just 125 acres, and although it is true that there is an absence of truly long holes, the 18 holes on offer provide a stiff test for any professional: quite simply because they demand the highest levels of precision and course management.

Indeed, so well laid out was the course that the revered architect, Alister Mackenzie, who, in 1926, was commissioned to look after the course's bunkering, was moved to say: "Never yet have I advised upon a course where, owing to the excellence of the design and construction work, the problems have been so simple." Praise indeed.

A classic example comes at the short par-four third. Standing on the tee, the player is invited to go for the green with his drive ... but to do so would be to invite considerable risk: the green that he is driving to is the smallest on the course and it is contoured to reward only the most precise of pitch shots. The smart play is a mid-iron followed by a wedge to the heart of the putting surface ... and hope to make a birdie from there.

As with most courses in recent times, Kingston Heath has been toughened up. Several greens have been rebuilt; a deep depression has been placed in front of the green on the highly reachable par-five seventh and, controversially, a new bunker was placed in the centre of the 11th fairway prior to the course's staging of the 2000 Australian Open.

The overriding impression of Kingston Heath, however, is a course that is one of the finest examples of golf architecture ... from any era.

ROYAL ADELAIDE

Royal Adelaide, Australia

Opened: 1906
Designer: Cargie Rymill, Alister Mackenzie
Yardage: 7,194
Par: 72
Major events: Australian Open 1910, 1923, 1926, 1932, 1935, 1938, 1962, 1998

When Alister Mackenzie visited the site of the Royal Adelaide golf course in 1926 – he had been commissioned to do some work on the course – he was moved to say: "One finds a most delightful combination of sand dunes and fir trees, a most unusual combination even at the best seaside courses. No seaside courses that I have seen possess such magnificent sand craters as those at Royal Adelaide."

And Mackenzie set about using the natural landscape to redesign the course that had initially been laid out by Cargie Rymill after the club had acquired the Seaton site back in 1904. Indeed, Royal Adelaide had a long history before Mackenzie had even arrived: it had hosted the Australian Open in both 1910 and 1923, the year that it had been granted the "Royal" prefix. However, Mackenzie moulded the landscape before him to create the nearest experience to a links course that you can find in Australia.

Not that you would think so when you first arrive at the site. The land is uncommonly flat and, unusually, a train line runs past the clubhouse, the first tee, the second green and the third tee. Any bad first impressions disappear the moment you step onto the course ... or to be more precise, the second tee. For

it is here that you get a flavour of a Mackenzie course: a long par five with strategic bunkering designed to punish the brave player who tries to reach the green in two.

The third is one of the greatest of Australia's short par fours (see box), before moving onto the fourth. Here you are faced with a blind tee shot over a huge patch of sandy wasteland, before the fairway curves away to the left.

The most famous hole on the course is the 11th. Indeed, Peter Thomson was moved to say that it

Royal Adelaide is another course that carries the Mackenzie trademark of classic bunkering. The challenge is considerable, though, and the course itself is the closest you will find in Australia to a true links experience.

FEATURE HOLE:
3rd – 291 yards,
par four

Alister Mackenzie made changes to every hole on the Royal Adelaide course except one: the third. In many ways the hole stands as the gateway to the Scot's work: before 1926, the sand dunes merely bordered the course; after Mackenzie had finished they became very much a part of it. The third, however, remained untouched because it remained one of the best short par fours in Australia – a country renowned for such holes. It is possible to reach the green in one with a perfect tee shot, but you dare not miss on the right, as the whole of the fairway on that side is protected by an enormous sand dune. The sensible play is to leave yourself a wedge to the long, narrow green.

Peter Thomson created much controversy when he tried to toughen up the Royal Adelaide course prior to it hosting the 1998 Australian Open.

would be regarded as the best hole in the continent if it appeared at a more critical juncture on the card. Called the "Crater Hole", it is a medium length par four with a restricted drive: a sandy crater crosses the fairway at the 250-yard mark and prevents the use of a driver. The long second needs to be fired towards the green that sits at the base of a sand dune covered in trees.

Others think that the 14th is the best hole on the course: a dog-leg right that is again characterized by the strategic placement of both bunkers and green. Only two of the best quality golf shots will gain reward on this hole. The final hole of real class comes at the 16th, a par three with a small green that demands extreme precision from the tee and which always seems to be the hole that is subject to the stiff sea breeze.

Royal Adelaide is a course of undeniable quality; so much so that it has hosted the Australian Open on nine occasions – the last of which caused considerable controversy. Peter Thomson, the five-time winner of the British Open, was charged with setting the course up.

It was the way in which he altered the course that brought in the criticism. Mounds were added to the flatter holes, the course was lengthened (to a staggering 7,200 yards) and the fairways were narrowed. Despite the flak, Thomson stuck to his guns: "If Australia really wants to stage a major then we need to present courses like St Andrews and US Open venues."

Mackenzie would not have been impressed. Writing in his book *The Spirit of St Andrews* in the early 1930s, he suggested: "Narrow fairways bordered by long grass make bad golfers. They do so by destroying the harmony and continuity of the game and in causing a stilted and cramped style, destroying all freedom of play."

Besides, even without the amendments, Royal Adelaide is such a fine course that it possesses the necessary armoury to defend itself against even the most talented of modern golfers.

ROYAL MELBOURNE

Melbourne, Victoria, Australia

Opened: 1931
Designers: Alister Mackenzie, Alex Russell
Yardage: 6,946
Par: 71
Major events: Australian Open 1905, 1907, 1909, 1912, 1913, 1921, 1924, 1927, 1933, 1939, 1953, 1963, 1984, 1985, 1987, 1991
President's Cup 1998
World Amateur Team Championship 1968
World Cup 1988

Sandy subsoils are the ideal ingredients to support golf courses as can be seen with the various Surrey clubs, those on the Lancashire coast and in many parts of Scotland. The same applies in Australia and especially in Melbourne, whose southern confines contain a 25 square mile area known as the Sandbelt. Here, the rolling terrain containing fine grasses and indigenous trees, reeds, heather and bracken, was considered the ideal site for the Royal Melbourne club to move to in the late 1920s.

The club had been founded as long ago as 1891, making it the oldest in Australia, but it had two other locations before eventually moving to its present site and building its reputation as one of the world's finest courses. The prime land was acquired in 1924, and club officials were in no doubt that they wanted "the best expert advice", irrespective of cost.

That advice was provided by Alister Mackenzie, the Scot who was later to go on to design Augusta National as well as many other top courses throughout the world. He began work in 1926 together with Alex Russell, the 1924 Australian Open champion, and the result was

**FEATURE HOLE:
8th – 305 yards,
par four**

This is another of the Sandbelt's great short par fours. It is a stiff test of an architect's skill to make something out of a hole that measures a fraction over 300 yards, but Mackenzie succeeds wonderfully here. Somewhat inevitably, the length of the hole inspires visions of glory: of driving the hole with a majestic tee shot and then holing out for an eagle. But the consequences of failure on this hole are dire indeed. All that can be seen from the tee as you look towards the green is the large bunker positioned between you and the flag: a bunker that is waiting to snaffle anything but the most precise tee shot ... all but the most confident are likely to feel inhibited by it. The hole tends to be more rewarding for the patient player who lays up and chips close to the pin.

the West course, which many feel is a masterpiece.

While Mackenzie's name is synon-ymous with the course, Russell also played a major role, and it was perhaps fitting that he should design and construct the neighbouring East course a little later. For championship purposes, a composite of the two courses is used, six holes of Russell's East linked with 12 from Mackenzie's West. The result is a layout of almost 7,000 yards and a tough par of 71.

Aesthetically, Royal Melbourne leaves something to be desired because, over the years, the city's development has seen it surrounded by roads, while houses back on to parts of the playing area. However, closer inspection reveals its true

quality, notably in the thoughtful arrangements of humps and ridges, adding character, not to mention the odd hazard.

Apart from the overall design, another significant feature of Royal Melbourne is the large greens, which are usually extremely fast. The credit for this belongs to the former head greenkeeper Claude Crockford, who was taken on to the staff in 1934. Such were his skills and devotion to duty that there are no truer or faster greens to be found anywhere; consequently, it takes the visitor some time to acclimatize and feel at home.

Crockford also carried out some redesign work, particularly with regard to the short seventh, which Mackenzie built with an elevated green that the members felt was a blind shot. They wanted it altered, so Crockford obliged by lowering it to where it could be seen. Even now, at just 148 yards, it is no pushover, with several very deep bunkers lying in wait for the wayward shot. In fact, bunkers were Mackenzie's signature, and there are 114 of various shapes, sizes and depths to be confronted or avoided if you are to come away with a decent score.

The 11th is generally regarded as the toughest hole on the course. From an elevated tee, this 455-yard par four presents a difficult drive to the elbow of the left-hand dog-leg, the fairway sloping left towards two large, luring traps. Turning left, the approach to a sloping green also requires accuracy to avoid a gaping bunker to the right of the putting surface.

Such has been Royal Melbourne's pedigree down the years that it has been a frequent host for the Australian Open and PGA Championships. It was also the venue for the World Cup in 1988, won by the Ozaki brothers from Japan, and the President's Cup in 1998.

Alister Mackenzie and Alex Russell have combined to produce the most challenging course in Australia and one of the finest in the world.

VALDERRAMA

Sotogrande, Cadiz, Spain

Opened: 1975
Designer: Robert Trent Jones
Yardage: 6,819
Par: 72
Major events: Ryder Cup 1997

The list of courses that bear the name of Robert Trent Jones is long and impressive, while his workmanship has become familiar throughout the world. When he designed Los Aves, in a spectacular location in the hills above Sotogrande in southern Spain, it was not regarded as particularly newsworthy. Most people were more familiar with Sotogrande Old, his also, and even when Los Aves became Sotogrande New, there was barely a ripple on the surface of the game. But in 1985, when a Bolivian tin millionaire and golf fanatic by the name of Jaime Ortiz-Patino, and seven of his golfing friends, acquired and improved the club, changing its name again to Valderrama, it was to have a far-reaching influence on the game, not only in Spain but also in Europe as a whole and around the world.

Trent Jones was brought back in to remodel the layout, describing it at the time as "polishing the diamond to improve the shot values in some areas".

Since then, Ortiz-Patino has made other changes on the way to turning Valderrama into what he calls the "Augusta of Europe".

There is no disputing now that Valderrama is a magnificent course in every sense of the word. Its quality is of the highest order, and such has been the refining, that it has become a severe test of even the best players, while its elevation into the nearest thing to Augusta in Europe has seen it become the permanent venue for the end-of-season European tour event, the Volvo Masters. Even more stunning was the awarding to Valderrama of the 1997 Ryder Cup matches, the first time that the contest was held outside Britain when Europe has been the host.

Thanks to its quality, its reputation for being a tough examination, and its agreeable climate, many national teams take the opportunity of going there to tune up for the season ahead. Some of Europe's leading tour professionals also use the course to hone their games, including Seve Ballesteros, one of its biggest fans, who used the facilities at Valderrama to warm up for one of his US Masters successes.

Europe's pros, almost to a man, admit that Valderrama is probably more difficult than any other course in Europe. The scoring certainly reflects that, and while its selection for the Ryder Cup was criticized in many quarters, it provided a fantastic battleground for the best from Europe as well as America.

Most of the holes are memorable for one reason or another, but among the most memorable is the short third, which measures around 170 yards but requires a solid shot to a severely bunkered green set into a hillside. Then there is the par-five 11th, where Trent Jones's redesign has left a sloping fairway with a nest of bunkers at the landing area followed by an uphill approach to the green which is

The lake that guards the front of the 17th green is a recent addition and was the inspiration of Severiano Ballesteros.

Course architect Robert Trent Jones considered the par-five fourth to be one of the best holes that he ever created: there is no questioning the hole's aesthetic appeal as an eye-catching waterfall cascades off the edge of the green.

difficult to judge accurately. Another testing par three is the 12th, which measures around 220 yards and is played from an elevated tee to a green set among cork trees. Anything off target is almost bound to catch one of the fearsome bunkers, while the green itself slopes from front to back and has many subtle undulations.

The 17th has also seen some changes in recent years, but this time Patino called in Ballesteros, and what used to be a long uphill par five, now has a lake guarding the front of the green. Anything short finds a watery grave, while anything too strong can leave you in clinging grass on the banking that surrounds the putting surface.

What is certain at Valderrama is that if something needs changing or improving, no expense is spared to see that it is done.

FEATURE HOLE:
4th – 516 yards, par five

The intention was to make Valderrama the "Augusta of Europe": the club has succeeded on many levels: the course is beautifully manicured and the course is tough. There is no more scenic hole than the fourth and according to the course's designer, Robert Trent Jones, there is none more challenging: "It's probably the best of all my par fives and, in my opinion, one of the great par fives in the world." To reach the green in two will require a long drive and an accurate three-wood: but it is a brave man indeed who takes that course of action, since the right-hand side of the green is protected by a scenic waterfall. The sensible play is to aim for the right-hand side of the fairway with the second shot and look to secure par, or better, with a precise pitch to the flag.

VICTORIA

Victoria, Australia

Opened: 1927
Designers: William Meader, Oscar Damman, Alister Mackenzie
Yardage: 6,801
Par: 72
Major events: Australian Open 1961, 1981, 2002

Set in the heart of Melbourne's Sandbelt and situated just across the road from the Royal Melbourne, the Victoria Golf Club is a course that is truly steeped in the history of golf in the Melbourne area.

The founder of the club was none other than William Meader, considered by many to be the forefather of golf in the state of Victoria. Meader helped establish the state's Golf Association in 1902 and founded the Victoria Golf Club, which was then located at Fishermen's Bend, the following year. In 1923, Meader was again the driving force behind the club's move to Cheltenham and, along with the help of the club's captain, Oscar Damman, laid out the course.

It was at this point that Lady Luck played a helping hand: there had been logistical problems laying out the course and its construction had been delayed. As it turned out the problems turned out to be a blessing, for they allowed Alister Mackenzie - a man who has influenced so many

of the courses in southern Australia - to advise on the bunkering for the finished course.

As with much of the Scot's work, it is the positioning of his bunkers that help define the character of the course: although the fairways are forgiving, they demand precision from the tee. This, along with the beautifully contoured greens, reminds you of the neighbouring Royal Melbourne course - another of Mackenzie's masterpieces.

A measure of the course's standing can be seen by the

The character of the course, like so many in southern Australia, was shaped by the skill of Alister Mackenzie: but his influence on Victoria was aided by luck - had the course's construction not been delayed, it would have been completed before the Scot's visit.

One of the few holes to receive attention in preparation for the 2002 Australian Open was the 17th. Former club member Peter Thomson decided to lengthen the hole and amended the bunkering and mounding around the green. The result toughened up the hole, a left-to-right dog-leg. A trio of bunkers await the con-servative tee shot and encourage the player to hit a fade around the corner – not too far, mind, or you will end up in the deep bunker strategically positioned on the right-hand corner. Only the perfect tee shot will allow you a chance at the green in two, but you cannot afford to miss on the left – it is guarded by a series of deep bunkers.

Victoria is one of the few courses that has not undergone radical changes in an attempt to protect it from today's big-hitters.

quality of some of the names of the members who learned their trade playing its holes: among them Peter Thomson, five-time winner of the British Open, three-time winner of the Australian Open and two-time winner of the World Cup, and Doug Bachli – who was the first Australian-born winner of the British Amateur Championship (in 1954, the same year that Thomson won the first of his British Open titles, at Birkdale).

The configuration of the holes draws its critics: particularly because both the front and the back nine finish with two par fives, but both the ninth and the 17th are world-class holes.

Indeed, it is the stretch of holes through nine to 13 that provide the real highlight of the course. The 585-yard ninth is a test of precision over big hitting: fairway bunkers are severe on both sides, but as you hit across the majestic tumbling

fairways, this is one of the classic Sandbelt par fives.

Mackenzie described the tenth as a "fine drive and pitch adventure", and it is the pitch shot to the superbly situated left-to-right sloping green that demands the player's attention. The green to the 404-yard 11th is guarded on all sides by deep bunkers and you have to keep the ball below the hole to assure a more straightforward putt. The 426-yard 12th is but a pitching wedge away from the Royal

Melbourne course and, like the holes of its neighbour, is a difficult and long par four – it is a dog-leg from left to right. The 13th is considered by many to be the best par four on the course – at 429 yards, it is one of the longest, and the approach to the green must be accurate – vast bunkers guard both sides of the green.

Unlike some courses, Victoria required little alteration in preparation for hosting the 2002 Australian Open – a little lengthening here and there. The tournament was controversial however; play had to be halted in the afternoon of the first day, due to "unplayable" greens ... Stuart Appleby described them as "Teflon coated".

That should not detract, however, from the fact that a round of golf at Victoria is one of the best playing experiences in Australia.

INDEX

All page numbers in italics refer to photographs
All page numbers in bold refer to main references

PICTURE CREDITS

The publishers would like to thank the following sources for their kind permission to reproduce the pictures in this book. The page numbers for each of the photographs are listed below, giving the page on which they appear in the book. Any location indicator: (T-top, B-bottom, L-left, R-right).

Corbis Images: /Royalty Free: 33

Getty Images: 150; /Robyn Beck/AFP: 68, 172; /Leonard Burt: 127; /David Cannon: 53, 100, 138, 188; /Timothy A. Clary/AFP: 50; /Michael Cohen: 195; /Christopher Condon/WireImage: 98; /Mark Dadswell: 268-269; /Adrian Dennis/AFP: 84, 85, 112; /Stephen Dunn: 176; /Mike Ehrmann: 201; /Stuart Franklin: 179; /Scott Halleran: 164; /Jeff Haynes/AFP: 113; /Richard Heathcote: 81; /Hulton Archive: 145BL, 166BL, 173R, 184, 198BL; /Carl Iwasaki: 202TR; /Craig Jones: 132, 165; /Robert W. Kelley: 198TR; /Ross Kinnaird: 69, 82, 114, 216TL; /Nick Laham: 66; /Streeter Lecka: 101; /Francisco Leong/AFP: 167; /Andy Lyons: 65, 147, 171, 180, 191; /Hunter Martin/WireImage: 49, 97; /Darren McNamara: 155; /Gary Newkirk: 144, 157, 196; /Lynn Pelham: 126; /Puttnam/Stringer: 125; /Andrew Redington: 4, 83, 115; /Tim Sloan/AFP: 51, 52; /Jamie Squire: 99; /Rob Tringali/Sportschrome: 67

Press Association Images: 88, 141TR, 166TR, 186R, 186B, 194BR, 206, 209L, 209BR, 212B; /Chris Bacon: 153R; /Barratts: 145TR, 202BL, 214BR; /Claudio Bresciani: 203BL; /Adam Butler: 187T; /Ben Curtis: 170, 211; /EPA: 6-7, 27, 46, 60, 93, 94, 95, 123T, 123B, 134, 139, 142, 153BR, 154, 156, 158TR, 163, 181, 182, 199, 200BR, 203R, 204, 205, 215TR, 215B; /Mike Egerton: 175; /Gareth Fuller: 29, 193; /Ross Kinnaird: 117B, 187B, 189; /Tony Marshall: 135, 183, 192; /Andrew Milligan: 136-137; /Don Morley: 161TL; /Rebecca Naden: 8-9, 149, 159TR, 159B, 200TL; /Tim Ockenden: 152, 158B; /S&G/Alpha: 10-11, 20, 22, 23, 25, 141B, 146, 148, 151, 160, 161BR, 162, 168, 173BL, 174, 177, 190L, 190B, 194L, 197, 210, 212TR, 214BL; /SMG: 169TR, 169B, 178, 185, 213; /Neal Simpson: 140, 143, 208; /Topham Picturepoint: 216R

The Bridgeman Art Library: /Private Collection/Christies Images: 12

Visions In Golf: /Richard Castka: 47, 63, 232-233; /GOLF Select: 270, 271, 272, 272-273, 278, 278-279; /Eric Hepworth: 242, 242-243; /Richard Hodkinson: 246; /Christer Hoglund: 38, 45, 48; /Michael Hobbs Golf Collection: 13, 14, 15, 16, 17, 19, 24, 39, 40, 54, 56, 57, 58, 70, 72, 75, 87, 89, 103, 104T, 104B, 117T, 119T, 121, 122, 207TR, 207BL, 217; /Mark Newcombe: 36-37, 42, 44, 61, 62, 74, 76, 77, 78, 79, 80, 90, 92, 96, 105, 106, 107, 108, 109, 110, 111, 119B, 129, 130L, 130R, 131, 218-219, 222, 223, 224, 224-225, 226-227, 230, 231, 232, 234, 236-237, 237, 244, 245, 247, 248, 248-249, 250, 251, 252, 253, 254, 254-255, 256, 257, 258, 258-259, 260, 260-261, 264, 265, 266, 267, 276, 277; /David Scaletti: 274-275; /Robert Walker: 64, 228-229, 235, 238, 238-239

Every effort has been made to acknowledge correctly and contact the source and/copyright holder of each picture, and Carlton Books Limited apologises for any unintentional errors or omissions, which will be corrected in further editions of this book.

Special thanks are due to Mark and Debbie Newcombe at Visions In Golf, whose efforts greatly rendered the burdens of picture research.